Fodor's 2nd Edition

W9-BNP-033

Puerto Rico

The Guide
for All Budgets

Completely
Updated

Where to Stay, Eat,
and Explore

On and Off
the Beaten Path

When to Go,
What to Pack

Maps, Travel Tips,
and Web Sites

Fodor's Travel Publications • New York, Toronto, London, Sydney, Auckland
www.fodors.com

Fodor's Puerto Rico

EDITOR: Laura M. Kidder

Editorial Contributors: Isabel Abislaimán, Carissa Bluestone, Priscilla Burgess, Mary Dempsey, Delinda Karle, John Marino, Caryn Nesmith, Cristina Córdova Suárez

Editorial Production: Kristin Milavec

Maps: David Lindroth, *cartographer;* Robert Blake and Rebecca Baer, *map editors*

Design: Fabrizio La Rocca, *creative director;* Guido Caroti, *art director;* Jolie Novak, *senior picture editor;* Melanie Marin, *photo editor*

Cover Design: Pentagram

Production/Manufacturing: Bob Shields

Cover Photo (Sentry Box, El Morro fortress in Old San Juan): Dave G. Houser

Copyright

Important Tip

Although all prices, opening times, and other details in this book are based on information supplied to us at press time, changes occur all the time in the travel world, and Fodor's cannot accept responsibility for facts that become outdated or for inadvertent errors or omissions. So **always confirm information when it matters,** especially if you're making a detour to visit a specific place.

Special Sales

Fodor's Travel Publications are available at special discounts for bulk purchases for sales promotions or premiums. Special editions, including personalized covers, excerpts of existing guides, and corporate imprints, can be created in large quantities for special needs. For more information, contact your local bookseller or write to Special Markets, Fodor's Travel Publications, 1745 Broadway, New York, NY 10019. Inquiries from Canada should be directed to your local Canadian bookseller or sent to Random House of Canada, Ltd., Marketing Department, 2775 Matheson Boulevard East, Mississauga, Ontario L4W 4P7. Inquiries from the United Kingdom should be sent to Fodor's Travel Publications, 20 Vauxhall Bridge Road, London SW1V 2SA, England.

PRINTED IN THE UNITED STATES OF AMERICA

10 9 8 7 6 5 4 3 2 1

CONTENTS

ON THE ROAD WITH FODOR'S

A TRIP TAKES YOU OUT OF YOURSELF. Concerns of life at home completely disappear, driven away by more immediate thoughts—about, say, what marvels will beguile the next day, or where you'll have dinner. That's where Fodor's comes in. We make sure that you know all your options, so that you don't miss something that's around the next bend just because you didn't know it was there. Mindful that the best memories of your trip might have nothing to do with what you came to Puerto Rico to see, we guide you to sights large and small all over the island. You might set out to just lounge on a beach, but back at home you find yourself unable to forget dancing to till dawn in a San Juan salsa club or spotting an endangered green parrot in El Yunque rain forest.

About Our Writers

Our success in showing you every corner of Puerto Rico is a credit to our extraordinary writers. Although there's no substitute for travel advice from a good friend who knows your style, our contributors are the next best thing—the kind of people you would poll for travel advice if you knew them.

Isabel Abislaimán, a writer-photographer who also happens to be a litigation lawyer, put her talents to work covering sights, hotels, sports outfitters, and shops in San Juan. She also revised the chapter's A to Z section. Isabel has contributed to the travel section of San Juan's Spanish-language newspaper, *El Nuevo Día*, and her photographs have appeared in collective exhibits at the Liga de Estudiantes de Arte de San Juan.

Cristina Córdova Suárez, who updated the Smart Travel Tips A to Z, is the publisher of *Voices*, a San Juan alternative newsweekly. The Puerto Rico native started her writing career at *PC Magazine* in New York and wrote for various other publications, including the *Village Beat, Foro/Forum, Spinning Free,* and the *Minneapolis Reader.* She returned home in 2000 and spent a year working at the *San Juan Star.*

An itch to travel has carried journalist **Mary Dempsey,** the writer of the Eastern Puerto Rico chapter, throughout Latin America and the Caribbean. Her writings from those journeys have appeared in numerous publications, including the *Los Angeles Times, Travel and Leisure, Americas,* and *Conde Nast Traveler.* She tackled her Fodor's assignment after spending two years in Puerto Rico, where she wrote for the *San Juan Star.* She's currently an editor at *Latin Trade* magazine, a Miami-based monthly covering business in the Caribbean and Central and South America.

A native of Michigan, **Delinda Karle** discovered the tropics on her first job with a Puerto Rican weekly business paper. She returned to the cold latitudes but found herself frequently traveling to warmer places. She left the *Cleveland Plain Dealer* in 1991 to write for the *San Juan Star,* the Associated Press, and Reuters in Puerto Rico, and she now freelances from Florida. Delinda wrote the Southern and Northwestern Puerto Rico chapters for the first edition and revised the Southern Puerto Rico chapter this time around.

John Marino, who reviewed San Juan restaurants and nightclubs, is city editor at the *San Juan Star.* He has written extensively about Puerto Rico and the Caribbean for several publications, including the *Washington Post,* the *New York Times, Gourmet, New York Newsday,* and Reuters. He lives with his wife and son in San Juan.

The island's northwestern reaches were covered by **Caryn Nesmith,** a Caribbean editor for the Associated Press. Caryn, who has lived on Puerto Rico four several years, was formerly with the *San Juan Star.*

You can rest assured that you're in good hands—and that no property mentioned in the book has paid to be included. Each has been selected strictly on its merits, as the best of its type in its price range.

How to Use This Book

Up front is Smart Travel Tips A to Z, arranged alphabetically by topic and loaded with tips, Web sites, and contact information. Destination: Puerto Rico helps get you in the mood for your trip. Subsequent chapters in the guide are arranged regionally. All city chapters begin with exploring information, with a section for each neighborhood (each recommending a good tour and listing sights alphabetically). All regional chapters are divided geographically; within each area, towns are covered in logical geographical order, and attractive stretches of road between them are indicated by the designation En Route. To help you decide what you'll have time to visit, all chapters begin with our writers' favorite itineraries. (Mix itineraries from several chapters, and you can put together a really exceptional trip.) The A to Z section that ends every chapter lists additional resources. At the end of the book you'll find Background and Essentials, including essays about San Juan and gambling strategies, a chronology that traces the island's history, followed by a Spanish vocabulary section.

Icons and Symbols

★ Our special recommendations
✕ Restaurant
🏠 Lodging establishment
✕🏠 Lodging establishment whose restaurant warrants a special trip
🐤 Good for kids (rubber duck)
☞ Sends you to another section of the guide for more information
⊠ Address
☎ Telephone number
◷ Opening and closing times
💶 Admission prices (those we give apply to adults; substantially reduced fees are almost always available for children, students, and senior citizens)

Numbers in white and black circles ③ ❸ that appear on the maps, in the margins, and within the tours correspond to one another.

For hotels, you can assume that all rooms have private baths, phones, TVs, and air-conditioning unless otherwise noted and that all hotels operate on the European Plan (with no meals) if we don't specify another meal plan. We always list a property's facilities but not whether you'll be charged extra to use them, so when pricing accommodations, do ask what's included. For restaurants, it's always a good idea to book ahead; we mention reservations only when they're essential or are not accepted. All restaurants we list are open daily for lunch and dinner unless stated otherwise; dress is mentioned only when men are required to wear a jacket or a jacket and tie. Look for an overview of local dining-out habits in Smart Travel Tips A to Z and in the Pleasures and Pastimes section that follows each chapter introduction.

Don't Forget to Write

Your experiences—positive and negative—matter to us. If we have missed or misstated something, we want to hear about it. We follow up on all suggestions. Contact the Puerto Rico editor at editors@fodors.com or c/o Fodor's at 1745 Broadway, New York, New York 10019. And have a fabulous trip!

Karen Cure
Editorial Director

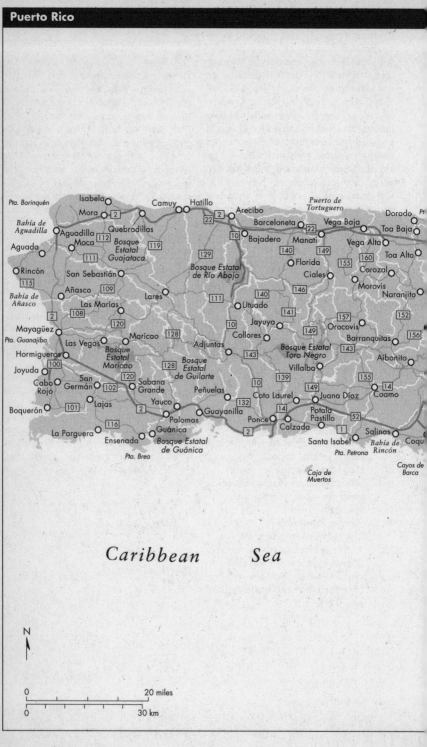

Caribbean Sea

N

0   20 miles
0   30 km

ATLANTIC OCEAN

Pta. Salinas
Old
San
Juan
San Juan
Piñones
Loíza
Cataño
187
22
2
Río Piedras
Cayo
Icacos
Bayamón
Guaynabo
Carolina
3
Río Grande
Luquillo
Isla de Culebra
1
Trujillo Alto
186
987
167
52
181
185
El Yunque
Fajardo
173
Aguas
Buenas
Gurabo
Ceiba
3
Sonda de Vieques
156
Juncos
53
Comerío
172
Caguas
191
31
Pasaje de Vieques
56
Cidra
1
San Lorenzo
30
Las Piedras
Naguabo
173
Cayey
181
Humacao
3
Isabel Segunda
200
Bosque
Estatal
Carite
53
Pta. Arenas
201
Pta. Este
52
15
184
Esperanza
ISLA DE VIEQUES
Guayama
Yabucoa
Maunabo
Patillas
Pta. Yeguas
53
qui
3
3
Arroyo
Cayos
Caribes
s de
ca

KEY

🚢 Ferry

🌴 Rain Forest

The Caribbean

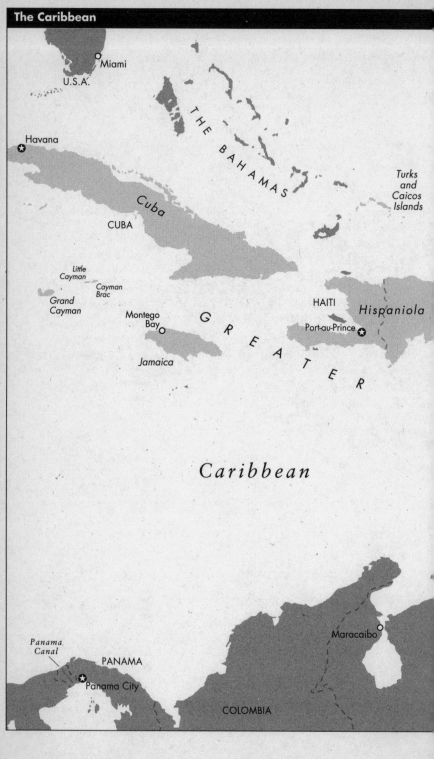

Miami

U.S.A.

THE BAHAMAS

Turks and Caicos Islands

Havana

Cuba

CUBA

Little Cayman

Cayman Brac

Grand Cayman

Montego Bay

Jamaica

G R E A T E R

HAITI

Hispaniola

Port-au-Prince

Caribbean

Panama Canal

PANAMA

Panama City

Maracaibo

COLOMBIA

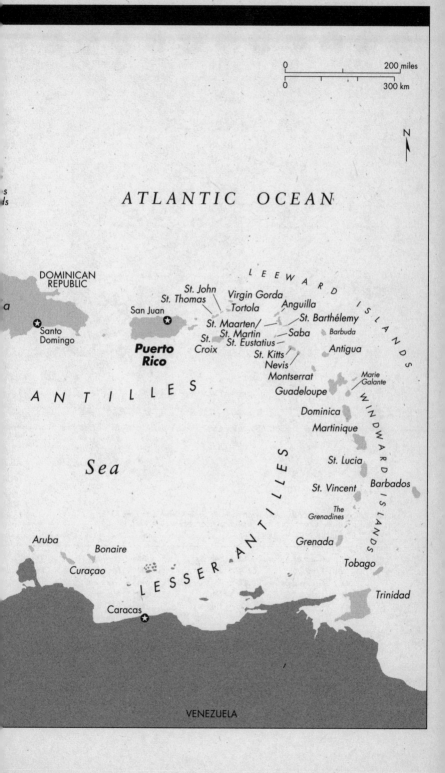

ATLANTIC OCEAN

0   200 miles
0   300 km

N

DOMINICAN
REPUBLIC

a

★ Santo
Domingo

*s
ds*

St. John
St. Thomas
San Juan
★

**Puerto
Rico**

A N T I L L E S

Sea

Virgin Gorda
Tortola
St. Maarten/
St. Martin
St. Eustatius
St.
Croix
St. Kitts
Nevis
Montserrat
Guadeloupe

L E E W A R D   I S L A N D S

Anguilla
St. Barthélemy
Saba
Barbuda

Antigua

Marie
Galante

Dominica

Martinique

St. Lucia

St. Vincent

The
Grenadines

Grenada

Barbados

W I N D W A R D   I S L A N D S

Tobago

Trinidad

Aruba   Bonaire
Curaçao

L E S S E R   A N T I L L E S

Caracas
★

VENEZUELA

x

World Time Zones

Numbers below vertical bands relate each zone to Greenwich Mean Time (0 hrs.).
Local times frequently differ from these general indications,
as indicated by light-face numbers on map.

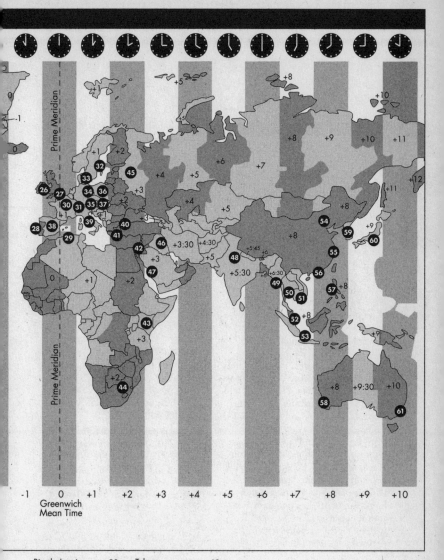

ESSENTIAL INFORMATION

AIR TRAVEL

BOOKING

When you book **look for nonstop flights** and **remember that "direct" flights stop at least once.** Try to avoid connecting flights, which require a change of plane.

CARRIERS

San Juan's large, busy Aeropuerto Internacional Luis Muñoz Marín is the regional hub of American Airlines, which flies nonstop daily from New York, Newark, Boston, Miami, Orlando, Fort Lauderdale, Los Angeles, and Saint Louis. Other major U.S. carriers serving San Juan include Continental, with daily nonstop service from Newark, Houston, and Cleveland; Delta, with daily nonstop service from Atlanta; Northwest, offering daily nonstop flights from Detroit, Memphis, and Minneapolis; United, which flies nonstop daily from Chicago and has weekend nonstop flights from New York and Washington, DC; US Airways, flying nonstop daily from Pittsburgh, Philadelphia, and Charlotte; and Spirit Air, which has two daily nonstop flights from Fort Lauderdale with connections from New York, Atlantic City, and Detroit.

Air Canada has Saturday flights to San Juan from Montréal with a stop in Toronto, and Canadian Airlines has weekly service—with a stop in Miami—from Toronto, Vancouver, and Calgary. British Airways serves San Juan from London, and Lufthansa's partner, Condor, flies every Saturday out of Frankfurt, Germany. LACSA connects San Juan to San José, Costa Rica. From Australia, you can take Qantas Airways from Sydney, Brisbane, Perth, Melbourne, and several other cities to Honolulu and Los Angeles for connections to Puerto Rico. Qantas also flies from Auckland, New Zealand, to Los Angeles.

Puerto Rico is also a good spot from which to hop to other Caribbean islands. American Airline's American Eagle serves many of the Lesser Antilles islands; Cape Air connects San Juan to Tortola, St. Thomas, and St. Croix; ALM travels to Jamaica, Aruba, Bonaire, and its base in Curaçao; and Leeward Islands Air Transport (LIAT), based in Antigua, flies to nearly all the Lesser Antilles islands. Vieques Air-Link connects San Juan with Puerto Rico's eastern islands of Vieques and Culebra.

➤ MAJOR U.S. AIRLINES: **American Airlines** (☎ 800/433–7300). **Continental** (☎ 800/231–0856). **Delta** (☎ 800/241–4141). **Northwest** (☎ 800/447–4747). **Spirit Air** (☎ 800/756–7117). **United** (☎ 800/538–2929). **US Airways** (☎ 800/428–4322).

➤ SMALLER AIRLINES: **ALM** (☎ 800/327–7230). **American Eagle** (☎ 800/433–7300). **Cape Air** (☎ 800/352–0714). **LIAT** (☎ 800/468–0482 or 787/791–0800 in Puerto Rico). **Vieques Air-Link** (☎ 888/901–9247 or 787/723–9882 in Puerto Rico).

➤ FROM ELSEWHERE IN THE WORLD: **Air Canada Vacations** (☎ 800/774–8993 in North America). **British Airways** (☎ 0845/722–2111 in the U.K.; 800/247–9297 in the U.S.). **Canadian Airlines** (☎ 800/426–7000 in North America). **Condor** (☎ 06107/939–229 in Germany; 800/524–6975 in the U.S.). **LACSA–Group Taca** (☎ 506/231–0033 in Costa Rica or 800/225–2272 in North America). **Qantas** (☎ 800/062–241 in Australia; 09/357–8700 in Auckland; 0800/808–767 elsewhere in New Zealand; 800/227–4500 in the U.S.).

CHECK-IN AND BOARDING

Due to heightened security, it's best to **check in at least three hours before**

flight time, even if you're flying from elsewhere in the United States. Assuming that not everyone with a ticket will show up, airlines routinely overbook planes. When everyone does, airlines ask for volunteers to give up their seats. In return, these volunteers usually get a certificate for a free flight and are rebooked on the next flight out. If there are not enough volunteers, the airline must choose who will be denied boarding. The first to get bumped are passengers who checked in late and those flying on discounted tickets, so get to the gate and check in as early as possible, especially during peak periods.

Always **bring a government-issued photo I.D. to the airport.** You'll be asked to show it before you are allowed to check in.

CUTTING COSTS

The least expensive airfares to Puerto Rico must usually be purchased in advance and are nonrefundable. It's smart to **call a number of airlines, and when you are quoted a good price, book it on the spot**—the same fare may not be available the next day. Always **check different routings** and look into using different airports. Travel agents, especially low-fare specialists (☞ Discounts and Deals), are helpful.

Consolidators are another good source. They buy tickets for scheduled international flights at reduced rates from the airlines, then sell them at prices that beat the best fare available directly from the airlines, usually without restrictions. Sometimes you can even get your money back if you need to return the ticket. Carefully read the fine print detailing penalties for changes and cancellations, and **confirm your consolidator reservation with the airline.**

When you **fly as a courier,** you trade your checked-luggage space for a ticket deeply subsidized by a courier service. There are restrictions on when you can book and how long you can stay.

Consider airline charter packages, which can offer savings. The disad-vantage is that such packages include stays in hotels or resorts that might not be your first choices (though you may be able to buy just the flight). Further, many companies have service to and from the island only once a week. There are penalties for extensions and cancellations on your part, though if charter companies don't fill their seats, they can cancel flights 10 days in advance and/or delay them by as much as 48 hours.

If you plan to use Puerto Rico as a base for exploring other Caribbean islands, **look for special island-hopping fares.** LIAT's Caribbean Super Explorer and Mini Explorer programs discount flights for unlimited travel for 30 days to any LIAT destination. In the past, ALM has also offered discounts on flights to multiple Caribbean destinations.

➤ CHARTER COMPANIES: **Air Charters Inc.** (☎ 787/724–6464). **Avitech Airplane and Helicopter Charters** (☎ 787/729–0000 or 787/729–0001). **Caribbean Helicorp, Inc.** (☎ 787/722–1984). **Charter Flights Caribbean Inc.** (☎ 787/791–1240). **Icarus Caribbean** (☎ 787/729–0001). **Inter Island Express** (☎ 787/253–1400). **M&N Aviation** (☎ 787/722–5980).

➤ CONSOLIDATORS: **Cheap Tickets** (☎ 800/377–1000). **Unitravel** (☎ 800/325–2222). **Up & Away Travel** (☎ 212/889–2345).

➤ COURIERS: **International Association of Air Travel Couriers** (✉ 220 S. Dixie Hwy. #3, Box 1349, Lake Worth, FL 33460, ☎ 561/582–8320).

➤ DISCOUNT PASSES: **ALM** (☎ 800/327–7230). **LIAT** (☎ 800/468–0482).

ENJOYING THE FLIGHT

For more legroom, **request an emergency-aisle seat.** Don't sit in the row in front of the emergency aisle or in front of a bulkhead, where seats may not recline. If you have dietary concerns, **ask for special meals when booking.** These can be vegetarian, low-cholesterol, or kosher, for example. On long flights, try to maintain a normal routine, to help fight jet lag. At night, **get some sleep.** By day, **eat light meals, drink water** (not alcohol), and **move around the cabin.**

FLYING TIMES

Nonstop flights to San Juan from New York are 3¾ hours; from Miami, 1½ hours; from Atlanta, 3½ hours; from Boston, 4 hours; from Chicago, 4¾ hours; from Los Angeles, 8 hours; from the United Kingdom, 5 hours; from Germany, 9¾ hours.

HOW TO COMPLAIN

If your baggage goes astray or your flight goes awry, complain right away. Most carriers require that you **file a claim immediately.**

➤ AIRLINE COMPLAINTS: U.S. Department of Transportation **Aviation Consumer Protection Division** (✉ C-75, Room 4107, Washington, DC 20590, ☎ 202/366–2220, airconsumer@ost.dot.gov, WEB www.dot.gov/airconsumer). **Federal Aviation Administration Consumer Hotline** (☎ 800/322–7873).

RECONFIRMING

Airlines flying in and out of Puerto Rico are reliable, but it's always best to **reconfirm flights.** Several San Juan and island hotels offer flight reconfirmation as a service of the concierge.

AIRPORTS

The Aeropuerto Internacional Luis Muñoz Marín (airline code SJU) is minutes east of downtown San Juan along the Baldorioty de Castro Highway (Route 26) in the coastal section of Isla Verde. San Juan's other airport, the small Aeropuerto Fernando L. Rivas Dominici (also known as the Isla Grande Airport), is near the city's Miramar section. From here you can catch Vieques Air-Link flights to Culebra, Vieques, and other destinations on Puerto Rico and throughout the Caribbean. (Note that although the Dominici airport was still operating at this writing, its future was uncertain.) Other Puerto Rican airports include Mercedita in the south coast town of Ponce, Eugenio María de Hostos in the west coast community of Mayagüez, Rafael Hernández in the northwestern town of Aguadilla, Antonio Rivera Rodríguez on Vieques, and Benjamín Rivera Noriega on Culebra.

➤ AIRPORT INFORMATION: **Aeropuerto Antonio Rivera Rodríguez** (☎ 787/741–8358). **Aeropuerto Benjamín Rivera Noriega** (☎ 787/742–0022). **Aeropuerto Eugenio María de Hostos** (☎ 787/833–0148). **Aeropuerto Fernando L. Rivas Dominici** (☎ 787/729–8711). **Aeropuerto Internacional Luis Muñoz Marín** (☎ 787/791–3840). **Aeropuerto Mercedita** (☎ 787/842–6292). **Aeropuerto Rafael Hernández** (☎ 787/891–2286).

TAXIS AND SHUTTLES

From the Aeropuerto Internacional Luis Muñoz Marín into San Juan, *taxis turísticos* charge set rates based on zones. Uniformed and badged officials will help you find a cab (look for the tourism company booth) and hand you a slip with your fare, which you present to your driver. To Isla Verde, the fare is $8; to Condado, $12; to Old San Juan, $16. If you don't hail one of these cabs (they're white and labeled "taxis turísticos"), you're at the mercy of the meter and the driver.

Airport Limousine Service provides exclusive prepaid town car service to Isla Verde ($50), Condado ($60), and Old San Juan ($75). The rates are by the trip, not per person. You can also arrange to have the driver take you to other parts of the island. Limousines of Dorado Transport Co-op serve hotels and villas in the Dorado area for $22 per person.

Many hotels offer guests transportation from the airport (either free or at a cost); when booking your room, get the lowdown. You should do the same if you're heading directly out onto the island and don't want to rent a car; many of the larger resorts run regular shuttles.

➤ TAXI AND SHUTTLE CONTACTS: **Airport Limousine Service** (☎ 787/791–4745). **Dorado Transport Co-op** (☎ 787/796–1214). **Taxis Turísticos** (☎ 787/721–2400).

DUTY-FREE SHOPPING

Puerto Rico isn't a duty-free island, but you'll find duty-free shops at Luis Muñoz Marín International Airport in San Juan. They're in the terminal boarding areas, and you'll have to show your boarding pass before loading up on watches, liquor, and perfume.

BOAT AND FERRY TRAVEL

The Autoridad de los Puertos (Port Authority) ferry between Old San Juan (Pier 2) and Cataño costs a mere 50¢ one-way. It runs daily every 15 or 30 minutes from 5:45 AM until 10 PM. The Fajardo port authority's 400-passenger ferries run between that east coast town and the out islands of Vieques and Culebra; both trips take 90 minutes. The vessels carry cargo and passengers to Vieques three times daily ($2 one-way) and to Culebra twice daily ($2.25 one-way). Additional vessels carry vehicles and large cargo to both islands each weekday morning at 9:30 AM and at 4 PM.

FARES AND SCHEDULES

Get schedules for the Culebra and Vieques ferries by calling the port authority in Fajardo, Vieques, or Culebra. You buy tickets at the ferry dock. Reservations aren't necessary unless you're transporting a vehicle, in which case you should make a reservation at least two weeks in advance and arrive one hour before the departure time.

➤ BOAT AND FERRY INFORMATION: **Autoridad de los Puertos** (☎ 787/788–1155 in San Juan; 787/863–4560 in Fajardo; 787/742–3161 in Culebra; 787/741–4761 in Vieques).

BUS TRAVEL

The Autoridad Metropolitana de Autobuses (AMA, or Metropolitan Bus Authority) operates *guaguas* (buses) that thread through San Juan, running in exclusive lanes on major thoroughfares and stopping at signs marked PARADA or PARADA DE GUAGUAS. The main terminals are at the Covadonga parking lot and Plaza de Colón in Old San Juan and the Capetillo Terminal in Río Piedras, next to the central business district. Most buses are air-conditioned and have wheelchair lifts and lock-downs.

Bus travel to outlying areas is less than comprehensive. Your best bet for travel to other parts of the island is by rental car or by *públicos*—"public cars," though most are actually 17-passenger vans. They have yellow license plates ending in "P" or "PD,"

and they scoot to towns throughout the island, stopping in each community's main plaza. They operate primarily during the day; routes and fares are fixed by the public service commission, but schedules aren't set, so you have to call ahead.

In San Juan, the main terminals are at Aeropuerto Internacional Luis Muñoz Marín and at Plaza Colón on the waterfront in Old San Juan. San Juan–based público companies include Blue Line for trips to Aguadilla and the northwest coast, Choferes Unidos de Ponce for Ponce, Línea Caborrojeña for Cabo Rojo and the southwest coast, Línea Boricua for the interior and the southwest, Línea Sultana for Mayagüez and the west coast, and Terminal de Transportación Pública for Fajardo and the east.

FARES AND SCHEDULES

In San Juan, bus fares are 25¢ or 50¢, depending on the route, and are paid in exact change upon entering the bus. Buses adhere to their routes, but schedules are fluid, to say the least. Count on a bus passing your stop every 20–30 minutes, less frequently on Sunday and holidays. Service starts at around 6 AM and generally lasts until 9 PM. For more information, call the AMA or pick up a schedule at the nearest bus station.

➤ BUS INFORMATION: **AMA** (☎ 787/729–1512 or 787/767–7979). **Blue Line** (☎ 787/765–7733). **Choferes Unidos de Ponce** (☎ 787/764–0540). **Línea Boricua** (☎ 787/765–1908). **Línea Caborrojeña** (☎ 787/723–9155). **Línea Sultana** (☎ 787/765–9377). **Terminal de Transportación Pública** (☎ 787/250–0717).

BUSINESS HOURS

BANKS AND OFFICES

Bank hours are generally weekdays 8–4 or 9–5, though a few branches are open Saturday 9–noon or 1. Post offices are open weekdays 7:30–4:30 and Saturday 8–noon. Government offices are open weekdays 9–5.

GAS STATIONS

Most stations are open daily from early in the morning until 10 PM or

11 PM. Numerous stations in urban areas are open 24 hours.

MUSEUMS AND SIGHTS

As a rule San Juan area museums are closed on Monday, and in some cases, Sunday. Hours otherwise are 9 or 10 AM to 5 PM, often with an hour off for lunch between noon and 2. Sights managed by the national parks service, such as Fuerte San Felipe del Morro and San Cristóbal, are open daily 9–5.

PHARMACIES

In cities, pharmacies are generally open 9–6 or 7 weekdays and on Saturday. Walgreens operates numerous pharmacies around the island; some are open 24 hours.

SHOPS

Street shops are open Monday through Saturday 9 to 6 (9–9 during Christmas holidays); mall stores tend to stay open until 9 or so. Count on convenience stores staying open late into the night, seven days a week. Supermarkets are often closed on Sunday, although some remain open 24-hours, seven days a week.

CAMERAS AND PHOTOGRAPHY

Frothy waves in a turquoise sea and palm-lined crescents of beach are relatively easy to capture on film if you **don't let the brightness of the sun on sand and water fool your light meter.** You must compensate or else work early or late in the day when the light isn't as brilliant and contrast isn't such a problem. Try to **capture expansive views** of waterfront, beach, or village scenes; consider shooting down onto the shore from a clearing on a hillside or from a rock on the beach. Or **zoom in on something colorful,** such as a delicate tropical flower or a craftsman at work—but always **ask permission to take pictures of locals or their property. Use a disposable underwater camera** to make your snorkeling and diving adventures more memorable.

➤ PHOTO HELP: **Kodak Information Center** (☎ 800/242–2424). *Kodak Guide to Shooting Great Travel Pictures,* available in bookstores or from Fodor's Travel Publications (☎ 800/533–6478; $16.50 plus $5.50 shipping).

EQUIPMENT PRECAUTIONS

Always **keep your film and tape out of the sun.** Carry an extra supply of batteries, and **be prepared to turn on your camera or camcorder** to prove to security personnel that the device is real. Always **ask for hand inspection of film,** which becomes clouded after repeated exposure to airport X-ray machines, and **keep videotapes away from metal detectors.**

On the beach, **be wary of sand and salt spray**—keep your camera and film in a sealed container or bag when not in use. Also, **don't leave your camera locked in your rental car's trunk** all day—heat can reduce the quality of the film. Never leave your gear unattended on the seats of your car or on the beach, and lock it in your hotel room safe when you go out.

FILM AND DEVELOPING

Film of all types is widely available in supermarkets, drugstores, souvenir shops, and photo shops. Count on paying about $7 for a 24-exposure roll of color-print film. In San Juan and other urban areas, numerous film developing shops and drugstores will get your prints made promptly, although seldom within the one-hour time frame that they advertise.

VIDEOS

The local standard for video players is the same as on the U.S. mainland–NTSC. Travelers from Australia, Britain, and New Zealand, where PAL is the standard, will have to wait until returning home to view their vacation.

CAR RENTAL

Rates start as low as $35 a day (plus insurance), with unlimited mileage. Discounts are often offered for long-term rentals, for cars that are booked more than 72 hours in advance, and to automobile association members. In addition, if you pay using an American Express or certain gold credit cards, you may not need to buy insurance (check with your credit-card company). All major U.S. car-rental agencies are represented on the island, but be sure to **look into local companies.** Most are reliable and some offer competitive rates.

If you're visiting during peak season or over holiday weekends **reserve your car before arriving on the island**—not only because of possible discounts but also to ensure that you get a car and that it's a reliable one. Faced with high demand, the agencies may be forced to drag out the worst of their fleet; waiting 'til the last minute could leave you stranded without a car or stranded with one on the side of the road.

You'll find offices for dozens of agencies at San Juan's Aeropuerto Internacional Luis Muñoz Marín, and a majority of them have shuttle service to and from the airport and the pickup point. Most rental cars are available with automatic or standard transmission. Four-wheel-drive vehicles aren't necessary unless you plan to go way off the beaten path or along the steep, rocky roads of Culebra or Vieques; in most cases a standard compact car will do the trick. **Always opt for air-conditioning.** You'll be glad you did when it's high noon and you're in a San Juan traffic jam.

➤ MAJOR AGENCIES: **Alamo** (☎ 800/327–9633). **Avis** (☎ 800/331–1084; 800/879–2847 in Canada; 02/9353–9000 in Australia; 09/525–1982 in New Zealand). **Budget** (☎ 800/527–0700; 0870/670–5000 in the U.K., through affiliate Europcar). **Dollar** (☎ 800/800–6000; 0124/622–0111 in the U.K., through affiliate Sixt Kenning; 02/9223–1444 in Australia). **Hertz** (☎ 800/654–3001; 800/263–0600 in Canada; 020/8897–2072 in the U.K.; 02/9669–2444 in Australia; 09/256–8690 in New Zealand). **National InterRent** (☎ 800/227–7368; National Europe: 020/8680–4800 in the U.K.).

➤ LOCAL AGENCIES: **Charlie Car Rental** (☎ 787/721–6525 or 800/289–1227). **L & M Car Rental** (☎ 787/791–1160 or 800/666–0807). **Target** (☎ 787/728–1447 or 800/934–6457).

CUTTING COSTS

To get the best deal, **book through a travel agent who will shop around.**

Do **look into wholesalers,** companies that do not own fleets but rent in bulk from those that do and often offer better rates than traditional car-rental operations. Payment must be made before you leave home.

➤ WHOLESALERS: **Auto Europe** (☎ 207/842–2000 or 800/223–5555, FAX 800–235–6321, WEB www. autoeurope.com).

INSURANCE

When driving a rented car you are generally responsible for any damage to or loss of the vehicle as well as for any property damage or personal injury that you may cause. Before you rent see what coverage your personal auto-insurance policy and credit cards already provide.

REQUIREMENTS AND RESTRICTIONS

A valid driver's license from your native country can be used in Puerto Rico for three months. In some cases the driver must be at least 25 years old.

SURCHARGES

Before you pick up a car in one city and leave it in another, **ask about drop-off charges or one-way service fees,** which can be substantial. Some rental agencies charge extra if you return the car before the time specified in your contract. To avoid a hefty refueling fee, **fill the tank just before you turn in the car,** but be aware that gas stations near the rental outlet may overcharge.

CAR TRAVEL

Several well-marked multilane highways link population centers. Route 26 is the main artery through San Juan, connecting Condado and Old San Juan to Isla Verde and the airport. Route 22, which runs east–west between San Juan and Camuy, and the Luis A. Ferré Expressway (Route 52), which runs north–south between San Juan and Ponce, are toll roads (35¢–50¢). Route 2, a smaller highway, travels along the west coast, and routes 3 and 53 traverse the east shore.

Five highways are particularly noteworthy thanks to their scenery and vistas. The island's tourism authorities have even given them special names. Ruta Panorámica (Panoramic Route) runs east–west through the central mountains. Ruta Cotorra (Puerto Rican Parrot Route) travels along the north coast. Ruta Paso Fino (Paso Fino Horse Route, after a horse breed) takes you north–south and west along the south coast. Ruta Coquí, named for the famous Puerto Rican tree frog, runs along the east coast. Ruta Flamboyán, named after the island tree, goes from San Juan through the mountains to the east coast.

AUTO CLUBS

➤ IN AUSTRALIA: **Australian Automobile Association** (☎ 02/6247–7311).

➤ IN CANADA: **Canadian Automobile Association** (CAA, ☎ 613/247–0117).

➤ IN NEW ZEALAND: **New Zealand Automobile Association** (☎ 09/377–4660).

➤ IN THE U.K.: **Automobile Association** (AA, ☎ 0990/500–600). **Royal Automobile Club** (RAC, ☎ 0990/722–722 for membership; 0345/121–345 for insurance).

➤ IN THE U.S.: **American Automobile Association** (☎ 800/564–6222).

EMERGENCY SERVICES

For extreme emergencies, dial 911. If your car breaks down, call the rental company for a replacement. Before renting, make sure you investigate the company's policy regarding replacement vehicles and repairs out on the island, and ask about surcharges that might be incurred if you break down in a rural area and need a new car.

GASOLINE

All types of fuel—unleaded regular, unleaded super-premium, diesel—are available by the liter. At this writing, the cost for regular gas was 32¢ a liter, which works out to roughly $1.22 a gallon. Most stations have both full- and self-service. Hours vary, but stations generally operate daily from early in the morning until 10 or 11 PM; in metro areas many are open 24 hours. Stations are few and far between in the central mountains

and other rural areas; plan accordingly. In cities, you can pay with cash and bank or credit cards; in the hinterlands cash is often your only option.

ROAD CONDITIONS

Puerto Rico has some of the Caribbean's best roads. That said, potholes, sharp turns, speed bumps, sudden gradient changes, and poor lighting can make driving difficult. **Be especially cautious when driving after heavy rains or hurricanes**; roads and bridges might be washed out or damaged. Many of the mountain roads are very narrow and steep, with unmarked curves and cliffs. Locals are familiar with such roads and often drive at high speeds, which can give you quite a scare. When traveling on a narrow, curving road, it's best to **honk your horn as you take any sharp turn.**

Traffic around cities—particularly San Juan, Ponce, and Mayagüez—is heavy at rush hours (weekdays 7–10 and 4–7).

ROAD MAPS

Most car-rental agencies give you a free map with your car; more detailed maps are available in bookstores, drugstores, and souvenir shops. Look for the *Puerto Rico Mapa de Carreteras* (about $7), by Metro Data Maps, which features an island map; a large metro map of San Juan; and insets of Aguadilla, Mayagüez, Arecibo, Ponce, and other large towns. Also, look for the free *Puerto Rico Travel Maps* at tourism company offices and information booths.

RULES OF THE ROAD

U.S. driving laws apply in Puerto Rico, and you'll find no problem with signage or directionals. Street and highway signs are most often in Spanish but use international symbols; brushing up on a few key Spanish terms before your trip will help. The following words and phrases are especially useful: *calle* (street), *calle sin salida* (dead end, no exit), *cruce de peatones* (pedestrian crossing), *cuidado* (caution), *desvío* (detour), *estación de peaje* (toll booth), *no entre* (do not enter), *prohibido adelantar* (no passing), *salida* (exit), *tránsito* (one way), *zona escolar* (school zone).

Distances are posted in kilometers (1.6 km to 1 mi), whereas speed limits are posted in miles per hour. Speeding and drunk-driving penalties are much the same here as on the mainland. Police cars often travel with their lights flashing, so it's difficult to know when they're trying to pull you over. If the siren is on, move to the right to get out of their way. If the lights are on, it's best to pull over—just be sure that the vehicle is a *marked* police car before doing so.

CHILDREN IN PUERTO RICO

With miles of beach and plenty of outdoor activities, the island is a paradise for the entire family, and Puerto Ricans are very family oriented. The Puerto Rico Tourism Company's free publication *Qué Pasa*—available at all their offices—lists children's events. **When, booking a hotel room, ask about children's activities.** Also, **if you're renting a car, arrange for a car seat** when you reserve.

FLYING

If your children are two or older, **ask about children's airfares.** As a rule, infants under two not occupying a seat fly at greatly reduced fares or even for free. When booking, **confirm carry-on allowances** if you're traveling with infants. In general, for babies charged 10% of the adult fare you are allowed one carry-on bag and a collapsible stroller; if the flight is full, the stroller may have to be checked or you may be limited to less.

Experts agree that it's a good idea to use safety seats aloft for children weighing less than 40 pounds. Airlines set their own policies: U.S. carriers usually require that the child be ticketed, even if he or she is young enough to ride free, since the seats must be strapped into regular seats. Do **check your airline's policy about using safety seats during takeoff and landing.** And since safety seats are not allowed everywhere in the plane, get your seat assignments early.

When reserving, **request children's meals or a freestanding bassinet** if you need them. But note that bulkhead seats, where you must sit to use the bassinet, may lack an overhead bin or storage space on the floor.

FOOD

Children tend to enjoy many Puerto Rican dishes, but there are plenty of options for those who shy away from new or different foods. You're never far from a Burger King or a Pizza Hut, and island supermarkets stock familiar brands of cereals, snacks, and other items. When thoroughly washed and/or peeled, fresh fruit is often a treat for even the most finicky eaters.

Many restaurants, including those in hotels, offer children's menus. Note that the legal drinking age on Puerto Rico is a loosely enforced 18.

LODGING

In general, kids are welcome at island resorts and hotels, many of which have children's activity centers or programs, wading pools, and baby-sitting services. Some resorts also have video games rooms, in-room videos, or in-room "movies on demand" with films for children and safeguards that allow you to block out adult flicks. When reserving your hotel room **ask about children's programs and amenities.**

Most hotels allow children under a certain age to stay in their parents' room at no extra charge, but some charge for them as extra adults; be sure to **find out the cutoff age for children's discounts.** Also ask about cribs and extra beds or cots.

➤ BEST CHOICES: **Candelero Resort at Palmas del Mar** (✉ Rte. 906 [Box 2020, Humacao 00792], ☎ 787/852-6000). **Condado Plaza Hotel and Casino** (✉ 999 Av. Ashford, Condado 00902, ☎ 787/721-1000 or 800/468-8588; 800/624-0420 direct to hotel). **Hilton Ponce & Casino** (✉ Rte. 14, 1150 Av. Caribe, La Guancha [Box 7419, 00732, Ponce], ☎ 787/259-7676 or 800/445-8667). **Inter-Continental San Juan Resort & Casino** (✉ 187 Av. Isla Verde, Isla Verde [Box 6676, 00914], ☎ 787/791-6100, 800/544-3008, or 800/443-2009). **Westin Río Mar Beach Resort** (✉ 6000 Río Mar Blvd., Barrio Palmer [Box 2006, 00721,

Río Grande], ☎ 787/888–6000).
**Wyndham El Conquistador Resort
and Country Club** (✉ 1000 Av. El
Conquistador [Box 70001, 00738,
Fajardo], ☎ 787/863–1000, 800/
996–3426, or 800/468–5228). **Wyndham El San Juan Hotel and Casino**
(✉ 6063 Av. Isla Verde, Isla Verde
[Box 2872, 00902], ☎ 787/791–
1000, 800/468–2818, or 800/996–
3426).

PRECAUTIONS

The sun can be the greatest danger to
children. Be sure to **stock up on sun
screen with an SPF of more than 28.**
Some island flowers—which are very
bright and attractive to children—are
actually poisonous. It's best to **en-
courage your kids to look but not
touch.** At the beach, watch out for
jellyfish, which are particularly abundant in winter, in the water or on the
sand and spiky sea urchins, which are
often embedded in rocks under water.

SIGHTS AND ATTRACTIONS

Puerto Rico offers many sights and
attractions that are particularly suitable for kids. Places that are especially appealing to children are
indicated by a rubber duckie icon (🦆)
in the margin.

The Museo del Niño (Children's
Museum) in Old San Juan has interactive exhibits. The Parque de las
Cavernas del Río Camuy (Río Camuy
Cave Park) offers an educational
video and a trolley ride through a
cave system. The Parque de las Ciencias Luis A. Ferré (Luis A. Ferré
Science Park) has a planetarium,
educational exhibits, and a small zoo.
The Parque Zoológico de Puerto Rico
(Puerto Rico Zoo) in Mayagüez
houses a wide array of animals.
There's also a lot to be said for flying
kites at El Morro and feeding pigeons
at Parque de Palomas in Old San Juan
as well as splashing about or building
sand castles at a beach just about
anywhere on the island.

➤ BEST CHOICES: **Museo del Niño**
(✉ 150 Calle Cristo, San Juan,
☎ 787/722–3791). **Parque de las
Cavernas del Río Camuy** (✉ Rte.
129, Km 18.9, Arecibo, ☎ 787/898–
3100). **Parque de las Ciencias Luis A.**

Ferré (✉ Rte. 167, Bayamón, ☎ 787/
740–6878). **Parque Zoológico de
Puerto Rico** (✉ Rte. 108, Miradero
Sector, Mayagüez, ☎ 787/834–8110).

SUPPLIES AND EQUIPMENT

American brands of baby food, dia-
pers, and other infant necessities are
easy to find in any grocery store, drug
store, or American chain such as
Walmart, Sams, or Kmart. Baby
formula is available in premixed and
powdered form. Note that most
supplies are more expensive than in
the United States; some premixed
formulas cost twice as much as they
would on the mainland.

COMPUTERS ON THE ROAD

It's easy to plug in at many hotels,
which are now frequently equipped
with dedicated fax/modem lines and
plenty of outlets. Still, it's a good idea
to carry an extra battery as well as a
small extension cord for those cases
when the only outlet is behind the
headboard of the bed.

Although the Internet is still a relatively new thing to many locals, more
and more copy shops and cybercafés
are popping up. Although service in
such places is reliable, your hotel's
business center is probably the best
place to surf the Web.

➤ INTERNET ACCESS: **Cigar Box**
(✉ Plazoleta de Isla Verde #6150,
L-15, Carolina, ☎ 787/253–2336).
CyberNet Café (✉ 1128 Av. Ashford,
Condado, San Juan, ☎ 787/724–
4033; ✉ 5575 Av. Isla Verde, Car-
olina, ☎ 787/791–3138). **Diner's
Restaurant** (✉ 357 Calle San Fran-
cisco, Old San Juan, San Juan,
☎ 787/723–4616).

CONSULATES

Australia and New Zealand don't
have consulates on Puerto Rico,
though Canada and the United Kingdom do.

➤ CONTACTS: **British Consulate**
(✉ Bank Trust Plaza, Suite 807, 265
Av. Ponce de León, Hato Rey, San
Juan, 00917, ☎ 787/758–9828).
Canadian Consulate (✉ 33 Calle
Bolivia, Hato Rey, San Juan 00917,
☎ 787/794–1205).

CONSUMER PROTECTION

Whenever shopping or buying travel services, **pay with a major credit card** so you can cancel payment or get reimbursed if there's a problem. If you're doing business with a particular company for the first time, **contact your local Better Business Bureau and the attorney general's offices** in your own state and the company's home state as well. Have any complaints been filed? Finally, if you're buying a package or tour, always **consider travel insurance** that includes default coverage (☞ Insurance).

➤ BBBs: **Council of Better Business Bureaus** (✉ 4200 Wilson Blvd., Suite 800, Arlington, VA 22203, ☎ 703/276–0100; 787/756–5400 in Puerto Rico, FAX 703/525–8277, WEB www.bbb.org).

CRUISE TRAVEL

Puerto Rico is a major cruise destination, and an embarkation point for several lines that ply the Caribbean. Cruising is a relaxing way to visit a destination, though it's not a way to get to know a place. The reason is time—most ships call at several ports per trip, spending a day or part of a day in port. Your onshore experience is limited to a few hours of sightseeing and/or shopping. That said, cruises offer sunshine, entertainment, and plenty of good food and drink for one price. For the best deals, **consult a travel agent who deals exclusively with cruise lines.** To get you started, pick up a copy of *Fodor's Caribbean Ports of Call,* a pocket primer for cruisers that's available at on-line retailers and bookstores everywhere.

Puerto Rico's main cruise-ship docks are in the San Juan metropolitan area. Most of the time, vessels dock at the piers in Old San Juan, though during the busy high season they often must dock at Isla Grande's Pan American Pier or Puerta de Tierra's Frontier Pier. Públicos, taxis, and tour buses meet passengers at the piers. Públicos have fixed fees from the piers to main tourist areas: $16 to and from the airport and Isla Verde, $10 to and from Condado and Mira-

mar, and $6 to and from Old San Juan and Puerta de Tierra. Monday and Tuesday are big days for ships to dock in the old city.

Lines that routinely have Puerto Rico on their itineraries include Carnival Cruise Lines, Celebrity Cruises, Club Med Cruises, Costa Cruise Lines, Cunard Lines, Holland America Lines, Norwegian Cruise Line, P&O Cruises, Princess Cruises, Radisson Seven Seas Cruises, Royal Olympic Cruises, Royal Caribbean International, Seabourn Cruise Line, and Sea Cloud Cruises.

➤ CRUISE LINES: **Carnival Cruise Lines** (✉ 3655 N.W. 87th Ave., Miami, FL 33178, ☎ 305/599–2600 or 800/327–9501). **Celebrity Cruises** (✉ 5200 Blue Lagoon Dr., Miami, FL 33126, ☎ 305/262–8322 or 800/437–3111). **Club Med Cruises** (✉ 40 W. 57th St., New York, NY 10019, ☎ 212/750–1687 or 800/258–2633). **Costa Cruise Lines** (✉ World Trade Center, 80 S.W. 8th St., Miami, FL 33130, ☎ 305/358–7352 or 800/462–6782). **Cunard Lines** (✉ 555 5th Ave., New York, NY 10017, ☎ 800/728–6273 or 800/221–4770). **Holland America Lines** (✉ 3000 Elliot Ave. W, Seattle, WA 98119, ☎ 800/426–0327). **Norwegian Cruise Line** (✉ 95 Merrick Way, Coral Gables, FL 33134, ☎ 305/445–0866 or 800/327–7030). **P&O Cruises** (✉ Richmond House, Terminus Terrace, Southampton, England S014 3PN, ☎ 084/5355–5333). **Princess Cruises** (✉ 10100 Santa Monica Blvd., Suite 1800, Los Angeles, CA 90067, ☎ 310/553–1770 or 800/421–0522). **Radisson Seven Seas Cruises** (✉ 600 Corporate Dr., Suite 410, Fort Lauderdale, FL 33334, ☎ 800/333–3333). **Royal Caribbean Cruise Line** (✉ 1050 Caribbean Way, Miami, FL 33132, ☎ 305/539–6000 or 800/327–6700). **Royal Olympic Cruises** (✉ 1805 3rd St., New York, NY 10022-7513, ☎ 800/872–6400; ✉ Triumph House, Suite 403-404, 189 Regent St., London, W1R 7WA, England, ☎ 207/734–0805 or 207/434–1180). **Seabourn Cruise Line** (✉ 55 Francisco St., Suite 710, San Francisco, CA 94133, ☎ 415/391–7444 or 800/929–9595). **Sea Cloud**

Cruises, Inc. (✉ 32-40 North Dean St., Englewood, NJ 07631, ☎ 201/227–9404 or 888/732–2568).

➤ ORGANIZATION: **Cruise Lines International Association** (✉ 500 5th Ave., Suite 1407, New York, NY 10010, ☎ 212/921–0066).

➤ PORT INFORMATION: **Autoridad de Puertos de Puerto Rico** (☎ 787/723–2260). **Terminal de San Juan** (☎ 787/729–8714).

CUSTOMS AND DUTIES

If you're coming from outside the United States, **keep receipts** for all purchases. Upon reentering the country, **be ready to show customs officials what you've bought.** If you feel a duty is incorrect or object to the way your clearance was handled, note the inspector's badge number and ask to see a supervisor. If the problem isn't resolved, write to the appropriate authorities, beginning with the port director at your point of entry.

IN AUSTRALIA

Australian residents who are 18 or older may bring home $A400 worth of souvenirs and gifts (including jewelry), 250 cigarettes or 250 grams of tobacco, and 1,125 ml of alcohol (including wine, beer, and spirits). Residents under 18 may bring back $A200 worth of goods. Prohibited items include meat products. Seeds, plants, and fruits need to be declared upon arrival.

➤ INFORMATION: **Australian Customs Service** (Regional Director, ✉ Box 8, Sydney, NSW 2001, ☎ 02/9213–2000 or 1300/363263; 1800/020504 quarantine-inquiry line, FAX 02/9213–4043, WEB www.customs.gov.au).

IN CANADA

Canadian residents who have been out of Canada for at least seven days may bring home C$500 worth of goods duty-free. If you've been away less than seven days but more than 48 hours, the duty-free allowance drops to C$200; if your trip lasts 24–48 hours, the allowance is C$50. You may not pool allowances with family members. Goods claimed under the C$500 exemption may follow you by mail; those claimed under the lesser exemptions must accompany you.

Alcohol and tobacco products may be included in the seven-day and 48-hour exemptions but not in the 24-hour exemption. If you meet the age requirements of the province or territory through which you reenter Canada, you may bring in, duty-free, 1.14 liters (40 imperial ounces) of wine or liquor *or* 24 12-ounce cans or bottles of beer or ale. If you are 16 or older you may bring in, duty-free, 200 cigarettes and 50 cigars. Check ahead of time with Revenue Canada or the Department of Agriculture for policies regarding meat products, seeds, plants, and fruits.

You may send an unlimited number of gifts worth up to C$60 each duty-free to Canada. Label the package UNSOLICITED GIFT—VALUE UNDER $60. Alcohol and tobacco are excluded.

➤ INFORMATION: **Canada Customs and Revenue Agency** (✉ 2265 St. Laurent Blvd. S, Ottawa, Ontario K1G 4K3, ☎ 204/983–3500, 506/636–5064, or 800/461–9999, WEB www.ccra-adrc.gc.ca).

IN NEW ZEALAND

Homeward-bound residents 17 or older may bring back $700 worth of souvenirs and gifts. Your duty-free allowance also includes 4.5 liters of wine or beer; one 1,125-ml bottle of spirits; and either 200 cigarettes, 250 grams of tobacco, 50 cigars, or a combination of the three up to 250 grams. Prohibited items include meat products, seeds, plants, and fruits.

➤ INFORMATION: **New Zealand Customs** (Head office: ✉ The Customhouse, 17–21 Whitmore St., Box 2218, Wellington, ☎ 09/300–5399 or 0800/428–786, WEB www.customs.govt.nz).

IN PUERTO RICO

U.S. citizens and legal residents need not clear customs in Puerto Rico when arriving from the mainland. Otherwise, clearing U.S. Customs in Puerto Rico is fast and efficient, provided you've filled out all customs forms and declared all items, including fruits and vegetables, plants and plant products, meat and meat products, and live animals and wildlife products. Pets and birds can enter Puerto Rico subject to certification, permits, inspection, and quarantine rules that vary with the animal and its origin.

When leaving Puerto Rico for the mainland, you must pass your bag through a checkpoint of the U.S. Department of Agriculture's (USDA) Animal and Plant Health Inspection Service (APHIS). The list of organic products that can be transported from Puerto Rico to the States includes avocados, bananas, breadfruits, citrus fruits, ginger, papayas, and plantains.

➤ INFORMATION: **USDA** (✉ ☎ 787/ 253–4510 or 787/253–4505 in Puerto Rico). **U.S. Customs Service** (✉ 1300 Pennsylvania Ave. NW, Washington, DC 20229, WEB www.customs.gov; inquiries ☎ 202/354–1000 or 787/ 253–4533; complaints c/o ✉ Office of Regulations and Rulings; registration of equipment c/o ✉ Resource Management, ☎ 202/927–0540).

IN THE U.K.

From areas outside the EU, including Puerto Rico, you may bring home, duty-free, 200 cigarettes or 50 cigars; 1 liter of spirits or 2 liters of fortified or sparkling wine or liqueurs; 2 liters of still table wine; 60 ml of perfume; 250 ml of toilet water; plus £136 worth of other goods, including gifts and souvenirs. If returning from outside the EU, prohibited items include meat products, seeds, plants, and fruits.

➤ INFORMATION: **HM Customs and Excise** (✉ Portcullis House, 21 Cowbridge Rd. E, Cardiff CF11 9SS, ☎ 029/2038–6423 or 0845/010– 9000, WEB www.hmce.gov.uk).

DINING

Throughout the island you'll find everything from French haute cuisine to sushi bars, as well as superb local eateries serving *comidas criollas,* traditional Caribbean-creole meals. Note that the *mesón gastronómico* label is used by the government to recognize restaurants that preserve culinary traditions. The restaurants we list are the cream of the crop in each price category. Properties indicated by a ✕☉ are lodging establishments whose restaurant warrants a special trip.

MEAL TIMES

Puerto Ricans' eating habits mirror those of their counterparts on the mainland United States: they eat breakfast, lunch, and dinner, though they don't tend to down coffee all day long. Instead, islanders like a steaming, high-test cup in the morning and another between 2 and 4 PM. They may finish a meal with coffee, but they never drink coffee *during* a meal.

Unless otherwise noted, the restaurants listed in this guide are open daily for lunch and dinner. People tend to eat dinner late in Puerto Rico; you may find yourself alone in the restaurant if you eat at 5 PM; at 6, business will pick up a little, and from 7–10, it may be quite busy.

RESERVATIONS AND DRESS

Reservations are always a good idea: we mention them only when they're essential or not accepted. Book as far ahead as you can, and reconfirm as soon as you arrive. We mention dress only when men are required to wear a jacket or a jacket and tie. Puerto Ricans generally dress up to go out, particularly in the evenings. And always remember: beach attire is only for the beach.

SPECIALTIES

Puerto Rican cooking uses lots of local vegetables: plantains are cooked a hundred different ways—as *tostones* (fried green), *amarillos* (baked ripe), and as chips. Rice and beans with tostones or amarillos are basic accompaniments to every dish. Locals cook white rice with *habichuelas* (red beans), *achiote* (annatto seeds), or saffron; brown rice with *gandules* (pigeon peas); and *morro* (black rice) with frijoles *negros* (black beans). Garbanzos and white beans are served in many daily specials. Assorted yams and other root vegetables such as yucca and yautía are served baked, fried, stuffed, boiled, mashed, and whole. *Sofrito*—a garlic, onion, sweet pepper, coriander, oregano, and tomato puree—is used as a base for practically everything.

Beef, chicken, pork, and seafood are rubbed with *adobo,* a garlic-oregano marinade, before cooking; the practice is said to date from the time of the Taínos. *Arroz con pollo* (chicken with rice), *sancocho* (beef or chicken and tuber soup), *asopao* (a soupy rice gumbo with chicken or seafood), and *encebollado* (steak smothered in onions) are all typical plates. Other traditional favorites, found in abundance during the Christmas holidays, are *lechón* (roast pork) and *pastelles*, a kind of Puerto Rican tamale made of meat and condiment stuffed inside plantain paste, which is then wrapped in a plantain leaf and tied off for boiling. The Cayey barrio of Guavaté, a pleasant 45-minute drive from San Juan, is known for its roast pork, and another favorite, *morcilla*, a black spicy sausage.

Fritters are a Puerto Rican specialty served in snack bars along the highways and beaches as well as at cocktail parties. You may find *empanadillas* (stuffed fried turnovers), *surrullitos* (cheese-stuffed corn sticks), *alcapurias* (stuffed green banana croquettes), and *bacalaitos* (codfish fritters).

Caribbean lobster (not as sweet as the Maine variety) is available mainly at small coastal restaurants, and there's always lots of fresh dolphinfish and red snapper. Conch is prepared in a chilled ceviche salad or stuffed inside fritters with tomato sauce. Local *pan de agua* is an excellent French-style bread, best hot out of the oven. It's also good toasted and should be tried as part of a *cubano* sandwich (roast pork, ham, Swiss cheese, pickles, and mustard). Local desserts include flans, puddings, and fruit pastes served with native white cheese. The renowned locally grown coffee is excellent served espresso-black or generously cut *con leche* (with hot milk).

WINE, BEER, AND SPIRITS

Puerto Rico isn't a notable producer of wine, but there are several well-crafted local beers to choose from. Legends trace the birthplace of the piña colada to any number of San Juan establishments, from the Caribe Hilton to a Calle La Fortaleza bar. Puerto Rican rum is popular mixed with cola (known as a *cuba libre*), soda, tonic, juices, or water, or served on the rocks or even straight up.

Rums range from light mixers to dark, aged sipping liqueurs. Look for Bacardí, Don Q, Ron Rico, Palo Viejo, and Barrilito. The drinking age in Puerto Rico is 18.

DISABILITIES
AND ACCESSIBILITY

As a commonwealth of the United States, Puerto Rico complies with regulations of the Americans with Disabilities Act (ADA). For information on accessibility in Puerto Rico, contact the Northeast Disability and Business Technical Assistance Center of the United Cerebral Palsy Associations of New Jersey.

Parking for travelers with disabilities is readily available in most places, and many towns have curbs cut to accommodate wheelchairs. Note that Old San Juan's cobblestone streets, narrow alleys, and steep hills are problematic for travelers in wheelchairs.

➤ LOCAL RESOURCES: **Northeast Disability and Business Technical Assistance Center** (⊠ 354 S. Broad St., Trenton, NJ 08608, ☎ 800/949–4232).

LODGING

Many of the newer accommodations offer rooms that comply with ADA rules. However, as is the case in all hotel bookings, **be sure that rooms are genuinely accessible.**

RESERVATIONS

When discussing accessibility with an operator or reservations agent, **ask hard questions.** Are there any stairs, inside *or* out? Are there grab bars next to the toilet *and* in the shower/tub? How wide is the doorway to the room? To the bathroom? For the most extensive facilities meeting the latest legal specifications, **opt for newer accommodations.**

SIGHTS AND ATTRACTIONS

Public attractions—including beaches as well as museums and galleries—are subject to ADA regulations. In some cases, however, phones, rest rooms, displays, and trails or other parts of a given sight aren't fully accessible to people with mobility, vision, or hearing problems.

In a quick survey of the island's top attractions, the following have limited accessibility: Hacienda Buena Vista in Ponce, Las Cabezas de San Juan in Las Croabas, El Morro and the Catedral de San Juan in Old San Juan, and the Bosque Nacional del Caribe (Caribbean National Forest), commonly known as El Yunque, in eastern Puerto Rico. (Note that a wheelchair-accessible trail with Braille markers is on the drawing board for El Yunque).

One of the most accessible sights for travelers with mobility problems is Balneario de Luquillo, a palm-lined public beach in eastern Puerto Rico. Its Mar Sin Barreras (Sea Without Barriers) includes a ramp that enables wheelchair users to take a dip.

TRANSPORTATION

San Juan's Luis Muñoz Marín International Airport is well equipped for travelers with disabilities. You disembark on flyways straight into the airport, thus avoiding the steep airplane stairway. Public rest rooms and phones are accessible, and, if necessary, airport personnel can help you through long walkways, through baggage claim, and through customs and immigration. Just be sure to **request wheelchairs and escorts when booking your flights.**

Most public buses are equipped with wheelchair lifts and lockdowns, and taxis and públicos can fit chairs in their trunks. Public parking lots have designated spots for travelers with disabilities, and although car-rental agencies don't issue tags or placards, you can use yours from home. With advance notice (at least a week) major car-rental agencies like Avis can equip vehicles with hand controls and other devices and deliver the car to you at the arrivals area. Wheelchair Getaway in San Juan offers transportation from airports and cruise-ship docks to San Juan hotels. The company also has city sightseeing tours.

➤ COMPLAINTS: **Aviation Consumer Protection Division** (☞ Air Travel) for airline-related problems. **Departmental Office of Civil Rights** (for general inquiries, ✉ U.S. Department of Transportation, S-30, 400 7th St. SW, Room 10215, Washington, DC 20590, ☎ 202/366–4648, FAX 202/366–3571, WEB www.dot.gov/ost/docr/index.htm). **Disability Rights Section** (✉ NYAV, U.S. Department of Justice, Civil Rights Division, 950 Pennsylvania Ave. NW, Washington, DC 20530; ☎ ADA information line 202/514–0301 or 800/514–0301; 202/514–0383 TTY; 800/514–0383 TTY, WEB www.usdoj.gov/crt/ada/adahom1.htm).

➤ TRANSPORTATION CONTACT: **Wheelchair Getaway** (☎ 800/868–8028 or 787/883–0131).

TRAVEL AGENCIES

In the United States, the Americans with Disabilities Act requires that travel firms serve the needs of all travelers. Some agencies specialize in working with people with disabilities.

➤ TRAVELERS WITH MOBILITY PROBLEMS: **Access Adventures** (✉ 206 Chestnut Ridge Rd., Rochester, NY 14624, ☎ 716/889–9096, dltravel@prodigy.net), run by a former physical-rehabilitation counselor. **CareVacations** (✉ 5-5110 50th Ave., Leduc, Alberta T9E 6V4, ☎ 780/986–6404 or 877/478–7827, FAX 780/986–8332, WEB www.carevacations.com), for group tours and cruise vacations. **Flying Wheels Travel** (✉ 143 W. Bridge St., Box 382, Owatonna, MN 55060, ☎ 507/451–5005, FAX 507/451–1685, thq@ll.net, WEB www.flyingwheels.com). **Tomorrow's Level of Care** (✉ Box 470299, Brooklyn, NY 11247, ☎ 718/756–0794 or 800/932–2012), for nursing services and medical equipment.

➤ TRAVELERS WITH DEVELOPMENTAL DISABILITIES: **New Directions** (✉ 5276 Hollister Ave., Suite 207, Santa Barbara, CA 93111, ☎ 805/967–2841 or 888/967–2841, FAX 805/964–7344, newdirec@silcom.com, WEB www.silcom.com/~newdirec). **Sprout** (✉ 893 Amsterdam Ave., New York, NY 10025, ☎ 212/222–9575 or 888/222–9575, FAX 212/222–9768, sprout@interport.net, WEB www.gosprout.org).

DISCOUNTS AND DEALS

Be a smart shopper and **compare all your options** before making decisions. A plane ticket bought with a promotional coupon from travel clubs, coupon books, and direct-mail offers may not be cheaper than the least expensive fare from a discount ticket agency. Always keep in mind that what you get is just as important as what you save.

DISCOUNT RESERVATIONS

To save money, **look into discount reservations services** with toll-free numbers, which use their buying power to get a better price on hotels, airline tickets, even car rentals. When booking a room, always **call the hotel's local toll-free number** (if one is available) rather than the central reservations number—you'll often get a better price. Always **ask about special packages or corporate rates.**

➤ AIRLINE TICKETS: ☎ **800/FLY–4–LESS.** ☎ **800/FLY–ASAP.**

➤ HOTEL ROOMS: **Hotel Reservations Network** (☎ 800/964–6835, WEB www.hoteldiscounts.com). **RMC Travel** (☎ 800/245–5738, WEB www.rmcwebtravel.com). **Steigenberger Reservation Service** (☎ 800/223–5652, WEB www.srs-worldhotels.com).

PACKAGE DEALS

Don't confuse packages and guided tours. When you buy a package, you travel on your own, just as though you had planned the trip yourself. Fly/drive packages, which combine airfare and car rental, are often a good deal.

ECOTOURISM

The Puerto Rico government and numerous private organizations are combatting the depletion of the island's natural resources. The Conservation Trust of Puerto Rico has acquired lands with ecological and historical significance. Among them are Las Cabezas de San Juan in Las Croabas—which contains several ecosystems common to Puerto Rico—and sections of the Bahía Fosforescente (Phosphorescent Bay) in La Parguera. El Yunque's 28,000 acres are managed by the U.S. Forest Service.

ELECTRICITY

Puerto Rico uses the same 110-volt AC (60-cycle), two-prong-outlet electrical system as in North America.

Plugs have two flat pins set parallel to each another. European visitors should bring adapters and converters, or call ahead to to see whether their hotel has them on hand.

EMERGENCIES

Emergencies are handled by dialing 911. You can expect a quick response by police, fire, and medical personnel, most of whom speak at least some English. San Juan's Turist Zone Police are particularly helpful to visitors.

➤ CONTACTS: **Ambulance, police, and fire** (☎ 911). **Air Ambulance Service** (☎ 800/633–3590 or 787/756–3424). **Dental Emergencies** (☎ 787/722–2351 or 787/795–0320). **Fire Department** (☎ 787/343–2330). **Medical Emergency** (☎ 787/754–2222). **Police** (☎ 787/343–2020). **Turist Zone Police** (☎ 787/726–7020; 787/726–7015 for Condado; 787/728–4770 or 787/726–2981 for Isla Verde). **Travelers' Aid** (☎ 787/791–1054 or 787/791–1034).

ENGLISH-LANGUAGE MEDIA

BOOKS

Most bookstores carry books in both English and Spanish, and you'll find the standard English-language paperbacks at supermarkets and drugstores, with prices comparable to those in the United States.

➤ BOOKSTORES: **Bell Book & Candle** (✉ 102 Av. de Diego, Santurce, ☎ 787/728–5000). **Borders** (✉ Plaza Las Américas, 525 Av. Franklin Delano Roosevelt, Hato Rey, ☎ 787/777–0916). **Castle Books** (✉ San Patricio Plaza, Guaynabo, ☎ 787/774–1790). **Cronopios** (✉ 255 Calle San José, Old San Juan, San Juan, ☎ 787/724–1815). **La Tertulia** (✉ Calle Amalia Marín y González, Río Piedras, ☎ 787/765–1148). **Thekes** (✉ Plaza Las Américas, 525 Av. Franklin Delano Roosevelt, Hato Rey, ☎ 787/765–1539).

NEWSPAPERS AND MAGAZINES

Puerto Rico's Pulitzer prize–winning *San Juan Star* is printed daily (45¢) in Spanish and English. It carries local and syndicated columnists as well as a good mix of local and international news. *Caribbean Business* offers a comprehensive weekly low-down on major local and international business issues. In addition, you can get copies of the *Wall Street Journal, New York Times, USA Today, Miami Herald,* and other dailies, most often at hotels and drugstores. For the most comprehensive weekly listing of activities and events in the San Juan metropolitan area, pick up a copy of *Voices,* the region's alternative newsweekly. Although most of the editorial content is in Spanish, the entertainment listings are completely in English.

RADIO AND TELEVISION

Most local TV programs are in Spanish, and consist of a mix of news, game shows, movies, soaps, and music videos. Some local shows broadcast in English, but the majority of English programming comes from cable-transmitted HBO, CNN, and others.

Radio programs run the gamut of Spanish talk shows, Miami-based English news broadcasts, evangelical religious broadcasts, and music of all sorts in both English and Spanish. Radio WOSO (1030 AM) is a local English-language radio station.

ETIQUETTE AND BEHAVIOR

In general, islanders have a strong sense of religion—as evidenced by the numerous Catholic patron-saint festivals held throughout the year. Family ties are also strong, and it's not unusual to see families piling onto the beaches on weekends for a day of fun and barbecue. Puerto Ricans tend to proffer a great deal of respect to their elders, in formal greetings, language, and general attitude.

Many islanders are conservative in dress and manners, despite a penchant for frenetic music and dance. Typical greetings between female friends and male and female friends and relatives is a kiss on the cheek, and the greetings "*Buenos días*" ("Good day"), "*Buenos tardes*" ("Good afternoon"), and "*Buenas noches*" ("Good evening") are among a host of formal and less formal colloquial greetings. The phrases are also said in departing.

Although you may be spending a great deal of time on the beach, it's important to **wear a shirt and shoes when entering any indoor business establishments.** It's considered highly disrespectful to enter a store or a restaurant in a bathing suit or other inappropriate attire.

Islanders' knowledge of U.S. culture is thorough. Many Puerto Ricans have spent a great deal of time stateside, and those who haven't inevitably have relatives or friends living on the mainland. U.S. music, dress, and attitudes have infiltrated the culture, especially among the young, but the overriding cues are Spanish-Caribbean. Indeed, Puerto Ricans have a strong sense of identity, marked by often-ferocious debates over the island's political destiny.

GAY AND LESBIAN TRAVEL

Although prevailing local attitudes toward same-sex couples are similar to those in the states, normal precautions regarding overt behavior stand: Puerto Ricans tend to be conservative in matters of sexuality and dress. You aren't likely to have any difficulty with the staffs at hotels or restaurants, though you may have a negative response from other patrons. Also be aware that other types of businesses may have practices that discriminate in more subtle ways (e.g., any man wearing an earring may be barred from entering).

In sophisticated San Juan, gays and lesbians will find it easy to mingle. There are gay-friendly hotels, restaurants, and clubs throughout the city, the beach at Ocean Park tends to attract a gay crowd, and the first Sunday in June sees a gay pride parade in Condado that's preceded by a week of events. The bohemian Old San Juan crowd is particularly friendly and—just as in Ocean Park and Condado—many businesses there are owned by gays or lesbians. Some also have a weekly "gay night." Other welcoming areas of the island include Boquerón in the southwest and the town of Fajardo and the out island of Culebra in the east. To find out more about events and gay-friendly businesses, pick up a copy of the *Puerto Rico Breeze,* the island's gay and lesbian newspaper.

➤ GAY- AND LESBIAN-FRIENDLY TRAVEL AGENCIES: **Different Roads Travel** (✉ 8383 Wilshire Blvd., Suite 902, Beverly Hills, CA 90211, ☎ 323/651–5557 or 800/429–8747, FAX 323/651–3678, leigh@west.tzell.com). **Kennedy Travel** (✉ 314 Jericho Tpke., Floral Park, NY 11001, ☎ 516/352–4888 or 800/237–7433, FAX 516/354–8849, inquire@kennedytravel.com, WEB www.kennedytravel.com). **Now, Voyager** (✉ 4406 18th St., San Francisco, CA 94114, ☎ 415/626–1169 or 800/255–6951, FAX 415/626–8626, WEB www.nowvoyager.com). **Skylink Travel and Tour** (✉ 1006 Mendocino Ave., Santa Rosa, CA 95401, ☎ 707/546–9888, FAX 707/546–9891, skylinktvl@aol.com), serving lesbian travelers.

HEALTH

Health care in Puerto Rico is among the best in the Caribbean, but expect long waits and often a less-than-pleasant bedside manner. At all hospitals and medical centers you'll find English-speaking medical staff, and many large hotels have an English-speaking doctor on call.

FOOD AND DRINK

Tap water is generally fine on the island; just avoid drinking it after storms (when the water supply can become mixed with sewage). Thoroughly wash or peel produce you buy in markets before eating it.

MEDICAL PLANS

No one plans to get sick while traveling, but it happens, so **consider signing up with a medical-assistance company.** Members get doctor referrals, emergency evacuation or repatriation, hot lines for medical consultation, cash for emergencies, and other assistance.

➤ MEDICAL-ASSISTANCE COMPANIES: **International SOS Assistance** (WEB www.internationalsos.com; ✉ 8 Neshaminy Interplex, Suite 207, Trevose, PA 19053, ☎ 215/245–4707 or 800/523–6586, FAX 215/244–9617; ✉ 12 Chemin Riantbosson, 1217 Meyrin 1, Geneva, Switzerland, ☎ 22/785–6464, FAX 22/785–6424; ✉ 331 N. Bridge Rd., 17-00, Odeon Towers, Singapore 188720, ☎ 338–7800, FAX 338–7611).

OVER-THE-COUNTER REMEDIES

All the U.S. brands of sunscreen and over-the-counter medicines (Tylenol, Advil, Robitussin, Nyquil, etc.) are available in pharmacies, supermarkets, and convenience stores.

PESTS AND OTHER HAZARDS

Most health problems encountered by visitors involve the trio of rum, sun, and blisters. Overindulgence has probably sidelined more travelers than any other health hazard. Use common sense. The sun is hot, so take precautions whether you're on the beach or hiking through a rain forest. **Limit your tanning** to 20 minutes at a time, and wear a T-shirt when the rays become too powerful. **Use a strong sunscreen,** wear a lightweight hat, and **drink plenty of water.** Wear comfortable walking shoes.

The ocean presents its own hazards. Some beaches along the north and west coasts have strong waves and undertows. Signs are often posted where and when the waves make it too dangerous to swim, but ask about the undertow conditions, which vary from season to season.

Avoid the long-spined sea urchin, often found in shallow water near shore, hidden among coral and rocks. Their strong barbs can pierce the skin and break off, resulting in painful swelling. Remove the fragments immediately, soak the injured area, and treat it with an antiseptic as soon as possible. Then see a doctor. Also, **stay clear of all forms of jellyfish,** which often wash up on shore, particularly in winter. Their tentacles are equipped with stinging organisms that detach when brushed. Splash the affected area with drying agents such as alcohol, talcum powder, or even sand, but avoid rubbing your skin or you may activate detached stingers. Then see a doctor.

When snorkeling or diving, **avoid touching live coral,** for the organism's safety as well as your own. All corals can be harmful, either causing a slow-healing gash or releasing toxins on contact. Fire and stinging corals do what their names suggest. If you accidentally touch them, seek treatment. Further, breaking coral, kicking it with your fins, or brushing it with your underwater camera can traumatize a reef's delicate ecological balance.

Bugs are, primarily, annoying— mosquitoes and sand gnats (no-see-ums) are the biggest problems, and can be warded off with a good repellent with DEET, available in all drugstores and pharmacies. Mosquito coils are also sold throughout the island. **Guard against mosquitoes at sunrise and sunset,** which is when the mosquitoes that carry *dengue* are active. If you develop a fever, fatigue, pin-size red spots, diarrhea, or nausea, see a doctor.

➤ HEALTH WARNINGS: **National Centers for Disease Control and Prevention** (CDC; National Center for Infectious Diseases, Division of Quarantine, Traveler's Health Section, ⊠ 1600 Clifton Rd. NE, M/S E-03, Atlanta, GA 30333, ☎ 888/232–3228 general information; 877/394–8747 travelers' health line; 800/311–3435 public inquiries, FAX 888/232–3299, WEB www.cdc.gov).

HOLIDAYS

Puerto Rico observes all U.S. federal holidays, as well as many local holidays. Most government offices and businesses shut down on holidays, with the exception of convenience stores and some supermarkets, pharmacies, and restaurants. Public transportation runs on abbreviated schedules, just as on Sunday. Public holidays in Puerto Rico include: New Year's Day, Three Kings Day (Jan. 6), Eugenio María de Hostos Day (Jan. 8), Dr. Martin Luther King Jr. Day (3rd Mon. in Jan.), Presidents' Day (3rd Mon. in Feb.), Palm Sunday, Good Friday, Easter Sunday, Memorial Day (last Mon. in May), Independence Day (July 4), Luis Muñoz Rivera Day (July 16), Constitution Day (July 25), José Celso Barbosa Day (July 27), Labor Day (1st Mon. in Sept.), Columbus Day (2nd Mon. in Oct.), Veterans' Day (Nov. 11), Puerto Rico Discovery Day (Nov. 19), Thanksgiving Day, and Christmas.

INSURANCE

The most useful travel insurance plan is a comprehensive policy that includes coverage for trip cancellation and interruption, default, trip delay, and medical expenses (with a waiver for preexisting conditions).

Without insurance you will lose all or most of your money if you cancel your trip, regardless of the reason. Default insurance covers you if your tour operator, airline, or cruise line goes out of business. Trip-delay covers expenses that arise because of bad weather or mechanical delays. Study the fine print when comparing policies.

If you're traveling internationally, a key component of travel insurance is coverage for medical bills incurred if you get sick on the road. U.K. residents can buy a travel insurance policy valid for most vacations taken during the year in which it's purchased (but check pre-existing-condition coverage). British and Australian citizens need extra medical coverage when traveling overseas. Always **buy travel policies directly from the insurance company;** if you buy them from a cruise line, airline, or tour operator that goes out of business you probably will not be covered for the agency or operator's default, a major risk. Before making any purchase, **review your existing health and homeowner's policies** to find what they cover away from home.

➤ TRAVEL INSURERS: In the U.S.: **Access America** (⊠ 6600 W. Broad St., Richmond, VA 23230, ☎ 804/285–3300 or 800/284–8300, FAX 804/673–1583, WEB www.accessamerica.com). **Travel Guard International** (⊠ 1145 Clark St., Stevens Point, WI 54481, ☎ 715/345–0505 or 800/826–1300, FAX 800/955–8785, WEB www.noelgroup.com). In Canada: **Voyager Insurance** (⊠ 44 Peel Center Dr., Brampton, Ontario L6T 4M8, ☎ 905/791–8700; 800/668–4342 in Canada).

➤ INSURANCE INFORMATION: In the U.K.: **Association of British Insurers** (⊠ 51–55 Gresham St., London EC2V 7HQ, ☎ 0171/600–3333, FAX 0171/696–8999, info@abi.org.uk,

WEB www.abi.org.uk). In Australia: **Insurance Council of Australia** (☎ 03/9614–1077, FAX 03/9614–7924).

LANGUAGE

The official languages are Spanish and English, in that order. Spanish prevails in everyday conversation, in commerce, and in the media. And although English is widely spoken, you'll probably want to take a Spanish phrase book along on your travels to rural areas. Hotel front desk staffs and restaurant staffs in large facilities speak English. Most business and government phones are manned by people who speak English (or will find someone who does), and telephone answering systems are bilingual. If you're stumped, call the Tourist Information line or the Traveler's Aid line.

➤ CONTACTS: **Tourist Information Line** (☎ 787/766–7777). **Traveler's Aid Line** (☎ 787/791–1054).

LANGUAGES FOR TRAVELERS

A phrase book and language-tape set can help get you started.

➤ PHRASE BOOKS AND LANGUAGE-TAPE SETS: *Fodor's Spanish for Travelers* (☎ 800/733–3000 in the U.S.; 800/668–4247 in Canada; $7 for phrasebook, $16.95 for audio set).

LODGING

San Juan's high-rise hotels on the Condado and Isla Verde beach strips cater primarily to the cruise-ship and casino crowd, though several target business travelers. Outside San Juan, particularly on the east coast, you'll find self-contained luxury resorts that cover hundreds of acres. In the west, southwest, and south—as well as on the islands of Vieques and Culebra—smaller inns, villas, condominiums, and government-sponsored *paradores* are the norm.

Before booking a room consider (and make a list of) your needs. Is it worth paying extra for a room overlooking the beach or the pool? Must the hotel even be on the beach? Rooms with garden or mountain views and properties away from the shore entirely often cost less. Which in-room amenities—air-conditioning, minibars,

safes, etc.—and on-site facilities are important to you? Do you want able to open your room windows and control the air-conditioning yourself? Do you need cable TV to keep up with CNN's financial news? Are you concerned about children's programs? Do you want a hotel with a dance club or a casino, or are you seeking peace? These are just some of the questions you should ask yourself.

The lodgings we list are the cream of the crop in each price category. We always list the facilities that are available—but we don't specify extra costs. When pricing accommodations, **always ask what's included and what costs extra.**

Assume that hotels operate on the **European Plan** (EP, with no meals), unless we specify that they're **all-inclusive** (including all meals and most activities) or use the **Breakfast Plan** (BP, with a full breakfast), **Continental Plan** (CP, with a Continental breakfast), **Modified American Plan** (MAP, with breakfast and dinner), or the **Full American Plan** (FAP, with all meals).

APARTMENT AND VILLA RENTALS

If you want a home base that's roomy enough for a family and comes with cooking facilities, **consider a furnished rental.** These can save you money, especially if you're traveling with a group. Home-exchange directories sometimes list rentals as well as exchanges.

➤ INTERNATIONAL AGENTS: **At Home Abroad** (✉ 405 E. 56th St., Suite 6H, New York, NY 10022, ☎ 212/421–9165, FAX 212/752–1591, athomabrod@aol.com, WEB http://member.aol.com/athomabrod/index.html). **Europa-Let/Tropical Inn-Let** (✉ 92 N. Main St., Ashland, OR 97520, ☎ 541/482–5806 or 800/462–4486, FAX 541/482–0660). **Hideaways International** (✉ 767 Islington St., Portsmouth, NH 03801, ☎ 603/430–4433 or 800/843–4433, FAX 603/430–4444, info@hideaways.com, WEB www.hideaways.com; membership $99). **Hometours International** (✉ Box 11503, Knoxville, TN 37939, ☎ 865/690–8484 or 800/367–4668, home-

tours@aol.com, WEB http://thor.he.
net/~hometour). **Vacation Home
Rentals Worldwide** (✉ 235 Kensington Ave., Norwood, NJ 07648,
☎ 201/767–9393 or 800/633–3284,
FAX 201/767–5510, vhrww@juno.com,
WEB www.vhrww.com). **Villas and
Apartments Abroad** (✉ 1270 Avenue
of the Americas, 15th floor, New
York, NY 10020, ☎ 212/897–5045
or 800/433–3020, FAX 212/897–5039,
vaa@altour.com, WEB www.vaanyc.
com). **Villas International** (✉ 950
Northgate Dr., Suite 206, San Rafael,
CA 94903, ☎ 415/499–9490 or 800/
221–2260, FAX 415/499–9491, villas@
best.com, WEB www.villasintl.com).

➤ LOCAL AGENTS: **Coconut Palms**
(✉ 2734 Calle 8, Rincón, 00677,
☎ 787/823–0147). **Connections**
(✉ Box 358, Esperanza, Vieques
00765, ☎ 787/741–0023). **Island
West Properties & Beach Rentals**
(✉ Rte. 413, Km 1.3, [Box 700,
Rincón 00677], ☎ 787/823–2323,
FAX 787/823–3254). **Puerto Rico
Vacation Apartments** (✉ Marabella
del Caribe Oeste S-5, Av. Isla Verde,
Isla Verde, San Juan 00979, ☎ 787/
727–1591 or 800/266–3639, FAX 787/
268–3604).

CAMPING

It's not safe or legal to simply to pitch
a tent in the woods or on a deserted
beach. The island's designated campgrounds—for tents and/or RVs—are
most often found at balnearios. Most
have cooking grills and bath houses.
Weekend camping at balnearios is
popular among Puerto Ricans, and
you'll find that the crowds are usually
in a party mood, with lots of music
and general merriment—not a setting
for peaceful communion with nature.

Other areas include a few private
camps along the north and northeast
coast and grounds in the Carite,
Guilarte, Toro Nego, Río Abajo, and
other state forests. To camp in nature
reserves or state forests, you must
get a permit from the Department
of Natural and Environmental Resources. **Request the permit at least
three weeks in advance.**

➤ CAMPING CONTACTS: **Department
of Natural and Environmental Resources** (☎ 787/724–3724 or 787/

724–3647). **Department of Sports
and Recreation** (☎ 787/721–2800 or
787/636–6340). **Tourist Information
Line** (☎ 787/766–7777).

HOME EXCHANGES

If you would like to exchange your
home for someone else's, **join a home-
exchange organization,** which will
send you its updated listings of available exchanges for a year and will
include your own listing in at least
one of them. It's up to you to make
specific arrangements.

➤ EXCHANGE CLUBS: **HomeLink
International** (✉ Box 47747, Tampa,
FL 33647, ☎ 813/975–9825 or 800/
638–3841, FAX 813/910–8144,
usa@homelink.org, WEB www.
homelink.org; $106 per year). **Inter-
vac U.S.** (✉ 30 Corte San Fernando,
Tiburon, CA 94920, ☎ 800/756–
4663, FAX 415/435–7440, WEB www.
intervacus.com; $90 yearly fee for a
listing, on-line access, and a catalog;
$50 without catalog).

HOSTELS

Currently, no hostels in Puerto Rico,
youth or otherwise, are sanctioned by
local or international organizations.

HOTELS

In the most expensive hotels, your
room will be large enough for two to
move around comfortably, with two
double beds (*camas matrimoniales*) or
one queen- or king-size bed, air-
conditioning (*aire acondicionado*), a
phone (*teléfono*), a private bath (*baño
particular*), an in-room safe, cable TV,
a hair dryer, iron and ironing board,
room service (*servicio de habitación*),
shampoo and toiletries, and possibly
a view of the water (*vista al mar*).
There will be a concierge and at least
one hotel restaurant and lounge, a
pool, a shop, and an exercise room or
spa. In Puerto Rico's smaller inns,
rooms will have private baths with
hot water (*agua caliente*), air-conditioning or fans, a double to king-size
bed, possibly room service, and
breakfast (Continental or full) included in the rates. In some hotels,
several rooms share baths—it's a
good idea to ask before booking. All
hotels listed in this guide have private
baths unless otherwise noted.

RESERVING A ROOM

➤ TOLL-FREE NUMBERS: **Best Western** (☎ 800/528–1234, WEB www. bestwestern.com). **Choice** (☎ 800/ 221–2222, WEB www.hotelchoice. com). **Doubletree and Red Lion Hotels** (☎ 800/222–8733, WEB www. doubletreehotels.com). **Embassy Suites** (☎ 800/362–2779, WEB www. embassysuites.com). **Hilton** (☎ 800/ 445–8667, WEB www.hiltons.com). **Holiday Inn** (☎ 800/465–4329, WEB www.holiday-inn.com). **Hyatt Hotels & Resorts** (☎ 800/233– 1234, WEB www.hyatt.com). **Inter-Continental** (☎ 800/327–0200, WEB www.intercontinental.com). **Marriott** (☎ 800/228–9290, WEB www. marriott.com). **Le Meridien** (☎ 800/ 543–4300, WEB www.forte-hotels. com). **Quality Inn** (☎ 800/228–5151, WEB www.qualityinn.com). **Ramada** (☎ 800/228–2828, WEB www.ramada. com). **Renaissance Hotels & Resorts** (☎ 800/468–3571, WEB www.hotels. com). **Ritz-Carlton** (☎ 800/241– 3333, WEB www.ritzcarlton.com). **Sheraton** (☎ 800/325–3535, WEB www. sheraton.com). **Wyndham Hotels & Resorts** (☎ 800/822–4200, WEB www. wyndham.com).

PARADORES

Some paradores are rural inns offering no-frills apartments, and others are large hotels; all must meet certain standards, such as proximity to an attraction or beach. Most have a small restaurant that serves local cuisine. They're great bargains (from $60 to $125 for a double room). You can make reservations by contacting the tourist board's Paradores of Puerto Rico.

➤ CONTACT: **Paradores of Puerto Rico** (☎ 800/866–7827, WEB www. prtourism.com).

MAIL AND SHIPPING

Puerto Rico uses the U.S. postal system, and all addresses on the island carry Zip codes. Major post office branches are at 153 Calle Fortaleza in Old San Juan, 163 Avenida Fernández Juncos in San Juan, 102 Calle Garrido Morales in Fajardo, 94 Calle Atocha in Ponce, and 60 Calle McKinley in Mayagüez.

You can buy stamps and aerograms and send letters and parcels in post offices. Stamp-dispensing machines can occasionally be found in airports, office buildings, and drugstores. You can also deposit mail in the stout, dark-blue, steel bins at strategic locations everywhere and in the mail chutes of large buildings; pickup schedules are posted.

To receive mail on the road, have it sent c/o General Delivery to your destination's main post office (use the correct five-digit zip code). You must pick up mail in person within 30 days and show a driver's license or passport.

➤ GENERAL INFORMATION: **Postal Services** (☎ 787/622–1756).

OVERNIGHT SERVICES

Post offices in major Puerto Rican cities offer express mail, next-day service to the U.S. mainland and to Puerto Rican destinations. In addition, you can send letters and packages via Federal Express or UPS, as well as through private mail companies such as Mail Boxes, Etc. The quickest way to ship via a courier service is to inquire with the concierge or front desk of your hotel. Staffers there can call for pickup. Hotels that offer business services will take care of the entire ordeal for you. Caveat emptor: courier delivery and pick-up is not available on Saturday, and "overnight" packages usually take two to three days.

➤ MAJOR SERVICES: **Federal Express** (☎ 787/793–9300). **UPS** (☎ 787/ 253–2877).

POSTAL RATES

For mail sent within the United States, you need a 37¢ stamp for first-class letters weighing up to 1 ounce (23¢ for each additional ounce) and 23¢ for postcards. You pay 80¢ for 1-ounce airmail letters and 70¢ for airmail postcards to most other countries; to Canada and Mexico, you need a 60¢ stamp for a 1-ounce letter and 50¢ for a postcard. An aerogram—a single sheet of lightweight blue paper that folds into its own envelope, stamped for overseas airmail—costs 70¢.

SHIPPING PARCELS

Many shops—particularly those in Old San Juan and Condado—will ship purchases for you. Shipping services are especially common at art galleries. **Pay by credit card, and save your receipts.** Make sure the proprietor insures the package against loss or damage, and ships it first class or by courier. Grab a business card with the proprietor's name and phone number so you can readily follow up with him or her if needed.

MONEY MATTERS

Puerto Rico, which is a commonwealth of the United States, uses the U.S. dollar as its official currency. Prices for most items are stable and comparable to those in the States, and that includes restaurants and hotel rates. As in many places, city prices tend to be higher than those in rural areas, but you're not going to go broke staying in the city: soft drinks or a cup of coffee run about $1; a local beer in a bar, $2.75; museum admission, $2.

Prices throughout this guide are given for adults. Substantially reduced fees are almost always available for children, students, and senior citizens. For information on taxes, *see* Taxes.

ATMS

Automated Teller Machines (ATMs; known as or ATHs here) are readily available and reliable in the cities; many are attached to banks, but you can also find them on the streets and in supermarkets. Just about every casino has one—the better to keep people in the game—as do many of the larger hotels. ATMs are found less frequently in rural areas. Look to local banks, such as Banco Popular.

CREDIT CARDS

Throughout this guide, the following abbreviations are used: **AE**, American Express; **D**, Discover; **DC**, Diners Club; **MC**, Master Card; and **V**, Visa.

➤ REPORTING LOST CARDS: **American Express** (☎ 800/441–0519). **Discover** (☎ 800/347–2683). **Diners Club** (☎ 800/234–6377). **MasterCard** (☎ 800/622–7747). **Visa** (☎ 800/847–2911).

CURRENCY

The U.S. dollar has 100 cents. Coins include the copper penny (1¢); the silvery nickel (5¢), dime (10¢), quarter (25¢), and half-dollar (50¢); and the golden $1 coin, replacing a now-rare silver dollar. Bills are in denominations of $1, $5, $10, $20, $50, and $100, all green and identical in size; designs vary. The exchange rate at this writing was 88¢ per Euro, $1.42 per British pound, 63¢ per Canadian dollar, 53¢ per Australian dollar, and 44¢ per New Zealand dollar.

OUTDOORS AND SPORTS

BEACHES

An island visit isn't complete without some time in the sand and sun. By law, everyone is welcome on Puerto Rico's *playas* (beaches), some of which—called balnearios—are maintained by the government. There are more than a dozen such beaches around the island, with dressing rooms; lifeguards; parking; and, in some cases, picnic tables, playgrounds, and camping facilities. Admission is free, and parking runs $2–$3. Hours vary, but most balnearios are open 9–5 daily in summer and Tuesday–Sunday the rest of the year.

BICYCLING

Selected areas—small towns, the central mountains, the southern coast—lend themselves to bike travel. In general, however, the roads are congested and distances are vast. Avoid the main thoroughfares in San Juan and Old San Juan: the traffic is too heavy and the fumes are too thick. East of the city, the bike trails in Piñones provide a beautiful beachfront escape. The entire southwest coast of Cabo Rojo also makes for good biking, particularly the broad beach at Boquerón. Vieques and Culebra are ideal for biking, as there's little traffic. If you're looking for a more challenging ride, head to the central mountains, particularly the Bosque Estatal de Toro Negro (Toro Negro State Forest) in Jayuya. The Puerto Rico Mountain Bike Association schedules events from March to October. Road bike events are organized throughout the year by the

Federación Puertorriqueña de Ciclismo.

Most airlines accommodate bikes as luggage, provided they are dismantled and boxed. For bike boxes, often free at bike shops, you'll pay about $5 from airlines (at least $100 for bike bags). International travelers can sometimes substitute a bike for a piece of checked luggage at no charge; otherwise, the cost is about $100. Domestic and Canadian airlines charge $25–$50.

➤ BIKE RENTALS: **Department of Sports and Recreation** (☎ 787/721–2800 or 787/636–6340).

➤ INFORMATION: **Federación Puertorriqueña de Ciclismo** (WEB www.federacionciclismopr.com). **Puerto Rico Mountain Bike Association** (WEB www.prmtb.com).

HIKING

In the east, El Yunque's 13 hiking trails loop past giant ferns, exotic orchids, sibilant streams and waterfalls, and broad trees reaching for the sun. You can even hike to the top of El Toro, the highest peak in the forest at 3,532 ft. The northwest's Bosque Estatal de Toro Negro and the south's Bosque Estatal de Guánica are also great places to hike.

➤ INFORMATION: **Bosque Estatal de Guánica** (Rte. 333 or 334, ☎ 787/821–5706). **Bosque Estatal de Toro Negro** (✉ Rte. 143, Km 31.8 Jayuya, ☎ 787/867–3040). **Department of Natural and Environmental Resources** (☎ 787/724–3724 or 787/724–3647). **El Yunque** (Centro de Información El Portal; ✉ Rte. 191, Km 4.3 [off Rte. 3], ☎ 787/888–1880).

GOLF

For aficionados worldwide, Puerto Rico is known as the birthplace of golf legend Chi Chi Rodríguez, who, at this writing, was planning to build an 18-hole golf course and golf school on Route 173 outside of Guayama in the south. Currently you'll find nearly 20 courses on the island, including several championship links. None of the courses is public, but plans for public facilities are on the table. Always call ahead for details on reserving tee times;

hours vary and several hotel courses give preference to guests or allow only allow guests to play. The Puerto Rican Golf Association is a good source for information on courses and tournaments.

➤ INFORMATION: **Puerto Rican Golf Association** (✉ 58 Calle Caribe, San Juan, ☎ 787/721–7742, WEB www.prga.org).

SCUBA DIVING AND SNORKELING

The diving is excellent off Puerto Rico's south, east, and west coasts as well as around its offshore islands. Popular among divers is tiny Desecheo Island, about 24 km (15 mi) off the coast of Rincón in the west. At depths of 20 ft to 120 ft, the rocky ocean floor around the base of the islet is full of coral and tropical fish, as well as several rock terraces and caverns. In the south, several reef-bordered cays lie off the Cabo Rojo area near walls that drop to 100 ft. In the east, many divers head to Fajardo, which is the jumping off point for Vieques and Culebra; the waters around these islets are full of diving possibilities. The nearest hyperbaric chamber is at the Hospital Universitario (University Hospital) in Río Piedras.

Do not fly within 24 hours of scuba diving.

➤ EMERGENCIES: **Hospital Universitario** (☎ 787/758–7910).

➤ INFORMATION: **Blue Caribe Dive Center** (✉ Calle Flamboyán, Esperanza, Vieques, ☎ 787/741–2522, WEB www.enchanted-isle.com/bluecaribe). **Desecheo Dive Shop** (✉ Rte. 413, Km 2.5, Rincón, ☎ 787/823–0390). **Sea Ventures Pro Dive Center** (✉ Puerto del Rey Marina, Rte. 3, Km 51.4, Fajardo, ☎ 787/863–3483 or 800/739–3483, WEB www.divepuertorico.com). **Tour Marine** (✉ Rte. 101, Km 14.1, Joyuda Sector, Puerto Real, Cabo Rojo, ☎ 787/851–9259). **Reef Link Divers** (✉ Carretera Fulladoza, inside Dinghy Dock restaurant, Dewey, Culebra, ☎ 787/742–0581).

PACKING

Although "casual" is the operative word for vacation clothes, wearing resort attire outside the hotel or at the casino will peg you as a tourist. Puerto Ricans, particularly in the cities, dress up to go out. Pack some dressy casual slacks and shirts, summer skirts for women, casual clothes for the resort, at least two bathing suits (to avoid having to wear that wet one from yesterday), and sturdy shoes for walking. A light sweater or jacket isn't a bad idea either.

In your carry-on luggage, **pack an extra pair of eyeglasses or contact lenses** and **enough of any medication you take** to last you a few days longer than the entire trip. You may also ask your doctor to write a spare prescription using the drug's generic name, since brand names may vary from country to country. In luggage to be checked, **never pack prescription drugs or valuables.** To avoid customs delays, carry medications in their original packaging. And don't forget to carry with you the addresses of offices that handle refunds of lost traveler's checks.

CHECKING LUGGAGE

How many carry-on bags you can bring with you is up to the airline. Most allow two, but not always, so make sure that everything you carry aboard will fit under your seat or in the overhead bin, and get to the gate early. Note that if you have a seat at the back of the plane, you'll probably board first, while the overhead bins are still empty.

If you are flying internationally, note that baggage allowances may be determined not by piece but by weight—generally 88 pounds (40 kilograms) in first class, 66 pounds (30 kilograms) in business class, and 44 pounds (20 kilograms) in economy.

Airline liability for baggage is limited to $1,250 per person on flights within the United States. On international flights it amounts to $9.07 per pound or $20 per kilogram for checked baggage (roughly $640 per 70-pound bag) and $400 per passenger for unchecked baggage. You can buy additional coverage at check-in for about $10 per $1,000 of coverage, but it excludes a rather extensive list of items, shown on your airline ticket.

Before departure, **itemize your bags' contents** and their worth, and label the bags with your name, address, and phone number. (If you use your home address, cover it so potential thieves can't see it readily.) Inside each bag, **pack a copy of your itinerary.** At check-in, **make sure that each bag is correctly tagged** with the destination airport's three-letter code. If your bags arrive damaged or fail to arrive at all, file a written report with the airline before leaving the airport.

PASSPORTS AND VISAS

When traveling internationally, **carry your passport even if you don't need one** (it's always the best form of I.D.) and **make two photocopies of the data page** (one for someone at home and another for you, carried separately from your passport). If you lose your passport, promptly call the nearest embassy or consulate and the local police.

ENTERING PUERTO RICO

U.S. citizens don't need passports to visit the island, but it's a good idea to carry a valid one anyway. Canadians need proof of citizenship (preferably a valid passport; otherwise bring a birth certificate with a raised seal along with a government-issued photo I.D.). Citizens of Australia, New Zealand, and the United Kingdom must have passports but don't need visas for stays of fewer than 90 days.

PASSPORT OFFICES

The best time to apply for a passport or to renew is in fall and winter. Before any trip, check your passport's expiration date, and, if necessary, renew it as soon as possible.

➤ AUSTRALIAN CITIZENS: **Australian State Passport Office** (☎ 131–232, WEB www.passports.gov.au).

➤ CANADIAN CITIZENS: **Passport Office** (to mail in applications: ✉ Dept. of Foreign Affairs and International Trade, Ottawa, Ontario K1A 0G3, ☎ 819/994–3500 or 800/567–6868, WEB www.dfait-maeci.gc.ca/passport/).

➤ NEW ZEALAND CITIZENS: **New Zealand Passport Office** (☎ 04/474–8100 or 0800/22–5050, WEB www.passports.govt.nz).

➤ U.K. CITIZENS: **London Passport Office** (☎ 0870/521–0410, 𝗪𝗘𝗕 www.passport.gov.uk).

REST ROOMS

Rest rooms you encounter in Puerto Rico will be not unlike those at home—some clean, some not so clean. Most public rest rooms at government facilities will be accessible for travelers with disabilities. Spanish for toilet is *baño*; men's room doors are labeled *caballeros*, ladies' room doors *damas*.

SAFETY

San Juan and Ponce, like most big cities, have their share of crime, so guard your wallet or purse on the city streets. **Avoid deserted beaches at night,** when muggings have been known to occur even on posh stretches such as those in Condado and Isla Verde. **Don't leave anything unattended on the beach.** Lock your valuables in the hotel safe, and stick to the fenced-in beach areas of your hotel. Always lock your car; if you must keep valuables in your vehicle, put them in the trunk.

Don't wear a waist pack, which pegs you as a tourist. Store only enough money in your wallet or purse to cover casual spending. Distribute the rest of your cash and any valuables (including credit cards and your passport) between a deep front pocket, an inside jacket or vest pocket, and a hidden money pouch. Do not reach for the money pouch once in public.

WOMEN IN PUERTO RICO

In the cities, women traveling solo are less likely to attract attention than elsewhere. Even so, men might still attempt to make conversation. Be polite but firm. A simple *"No, gracias"* ("No, thanks") is usually enough to discourage them. Avoid drinking alone in bars and walking on deserted beaches—day or at night—or along dark, empty streets. Getting into an unmarked car identified by the driver as a taxi is a bad idea. It's also best not to don revealing attire or to wear swimsuits anywhere but at the beach or by the pool. If you carry a purse, choose one with a zipper and a thick strap that you can drape across your body; adjust the length so that the purse sits in front of you at or above hip level.

SENIOR-CITIZEN TRAVEL

To qualify for age-related discounts, **mention your senior-citizen status up front** when booking hotel reservations (not when checking out) and before you're seated in restaurants (not when paying the bill). When renting a car, ask about promotional car-rental discounts, which can be cheaper than senior-citizen rates.

➤ EDUCATIONAL PROGRAMS: **Elderhostel** (✉ 75 Federal St., 3rd floor, Boston, MA 02110, ☎ 877/426–8056, 𝗙𝗔𝗫 877/426–2166, 𝗪𝗘𝗕 www.elderhostel.org). **Interhostel** (✉ University of New Hampshire, 6 Garrison Ave., Durham, NH 03824, ☎ 603/862–1147 or 800/733–9753, 𝗙𝗔𝗫 603/862–1113, 𝗪𝗘𝗕 www.learn.unh.edu).

SHOPPING

Shopping in Puerto Rico differs little from shopping in North America: cash, of course, is always accepted, and in most cases traveler's checks and major credit cards are fine. Street vendors selling crafts and other items are likely to accept cash only; they're also open to bargaining, which isn't a common practice in shops and boutiques.

Although there are a few duty-free shops in the terminal boarding areas at San Juan's Luis Muñoz Marín International Airport, Puerto Rico isn't a duty-free island. You can, however, find excellent prices on china, crystal, jewelry, and designer fashions.

SMART SOUVENIRS

Shopping for local crafts can be gratifying: you'll run across a lot of tacky items, but you can also find some treasures, and in many cases you can watch the artisans at work. For guidance, contact the Puerto Rico Tourism Company's Asuntos Culturales (Cultural Affairs Office). Popular items include *santos* (small hand-carved figures of saints or religious scenes), hand-rolled cigars, Panama hats, handmade *mundillo* lace from Aguadilla, *veijigantes* (colorful festival masks made of papier-mâché and/or coconut husks), and fancy men's shirts called *guayaberas*. Also, some folks swear that Puerto Rican rum is the best in the world, and locally grown and processed coffee is of a very high quality.

➤ INFORMATION: **Puerto Rico Tourism Company's Asuntos Culturales** (☎ 787/723–0692).

WATCH OUT

Remember, Puerto Rico is not duty-free, and shopkeepers who tell you otherwise are trying to scam you.

STUDENTS IN PUERTO RICO

Puerto Rico is well within the budget of students and is tailor-made for the adventurous. To beat the costs of traveling alone, hook up with educational institutions that use the island for research. Educational trips where you help out in projects are often inexpensive but might require a time commitment of several weeks.

➤ I.D.s AND SERVICES: **Council Travel** (✉ 205 E. 42nd St., 15th floor, New York, NY 10017, ☎ 212/822–2700 or 888/226–8624, FAX 212/822–2719, WEB www.counciltravel.com). **Travel Cuts** (✉ 187 College St., Toronto, Ontario M5T 1P7, Canada, ☎ 416/979–2406 or 888/838–2887, FAX 416/979–8167, WEB www.travelcuts.com).

TAXES

Accommodations incur a tax: for hotels with casinos it's 11%, for other hotels it's 9%, and for government-approved paradores it's 7%. Ask your hotel before booking. The tax, in addition to each hotel's discretionary service charge (it usually ranges from 5%–12%), can add a hefty 12%–23% to your bill. There's no sales tax on Puerto Rico. Airport departure taxes are usually included in the cost of your plane ticket rather than being collected at the airport.

TAXIS

In San Juan, the Puerto Rico Tourism Company's authorized taxis—painted white and displaying the *garita* (sentry box) logo and TAXI TURÍSTICO label—charge set rates depending on the destination. They run from Aeropuerto Internacional Luis Muñoz Marín and the cruise-ship piers to Isla Verde, Condado/Ocean Park, and Old San Juan, with rates from $6 to $16. They also offer city tours, which start at $30 per hour. Metered cabs authorized by the Public Service Commission start at $1 and charge 10¢ for every additional ⅓ mi, 50¢ for every suitcase. Waiting time is 10¢ for each 45 seconds. The minimum charge is $3 and there is an extra $1 night charge between 10 PM and 6 AM. There are also cab stands in Old San Juan on Calle Cristo, across from El Convento Hotel; by the Plaza de Armas; and across from the Tapia Theater. The best thing to do anywhere else is to call for a cab.

Tourist taxis do exist in other island cities, but you usually have to call for one. Although some are metered, most have fixed fees they charge for specific destinations. Always **confirm taxi fares with the driver before setting out.**

Líneas are private taxis you share with three to five other passengers. There are more than 20 companies, each usually specializing in a certain region. Most will arrange door-to-door service. Check local Yellow Pages listings under *Líneas de Carros*. They're affordable and are a great way to meet people, but be prepared to wait: they usually don't leave until they have a full load.

TELEPHONES

All U.S. phone numbers consist of a three-digit area code and a seven-digit local number. Puerto Rico's main area code is 787, but all new numbers are being given a 939 area code. Toll-free numbers (prefix 800, 888, or 877) are widely used in Puerto Rico, and many can be accessed from North America. You can also access many North American toll-free numbers from the island.

Cell phones are a viable alternative to using local service if you need to keep records of your bills. Call your cell phone company before departing to get information about activation and roaming charges. Companies that have service on the island include Cellular One and Sprint.

DIRECTORY AND OPERATOR ASSISTANCE

Dial 411 for directory assistance, and dial 0 for operator-assisted calls. Operators generally speak English.

INTERNATIONAL CALLS

For direct international calls to the United Kingdom, Australia, New Zealand, and elsewhere dial "011" followed by the country code, area code, and number. Dial 00 for the international long-distance operator.

LOCAL CALLS

You must always **dial the area code and the number when making calls on the island.**

LONG-DISTANCE CALLS

If the call is outside of your zone but still on the island or it's to (or from) the United States or Canada, simply dial a "1" before the area code and the number. The same procedure applies for calls to many other Caribbean islands.

LONG-DISTANCE SERVICES

AT&T, MCI, and Sprint access codes make calling long-distance relatively convenient, but you may find the local access number blocked in many hotel rooms. First ask the hotel operator to connect you. If the hotel operator balks, ask for a local operator, or dial the local operator yourself. One way to improve your odds of getting connected to your long-distance carrier is to travel with more than one company's calling card (a hotel may block Sprint, for example, but not MCI). If all else fails, call from a pay phone.

➤ ACCESS CODES: **AT&T Direct** (☎ 787/725–0300). **Cellular One** (☎ 787/505–2273 or 787/505–4636). **MCI WorldPhone** (☎ 787/782–6244 or 800/939–7624). **Sprint International Access** (☎ 800/473–3037 or 800/298–3266).

PHONE CARDS

Phone cards are widely available. The Puerto Rico Telephone Company sells its "Ring Cards" in various denominations that can be used for both local and international calls. They're available in shops, supermarkets, and drugstores as well as from the phone company.

➤ INFORMATION: **Ring Cards** (☎ 800/ 981–9105).

PUBLIC PHONES

Pay phones, which are abundant in tourist areas, use coins or prepaid phone cards; some accept credit cards. Local calls run 10¢ to 25¢, and on-island, long-distance calls cost about 50¢.

TIME

Puerto Rico operates on Atlantic standard time, which is one hour later than the U.S. Eastern standard time in winter. The island does not adjust for the U.S.'s Daylight Savings time. This means that when it's noon on a winter day in New York, it's 1 PM in Puerto Rico. In summer, Puerto Rico and the east coast of the United States are on the same time, and three hours ahead of the west coast. Sydney is 14 hours ahead of Puerto Rico, Auckland is 16 hours ahead, and London is 4 hours ahead.

➤ CONTACT: **Time Information** (☎ 787/728–9595).

TIPPING

Some hotels automatically add a 5%– 12% service charge to your bill. Check ahead to confirm whether this charge is built into the room rate or will be tacked on at check out. Some smaller hotels might charge extra (as much as $5 per day) for use of air-conditioning, called an "energy tax." Tips are expected, and appreciated, by restaurant waitstaff (15%–20% if a service charge isn't included), hotel porters ($1 per bag), maids ($1–$2 a day), and taxi drivers (10%–15%).

TOURS AND PACKAGES

Because everything is prearranged on a prepackaged tour or independent vacation, you'll spend less time planning—and often get it all at a good price.

BOOKING WITH AN AGENT

Travel agents are excellent resources. But it's a good idea to collect brochures from several agencies as some agents' suggestions may be influenced by relationships with tour and package firms that reward them for volume sales. If you have a special interest, **find an agent with expertise in that area**; ASTA (☞ Travel Agencies) has a database of specialists worldwide.

Make sure your travel agent knows the accommodations and other services of the place they're recommending. Ask about the hotel's location, room size, beds, and whether it has a pool, room service, or programs for children, if you care about these. Has your agent been there in person or sent others whom you can contact?

Do some homework on your own, too: local tourism boards can provide information about lesser-known and small-niche operators, some of which may sell only direct.

BUYER BEWARE

Each year consumers are stranded or lose their money when tour operators—even large ones with excellent reputations—go out of business. So **check out the operator.** Ask several travel agents about its reputation, and try to **book with a company that has a consumer-protection program.** (Look for information in the company's brochure.) In the United States, members of the National Tour Association and the United States Tour Operators Association are required to set aside funds to cover your payments and travel arrangements in the event that the company defaults. It's also a good idea to choose a company that participates in the American Society of Travel Agents' Tour Operator Program (TOP); ASTA will act as mediator in any disputes between you and your tour operator.

Remember that the more your package or tour includes the better you can predict the ultimate cost of your vacation. Make sure you know exactly what is covered, and **beware of hidden costs.** Are taxes, tips, and transfers included? Entertainment and excursions? These can add up.

➤ TOUR-OPERATOR RECOMMENDA-TIONS: **American Society of Travel Agents** (☞ Travel Agencies). **National Tour Association (NTA;** ✉ 546 E. Main St., Lexington, KY 40508, ☎ 606/226–4444 or 800/682–8886, WEB www.ntaonline.com). **United States Tour Operators Association** (USTOA; ✉ 342 Madison Ave., Suite 1522, New York, NY 10173, ☎ 212/599–6599 or 800/468–7862, FAX 212/599–6744, ustoa@aol.com, WEB www.ustoa.com).

GUIDED TOURS

You can see Old San Juan from the free trolley or on self-guided walking tours; look for them in copy of *Qué Pasa*, which is available at all tourist offices and hotels. The Caribbean Carriage Company will take you around Old San Juan in a horse-drawn buggy. Call the company or hop one of their carriages at Plaza Dársenas near Pier 1. Tours cost about $30 per half hour.

If you'd like to explore other parts of the island but don't want to rent a car, several companies offer tours. Most San Juan hotels have a tour desk that can make arrangements for you. The three standard half-day tours ($20–$30) are of Old and "new" San Juan; Old San Juan and the Bacardi Rum Plant; and Playa Luquillo and El Yunque rain forest. All-day tours ($25–$45) can include a trip to Ponce, a day at El Comandante Racetrack, or a combined tour of the city and El Yunque rain forest.

Leading operators include Normandie Tours, Rico Suntours, Tropix Wellness Outings, and United Tour Guides. Cordero Caribbean Tours runs tours in air-conditioned limousines for an hourly rate. Wheelchair Getaway offers sightseeing tours of San Juan as well as wheelchair transport between the airports and cruise-ship docks and city hotels.

➤ LOCAL TOUR COMPANIES: **Caribbean Carriage Company** (☎ 787/797–8063). **Cordero Caribbean Tours** (☎ 787/786–9114; 787/780–2442 evenings). **Normandie Tours, Inc.** (☎ 787/722–6308). **Rico Suntours** (☎ 787/722–2080 or 787/722–6090). **Tropix Wellness Outings** (☎ 787/268–2173). **United Tour Guides** (☎ 787/725–7605 or 787/723–5578). **Wheelchair Getaway** (☎ 787/883–0131).

TRAIN TRAVEL

As of this writing, the island's only operating trains were small-gauge sugarcane trains used to haul crops from the fields. San Juan, however, has embarked on construction of an elevated urban train system. Due for completion in 2004, it will connect the city with the suburbs of Bayamón, Guaynabo, Santurce, Río Piedras, and Carolina. The system is slated to have 16 city stops and will also serve Aeropuerto Internacional Luis Muñoz Marín.

TRAVEL AGENCIES

A good travel agent puts your needs first. Look for an agency that has been in business at least five years, emphasizes customer service, and has someone on staff who specializes in your destination. In addition, **make sure the agency belongs to a professional trade organization.** The American Society of Travel Agents (ASTA), with 24,000 agents in some 140 countries, is the largest and most influential in the field. Operating under the motto "Integrity in Travel," it maintains and enforces a strict code of ethics and will step in to help mediate any agent-client disputes if necessary. ASTA also maintains a Web site that includes a directory of agents. (If a travel agency is also acting as your tour operator, *see* Buyer Beware *in* Tours and Packages.)

➤ LOCAL AGENT REFERRALS: **American Society of Travel Agents** (ASTA; ✉ 1101 King St., Suite 200, Alexandria, VA 22314, ☎ 800/965–2782 24-hr hot line, FAX 703/739–3268, WEB www.astanet.com). **Association of British Travel Agents** (✉ 68–71 Newman St., London W1T 3AH, ☎ 020/7637–2444, FAX 020/7637–0713, WEB www.abtanet.com). **Association of Canadian Travel Agents** (✉ 130 Albert St., Suite 1705, Ottawa, Ontario K1P 5G4, ☎ 613/237–3657, FAX 613/237–7052, WEB www.acta.ca). **Australian Federation of Travel Agents** (✉ Level 3, 309 Pitt St., Sydney, NSW 2000, ☎ 02/9264–3299, FAX 02/9264–1085, WEB www.afta.com.au). **Travel Agents' Association of New Zealand** (✉ Level 5, Tourism and Travel House, 79 Boulcott St., Box 1888, Wellington 6001, ☎ 04/499–0104, FAX 04/499–0827, WEB www.taanz.org.nz).

VISITOR INFORMATION

In addition to the Puerto Rico Tourism Company's *Qué Pasa,* pick up the Puerto Rico Hotel and Tourism Association's *Bienvenidos* and *Places to Go.* Among them you'll find a wealth of information about the island and its activities. All are free and available at tourism offices and hotel desks. The Puerto Rico Tourism Company has information centers at the airport, Old San Juan, Ponce, Aguadilla, and Cabo Rojo. Most island towns also have a tourism office in their city hall.

➤ TOURIST INFORMATION: **Puerto Rico Tourism Company** (✉ Box 902-3960, Old San Juan Station, San Juan, PR 00902-3960, ☎ 787/721–2400, WEB www.gotopuertorico.com). From the States, you can call the New York office toll-free (☎ 800/223–6530). Other branches: (✉ 3575 W. Cahuenga Blvd., Suite 560, Los Angeles, CA 90068, ☎ 213/874–5991; ✉ 901 Ponce de León Blvd., Suite 101, Coral Gables, FL 33134, ☎ 305/445–9112).

WEB SITES

Do check out the World Wide Web when planning your trip. You'll find everything from weather forecasts to virtual tours of famous cities. Be sure to **visit Fodors.com** (www.fodors.com), a complete travel-planning site. You can research prices and book plane tickets, hotel rooms, rental cars, vacation packages, and more. In addition, you can post your pressing questions in the Travel Talk section. Other planning tools include a currency converter and weather reports, and there are loads of links to travel resources.

You can get basic information about Puerto Rico from **www.puertoricowow.com** and **www.gotopuertorico.com.** Maps are available at **www.travelmaps.com.** For information on conferences and conventions, see the Puerto Rico Convention Center Web site at **www.prconvention.com** or the Puerto Rico Convention Bureau at **www.meetpuertorico.com.** In addition, many of the hotels and attractions throughout the island have their own Web sites.

WHEN TO GO

High season runs from mid-December through mid-April. Winter hotel rates are 25%–40% higher than off-season rates, and hotels tend to be packed. San Juan is also a commercial town, and hotels, save for the short season around Christmas and New Year's, are busy year-round with international business travelers. This doesn't mean the island won't have rooms in winter—rarely is space completely unavailable—but if you plan to beat that winter sleet in Duluth, **make arrangements for flights and hotel space a few months ahead of time.**

A fun and often less expensive time to visit is during the "shoulder" seasons of fall and spring. The weather is—still—perfect, and the tourist crush is less intense.

CLIMATE

Puerto Rico's weather is moderate and tropical year-round, with an average temperature of about 82°F (26°C). Essentially, there are no seasonal changes, although winter sees cooling (not cold) breezes from the north, and temperatures in higher elevations drop by as much as 20 degrees. Hurricane season in the Caribbean runs July through November.

The following are average daily maximum and minimum temperatures.

SAN JUAN

Jan.	70F	21C	May	74F	23C	Sept.	75F	24C
	80	27		84	29		86	30
Feb.	70F	21C	June	75F	24C	Oct.	75F	24C
	80	27		85	29		85	29
Mar.	70F	21C	July	75F	24C	Nov.	73F	23C
	81	27		85	29		84	29
Apr.	72F	22C	Aug.	76F	24C	Dec.	72F	22C
	82	28		85	29		81	27

➤ FORECASTS: **Puerto Rico Weather** (☎ 787/253–4586). **Weather Channel Connection** (☎ 900/932–8437), 95¢ per minute from a Touch-Tone phone.

FESTIVALS AND SEASONAL EVENTS

➤ DEC.: The Puerto Rico National Folkloric Ballet performs its highly anticipated **Annual Criollísimo Show** regularly during the month. The dance blends modern ballet with Puerto Rican and Caribbean music and themes. Look to the Teatro Tapia in Old San Juan or the Centro de Bellas Artes Luis A. Ferré in Santurce for schedules.

➤ EARLY DEC.: For 10 days in early December, **Humacao's Fiesta Patronale** celebrates the Virgin of the Immaculate Conception; the festival coincides with the city's sprucing up for Christmas.

➤ MID-DEC.: Cataño's Bacardí Rum Plant hosts the **Bacardí Artisan's Fair.** With local crafts, children's activities,

folk bands, and food and drink kiosks, it's arguably the largest event of its kind in the Caribbean. If you've got a hankering for loud engines and sea spray, visit the exciting **Puerto Rico International Offshore Cup** speed-boat races held every year in Fajardo, where local and international teams compete for prize money and prestige.

➤ LATE DEC.: The annual **Hatillo Festival de los Mascaras** honors the mask-making traditions of the northwestern town of Hatillo, where colorful masks used in religious processions have been crafted for centuries. **Navidades,** or Christmas, features costumed nativity processions, music concerts, and other festivities islandwide during the week leading to one of the busiest holidays of the year.

➤ JAN.: The annual season of the **Puerto Rico Symphony Orchestra** begins with classical and pop performances by the island's finest orchestra. Concerts are held in San Juan.

➤ JAN. 6: The traditional **El Día de los Tres Reyes** (Three Kings Day) is a time of gift-giving and celebration. Sculptures of the gift-bearing three wise men, in wood or wire decorated with Christmas lights, appear in towns around the island, accompanied by music, puppet shows for children, and feasts.

➤ LATE JAN.: The annual **Las Fiestas de la Calle San Sebastián** (San Sebastián Street Festival), named after the street in Old San Juan where the festival originated, features several nights of live music in the plazas as well as food festivals and *cabezudos* parades, where folk legends are caricatured in oversize masks.

➤ LATE JAN.–EARLY FEB.: Each year the Puerto Rico film industry picks talent to honor in the **Puerto Rico International Film Festival.** International stars such as Benicio Del Toro and Chita Rivera attest to the power of Puerto Rican influence in the arts, and the San Juan film festival showcases island-made films and works from around the world.

➤ EARLY FEB.: Coamo's **San Blas de Illescas Half Marathon** has been running, literally, since 1957. The race, in honor of the town's patron saint and part of its fiesta patronale, covers 21 km (13 mi) in the hills of the central town; it's so popular that competitors come from the world over, and the streets are lined with some 200,000 spectators.

➤ MID-FEB.: Ponce's **Danza Week** of cultural activities celebrates the *danza,* a colonial-era dance similar to the waltz.

➤ LATE FEB.: The mountain towns of Maricao and Yauco, centers of the island's coffee-growing region, host the annual **Festival de Café** (Coffee Harvest Festival), honoring both crops and farmers. It takes place at the towns' plazas, with exhibits of coffee and harvesting equipment as well as with local bands, folk crafts, and food and drink kiosks.

➤ FEB.–EARLY MAR.: The weeks preceding Lent have special significance for Catholicism and other religions, and Puerto Rico celebrates its **Carnivales,** or Carnivals, with vigor. The flamboyant celebrations,

held island-wide but with particular energy in Ponce, are complete with float parades, folk music, local foods, Carnival Queen pageants, and music competitions.

➤ MAR.: The two-day **Dulce Sueño Paso Fino Fair,** showcasing the island's famous Paso Fino horses, is held in the town of Guayama. Paso Finos are bred and trained to walk with a distinctive, smooth gait, and the horses and their trainers are held in high regard.

➤ MID-MAR.: The Puerto Rico Tourism Company sponsors the annual **International Artisans' Festival,** with folk art, carvings, leather work, and other crafts from islanders and international artists.

➤ APR.: Fajardo's **Festival de Chiringas** (Kite Festival) features demonstrations and flying competitions, as well as food and drink booths. The annual **Regata de Veleros Copa Kelly** (Kelly Cup Sailboat Regatta) takes place off the coast of Fajardo. Not only for professionals in the tourism industry, the **Tourism Fair** highlights island attractions and activities, as well as local crafts and artisans' creations.

➤ LATE APR.–MAY: Isabela's **Festival de Mundillo** (Bobbin Lace Festival) showcases delicate, woven lace with demonstrations and exhibits.

➤ MAY: Bayamón's **Chicharrón Festival** celebrates the island's famous puffy, pork-rind fritter. The city has become known for this treat thanks to the many *chicharronero* carts that line Route 2 on the way into town. The Fajardo **Festival de Bomba y Plena** turns the spotlight on Puerto Rico's lively Afro-influenced music and dance.

➤ LATE MAY–EARLY JUNE: The annual **Heineken JazzFest** attracts some 15,000 aficionados to San Juan for four days of outdoor concerts by the likes of David Sánchez, George Benson, Nestor Torres, and Spyro Gyra.

➤ EARLY JUNE: The annual **Casals Festival** honors the late, great cellist Pablo Casals, who lived in Old San Juan. The 10 days of classical music performances feature the Puerto Rico Symphony Orchestra as well as soloists from the island and around the world.

➤ JUNE: In San Juan, the **Fiesta de San Juan Bautista or Noche de San Juan** (San Juan Bautista Festival) honors city patron St. John the Baptist with a week of parades, music, dance, and, ultimately, a traditional backward walk into the ocean to bring good luck in the ensuing year.

➤ LATE JUNE–JULY: Gardenias, lilies, begonias, and thousands of tropical plants are showcased at Aibonito's annual **Fiesta de Flores** (Flower Festival).

➤ JULY: Loíza's **Fiesta de Santiago Apóstal** (St. James Festival), held in July, honors Puerto Rico's African traditions and the apostle St. James with a carnival of street parades, music, and dancing.

➤ EARLY JULY: Río Grande celebrates its **Carnivale**, between the first and second week of July with music competitions, parades, and feasts.

➤ MID-JULY: The **Barranquitas Fería de Artesanía** (Barranquitas Artisans' Fair) offers spots to more than 200 local artisans to display their pottery, wood carvings, leather bags and belts, basketry, and other handiwork.

Around July 16, such coastal towns as Naguabo, Ceiba, and Humacao conduct religious processions honoring the **Virgen del Carmen.** Offerings of flowers from the *flamboyán* tree are made to this virgin, the patron saint of the fishermen, and festivities continue into the evening.

➤ LATE AUG.–EARLY SEPT.: Anglers of all stripes try their hand at snagging blue marlin and other game fish in the largest fishing competition in Puerto Rico, the **International Billfish Tour-**nament. The strongest tackle might prevail—marlins can weigh as much as 900 pounds.

➤ EARLY OCT.: **Naguabo's fiesta patronale** honors Our Lady of the Rosary the first 10 days of October.

➤ LATE OCT.: The northern town of Corozal hosts the **Festival del Platano** (Plantain Festival), which highlights this versatile staple of Puerto Rican cuisine.

➤ OCT.: Arecibo, on the north coast, holds the **Cetí Festival,** named after a tiny, sardinelike fish found in the area and considered a culinary delicacy.

➤ NOV.–JAN.: The boys of summer are actually the boys of winter in Puerto Rico: in October the **baseball season** commences. Fans follow the games, played at various island stadiums, with the fervor of sports enthusiasts anywhere. Major-league players often travel to Puerto Rico to play with the island's six pro teams.

➤ MID-NOV.: The **Festival of Puerto Rican Music,** held in San Juan and other locations, celebrates the vibrancy of the island's folk music, highlighted by a contest featuring the *cuatro,* a traditional guitar with five double strings.

➤ LATE NOV.: Luquillo hosts the three-day **Festival de Platos Tipicos** (Festival of Typical Dishes), highlighting food and drink prepared with coconut.

➤ LATE NOV.: The central mountain areas hold an annual **Joyuya Indian Festival,** honoring the island's indigenous Taíno culture with crafts demonstrations, ceremonies, and guided visits to Taíno sites in the area.

1 DESTINATION: PUERTO RICO

More Than Just a Day at the Beach

What's Where

Pleasures and Pastimes

Fodor's Choice

Great Itinerary

MORE THAN JUST A DAY AT THE BEACH

PUERTO RICO is unique among Caribbean destinations because of the shear breadth of experiences available to you. If you crave a luxury resort, you'll find several world-class options to choose from. If you're a nature lover, you'll find an abundance of wonders to explore. If you're a surfer or an art aficionado, a golfer or a history buff, a deep-sea diver or a gourmet, you'll find satisfaction here. And perhaps foremost, lending a distinctive flavor to any Puerto Rico experience, you'll find a sophisticated, centuries-old culture—a mix of Native American, Spanish, African, and contemporary U.S. influences.

Puerto Rico's role in the New World began early. Somewhere along the western coast (the spot is disputed), Christopher Columbus landed on his second voyage, claiming the island for Spain on November 19, 1493. Another famous explorer, Ponce de León, had a more lasting impact, helping to establish Spanish rule when not searching for the elusive Fountain of Youth. But for many generations before the arrival of European settlers, there was a thriving indigenous culture here. The Taínos, believed to have numbered 30,000 at the time of Columbus's landing, called the island Boriquén, and to this day Puerto Ricans refer to themselves as Boriquas. Most historical accounts have the Taínos quickly dying out after Spanish settlement, but current University of Puerto Rico studies suggest that Taíno DNA is still evident in the genetic makeup of present-day Puerto Ricans. Researchers say this may indicate that the Taínos were far more numerous than was previously thought, and that they did not disappear so soon after the arrival of Europeans.

Spain would ward off Dutch and English aggression to rule the island until 1898, when the United States took it over as part of the spoils from the Spanish-American war. Since 1952 Puerto Rico has had U.S. commonwealth status, calling itself an *estado libre asociado* (free associated state)—a term that conveys some of the complexities and contradictions of the relationship. Puerto Ricans are U.S. citizens, but their single representative in congress has only a symbolic vote. The island receives government funds for social, health, education, and infrastructure programs, and Puerto Ricans are found in the U.S. military in numbers proportionately greater than those of many full-fledged states. But Puerto Rico residents don't pay federal taxes, and they aren't allowed to vote in presidential elections.

In day-to-day life, the contrast between U.S. influences and the more long-standing Spanish, African, and Native American cultural mix is in ample evidence: American-style malls and fast-food restaurants compete with small, family-run places that have a distinctly traditional feel. Spanish is the mother tongue, but English is also an "official language" and is widely spoken, particularly in and around San Juan. For visitors from the mainland United States, the relationship provides undeniable advantages—you don't need to clear customs or exchange currency, and when you touch down in San Juan's Luis Muñoz Marín International Airport you'll be in an easily negotiated bilingual environment.

If you're like most visitors, your discovery of Puerto Rico will begin in Vieja San Juan (Old San Juan), a largely restored historic city dating from the 16th century that's a magical place. On a mile-square peninsula to the northwest of the greater metropolitan area, it has open plazas and parks, a sweeping bayside promenade, and some of the New World's best examples of Spanish architecture.

The old city's bluestone streets climb from the Bahía de San Juan (San Juan Bay) to a long headland overlooking the Atlantic. The oceanside bluff, which runs along Calle Norzagaray, is bound at either end by two great fortresses, Fuerte San Cristóbal to the east and Fuerte San Felipe del Morro (El Morro) to the west, testifying to the city's past as a military stronghold. El Morro is particularly imposing, its massive walls melding with the promontory on which it sits, rising to split bay from ocean.

As you explore the city, at every turn you're likely to encounter a new pleasure, from the central Plaza de Armas, where you can linger over a *café con leche* (coffee with milk) and watch schoolchildren chase pigeons, to the serene gardens of the Casa Blanca, built originally as a home for Puerto Rico's first governor, Ponce de León, in 1521, to the extraordinary folkart collection of the Museo de las Américas. Along with the fortresses, there are numerous churches—some dating from the 16th century—mansions from the 19th-century, and art deco masterpieces. Most buildings are only one or two stories tall and painted in bright pastels that radiate under the Caribbean sun.

Although filled with history, Old San Juan doesn't live in the past; it's a flourishing cultural center, with the island's greatest concentration of top-flight restaurants, galleries, shops, and nightspots, attracting artists, intellectuals, and all manner of other *sanjuaneros*. On weekends, particularly, the city can feel like one big party after dark, with salsa and jazz pulsing from the doorways and open windows of bars and restaurants, and revelers spilling onto the streets. The young and beautiful strut side by side with San Juan's professional set and distinguished elders who have seen it all a thousand times before. The people you encounter on these streets are as charming and varied as the beautiful buildings that surround them.

Greater San Juan is an urban anomaly in the Caribbean. There are, of course, the trademark beaches, from the Miami-style Condado and Isla Verde areas to low-key Ocean Park and undeveloped Piñones. But in and around San Juan you can also watch major-league baseball stars in action during Puerto Rico's Winter League, take in a world-class ballet or theatrical production, go to the horse races, or visit one of several fine museums. And everywhere, from makeshift clubs to concert halls, there's music in the air.

The Santurce area, San Juan's urban center, is in the throes of a revival, with old theaters and grand, pre-war apartment buildings undergoing renovation. The Museo de Arte de Puerto Rico, the island's largest art museum, is here with works—from the 17th century to the present—by island artists and renowned international artists as well. It joins Puerto Rico's premier music and theater venue, the Centro de Bellas Artes Luis A. Ferré,

to make Santurce the Caribbean's pre-eminent spot for high culture.

Hato Rey, home of Puerto Rico's financial district—a single row of gleaming office towers known as the Golden Mile—has some of San Juan's finest restaurants. The range of dining choices reflects the city's cosmopolitan character: there's everything from Chinese to Italian to Mexican to Middle Eastern to Spanish. The construction of an urban train system, whose first phase will run from the suburbs of Bayamón to Santurce, will accent the district's modern feel, with a futuristic, elevated track weaving through the glass-and-steel office buildings.

In Río Piedras you'll find the main campus of the Universidad de Puerto Rico, built in the fashion of traditional British and U.S. schools, but with beautiful tropical landscaping. There are music, theater, and other performances given at university facilities, which also include museums and libraries.

Overall, San Juan's rapid pulse is what distinguishes life there from life *en la isla* (out on the island), the term Puerto Ricans use for everything that's not part of the city. The distinction is as much psychological as geographical; it implies a freedom from stress, an embrace of tradition, and the power and beauty of nature.

WHETHER YOU'RE driving up the northern face of the Cordillera mountain range for a lunch of roast pork, fried rice, and chickpeas on the back porch of a mountain inn, or rumbling down the range's southern side toward the Caribbean coastline, where the water is gentler, calmer, and bluer than in the north, you'll know "en la isla" when you find it. It's a place that includes virgin rain forests, bioluminescent bays, labyrinthine limestone caves, and mile after mile of white sand beaches. You can also find it on the tip of your tongue—just try an *empanadilla* (stuffed fried turnover) washed back by a cold beer at one of the open-air food stalls scattered along the coasts from Boquerón in the west to Luquillo in the east.

Among the natural attractions, star treatment goes to the Bosque Nacional del Caribe (Caribbean National Forest), popularly known as El Yunque. This rain forest encompasses a huge, anvil-shape mountaintop that dominates the skyline on the roadway east from San Juan to Fajardo. The Taínos considered the area sacred ground, and as you hike the numerous trails you understand why. Waterfalls slice through the forest; mammoth ferns, pines, and Sierra palms refract the sunlight through a lime-green canopy; more than 200 species of birds make the forest home, including the rare Puerto Rican green parrot. El Yunque is less than an hour's drive from downtown San Juan, but it feels like the other side the world.

On the eastern coast, the Fajardo region is a hot spot for boating and diving, and nearby Balneario de Luquillo is one of Puerto Rico's prettiest and most popular beaches. Fajardo also serves as the departure point for trips to the offshore islets of Vieques and Culebra. Both are known as places to get away from it all, considered by some to be the last pieces of unspoiled paradise in the Caribbean—a status that's ironically due in part to the presence of the U.S. Navy, which has kept much of the land undeveloped in order to use it for bombing exercises. (The navy discontinued exercises on Culebra some years ago; its activities on Vieques are a subject of heated controversy.) At night, thousands of tiny bioluminescent dinoflagellates light up Vieques's Bahía Mosquito (Mosquito Bay, also known as Bioluminescent Bay or Phosphorescent Bay), creating one of Puerto Rico's most novel and spectacular natural phenomena.

I**F YOU TRAVEL SOUTH** of the central mountains, you enter a part of the island that is noticeably removed from the influences of San Juan. The urban center here is Ponce, which has long been an important port. The overland trip from the north was, until recently, an arduous journey, which in large part explains the distinctive identity of Ponce and the south. The climate here is also different, both drier and warmer. Where the north has El Yunque, the south has the Bosque Estatal de Guánica (Guánica State Forest), a United Nations Biosphere Reserve that's a strangely beautiful collection of twisted, bonsailike trees and towering cacti.

Ponce itself has a well-preserved downtown, with a large main square, Plaza las Delicias, that's filled with broad tile walkways, shade trees, and flower gardens. Its centerpiece is an opulent fountain with water-spewing lions built for the 1939 World's Fair, but its most photographed landmark is undoubtedly the Parque de los Bomberos, a red-and-black, Victorian-style firehouse that dates from 1883.

In its heyday, from the 1850s through the 1930s, Ponce was a center of politics and culture as well as commerce, spawning some of Puerto Rico's most revered artists and civic leaders. The period also marked an architectural flowering that's still evident in the neighborhoods surrounding the main plaza, where you'll see a whimsical mix of Caribbean, European, and North American influences in the carefully maintained houses. To the north of the city are two historical treasures: Hacienda Buena Vista, a restored 19th-century coffee plantation, and Centro Ceremonial Indígena de Tibes (Tibes Indian Ceremonial Center), a pre-Taíno burial ground dating from AD 700 that's an extremely important archaeological site.

To the west of Ponce, in the island's southwest corner, are some of Puerto Rico's finest beaches, stretching from Guánica to Cabo Rojo. The Caribbean coast is calmer than that in the north, and its shallow waters are filled with reefs that teem with sea life. A vast underwater shelf extending from Ponce to the Mona Channel west of the island provides great snorkeling and scuba-diving spots.

The western coast has Mayagüez, Puerto Rico's third-largest city, and, farther north, the hip town of Rincón, epicenter of the island's surfing scene. Karst country, extending along the northwest corridor, is marked by haystack-shape hills and a network of caves that were formed many millennia ago as the island rose from the sea; you can explore them at the Parque de las Cavernas del Río Camuy (Río Camuy Cave Park). Also in the region is a man-made wonder, Observatorio de Arecibo (Arecibo Observatory), home to one of the world's largest satellite dishes, spanning more than 20 acres.

If you're looking for cool breezes and majestic views, spend some time in the central mountains, which undulate between 1,000 ft and 3,000 ft above sea level as they span the island east to west. There are many inns throughout the area, some of them renovated plantation homes, as well as a number of restaurants and out-door barbecues of high repute that you can reach on a day trip from San Juan. You'll also be rewarded by the vistas; at some points you can see both the Caribbean Sea and the Atlantic Ocean from the same location.

IF YOU SPEND THE TIME to enjoy even a few of Puerto Rico's treasures, you'll inevitably get a feel for its people. It's immediately clear that the island has its own vibrant, self-sustaining culture; no one could mistake it for a developer's attempt to create a tourist fantasy. The hotels, restaurants, and nightclubs have been de-signed with an eye toward the tastes of the locals—a strong market on an island where tourism accounts for less than 10% of the economy. This means you're as likely to meet a Puerto Rican staying at your hotel as one working there. The same goes for restaurants and bars—which makes it all the easier to get to know Puerto Ricans, who are among the best hosts in the world. They're genuinely friendly and proud of their island, and they can impress you on many levels, from their *criollo* (creole) cuisine, to their artis-tic achievements, to their music—whether it be salsa, *bomba,* jazz, or pop.

Puerto Ricans are masters at having a good time; you can feel the whole island coming alive on typical weekend nights. If you have the opportunity, attend one of the *fiestas patronales* (patron saint fes-tivals) that towns large and small hold throughout the year. They're a mix of good food, good drink, and great music, often provided by the island's top per-formers and usually free of charge.

Puerto Rico will wow you with its gor-geous beaches and deep blue waters. If all you want is to sit on the sand and enjoy a piña colada, there's no better place to do it. But if you want something more, this island is rich with possibilities.

— John Marino

WHAT'S WHERE

Destination chapters in *Fodor's Puerto Rico* are arranged geographically. They start with San Juan, the first destination for most visitors, and move to the inland rain for-est and coastal regions of the east, on to the southern mountains and shores, and around to the island's northwestern reaches.

San Juan

San Juan, buffed by Atlantic Ocean cur-rents and gentle trade winds, sits on the island's northeast coast, a bit more than a two-hour drive from the west coast, about an hour's drive from the eastern shores, and about an hour from the town of Ponce, on the south coast. It's gener-ally a flat town, with mountain ranges to the east and to the south, near the is-land's center.

Eastern Puerto Rico

Although eastern Puerto Rico encom-passes several thriving communities, all have a slow pace and a somewhat provincial outlook on life. They also tend to hang on to traditions, something that is re-flected in the music, food, and art of the region. The east coast begins just outside San Juan and follows the Atlantic Ocean down to where it meets the Caribbean. Outer island Vieques sits squarely off the central coast; smaller sister island Cule-bra floats east of the northeasternmost cor-ner of the "main island." The shore is placid in some spots, banked by the remains of coconut plantations, and rugged in others, especially north of Fajardo, where bluffs overlook the ocean. Much of it lies in the foothills of mountains, including El Yunque rain forest.

Southern Puerto Rico

Stretching from Puerto Rico's central mountains to the Caribbean Sea and some 90 mi along the southern coast, southern Puerto Rico encompasses lush forests, such as in the Bosque Estatal Carite in the southeastern part of the island, as well as tropical dry forests such as the Bosque Es-tatal de Guánica on the southwestern coast. In general, this area is drier than other parts of the island, and numerous forms of cacti are abundant. You'll find homes scattered through the area, picturesque mountain towns, seaside fishing villages, and Puerto Rico's second-largest urban hub, Ponce.

Northwestern Puerto Rico

The north coast, which skirts the Atlantic Ocean, was formerly the home of many coconut and fruit plantations, and trees are still abundant in the area. The jagged coastline is also known for its world-class surfing beaches. The area just inland is dominated by limestone karst terrain, where huge cliffs and sinkholes in the porous ground create a surreal feeling. Tropical vegetation fills the area still farther inland, near the Cordillera Central, where the island's tallest peak, Cerro de Punta, looms 4,390 ft above sea level. A casual, laid-back atmosphere is the norm in this region, which is dotted with small hotels and restaurants.

PLEASURES AND PASTIMES

Beaches

Beaches rim the island. Sanjuaneros often pack the sandy stretches lining the neighborhoods of Puerta de Tierra, Condado, Ocean Park, and Isla Verde as well as such east-coast beaches as Luquillo. Those seeking solitude will find it on the outer islands of Vieques and Culebra, where the beaches are wide, spectacular, and often uncrowded. To the south, several strands are broad and inviting, with plenty of seaside bars and restaurants where you can while away the hours. The west coast near the town of Rincón is noted for its big waves and is popular with surfers.

Dining

Many Puerto Rican chefs have taken cues from the international set, and "world cuisine" is the buzzword at trend-conscious restaurants. Throughout the island you'll find everything from French haute cuisine to sushi bars, as well as superb local eateries serving *comidas criollas,* traditional Caribbean-creole meals. If you're looking for authentic Puerto Rican cuisine, one indication is the *mesón gastronómico* label used by the government to recognize restaurants that preserve culinary traditions. There are more than 40 such establishments island-wide.

Festivals

Puerto Rico's festivals are colorful and inclined toward lots of music and feasting. The towns and villages are particularly loyal to their patron saints, and every year each

of the island's 78 municipalities celebrates a *fiesta patronale* (patron saint festival). Though religious in origin, these festivities feature processions, sports events, folklore shows, feasting, music, and dance, and they often highlight local crafts (such as the delicate *mundillo* lace of Aguadilla). They last about 10 days, with more activities on weekends than on weekdays. Several towns and regions also have pre-Lenten Carnivals, complete with parades, folk music, local dishes, a Carnival Queen pageant, and music competitions. All are in early to late February, sometimes into March. The island calendar is also full year-round with street fêtes, sporting competitions, and cultural and arts festivals.

Gambling

The time when one of the main tourism activities in Puerto Rico was gambling has passed, but casinos still draw crowds. Today, rather than high rollers out for a week of intense dice and card games, the casinos tend to be filled with couples looking for fun and a chance to hit the jackpot. Games generally include slot machines, blackjack, roulette, craps, Caribbean stud poker (a five-card stud game), and *pai gow* poker (a combination of American poker and the ancient Chinese game of pai gow, which employs cards and dice). Hotels that house casinos have live entertainment most weekends, restaurants, and bars.

Music

Music is the heart and soul of Puerto Rico. Take the instruments from the days of the Taíno Indians—the *guiro* (scratch gourd) and the *fotuto* (conch shell)—and blend them with the drums and rhythms of Africa that took root on the island's sugarcane-lined coasts. To this mixture, stir in the Spanish-Moorish–influenced music of the inland farmers and mountain folk—the *trovadores,* who still perform their improvised songs accompanied by the *cuatro* (five-double-string Spanish guitar). Let all this simmer for a couple centuries, and there you have it.

The island's brash Latin sound is best exemplified by the highly danceable salsa, especially as interpreted by such entertainers as the late, great Tito Puente and pop sensation Ricky Martin. Salsa, Spanish for "sauce" (as in the sauce that energizes the party) is a fusion of West African percussion and jazz with a swing beat. Two of its predecessors, *bomba* and *plena,* can still be heard today. Bomba is African-based drum and dance music in which a lead singer often leads a chorus of singers in a call-and-response interplay, similar to Cuba's rumba music. Plena is a more melodic country music that makes use of the cuatro as well of scratch gourds.

Other Latin beats heard on the island, with origins in the Caribbean, Latin America, and Spain, are mambo, merengue, flamenco, cha-cha, and rumba. Increasingly, young musicians are experimenting with new forms, including urban dance music, rap, and Spanish-language rock and pop. Fiel a la Vega and Sol de Menta compose and perform danceable rock tunes without losing their island roots, and heavy metal band Puya has been making its marks in stateside markets. Vico C is one of the island's most famous rappers, known for weaving urban tales with a positive message.

FODOR'S CHOICE

No two people will agree on what makes a perfect vacation, but it's fun and helpful to know what others think. We hope you'll have a chance to experience some of Fodor's Choices yourself in Puerto Rico. For detailed information about each entry, refer to the appropriate chapter.

Beaches

Balneario de Luquillo. This beautiful beach has all the trimmings—including lifeguards, changing rooms, and nearby kiosks where you can find tasty local cuisine and piña coladas. It also has something extra: ocean access for wheelchair users.

Cabo Rojo Beaches. The strips of sand stretching along such beaches as Boquerón, El Combate, Buyé, and the more secluded La Playuela are some of the island's most gorgeous.

Playa Crashboat, Aguadilla. The picturesque boats lining the shores here are just part of the appeal. The water has a shimmering, glasslike look and is great for swimming and snorkeling. The shoreline has picnic tables and playground areas.

Playa Flamenco, Culebra. Imagine a long curve of white sand and azure-tinted water. Palm trees wave in the wind. No one is there to claim the spot as theirs. That's what you'll find at this Culebra beach.

Playa de Isla Verde, San Juan. There's a reason this spot is the site for some of the toniest resorts in San Juan—the beach, wide and warm and kissed by the surf, seems to go on forever.

Dining

Horned Dorset Primavera, Rincón. The five-course prix-fixe dinner here is known throughout the island. French cuisine is laced with tropical touches to create subtle, sophisticated meals. $$$$

Ajili Mojili, San Juan. Here you'll find classic Puerto Rican dishes given an upscale twist and served with a mix of efficiency and island charm. $$–$$$$

Mark's at the Meliá, Ponce. This restaurant gets points for being right in the center of town in the Meliá Hotel on Plaza las Delicias. Award-winning chef Mark French serves up consistently outstanding food—an eclectic mix of Caribbean and international cuisine. $$–$$$$

Café Blu, Vieques. Take scrumptious food, add an elegant setting, and you've got this posh restaurant. From the tuna to the trout, every dish is exquisite. $$–$$$

Café Media Luna, Vieques. For lovers of exotic spices, this local favorite is heaven. Everything from Asian to Middle Eastern fare joins tropical cuisine for a meld that is incomparable. $$–$$$

Parrot Club, Old San Juan. The relaxed yet stylish environment here seems to have struck a chord with sanjuaneros, who are quickly turning this Nuevo Latino restaurant into an institution. $$–$$$

Sand and the Sea, Cayey. The open balcony at this mountaintop restaurant may have the best view on the island—it's especially breathtaking at sunset. Piano music, a fireplace, and good food make for a memorable experience. $$

El Picoteo, Old San Juan. El Convento Hotel's stylish tapas bar is nothing if not flexible—stop in for an early cocktail and an appetizer, have a full meal, or end the evening with dessert or a nightcap. $–$$

La Fonda del Jibarito, Old San Juan. There are excellent family-run restaurants serving traditional Puerto Rican fare all over the island—this happens to be one of the best. $

Lodging

El Convento Hotel, Old San Juan. You wouldn't recognize the El Convento as the Carmelite convent it was 350 years ago; today it's luxurious and hip, a fine example of what sensitive planning and a good decorator can achieve. $$$$

Horned Dorset Primavera, Rincón. This west-coast inn is the place to go to get away from it all in luxury. There are no phones, TVs, or radios in the antique-trimmed rooms, a secluded beach is steps away, and plunge pools dot the manicured grounds. $$$$

Wyndham El Conquistador Resort and Country Club, Fajardo. Hanging off a bluff just above the Atlantic Ocean this giant, self-contained complex aims to meet all of your needs—and succeeds. $$$$

Wyndham El San Juan Hotel & Casino, San Juan. Put on your dancing gear and salsa the night away in the immense, mahogany-paneled lobby of the landmark El San Juan, where on Saturday night it's the place to see and be seen. This is also one of San Juan's finest hotels. $$$$

Inn on the Blue Horizon, Vieques. No phones, no televisions, no noise—just privacy and pampering at this hotel made up of six villas and a main house. $$$–$$$$

Hacienda Tamarindo, Vieques. A tamarind tree rises up through three stories in the lobby, and the outdoor pool is touted as one of Puerto Rico's most beautiful, sitting on a hilltop overlooking Vieques. It's a formula for whimsical bliss. $$–$$$

Mary Lee's by the Sea, Guánica. Tranquillity reigns at this colorful complex of apartments and suites with fully equipped kitchenettes. It's a wonderful place to escape after a day of sun and sea. $$

Villas del Mar Hau, Isabela. A row of brightly colored cottages lines the Montones Beach, and the whole area is dotted with palm and pine trees. There are outdoor sports facilities where active children and adults can work up a sweat, and horseback riding is available. $$

Museums

Fuerte San Felipe del Morro, Old San Juan. El Morro is solid as a rock and even today seems impenetrable. Take a guided tour and see why San Juan was able to fend off invaders for 400 years.

Hacienda Buena Vista, Ponce. The grounds of this former coffee plantation are meticulously maintained, and the guided tours, offered in English and Spanish, are as informative as they come. You'll know how it felt to be a settler taming the wilderness.

Museo de las Américas, Old San Juan. The Museum of the Americas, housed in the impressive 1864 Cuartel de Ballajá military barracks in Old San Juan, has extraordinary folk art collected from throughout North and South America.

Museo de Arte de Ponce. The breadth and quality of both European and Puerto Rican art found here is astounding. The collection of Pre-Raphaelite paintings is truly world class.

Museo de Arte de Puerto Rico, San Juan. The island's premier art museum scours the island for interesting pieces, displays works by contemporary local artists, hosts retrospectives of such island masters as Rafael Tufiño, and mounts shows by international artists.

Natural Wonders

Bahía Mosquito, Vieques. The magnificence of gliding through the sparkling sea creatures at this bioluminescent bay is almost beyond description. Forget special effects and high-tech trickery; here nature beats them hands down.

Bosque Estatal de Guánica. This dry forest is an amazing site with its various forms of cacti and abundant bird life. Hiking here may not be for everyone—it's hot and arid—but you'll love it if you're interested in exotic flora and birds.

Parque de las Cavernas de Río Camuy, Arecibo. The caves are nestled in the island's limestone karst country just south of Arecibo. The tram ride down to them—through wild bamboo and banana plants—is worth the price of admission alone. The large Clara Cave de Empalme is a natural wonder of stalactites, stalagmites, and unique cave life.

El Yunque. With 100 billion gallons of precipitation annually, this protected area truly is a rain forest. Among its sights are 240 tree species and 68 types of birds, including the endangered Puerto Rican green parrot.

GREAT ITINERARY

Highlights of Puerto Rico

Eleven days.

You can loop around the entire island in a day with a few stops along the way. But, to get the most of Puerto Rico's diverse cultural offerings as well as its sunny beaches, colorful towns, and mountain landscapes it's best to divide the drive into a series of short segments. And remember, from wherever you are, you can return to San Juan in two to three hours.

San Juan (*two days*). The old city's forts, museums, and shops will keep you busy for a full day. On the second day, spend the morning on a beach—perhaps Condado or Isla Verde—and the afternoon visiting the Puerto Rico Art Museum and the Plaza del Mercado in Santurce or venturing across San Juan Bay to Cataño for a tour of the Bacardí Rum Factory. Evening dining and nightlife options abound in San Juan. ☞ *Chapter 2.*

Fajardo and the Out Islands (*two days*). Get an early start and head east for a hike in El Yunque rain forest. Afterward travel to Luquillo Beach for some late-afternoon rays and the area's famous fritters before driving to Fajardo for the night. The next day travel (by plane or ferry) to Vieques or Culebra. On Vieques you can lounge on a pristine beach and visit the bioluminescent Mosquito Bay. Culebra is a quieter island, where sand, sea, and sun blot out life's cares. ☞ *Chapter 3.*

Ponce and Environs (*two days*). From Fajardo take Route 3 south to Route 182, the Panoramic Route. Follow it toward Cayey, passing through the Carite State Forest, with its stands of palms, Honduras mahogany, and Spanish cedars. Stop for lunch at a *lechonera* (stand that

serves slow-roasted meats) outside the park or at a restaurant in Cayey before taking Route 52 to Ponce. Spend the next day touring this historic city and visiting the Hacienda Buena Vista or the Tibes Indian Ceremonial Center. You can spend another night in Ponce or continue your drive to Guánica and overnight there. ☞ *Chapter 4.*

Guánica to San Germán (*two days*). Spend a day on one of the beaches near Guánica or take a day-trip to Gilligan Island with its sandy stretches and coral reefs. In the evening, make your way to the bioluminescent bay, La Parguera, just outside town. The next morning, visit Guánica State Forest, a dry tropical dry forest with cacti and gumbo limbo trees. Afterward, travel northwest to Cabo Rojo, with its lighthouse, and head inland on Route 102 to San Germán for lunch and a stroll past the town's many beautiful buildings. Spend the night here or in Cabo Rojo. ☞ *Chapter 4.*

Rincón (*one day*). From San Germán, continue inland on Route 102; in Sábana Grande, pick up Route 120 and follow it through the Maricao State Forest to the western end of the Panoramic Route. Follow this route back to the coast and the town of Mayagüez. Stop for some lunch and a trip to the zoo before taking Route 2 and then Route 115 to Rincón. Spend the next morning on the beach before heading inland yet again. ☞ *Chapter 5.*

Jayuya to San Juan (*two days*). From Rincón, work your way back to Route 2, and follow it to the scenic Route 111. Make a brief stop in Lares before visiting the Río Camuy Cave Park and/or the Caguana Indian Ceremonial Center. Head inland still farther to Utuado or Jayuya, both of which are good places to spend the night. The next day, visit the Toro Negro State Forest, learn more about the Taíno Indians at the Museo Cemí, and see the petroglyphs on La Piedra Escrita. In the afternoon, return west along Route 111 and pick up Route 129 north to the Arecibo Observatory. Make your way north to the town of Arecibo and return to San Juan on Route 22. ☞ *Chapter 5.*

2 SAN JUAN

Beneath the surface—beneath the highways and malls, the Pizza Huts and Texacos—the Latin Caribbean is here. It's in the beat-heavy music that thumps from your cabbie's radio, in the insouciant swagger of a young *sanjuanero* walking down the boulevard, in the limpid waters of the Bahía de San Juan, and in the swaying palms that line the beaches. This is the land of salsa, of hot coffee and sugared mallorcas; it has a Spanish mother and an American uncle.

by Karl Luntta
and John
Marino

Updated by
John Marino
and Isabel
Abislaimán

S AN JUAN IS PARADISE'S BABY IN AN URBAN COMFORTER. Puerto Rico's sprawling capital is bordered to the north by the Atlantic and to the east and west by bays and lagoons. More than a third of the island's 4 million citizens are proud to call themselves *sanjuaneros*. They go about their business surrounded by the antique and the modern, the commercial and the residential, the man-made and the natural.

By 1508 the explorer Juan Ponce de León had established a colony in an area now known as Caparra, southeast of present-day San Juan. He later moved the settlement north to a more hospitable peninsular location. In 1521, after he became the first colonial governor, Ponce de León switched the name of the island—which was called San Juan Bautista in honor of St. John the Baptist—with that of the settlement of Puerto Rico (Rich Port). The capital of paradise was born.

Defended by the imposing Fuerte San Felipe del Morro (El Morro), Puerto Rico's administrative and population center helped to keep the island firmly in Spain's hands until 1898, when it came under U.S. control after the Spanish-American War. Centuries of Spanish rule left an indelible imprint on the city, particularly in the walled area now known as Old San Juan. Its cobblestone streets are lined with brightly painted, well-preserved colonial structures, and the area has been a U.S. National Historic Zone since 1950.

Old San Juan is a monument to the past, but the rest of the city is firmly in the here and now. It draws migrants from elsewhere on the island to jobs in its businesses and industries. It captivates both residents and visitors with its vibrant lifestyle as well as its balmy beaches, pulsing nightclubs, and mesmerizing museums. Wrap yourself up in even one small patch of the urban comforter, and you may never want to leave this baby.

Pleasures and Pastimes

Architecture
San Juan has been under construction for nearly 500 years. The old city's colonial Spanish row houses—brick with plaster fronts painted in pastel blues, oranges, and yellows—line narrow streets and alleys paved with *adoquines* (blue-gray stones originally used as ballast in Spanish ships). Several churches, including the Catedral de San Juan, were built in the ornate Spanish Gothic style of the 16th century. The massive, white-marble El Capitolio, home of Puerto Rico's legislature, was completed in 1929. The gleaming high-rise resorts along the beaches in Condado and Isla Verde and the glistening steel-and-glass towers in the business and financial district of Hato Rey belong to the end of the 20th century.

Beaches
Just because you're staying in the city doesn't mean you'll have to forgo time on the *playa*. San Juan's beaches are among the island's best, and Condado, Isla Verde, and Ocean Park—to name just a few sandy stretches—are always abuzz. The government maintains 13 *balnearios* (public beaches), including two in the San Juan metro area. They're gated and have dressing rooms, lifeguards, parking, and in some cases picnic tables, playgrounds, and camping facilities. Admission is free; hours are generally 9–5 daily in summer and 9–5 Tuesday–Sunday the rest of the year.

Music

Music is a source of Puerto Rican pride, and it seems that, increasingly, everyone wants to live that *vida loca* espoused by Puerto Rico's own Ricky Martin. The brash Latin sound is best characterized by the music–dance form salsa, which shares not only its name with the word "sauce," but also its zesty, hot flavor. This fusion of West African percussion, jazz (especially swing and Big Band), and other Latin beats (mambo, merengue, flamenco, cha-cha, rumba) is sexy and primal. Dancing to it is a chance to let go of inhibitions.

EXPLORING SAN JUAN

San Juan's metro area stretches for a dozen miles along the north coast, and defining the city is rather like assembling a puzzle. Its neighborhoods are irregular and sometimes overlapping, not easily pieced together.

West from Luis Muñoz Marín Airport is Isla Verde, a stretch of high-rise apartment complexes and hotels, many of which sit directly on a superb, sandy beach. West of Isla Verde is the more sedate Ocean Park, a residential neighborhood of low-lying buildings on another fine patch of beach, with several outstanding small hotels and restaurants and a few shops. South of Ocean Park lies Santurce, a combined residential and business district with wide roads, plenty of commercial activity, and a growing artistic vitality thanks to the Museo de Arte de Puerto Rico on De Diego Avenue. The city's core is several miles south of Santurce, in a collection of neighborhoods including Hato Rey, a busy financial district where you'll find the large Plaza las Américas Mall, and the mostly residential Río Piedras area, home of the Universidad de Puerto Rico (University of Puerto Rico) and its museum and botanical garden.

Back along the north coast and west of Ocean Park is Condado, on a thin strip of land between the ocean and the Laguna del Condado (Condado Lagoon). Here the buzz is all about tourism: hotels crowd the beach, and tony shops and restaurants line the main drag, Avenida Ashford. Heading west from Condado will bring you to the Puerta de Tierra Peninsula, between the ocean to the north and Bahía de San Juan (San Juan Bay) to the south, where there are several resort hotels and two noteworthy parks, the Parque de Tercer Milenio (Third Millennium Park) and the Parque Muñoz Rivera. Finally, west of Puerta de Tierra is famous Old San Juan, the focal point and showplace of the island's rich history, where you will find the city's finest museums and shops, as well as excellent dining and lodging. It's a soulful feast, indeed.

Great Itineraries

IF YOU HAVE 3 DAYS

It's only fitting that you spend the first day on a *playa* (beach). Choose from the city's finest at Condado, Ocean Park, or Isla Verde, and park yourself in a rented chair with a good book, a cold drink, and plenty of sunscreen. On the second day, take a walking tour of Old San Juan. Ramble through the cobblestone streets and get caught up in the many shops and sights, but save plenty of time for exploring the turrets, towers, and dungeons of El Morro, the original fortress on a rocky promontory at the old city's northwestern tip. Spend the morning of the third day back on the beach. Return to Old San Juan for an early lunch and some shopping along Calle Fortaleza and Calle Cristo. Hop the ferry across the bay to Cataño for a tour of the Bacardí Rum Plant. The last tour is at 4, and if you time it right, you'll catch beautiful sunset views of Viejo San Juan on the ferry ride back.

IF YOU HAVE 5 DAYS

Nothing is more restful than sun, sand, and sea waves—so by all means, start your visit with a day on the beach. Spend all of the second and the third days exploring Old San Juan and touring the Bacardí Rum Plant in Cataño. At some point—in between sunbathing and sightseeing—make arrangements to visit the 28,000-acre Bosque Nacional del Caribe (Caribbean National Forest) on the fourth day. You can either rent a car and head out yourself or sign on to a tour through your hotel. El Yunque, as this park is affectionately known, is 43 km (26 mi) southeast of San Juan (about an hour's drive). It has 100-ft-high trees, dramatic mountain ranges, and walking trails leading to cool, soothing waterfalls. Alternatively, you could head east for a day of golf on one of the region's championship courses. On the fifth day, it's back to the beach for some (more) well-deserved rest.

IF YOU HAVE 7 DAYS

Follow the five-day itinerary above. On the sixth day, head for the Santurce district, and immerse yourself in island art at the Museo de Arte Contemporáneo de Puerto Rico, the Museo de Arte de Puerto Rico, or both. Afterward, wander through the produce at the Plaza del Mercado, with a fresh papaya or soursop shake in hand, and have your palm read. Be sure to note the giant bronze sculptures of avocados by artist by Annex Burgos. On the morning of the seventh day, hit the beach once more, then head to Avenida Ashford in Condado for an afternoon of shopping in its ritzy boutiques or visit the Jardín Botánico on the campus of the Universidad de Puerto Rico in the Río Pedras district.

When to Tour San Juan

The high season is roughly mid-December through mid-April. Winter hotel rates are 25%–40% higher than in the off season, and hotels tend to be packed, though rarely entirely full. A winter visit may allow you to participate in several colorful annual events on the San Juan social calendar. The January San Sebastián Street Festival, held in Old San Juan, consists of several nights of live music in the plazas, food festivals, and *cabezudos* (parades), in which folk legends are caricatured using oversize masks. A near-winter festival, the mid-November Festival of Puerto Rican Music, is held both in San Juan venues and out on the island. The festival celebrates Puerto Rico's traditional *plena* and *bomba* folk music with competitions and concerts.

A less expensive time to visit San Juan is during the "shoulder" seasons of fall and spring, when the weather is still fantastic and the tourist crush is less intense. Weather in San Juan is moderate and tropical year-round, with an average temperature of about 82°F (26°C). And while it's true that much of the summer encompasses the hurricane season, San Juan is still an attractive destination during those months—many accommodations charge the lowest rates of the year, restaurant reservations are easier to come by, and the streets are free of tourists.

Old San Juan

Old San Juan is compelling. Its 16th-century cobblestone streets, ornate Spanish town houses with wrought-iron balconies, busy plazas, and museums are all the repositories of the island's history. Founded in 1521 by the Spanish explorer Juan Ponce de León, Old San Juan (Viejo San Juan in Spanish) sits on a peninsula separated from "new" San Juan by a couple of miles and a couple of centuries. It has a culture unto itself, reflecting the sensibilities of the stylish professionals, the bohemian art crowd, and the skateboarding teenagers who populate its streets. Ironically, it's youthful and vibrant. You'll find more streetside cafés and restaurants, more contemporary art galleries, more musicians playing in plazas, than anywhere else in San Juan.

At the northwest end of Old San Juan, Calle Norzagaray leads to El Morro, the old city's defense bastion. On the north side of Calle Norzagaray, you'll note a small neighborhood at the foot of an embankment, bordering the ocean—this is La Perla, a rough neighborhood that you would do best to avoid. The west end of the Old City faces San Juan Bay, and it's here that the stone walls of the original city are most in evidence. On Old San Juan's south side, you'll find the commercial and cruise-ship piers that jut into San Juan Harbor.

Numbers in the text correspond to numbers in the margin and on the Old San Juan map.

A Good Walk

Start at the central **Plaza de Armas** ①, bordered by calles San Francisco, San José, and Cruz. From here you can branch out, much like following the spokes of a wheel, to various parts of the old city. On the north side of the plaza is the **Alcaldía** ②, the former city hall built between 1604 and 1789. On the west side of the plaza, the regal **La Intendencia** ③, once the Spanish Treasury building, now houses Puerto Rico's State Department.

A block to the west is Calle Cristo and its many galleries and clothing outlets. Head south on Cristo and follow it to its end and the **Capilla del Cristo** ④, an ornate 18th-century chapel. You can gaze through the gates at the ornate altar, but note that it's open only on Tuesday. To the right of the chapel is the **Parque de las Palomas** ⑤, roost for many of the city's pigeons. A few steps north, also on Calle Cristo, is the **Casa del Libro** ⑥, home to rare books and exhibits on bookbinding. Next door, the **Centro Nacional de Artes Populares y Artesanías** ⑦ displays island crafts. Walk a block north from the Casa del Libro and go left on Calle Fortaleza and right on Calle Recinto Oeste to reach **La Fortaleza** ⑧, the imposing former bastion now used as the governor's residence. Head east on Calle Fortaleza and south on Calle Cristo back to the Parque de las Palomas. A block and a half east of here, on Calle Tetuán, is the **Casa de Ramón Power y Giralt** ⑨, the restored home of an 18th-century naval hero and politician.

From Casa de Ramón Power y Giralt, head back west to Calle Cristo and walk north for two blocks to find the looming **Catedral de San Juan** ⑩. Across the street from the cathedral is one of the city's premier hotels, El Convento, which is in what was once a Carmelite convent. Adjacent to the hotel, the Plaza de Catedral is the site of the small but absolutely child-friendly **Museo del Niño** ⑪, which has natural-history exhibits and educational interactive displays. Heading west from the Museo del Niño on Caleta de las Monjas you'll find a small plaza, the **Plazuela de la Rogativa** ⑫. The statue here of a priest and three women commemorates the historic moment when British attackers were frightened off by torches of a religious procession, or *rogativa,* which they mistook for Spanish reinforcements.

Head north on Calle Cristo (which runs in front of the Museo del Niño) until you reach the white stucco **Iglesia de San José** ⑬, one of the oldest churches in the western hemisphere, on the Plaza San José. On the plaza's east end are two museums: the two-story **Museo Pablo Casals** ⑭ celebrates the life and art of the famous cellist, and the **Museo de Nuestra Raíz Africana** ⑮ investigates African influences on Puerto Rico's culture. Also on the plaza, to the west of the church, is the 1532 **Convento de los Dominicos** ⑯, now home to the bookshop of the Instituto de Cultura Puertorriqueña (Institute of Puerto Rican Culture), where you can buy folk crafts. A short walk west on Calle San Sebastián will bring you to the **Casa Blanca** ⑰, built in 1521 as a home for Ponce de León, and rebuilt in 1523 after a hurricane destroyed the original.

Traveling north on Calle Cristo from Plaza San José will bring you to Calle Norzagaray; to the east is the **Museo de Arte y Historia de San Juan** ⑱, once a bustling marketplace and now an art and history museum. West on Calle Norzagaray, you'll pass the large Plaza de Quinto Centenario, a tribute to the quincentennial of Columbus's voyages. On its west side is the Cuartel de Ballajá, a three-story structure that once served as a military barracks. Today the second floor is home to the **Museo de las Américas** ⑲ and its rotating exhibits of Latin American art. The next building west of the Cuartel is the old Asilo de Beneficencia, once a hospital for indigents and now the headquarters of the Instituto de Cultura Puertorriqueña. On its first floor is the tiny **Museo del Indio** ⑳, a museum that traces the indigenous Taíno culture of Puerto Rico through artifacts and a short video presentation. Finally, look to the west across a wide field. The massive stone structure on the hill is **Fuerte San Felipe del Morro** ㉑, also known as El Morro, the city's premier defense bastion, built between 1540 and 1783.

Head east from El Morro along Calle Norzagaray to Old San Juan's second fort. **Fuerte San Cristóbal** ㉒, built in the 18th century, guarded the north end of the city. At its base is the **Plaza de Colón** ㉓, bordered by Calle San Francisco and Calle O'Donell and adorned with a large statue of Christopher Columbus. At the plaza's south end, across Calle Fortaleza on Calle Recinto Sur, stands the **Teatro Tapia** ㉔, which has been hosting performances since 1832. Head south and east on Calle Recinto Sur to **Paseo de la Princesa** ㉕, a long, wide promenade that stretches to the Bahía de San Juan, and passes La Princesa, once the Old City's jail and now home to the Puerto Rican Tourism Company's offices.

TIMING AND PRECAUTIONS

Old San Juan is, in effect, a small neighborhood, approximately seven city blocks square with numerous side streets, alleys, and hidden plazas. In strictly geographical terms, it's easily traversed in a day, but lingering is what Old San Juan is all about. To truly appreciate the numerous museums, galleries, and cafés requires two or three days—and the walk described above is designed with that in mind. If you're limited to a day, you'll need to pick and choose sights according to your interests. It can be done—it's just not quite so rewarding.

Don't consider driving in Old San Juan unless you have a penchant for sitting in traffic jams for much of the waking day. Old San Juan is a walking city, with narrow one-way streets, narrower alleys, sparse parking, and sights and shops all packed together in an area hardly larger than half a square mile. Some of the streets are steep, and the cobblestones will wreak havoc on high heels, so dress comfortably. Wear walking shoes, a hat, and sunscreen—and drink plenty of water. Old San Juan is generally a safe area, but keep in mind that pickpockets visit the same places as tourists. Keep money and credit cards in money belts and avoid carrying open handbags. Street hustlers are few and far between, but you will find the occasional, mostly harmless, indigent asking for money.

If you get tired, free trolleys swing through Old San Juan all day, every day—they depart from the Covadonga parking lot at the main bus terminal area across from Pier 4 and take two routes through the Old City. One route heads north to Calle Norzagaray then west to El Morro (the trolley doesn't go into El Morro, but drops you off at the

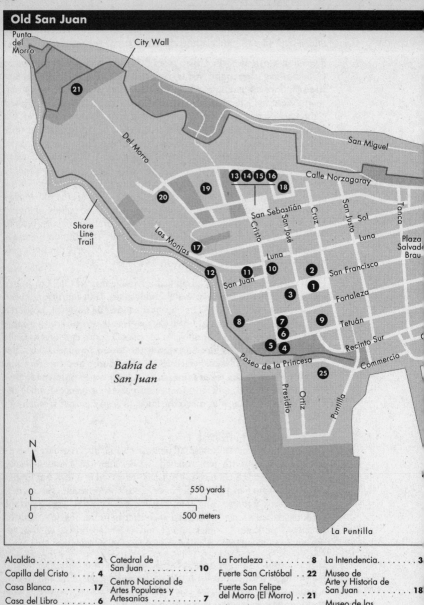

Punta del Morro

City Wall

San Miguel

Calle Norzagaray

Del Morro

Shore Line Trail

Las Monjas

San Sebastián

Cristo

San José

Cruz

San Justo

Sol

Tanca

Plaza Salvado Brau

Luna

San Juan

San Francisco

Fortaleza

Tetuán

Recinto Sur

Commercio

Paseo de la Princesa

Bahía de San Juan

Presidio

Ortiz

Puntilla

N

| 0 | 550 yards |
| 0 | 500 meters |

La Puntilla

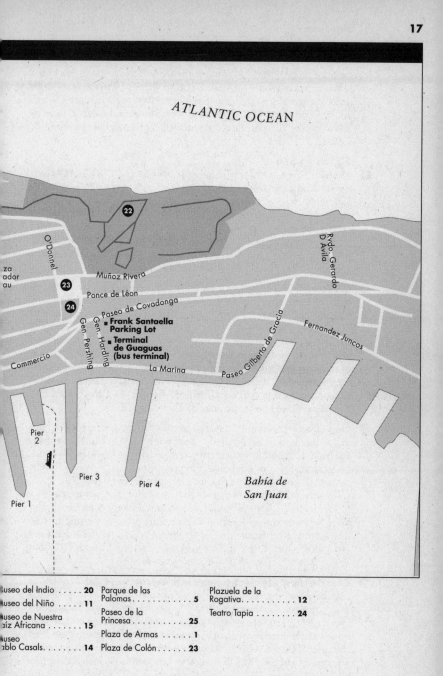

ATLANTIC OCEAN

22

O'Donnel

za
ador
au

Muñoz Rivera

Rvdo. Gerardo
D Avila

23

Ponce de Léon

24

Paseo de Covadonga

**Frank Santaella
Parking Lot**

Gen. Harding

**Terminal
de Guaguas
(bus terminal)**

Gen. Pershing

Fernandez Juncos

Paseo Gilberto de Gracia

Commercio

La Marina

Pier
2

Pier 3

Pier 4

*Bahía de
San Juan*

Pier 1

long footpath leading to the fort), then south along Calle Cristo to For-taleza, San Justo, and back along Calle Gilberto Concepción de Gra-cia (also called Calle la Marina) to the piers. Another takes you to the Plaza de Armas, south on Calle San José, then back to the piers. Both make regular stops (at signs marked PARADA) on their routes. When you're finished touring, taxis can be found in several spots: in front of Pier 2, on the Plaza de Armas, or on Calle O'Donell near the Plaza de Colón.

Sights to See

❷ Alcaldía. This city hall was built between 1604 and 1789. In 1841, ex-tensive alterations were made so that it would resemble Madrid's city hall, with arcades, towers, balconies, and an inner courtyard. Reno-vations have refreshed the facade of the building and some interior rooms, but the architecture remains true to its colonial style. A municipal tourist information center and an art gallery with rotating exhibits are on the first floor. ⊠ *153 Calle San Francisco, Plaza de Armas, Old San Juan,* ☎ *787/724–7171 Ext. 2391.* 🎟 *Free.* ⊙ *Weekdays 8–4.*

❹ Capilla del Cristo. According to legend, in 1753 a young horseman named Baltazar Montañez, carried away during festivities in honor of San Juan Bautista (St. John the Baptist), raced down Calle Cristo and plunged over its steep precipice. A witness to the tragedy promised to build a chapel if the young man's life could be saved. Historical records main-tain the man died, but legend contends that he lived. (Another version of the story has it that the horse miraculously stopped before plung-ing over the cliff.) Regardless, this chapel was built, and inside is a small silver altar dedicated to the Christ of Miracles. ⊠ *Calle Cristo, Old San Juan,* ☎ *no phone.* 🎟 *Free.* ⊙ *Tues. 10–3:30.*

⓱ Casa Blanca. The original structure on this site was a frame house built in 1521 as a home for Ponce de León. But he died in Cuba never hav-ing lived in it, and it was virtually destroyed by a hurricane in 1523, after which his son-in-law had the present masonry home built. His descendants occupied the house for 250 years. From the end of the Span-ish-American War in 1898 to 1966, it housed the U.S. Army commander in Puerto Rico. A museum devoted to archaeology is on the second floor. Select rooms, with period furniture, are open for viewing as well. The surrounding garden, cooled by fountains, is a tranquil spot for a restorative pause. ⊠ *1 Calle San Sebastián, Old San Juan,* ☎ *787/724–4102.* 🎟 *$2.* ⊙ *Tues.–Sat. 9–noon and 1–4:30.*

❻ Casa del Libro. This 18th-century building contains exhibits of books and bookbinding techniques—it's dedicated to the artistry of the printed word. The museum's 6,000 books, sketches, and illustrations include some 200 rare volumes produced before 1501, as well as what appears to be legal writing on a fragment of clay, thought to date from the time of Christ. Also on hand are several antique printing presses, one constructed in 1812 in France and brought to Puerto Rico in the mid-19th century. ⊠ *255 Calle Cristo,* ☎ *787/723–0354.* 🎟 *$2 do-nation suggested.* ⊙ *Tues.–Sat. 11–4:30.*

☞ ❾ Casa de Ramón Power y Giralt. The restored home of 18th-century naval hero Don Ramón Power y Giralt is now the headquarters of the Con-servation Trust of Puerto Rico. On site are several displays highlight-ing the physical, cultural, and historical importance of land and properties on the island under the trust's aegis. You'll find a display of musical in-struments that you can play, a bird diorama with recorded bird songs, an active beehive, and a seven-minute movie discussing the trust's ef-forts. Displays are in Spanish; the movie is in English or Spanish. A gift shop sells toys and Puerto Rican candies. ⊠ *155 Calle Tetuán, Old San*

Juan, ☎ *787/722–5834,* WEB *www.fideicomiso.org.* ✉ *Free.* ◷ *Tues.–Sat. 10–4.*

❿ Catedral de San Juan. The Catholic shrine of Puerto Rico had humble beginnings in the early 1520s as a thatch-top, wooden structure. Hurricane winds tore off the thatch and destroyed the church. It was reconstructed in 1540, when it was given a graceful circular staircase and vaulted Gothic ceilings. Most of the work on the present cathedral, however, was done in the 19th century. The remains of Ponce de León are in a marble tomb near the transept. ⊠ *153 Calle Cristo, Old San Juan,* ☎ *787/722–0861.* ✉ *$1 donation suggested.* ◷ *Weekdays 8:30–4; masses Sat. at 7* PM, *Sun. at 9* AM *and 11* AM, *weekdays at 12:15* PM.

❼ Centro Nacional de Artes Populares y Artesanías. Run by the Institute of Puerto Rican Culture, the Popular Arts and Crafts Center is in a colonial building next to the Casa del Libro, and is a superb repository of island crafts, some of which are for sale. ⊠ *253 Calle Cristo,* ☎ *787/722–0621.* ✉ *Free.* ◷ *Mon.–Sat. 9–5.*

❶❻ Convento de los Dominicos. Built by Dominican friars in 1523, this convent often served as a shelter during Carib Indian attacks and, more recently, as headquarters for the Antilles command of the U.S. Army. Now home to some offices of the Institute of Puerto Rican Culture, the beautifully restored building contains religious manuscripts, artifacts, and art. The institute also maintains a book and music shop on the premises, and occasionally classical concerts are held here. ⊠ *98 Calle Norzagaray, Old San Juan,* ☎ *787/721–6866.* ✉ *Free.* ◷ *Mon.–Sat. 9–5.*

❽ La Fortaleza. Sitting on a hill overlooking the harbor, La Fortaleza, the western hemisphere's oldest executive mansion in continuous use, was built as a fortress. It was attacked numerous times and taken twice, by the British in 1598 and by the Dutch in 1625. Numerous changes to the original primitive structure, constructed in 1540, over the past four centuries have resulted in the present collection of marble and mahogany, medieval towers, and stained-glass galleries. The building is still the official residence of the island's governor, and much of its interior is closed to visitors. Guided tours of the extensive gardens and selected rooms are conducted every hour on the hour in English, on the half hour in Spanish; both include a short video presentation. ⊠ *Calle Recinto Oeste, Old San Juan,* ☎ *787/721–7000 Ext. 2211 or 2358.* ✉ *Free.* ◷ *Weekdays 9–4.*

| NEED A BREAK? | On your hike up hilly Calle Cristo, stop at **Ben & Jerry's** (⊠ 61 Calle Cristo, Old San Juan, ☎ 787/977–6882) at the corner of Calle Sol. You can savor Vermont ice cream under a palm tree or enjoy fresh fruit smoothies next to a Green Mountain cow—depending on how you look at it. Olympic gymnast Michelle Campi and her mother, Celí Williams, have made this ice cream parlor one of the friendliest hangouts in Old San Juan. |

☝ ㉒ Fuerte San Cristóbal. This stone fortress, built between 1634 and 1785, guarded the city from land attacks. Even larger in structure (but not in area covered) than El Morro, San Cristóbal was known in the 17th and 18th centuries as the Gibraltar of the West Indies. Five free-standing structures are connected by tunnels, and restored units include an 18th-century barracks. You're free to explore the gun turrets, officers' quarters, and passageways. Along with El Morro, San Cristóbal is a National Historic Site administered by the U.S. Park Service. Guides conduct tours in Spanish and English. ⊠ *Calle Norzagaray, Old San Juan,* ☎ *787/729–6960,* WEB *www.nps.gov/saju.* ✉ *$2.* ◷ *Daily 9–5.*

★ 21 **Fuerte San Felipe del Morro.** On a rocky promontory at the northwestern tip of the old city is El Morro (which translates as "promontory"), a fortress built by the Spaniards between 1540 and 1783. Rising 140 ft above the sea, the massive six-level fortress covers enough territory to accommodate a 9-hole golf course. It is a labyrinth of dungeons, ramps, barracks, turrets, towers, and tunnels. Built to protect the port, El Morro has a commanding view of the harbor. You're free to wander throughout. The cannon emplacement walls are thick as a child's arm is long, and the dank secret passageways are a wonder of engineering. The fort's small but enlightening museum displays ancient Spanish guns and other armaments, military uniforms, and blueprints for Spanish forts in the Americas. There's also a gift shop. The fort is a national historic site administered by the U.S. Park Service. Tours and a video are available in English. ✉ *Calle Norzagaray, Old San Juan,* ☎ *787/729–6960,* WEB *www.nps.gov/saju.* *$2.* *Daily 9–5.*

13 **Iglesia de San José.** With its vaulted ceilings, this church is a splendid example of 16th-century Spanish Gothic architecture. It was built under the supervision of Dominican friars in 1532, making it one of the oldest churches in the western hemisphere. The body of Ponce de León, the Spanish explorer who came to the New World seeking the Fountain of Youth, was buried here for almost three centuries before being moved to the Catedral de San Juan in 1913. ✉ *Calle San Sebastián, Plaza de San José,* ☎ *787/725–7501.* *$1 donation suggested.* *Mon.–Sat. 8:30–4; mass Sun. at 12:15* PM.

3 **La Intendencia.** From 1851 to 1898, this three-story neoclassical building was home to the Spanish treasury; now it's the headquarters of Puerto Rico's State Department. You can go inside, where the wide interior courtyard, typical of colonial architectural, is framed by the high arcades of the perimeter walkways. ✉ *200 Calle San José, at Calle San Francisco, Old San Juan,* ☎ *787/722–2121 Ext. 230.* *Free.* *Weekdays 8–noon and 1–4:30. Tours in Spanish at 2 and 3, in English at 4.*

18 **Museo de Arte y Historia de San Juan.** A bustling marketplace in 1855, this handsome building is now the modern San Juan Museum of Art and History. You'll find exhibits of Puerto Rican art and audiovisual shows that present the island's history. Concerts and other cultural events take place in the huge interior courtyard. ✉ *150 Calle Norzagaray, at Calle MacArthur, Old San Juan,* ☎ *787/724–1875.* *Free.* *Tues.–Sun. 10–4.*

★ 19 **Museo de las Américas.** One of the finest collections of its type in Puerto Rico, the Museum of the Americas is on the second floor of the imposing former military barracks, Cuartel de Ballajá. Most exhibits rotate, but the focus is on the popular and folk art of Latin America. The permanent exhibit, "Las Artes Populares en las Américas," has religious figures, musical instruments, basketwork, costumes, and farming and other implements of the Americas. The old military barracks, big and boxy in a neoclassical style and painted green and peach, was built between 1854 and 1864, and its immense inner courtyard is used for concerts and private events such as weddings. With a little notice, the staff can take you on a guided tour. ✉ *Calle Norzagaray and Calle del Morro, Old San Juan,* ☎ *787/724–5052,* WEB *www.museolasamericas.org.* *Free.* *Tues.–Fri. 10–4, weekends 11–5.*

20 **Museo del Indio.** The Instituto de Cultura Puertorriqueña (Institute of Puerto Rican Culture) maintains the small Museum of the Indian as a repository of ancient Taíno artifacts and information regarding Taíno

life some 500 years ago. The short tour starts with a five-minute video describing the island's geophysical origins, and displays include Taíno religious figures carved from rock, digging and fishing implements, and a replica of a Taíno home. The museum is in the institute's headquarters in the Asilo de Beneficencia, once a hospital for the poor. ⊠ *Calle Beneficencia, at Calle del Morro,* ☎ *787/724–0700,* WEB *www.icp. gobierno.org.* ☞ *$1.* ☉ *Tues.–Sat. 10–4.*

👆 ⑪ **Museo del Niño.** This three-floor, hands-on "museum" is pure fun for kids. There are games to play, clothes for dress-up, a mock plaza with market, even a barber shop where children can play (no real scissors here). One of the newer exhibits is an immense food-groups pyramid, where children can climb to place magnets representing different foods. Older children will appreciate the top-floor garden where bugs and plants are on display, and the little ones can pretend to go shopping or to work at a construction site. For infants, there's a playground. Note that the museum's ticket window closes an hour before the close of the museum. ⊠ *150 Calle Cristo,* ☎ *787/722–3791,* WEB *www.muesodelninopr.org.* ☞ *$2.50.* ☉ *Tues.–Thurs. 9–3:30, Fri. 9–5, weekends 12:30–5.*

⑮ **Museo de Nuestra Raíz Africana.** The Institute of Puerto Rican Culture created this museum to help Puerto Ricans understand African influences in island culture. On display over two floors are African musical instruments, documents relating to the slave trade, and a list of African words that have made it into popular Puerto Rican culture. ⊠ *101 Calle San Sebastián, Plaza de San José, Old San Juan,* ☎ *787/ 724–0700 Ext. 4239,* WEB *www.icp.gobierno.org.* ☞ *Free.* ☉ *Tues.– Sat. 9:30–5, Sun. 11–5.*

⑭ **Museo Pablo Casals.** The small, two-story Pablo Casals Museum contains memorabilia of the famed cellist, who made his home in Puerto Rico from 1956 until his death in 1973. Manuscripts, photographs, and his favorite cellos are on display, in addition to recordings and videotapes (shown on request) of Casals Festival concerts, which he instituted in 1957. The festival is held annually in June. ⊠ *101 Calle San Sebastián, Plaza de San José, Old San Juan,* ☎ *787/723–9185.* ☞ *$1.* ☉ *Tues.–Sat. 9:30–5:30.*

👆 ⑤ **Parque de las Palomas.** Never have birds had it so good. The small, shaded park bordering Old San Juan's Capilla del Cristo has a large stone wall with pigeonholes cut into it. Hundreds of pigeons roost here, and the park is full of cooing local children chasing the well-fed birds. There's a small kiosk where you can buy refreshments and bags of seed to feed the *palomas*. Stop to enjoy the wide views over the bay.

㉕ **Paseo de la Princesa.** This street down at the port is spruced up with flowers, trees, benches, street lamps, and a striking fountain depicting the various ethnic groups of Puerto Rico. Take a seat and watch the boats zip across the water. At the west end of the paseo, beyond the fountain, is the beginning of a shoreline path that hugs Old San Juan's walls and leads to the city gate at Calle San Juan.

❶ **Plaza de Armas.** The old city's original main square was once used as military drilling grounds. Bordered by calles San Francisco, Rafael Codero, San José, and Cruz, it has a fountain with 19th-century statues representing the four seasons, as well as a bandstand and a small café. This is a central meeting place in Old San Juan, and you're likely to encounter everything from local bands to artists sketching caricatures to street preachers imploring the wicked to repent.

Close-Up

PEACEFUL MUSIC

CELLIST PABLO CASALS was one of the 20th century's most influential musicians. Born in Catalonia in 1876, he studied in Spain and Belgium, settled for a time in Paris, then returned to Barcelona. Tours in Europe, the United States, and South America brought him artistic and financial success and opportunities to collaborate with other prominent musicians.

By the advent of the Spanish Civil War, he was an internationally famous musician, teacher, and conductor. He was also an outspoken supporter of a democratic Spain. Forced into exile by Franco's regime, Casals arrived in Puerto Rico, his mother's birthplace, in 1956. There, the 81-year-old maestro continued to work and teach. He established the Casals Festival of Classical Music, making it a home for sublime orchestral and chamber works. During two weeks each June, the Puerto Rico Symphony Orchestra is joined by musicians from all over the world.

In Catalan, Casal's first name is "Pau," which appropriately enough means "peace." He and his friend Albert Schweitzer appealed to the world powers to stop the arms race, and he made what many experts say is his greatest work—an oratorio titled "The Manger"—his personal message of peace. Casals died in Puerto Rico in 1973, but his many legacies live on. His favorite instruments, his recordings, and some of his many awards, are preserved at the Museo Pablo Casals.

— Karen English

NEED A BREAK? At **Café 4 Estaciones,** on the Plaza de Armas in Old San Juan, tables and chairs sit under a canvas canopy surrounded by potted plants. It's the perfect spot to put down your shopping bags and rest your tired feet. Grab a *café con leche* (coffee with hot milk), an espresso, or cold drink, and watch the children chase the pigeons.

㉓ Plaza de Colón. A statue of Christopher Columbus stands atop a high pedestal in this bustling Old San Juan square. Originally called St. James Square, it was renamed in honor of Columbus on the 400th anniversary of his arrival in Puerto Rico. Bronze plaques on the statue's base relate various episodes in the life of the great explorer. On the north side of the plaza is a terminal for buses to and from San Juan.

⑫ Plazuela de la Rogativa. According to legend, the British, while laying siege to the city in 1797, mistook the flaming torches of a rogativa—religious processions—for Spanish reinforcements, and beat a hasty retreat. In this little plaza, statues of a bishop and three women commemorate the legend. The monument was created in 1971 by the artist Lindsay Daen to mark the old city's 450th anniversary. ⊠ *Caleta de las Monjas, Old San Juan.*

㉔ Teatro Tapia. Named after the Puerto Rican playwright Alejandro Tapia y Rivera, this municipal theater was built in 1832 and remodeled in 1949 and again in 1987. It showcases ballets, plays, and operettas. Stop by the box office to find out what's showing. ⊠ *Calle Fortaleza, Plaza de Colón, Old San Juan,* ☎ 787/722–0407.

Greater San Juan

Modern San Juan is a study in congested highways and cement-block housing complexes, as well as the ritzy resorts of the Condado and Isla Verde shoreline. Sightseeing in the modern city requires more effort than it does in Old San Juan—the sights are scattered in the suburbs, accessible by taxi, bus, or a rental car, but not by foot.

Avenidas Muñoz Rivera, Ponce de León, and Fernández Juncos are the main thoroughfares that cross Puerta de Tierra, just east of Old San Juan, to the business and tourist districts of Condado and Isla Verde. Puente Dos Hermanos (Bridge of the Brothers) connects Puerta de Tierra with Condado's avenidas Ashford and Isla Verde, which goes through Ocean Park and on to Isla Verde. The G. Esteves and San Antonio bridges also connect Puerta de Tierra to "new" San Juan.

Due south of the Laguna del Condado is Miramar, a residential area with fashionable turn-of-the-20th-century homes and a few hotels and restaurants. East of Miramar and south of Ocean Park is Santurce, another business and residential area characterized by high-rise office and apartment complexes. South of that is the Golden Mile—Hato Rey, the city's financial and banking hub. Isla Verde, with its glittering beachfront hotels, casinos, discos, and public beach, is to the east, near the airport.

Numbers in the text correspond to numbers in the margin and on the Greater San Juan map.

A Good Tour

Heading east from Old San Juan on Avenida Ponce de León brings you to **El Capitolio** ㉖, Puerto Rico's magnificent capitol building. At the east end of Puerta de Tierra is the Caribe Hilton hotel, where you'll find the small bastion **Fuerte San Gerónimo** ㉗, which once guarded an entrance to San Juan Bay. Avenida Baldorioty de Castro (Route 26) leads into Miramar, then Santurce, where the Route 37 Exit (Avenida José de Diego) brings you to the **Museo de Arte de Puerto Rico** ㉘, a former hospital that has been transformed into the island's most ambitious art museum. Farther south on José de Diego at Avenida Ponce de León is the **Centro de Bellas Artes Luis A. Ferré** ㉙, the boxy, white performing-arts center.

Minutes from the arts center, west on Avenida Fernández Juncos, then left on Calle Sagrado Corazón, is the Universidad del Sagrado Corazón (Sacred Heart University) and its **Museo de Arte Contemporáneo de Puerto Rico** ㉚, with a fine collection of contemporary Puerto Rican art. From the university, it's a straight ride south on Avenida Ponce de León (Route 25) to the Río Piedras district, where you'll find the **Universidad de Puerto Rico** ㉛ and its Museo de Historia, Antropología y Arte. Less than a mile to the west, at the junction of routes 1 and 847, is the university's Jardín Botánico, a 75-acre garden. If you're looking for a place to jog or play tennis, visit the **Parque Central Municipo de San Juan** ㉜ in Miramar, at the Calle Cerra Exit off Avenida John F. Kennedy (Route 2), northwest of the university.

TIMING

Depending on what mode of transportation you choose, you can see these sights in a day, two if you linger. Buses are the least expensive but most time-consuming way to travel. Taxis are more convenient and you won't get lost—consider hiring a taxi by the hour and covering your selected sights in a couple of hours. Taxis charge $30 per hour for city tours, but the rate can be negotiable for long stretches of time. If you choose to rent a car, get a good map. San Juan's roads are well

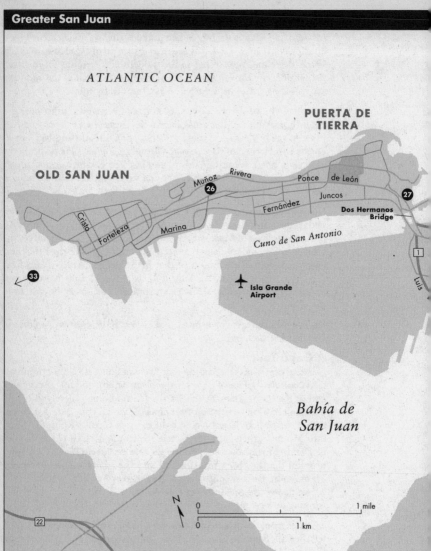

ATLANTIC OCEAN

PUERTA DE TIERRA

OLD SAN JUAN

Muñoz Rivera

26

Ponce de León

Juncos

Fernández

Dos Hermanos Bridge

Cristo

Fortaleza

Marina

27

Caño de San Antonio

1

33

✈ **Isla Grande Airport**

Luis

Bahía de San Juan

N

| 0 | | 1 mile |
| 0 | | 1 km |

22

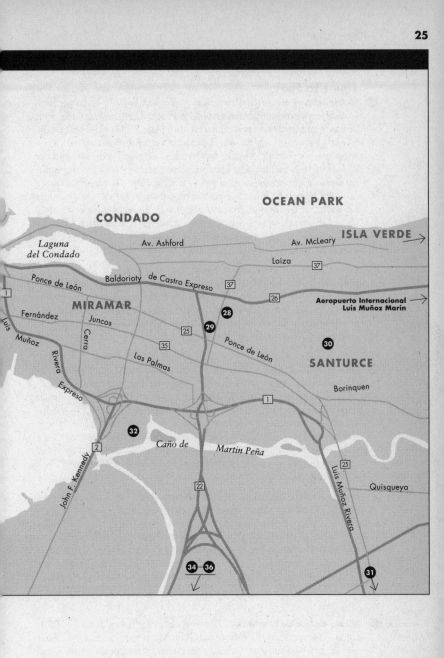

marked, but one-way streets pop up out of nowhere and traffic jams at rush hour are frequent.

Sights to See

26 El Capitolio. Puerto Rico's capitol is a white marble building with Corinthian columns that dates from the 1920s. The grand rotunda, with mosaics and friezes, was completed in the late 1990s. The seat of the island's bicameral legislature, the capitol contains Puerto Rico's constitution and is flanked by the modern buildings of the Senate and the House of Representatives. There are spectacular views from the observation plaza on the capitol's sea side. Pick up a booklet about the building from the House Secretariat on the second floor. Guided tours are by appointment only. You can also watch the legislature in action—note that the action is in Spanish—on select days, most often Monday and Tuesday. ⊠ *Av. Ponce de León, Puerta de Tierra,* ☎ *787/724–8979.* ☎ *Free.* ☉ *Daily 8:30–5.*

29 Centro de Bellas Artes Luis A. Ferré. This completely modern facility, the largest of its kind in the Caribbean, hosts the yearly Pablo Casals Festival in June and has a full schedule of concerts, plays, and operas throughout the year. The entrance wall is characterized by an immense mural by artist Jaime Suárez. Stop by the ticket office for a list of current shows. ⊠ *Av. José de Diego and Av. Ponce de León, Santurce,* ☎ *787/725–7334.*

27 Fuerte San Gerónimo. At Puerta de Tierra's eastern tip, behind the splashy Caribe Hilton, this tiny fort is perched over the Atlantic like an afterthought. Added to San Juan's fortifications in the 18th century, it barely survived the British attack of 1797. Restored in 1983 by the Institute of Puerto Rican Culture, it's now leased by the Caribe Hilton for private functions. The buildings are empty and the structure itself is the attraction, but it's free and open to the public (accessed from the Caribe Hilton entrance). ⊠ *Calle Rosales, Puerta de Tierra,* ☎ *787/724–5477.*

★ **30 Museo de Arte Contemporáneo de Puerto Rico.** The Universidad del Sagrado Corazón (Sacred Heart University) is the home of the Museum of Contemporary Puerto Rican Art, containing a wide range of painting, sculpture, photography, and new-media art by both established and up-and-coming Puerto Rican artists. Exhibits, in several rooms on the large second floor of the university's Barat Building, change once or twice per year. ⊠ *Calle San Antonio and Calle Rosales, Santurce,* ☎ *787/268–0049,* WEB *museocontemporaneopr.org.* ☎ *Free.* ☉ *Mon.– Sat. 9–5.*

★ **28 Museo de Arte de Puerto Rico.** The west wing of this ambitious 130,000-square-ft museum is the former San Juan Municipal Hospital, a 1920s neoclassical building that contains a permanent collection of Puerto Rican art dating from the 17th century to the present. The newly constructed east wing is dominated by a five-story-tall stained-glass window, the work of local artist Eric Tabales, that towers over the museum's Grand Hall and faces a 5-acre garden. In the east wing there are galleries for changing exhibits, an interactive Family Gallery, and a 400-seat theater that's worth seeing for the stage's remarkable lace curtain alone. The garden has a sculpture trail, a pond, and a variety of native flora. ⊠ *300 Av. José De Diego, Santurce,* ☎ *787/977–6277,* WEB *www.mapr.org.* ☎ *$5.* ☉ *Tues. and Thurs.–Sun. 10–5, Wed. 10–8.*

NEED A BREAK?
While in Santurce, drop by **Plaza del Mercado,** a produce market surrounded by restaurants where you can have fresh fish for lunch at reasonable prices. The area also has many *botánicas,* small stores that sell

herbs, candles, and religious items. There may even be an in-house card- or palm-reader ready to show you your future.

③ **Parque Central Municipo de San Juan.** Southeast of Miramar, Avenida Muñoz Rivera skirts the northern side of the mangrove-bordered San Juan Central Municipal Park. Built for the 1979 Pan-American Games, it's dry and dusty but, with several miles of trails and inexpensive tennis courts, it's a good place to work off some of San Juan's rich desserts. It has a sports shop and a cafeteria. ✉ *Calle Cerra, exit on Rte. 2, Santurce,* ☎ *787/722–1646.* ▭ *75¢ per vehicle.* ☉ *Mon. 2–10, Tues.–Thurs. 6:30 AM–10 PM, Fri. 6:30 AM–9 PM, weekends 6:30 AM–6 PM.*

③ **Universidad de Puerto Rico.** The southern district of Río Piedras is home to the University of Puerto Rico, between Avenida Ponce de León and Avenida Barbosa. The campus is one of the two performance venues for the Puerto Rico Symphony Orchestra. (The other is the Centro de Bellas Artes Luis A. Ferré in Santurce.) Theatrical productions and other concerts are also scheduled here.

The university's **Museo de Historia, Antropología y Arte** (Museum of History, Anthropology, and Art) has archaeological and historical exhibits that deal with the Native American influence on the island and the Caribbean, the colonial era, and the history of slavery. Art displays are occasionally mounted; the museum's prize exhibit is the painting *El Velorio* (The Wake), by the 19th-century artist Francisco Oller. ✉ *Next to main university entrance on Av. Ponce de León, Río Piedras,* ☎ *787/764–0000 Ext. 2452.* ▭ *Free.* ☉ *Mon.–Wed. and Fri. 9–4:30, Thurs. 9–9, weekends 9–3.*

The university's main attraction is the **Jardín Botánico** (Botanical Garden), a 75-acre forest of more than 200 species of tropical and subtropical vegetation. Gravel footpaths lead to a graceful lotus lagoon, a bamboo promenade, an orchid garden with some 30,000 plants, and a palm garden. Signs are in Spanish and English. Trail maps are available at the entrance gate, and groups of 10 or more can arrange guided tours ($25). ✉ *Intersection of Rtes. 1 and 847 at entrance to Barrio Venezuela, Río Piedras,* ☎ *787/767–1710.* ▭ *Free.* ☉ *Daily 9–4:30.*

San Juan Environs

The metro suburbs of Cataño, Bayamón, and Guaynabo, west and south of San Juan, are separate municipalities but in many ways are indistinguishable from the city itself. Cataño, bordered by the Bahía de San Juan in the north, is an industrial suburb, perhaps most noted for its Bacardí Rum Plant. Bayamón, 15–30 minutes from central San Juan depending on traffic, has an attractive central park bordered by historic buildings. Guaynabo is a mix of residential and industrial areas, and is worth visiting for its historical importance—Juan Ponce de León established the island's first settlement here in Caparra, and you can visit the ruins of the original fortification.

A Good Tour

Make your way to Old San Juan and Pier 2 at the south end of the old city for the ferry to Cataño. Once there, take a quick taxi or bus ride to the **Bacardí Rum Plant** ㉝. The plant tour will lead you through the process of distilling the spirits, and its small museum displays the history of the Bacardí family.

To reach the 42-acre **Parque de las Ciencias Luis A. Ferré** ㉞, take Route 22 south from San Juan's Avenida Ponce de León to Bayamón and head south on Route 167. A great stop for children, the park has a plane-

ART INVASION

PUBLIC ART IS TRANSFORMING the Puerto Rican capital: here, a monolithic metal dove; there, avocados so big you can stretch out on them. The stained-glass blades of a windmill spin above an oceanfront drive. A bright red jack towers over children at play in a park. These are just some of the 25 works by local artists that the city commissioned from 1996 to 2000, when Governor Sila Marí Calderón was its mayor. Part of a $3 million urban art project, the pieces range from realistic to abstract, and many were installed as part of larger renovations of parks, plazas, and markets.

Often the works seem perfectly at home in their environments. "Platanal," by Imel Sierra Cabreras, has translucent panels that run across the ceiling of the restored Plaza del Mercado in Santurce. The avocados in "My Favorite Fruit" by Annex Burgos seem to spill from the entrance of this marketplace and across its front plaza. Although the large jack by María Elena Perales is a bit surreal, it's an appropriate addition to a playground in Parque Central Municipo de San Juan.

Some pieces attempt to soften or enliven their surroundings. Carmen Inés Blondet, whose "Fire Dance" is a collection of 28- to 35-ft spirals, seems an abstract forest in the midst of the concrete jungle. The iron spirals are interspersed with benches across a small plaza beneath an expressway. Crabs were once a common sight in Santurce (hence the name of the baseball team, the Santurce Crabbers), so Adelino González's benches for the area are bronze crabs. "Wind-

mills of San Juan," by Eric Tables, is a whimsical tribute to the coast and its ocean breezes. The steel tower, with its rotating wheel of color, is on a restored oceanside drive in Ocean Park.

The works haven't been without controversy. Many residents found "Paloma," the metallic dove that towers over a busy Condado intersection ugly; others went so far as to assert that it was the cause of traffic jams. Mayor Jorge Santini even threatened to remove it during his campaign. But it appears to be here to stay. To soften the piece, a fountain was added to its base and it's now especially beautiful at night when the water is illuminated.

As a whole, however, the statues have made San Juan more interesting. And public art is about to go islandwide. In January 2002 Governor Calderón unveiled plans for the Puerto Rico Public Art Project. Its budget of $15 million is slated to fund about 100 new works over the course of three years. Twenty-one locations have been selected by an independent committee of art experts. In San Juan, these include stations of the still-under-construction urban train, the Luis Muñoz Marín International Airport, and several government buildings and city parks. The committee also envisions installing works at nature reserves, along highways, and in school playgrounds across the island. Soon, perhaps, that new bus stop, lifeguard station, or street-vendor stand you see will truly be a work of art.

— John Marino

tarium and a science and physics museum examining the wonders of space. Bayamón's central park on Calle Santiago Veve contains several historic buildings and a church, as well as, in the old city hall, the **Museo de Arte y Historia de Francisco Oller** ㉟, dedicated to the life and work of a famous Puerto Rican artist. From the science park, head south again on Route 167, then left (east) on Route 2 into Guaynabo. You'll come to the **Caparra Ruins** ㊱, the site of one of San Juan's first settlements, with its small museum.

TIMING

Plan to spend half a day traveling to and touring the Bacardí plant. It's best to visit the sights in Bayamón and Guaynabo on a separate day. They're about 30 minutes from central San Juan and you'll need a rental car or taxi to reach them. Be advised of the infamous traffic known as *el tapón de Bayamón* (Bayamón's traffic jam), which also rhymes with *chicharrón de Bayamón* (the area's famous pig-skin fritters).

Sights to See

㉝ **Bacardí Rum Plant.** The first Bacardí rum distillery was built in 1862 in Cuba, but it was confiscated by the Castro regime in 1960, and the Bacardí family was exiled. Over the years the rum brand has grown, with distilleries in Spain, Mexico, Panama, and Brazil. The Puerto Rico plant was built in the 1950s and is one of the world's largest, with the capacity to produce 100,000 gallons of spirits a day and 221 million cases a year. You can take a 45-minute tour of the bottling plant, museum (called the Cathedral of Rum), and distillery, and there's a gift shop. Yes, you'll be offered a sample. ⊠ *Bay View Industrial Park, Rte. 888, Km 2.6, Cataño,* ☎ *787/788–1500 or 787/788–8400.* ⌦ *Free.* ☉ *Tours every 30 mins Mon.–Sat. 9–10:30 and noon–4.*

NEED A BREAK?   A *cuba libre* (Coca-Cola with rum and lime) is the perfect complement to the view of El Morro and Old San Juan across the bay from the bar window at **Morgan's Steak & Sea Food** (⊠ 94 Av. Las Nereidas, Cataño, ☎ 787/275–0850). If you come at sunset, you might be tempted to have two. And beware of the charms of the *música bohemia* (nostalgic, sultry music) or you might miss the last ferry back to the old city.

㊱ **Caparra Ruins.** In 1508 Ponce de León established the island's first settlement here. The ruins—a few crumbling walls—are what remains of an ancient fort. The small Museo de la Conquista y Colonización de Puerto Rico (Museum of the Conquest and Colonization of Puerto Rico) contains historical documents, exhibits, and excavated artifacts, though you can see the museum's contents in less time than it takes to say the name. Both the ruins and the museum are maintained by the Puerto Rican government's museums and parks division. ⊠ *Rte. 2, Km 6.6, Guaynabo,* ☎ *787/781–4795,* WEB *www.icp.gobierno.pr.* ⌦ *Free.* ☉ *Tues.–Sat. 8:30–4:30.*

㉟ **Museo de Arte y Historia de Francisco Oller.** In Bayamón's central park you'll find the 18th-century Catholic church of Santa Cruz and the neoclassical former city hall, which now houses the Francisco Oller Art and History Museum. Oller (1833–1917) was one of the most accomplished artists of his time, and in Puerto Rico is best known for his painting *El Velorio* (*The Wake,* on display at the Museo de Historia, Antropolgía y Arte at the University of Puerto Rico), which depicts the futility of a wake for a peasant child. ⊠ *Calle Santiago Veve, Bayamón,* ☎ *787/787–8620.* ⌦ *Free.* ☉ *Tues.–Sat. 9–4.*

♻ ③④ **Parque de las Ciencias Luis A. Ferré.** The 42-acre Luis A. Ferré Science Park contains a collection of intriguing activities and displays. The Transportation Museum has antique cars and the island's oldest bicycle. In the Rocket Plaza, children can experience a flight simulator, and in the planetarium, the solar system is projected on the ceiling. On site as well are a small zoo and a natural science exhibit. The park is popular with Puerto Rican schoolchildren, and, although it's a bit of a drive from central San Juan, it's a good activity for the family. ⊠ *Rte. 167, Bayamón,* ☎ *787/740–6878.* ☞ *$5.* ☉ *Wed.–Fri. 9–4, weekends and holidays 10–6.*

DINING

In cosmopolitan San Juan, European, Asian, and Middle Eastern eateries vie for your attention with family-owned restaurants specializing in seafood or *comida criolla* (creole cooking). U.S. chains such as McDonald's and Pizzeria Uno compete with chains like Pollo Tropical specializing in local cuisine. Although each of the city's large hotels has two or more fine restaurants, the best dining is often in stand-alone establishments—don't be shy about venturing to such places.

Dress codes vary greatly, though a restaurant's price category is a good indicator of its formality. For less expensive places, anything but beachwear is fine. Ritzier eateries will expect collared shirts for men (jacket and tie requirements are rare) and chic attire for women. When in doubt, do as the Puerto Ricans often do and dress up.

For breakfast outside of your hotel, cafés are your best bet. It's rare for such establishments to close between breakfast and lunch; it's slightly more common for restaurants to close between lunch and dinner, though. Dinner is generally served late; if you arrive at a restaurant before 7 PM, you may be the only diners. Although some places don't accept reservations, it's always a good idea to make them for dinner whenever possible. This is especially true during the November–April busy season and on weekends at any time of the year.

CATEGORY	COST*
$$$$	over $35
$$$	$25–$35
$$	$15–$25
$	under $15

per person for a main course at dinner

Old San Juan

Cafés

$–$$ ✕ **La Bombonera.** Strong coffee and excellent pastries make this café, a landmark that was established in 1903, very popular in the morning—particularly on Sunday. All this even though the waiters are grumpy and give the appearance of having worked here since day one. It's open from 7:30 AM to early evening, and full breakfasts are served 'til 11 AM. ⊠ *259 Calle San Francisco, Old San Juan,* ☎ *787/722–0658. AE, MC, V.*

$–$$ ✕ **Café Berlin.** Tasty vegetarian fare prevails at this casual café, bakery, and delicatessen overlooking Plaza Colón. The salads are particularly creative, but there's also an assortment of nonvegetarian dishes, and the pastries, fresh juices, and Puerto Rican coffees are perfect after a day of touring Old San Juan. ⊠ *407 Calle San Francisco, Old San Juan,* ☎ *787/722–5205. AE, MC, V.*

$–$$ ✗ **Café Zaguan.** Works by local artists adorn the inside of this narrow, cozy café, and tables outside on the plaza are great places to people-watch. For lunch (weekdays only) there are great deli sandwiches and wraps; the California wrap is particularly good with chicken breast, tomato, and avocado stuffed inside a tomato or spinach tortilla. The dinner menu is a little more formal: try the red snapper served in a velvety coconut sauce or the grilled chicken with mango and chipotle sauce. Pop bands often play after dinner on weekends. ✉ *359 Calle Tetuán, Old San Juan,* ☎ *787/724–3359. AE, MC, V.*

$–$$ ✗ **Cafeteria Mallorca.** The specialty here is the *mallorca,* a sweet pastry that's buttered, grilled, and then sprinkled with powdered sugar.
★ Wash one down with a terrific cup of *café con leche* (coffee with milk). For something more substantial, try the breakfast mallorca, which has ham and cheese. The waitstaffers—all dressed in crisp green uniforms and caps—are attentive. ✉ *300 Calle San Francisco, Old San Juan,* ☎ *787/724–4607. MC, V. Closed Sun.*

Caribbean

$$ ✗ **Casa Borinquen.** A portrait of independence leader Pedro Albizu Campos adorns the building's facade, a holdover from before restoration work, when a group of artists turned the crumbling walls into the "Museo sin Techo" ("Roofless Museum"). Today it's a bright, attractive restaurant serving radically delicious local cuisine. The vegetarian dishes are made with local produce, shrimp is served with *acerola* (a local fruit similar to a cherry but not as sweet) sauce and mashed casava, and pork loin comes with fresh corn relish. ✉ *109 Calle San Sebastián, Old San Juan,* ☎ *787/725–0888. AE, D, MC, V. Closed Mon.*

$ ✗ **La Fonda del Jibarito.** Sanjuaneros have favored this casual, family-run restaurant for years. The back porch is filled with plants, the
★ dining room is filled with fanciful depictions of Calle Sol (the street outside), and the ever-present owner, Pedro J. Ruiz, is filled with the desire to ensure that everyone's happy. The conch ceviche and chicken fricassee are among the specialties. ✉ *280 Calle Sol, Old San Juan,* ☎ *787/725–8375. Reservations not accepted. AE, MC, V.*

Contemporary

$$–$$$ ✗ **Carli Café Concierto.** The Banco Popular building dominates the Old
★ San Juan skyline. On its ground floor, you'll find this intimate bistro, with rust-hue walls and black-marble tables. Have a seat indoors or on the streetside patio, and dine on such international savories such as seared loin of lamb or spinach-and-ricotta ravioli in pesto sauce. The genial owner and host, Carli Muñoz, is a pianist who toured with the Beach Boys (note the gold album on the wall). Many evenings he plays the Steinway grand piano, often accompanied by singers and musicians who happen to drop in. ✉ *Plazoleta Rafael Carrión, Calle Recinto Sur and Calle San Justo, Old San Juan,* ☎ *787/725–4927. AE, MC, V.*

$$–$$$ ✗ **Parrot Club.** The cuisine is inventive, the decor is colorful, and the
★ staff is casual but efficient. Stop by the bar for the speciality passion-fruit drink before moving to the adjacent dining room or the back courtyard. The menu has contemporary variations of Cuban and Puerto Rican classics. You might start with mouthwatering crabcakes or tamarind-barbecued ribs, followed by blackened tuna in a dark rum sauce or *churrasco* (barbecued steak) with *chimichurri* (a green sauce made with herbs, garlic, and tomatoes). ✉ *363 Calle Fortaleza, Old San Juan,* ☎ *787/725–7370. Reservations not accepted. AE, DC, MC, V.*

$–$$ ✗ **Amadeus.** A trendy crowd enjoys such nouvelle Caribbean appetizers as buffalo wings or plantain mousse with shrimp, and entrées such as ravioli with a goat cheese–and–walnut sauce or Cajun-grilled mahimahi. The front dining room is attractive—whitewashed walls, dark wood, white tablecloths, ceiling fans—and an interior courtyard

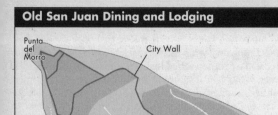

Old San Juan Dining and Lodging

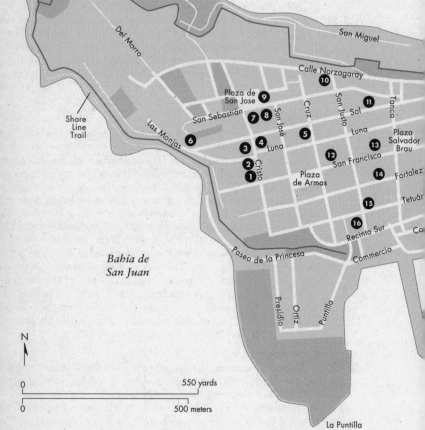

Punta del Morro

City Wall

Del Morro

San Miguel

Calle Norzagaray

⑩

Plaza de San Jose ⑨

⑪

Shore Line Trail

San Sebastián

Las Monjas

⑦ ⑧

San José

Sol

Tanca

Cruz

San Justo

Luna

Plaza Salvador Brau

⑥

③ ④

Luna

⑤

⑬

Cristo

⑫

San Francisco

②

Plaza de Armas

⑭

Fortalez

①

⑮

Tetuár

⑯

Recinto Sur

Co

Bahía de San Juan

Paseo de la Princesa

Commercio

Presidio

Ortiz

Puntilla

N

0 _____ 550 yards

0 _____ 500 meters

La Puntilla

Dining

Amadeus	**8**
La Bella Piazza	**26**
La Bombonera	**12**
Café Berlin	**27**
Café Zaguan	**21**
Cafeteria Mallorca	**13**
Carli Café Concierto	**16**

Casa Borinquen	**9**
La Chaumière	**22**
Chef Marisoll	**1**
Dragonfly	**24**
La Fonda del Jibarito	**11**
King and I Thai Restaurant	**18**
La Mallorquina	**15**
La Ostra Cosa	**2**

Parrot Club	**25**
El Patio de Sam	**7**
Il Perugino	**4**
El Picoteo	**3**
La Querencia	**5**
Tantra	**23**
Transylvania	**19**
Yukiyú	**17**

Lodging

Caleta Guesthouse	**6**
El Convento Hotel	**3**
Gallery Inn	**10**
Hotel Milano	**14**
Wyndham Old San Juan Hotel & Casino	**20**

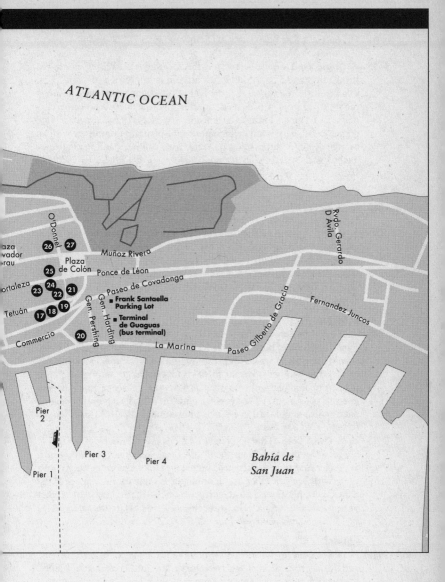

ATLANTIC OCEAN

O'Donnell

aza
vador
erau

26 27

Muñoz Rivera

Plaza
de Colón

25

Ponce de Léon

ortaleza

23 24

Paseo de Covadonga

22 21

■ Frank Santaella
Parking Lot

Tetuán

17 18 19

■ Terminal
de Guaguas
(bus terminal)

Commercio

20

La Marina

Gen. Harding

Gen. Pershing

Rvdo. Gerardo
D'Avila

Fernandez Juncos

Paseo Gilberto de Gracia

Pier
2

Pier 3

Pier 4

Bahía de
San Juan

Pier 1

leads to a romantic back dining room with printed tablecloths, candles, and exposed brick. There's also a seating area on Plaza San José. ✉ *106 Calle San Sebastián, Old San Juan,* ☎ *787/722–8635. AE, MC, V. No lunch Mon.*

$–$$ ✕ **Dragonfly.** Don't leave town without eating here. With Chinese-red furnishings and a charming staff outfitted in kimonos and satin shirts, this hip little restaurant has the feel of an elegant opium den. Surely the frequent lines outside its door attest to the seductive power of chef Roberto Trevino's Latin-Asian cuisine. The *platos* (large appetizers) are meant to be shared and include pork-and-plantain dumplings with an orange dipping sauce; spicy, perfectly fried calimari; and Peking-duck nachos with wasabi sour cream. ✉ *364 Calle La Fortaleza, Old San Juan,* ☎ *787/977–3886. Reservations not accepted. AE, MC, V.*

Continental

$$–$$$ ✕ **Chef Marisoll.** On two sides of a Venetianesque courtyard surrounded by ornate balconies, this restaurant with dark woods and high ceilings, serves international dishes that look as good as they taste (the chef was once an interior designer). Try the duck Caesar salad or the cream of exotic mushroom soup to start; entrées include beef tenderloin and salmon fillet. For dessert, the crème caramel is a classic. ✉ *202 Calle Cristo, Old San Juan,* ☎ *787/725–7454. AE, MC, V. Closed Mon. No lunch Sun.*

Eclectic

$–$$$ ✕ **El Patio de Sam.** A warm interior of dark wood and faux brick and a great selection of beers make Sam's a popular late-night spot. The menu consists mostly of steaks and seafood, with a few native dishes mixed in. Try the Samuel's Special pizza—mozzarella, tomato sauce, beef, pepperoni, and black olives—which feeds two or three people. The flan melts in your mouth. There's entertainment (usually a guitarist singing old Spanish standards) every night but Sunday. ✉ *102 Calle San Sebastián, Old San Juan,* ☎ *787/723–1149. AE, D, DC, MC, V.*

$–$$ ✕ **La Ostra Cosa.** The menu here includes everything from oysters to burgers, but most people come for the large, succulent prawns, which are grilled and served with garlic butter. Opt for a seat in the back courtyard: with bougainvillea and moonlight, it's one of the city's prettiest alfresco dining spots. The gregarious owner, Alberto Nazario, brother of pop star Ednita Nazario, truly enjoys seeing his guests satisfied. ✉ *154 Calle Cristo, Old San Juan,* ☎ *787/722–2672. AE, MC, V.*

French

$$$–$$$$ ✕ **La Chaumière.** With black-and-white floor tiles, a beamed ceiling, and floral-print curtains, this two-story restaurant evokes rural France. It has been under the same management since 1969, and with all that experience the service is smooth. Daily specials augment a menu of stellar French classics, including onion soup, rack of lamb, scallops Provençale, and chateaubriand for two. ✉ *367 Calle Tetuan, Old San Juan,* ☎ *787/722–3330. AE, DC, MC, V. Closed Sun. No lunch.*

Indian

$–$$$ ✕ **Tantra.** San Juan's first Indian restaurant is in the up-and-coming area known as SoFo. The menu has traditional tandoori and curry dishes as well as such inventive surprises as salmon-stuffed beef tenderloin in a casava puree. The earthtone interior invites you to linger, and many patrons do so for an after-dinner puff on an Asian water pipe. ✉ *356 Calle La Fortaleza, Old San Juan,* ☎ *787/977–8141. AE, MC, V. Closed Mon.*

Italian

$$–$$$ **✕ Il Perugino.** The intimate 200-year-old building seems the perfect
★ place to dine on classic carpaccios, homemade pastas, hearty main
courses, and exquisite desserts. Try the black fettuccine with crayfish
and baby eels or the rack of lamb in a red-wine sauce with aromatic
herbs. The extensive wine cellar, housed in the former cistern, is sure
to contain the perfect complement to your meal. ⊠ *105 Calle Cristo,
Old San Juan,* ☎ *787/722–5481. MC, V.*

$$ **✕ La Bella Piazza.** The narrow dining room has Roman columns,
gold-leaf flourishes, and arched doorways that lead to an interior ter-
race. You'll find such quintessentially Italian appetizers as calamari *in
padella* (lightly breaded and sautéed in olive oil, parsley, and garlic)
and such archetypal pasta dishes as fusilli *amatriciana* (in a crushed
bacon, tomato, and red-pepper sauce). Main courses include *saltinbocca
alla romana* (veal and prosciutto in a sage, white-wine, and butter sauce)
and *medaglioni al Chianti* (beef medallions in a spicy Chianti sauce).
⊠ *355 Calle San Francisco, Old San Juan,* ☎ *787/721–0396. AE, MC,
V. Closed Wed.*

Japanese

$$–$$$ **✕ Yukiyú.** Old San Juan's only Japanese restaurant maintains high stan-
dards despite the lack of competition. If you're craving sushi, you
should make a beeline for this establishment; if you prefer your meals
cooked, you'll find a selection of beef, chicken, and seafood dishes, all
prepared under the watchful eye of chef Igarashi. There's a Zenlike aus-
terity to the surroundings, but the staff is friendly, and the clientele is
unpretentious. ⊠ *311 Calle Recinto Sur, Old San Juan,* ☎ *787/721–
0653. AE, D, MC, V.*

Latin

$$–$$$$ **✕ La Mallorquina.** It's said to date from 1848, making it what many
consider the island's oldest restaurant. The food consists of such basic
Puerto Rican and Spanish fare as *asopao* (a stew with rice and seafood)
and paella, but it's really the atmosphere that recommends the place.
Friendly, nattily attired staffers zip between tables amid the peach-colored
walls and the whir of ceiling fans. ⊠ *207 Calle San Justo, Old San Juan,*
☎ *787/722–3261. AE, MC, V. Closed Sun.*

$$–$$$$ **✕ La Querencia.** Inside a Spanish colonial building, large wooden ta-
★ bles, muted-green stone walls, and weekend performances by Spanish
guitarists make this restaurant seem downright rustic. It's also a tad
bohemian: the owners, a Spaniard and a *puertorriqueña* with back-
grounds in the arts, think of it as a gallery as well as a restaurant, and
works by local and Spanish artists hang on the walls. The fare is Span-
ish, but Mediterranean and Caribbean flavors help to create such in-
spired dishes as lamb loin with coconut and dried-fruit couscous, duck
breast crusted with casava, and hearty Puerto Rican seafood stew. Reser-
vations are recommended on weekends. ⊠ *100 Calle Cruz, Old San
Juan,* ☎ *787/725–1304. AE, MC, V.*

Romanian

$$ **✕ Transylvania.** Despite the portraits of Vlad-like characters and the
medieval weaponry on its stone walls, this Romanian restaurant is wel-
coming—this is, after all, the sunny Caribbean. There's goulash, a red-
meat lover's platter called Dracula's Feast, and such surprisingly
contemporary dishes as walnut-crusted chicken in a caper cream sauce.
The bar attracts an affable expatriot crowd. ⊠ *317 Calle Recinto Sur,
Old San Juan,* ☎ *787/977–2328. AE, MC, V.*

Spanish

$–$$
★
✕ **El Picoteo.** Many patrons make a meal of the appetizers that dominate the menu at this chic tapas bar. Entrées such as paella are also noteworthy. There's a long, lively bar inside; one dining area overlooks the hotel El Convento's courtyard, and the other takes in the action along Calle Cristo. Even if you have dinner plans elsewhere, consider stopping here for a cocktail or a nightcap. ⊠ *El Convento Hotel, 100 Calle Cristo, Old San Juan,* ☎ *787/723–9621. AE, D, DC, MC, V.*

Thai

$$–$$$
✕ **King and I Thai Restaurant.** The walls of this long, narrow, well-established restaurant are covered with mirrors and murals of aquarium scenes. The heat has been turned down in most dishes, but if you're a fan of spicy Thai cuisine you can ask to have it fired back up. The coconut shrimp and the *kari gang ped* (chicken served in a pungent curry sauce) are among the specialties. The service is superb. ⊠ *315 Calle Recinto Sur, Old San Juan,* ☎ *787/725–8401. AE, D, MC, V.*

Greater San Juan

Cafés

$–$$
✕ **Kasalta Bakery, Inc.** Make your selection from the display cases full of luscious pastries and other tempting treats. Walk up to the counter and order a sandwich (try the Cubano) or such items as the meltingly tender octopus salad and the savory *caldo gallego* (a soup of fresh vegetables, sausage, and potatoes). Wash everything down with a cold drink or a café con leche that's guaranteed to be strong. ⊠ *1966 Calle McLeary, Ocean Park,* ☎ *787/727–7340. AE, MC, V.*

$
✕ **La Patisserie.** Everything—from the pastries to the pastas—is delicious at this café on a quiet stretch of the Condado strip. For breakfast there are wonderful omelettes stuffed with fresh vegetables and imported cheeses. For lunch or an early dinner there are sandwiches—from pastrami to king crab, on croissants, baguettes, or other breads—as well as pasta dishes and salads. The pecan pie is the best in San Juan. ⊠ *1504 Av. Ashford, Condado,* ☎ *787/728–5508. AE, MC, V.*

Caribbean

$$–$$$$
★
✕ **Ajili Mojili.** The traditional Puerto Rican food is prepared with a flourish and served in an attractive plantation-style setting. Sample the fried cheese and *yautía* (a tuber similar to a potato) dumplings with the house sauce, a tomato, herb, garlic, and shaved almond concoction. The *mofongo*, a mashed plantain casserole with seafood or meat, is wonderful, as is the plantain-crusted shrimp in a white-wine herb sauce. ⊠ *1052 Av. Ashford, Condado,* ☎ *787/725–9195. AE, DC, MC, V. No lunch Sat.*

$$–$$$$
✕ **Casa Dante.** The self-proclaimed "casa del mofongo" is a good place to try this Puerto Rican specialty of plantains mashed with garlic and other ingredients. You can get it with seafood, chicken, or beef in a red sauce, or as a side dish to a churrasco or sautéed red snapper. The bright dining room has tourist photos of Puerto Rico covering its walls and is a favorite of families. ⊠ *39 Calle Loíza, Punta Las Marías,* ☎ *787/726–7310. AE, MC, V. Closed Mon.*

$$
✕ **Yerba Buena.** This "corner of South Beach in the Condado" serves Latin Caribbean food in contemporary trappings. The Cuban classic *ropa vieja* (meat cooked so slowly that it becomes tender shreds) comes in a stylish plantain nest. The shrimp has a coconut-and-ginger sauce, the halibut fillet one of mango and Grand Marnier. The restaurant claims to use the "original" recipe for its *mojito,* Cuba's tasty rum, lime, and mint drink. ⊠ *1350 Av. Ashford, Condado,* ☎ *787/721–5907. AE, MC, V. Closed Sun.*

$-$$ ✕ **Havana's Café.** Photos of Old Havana line the walls of this Cuban restaurant in the heart of Santurce, just off Avenida Ponce de León. Crowds pack in for lunch and dinner because the food here, down to the *moros y cristianos* (black beans and rice), is fresh and lovingly prepared. ⊠ *409 Calle Del Parque, Santurce,* ☎ *787/725–0888. AE, MC, V. Closed Mon.*

$-$$ ✕ **Tropical Restaurant.** For years, locals have favored this unpretentious Cuban restaurant for its reasonably priced Latin classics. Years of experience at preparing steak in brandy sauce, lobster stew, and chicken in rice show up in the final product. For dessert, the *dulce de leche* (a sweet milk pudding) and the flan are good bets. ⊠ *1214 Av. Ashford, Condado,* ☎ *787/724–3760. AE, MC, V.*

Chinese

$-$$$$ ✕ **Great Taste Chinese Restaurant.** The kitchen is open until 2 AM, and the menu has dim sum offerings and several regional classics whose quality rivals that of anything served in New York City's Chinatown. The restaurant is in a faded condominium complex, and canned disco music plays through cheap speakers, but the view over the Laguna del Condado is beautiful. ⊠ *1018 Av. Ashford, Condado,* ☎ *787/721–8111. AE, D, DC, MC, V.*

Contemporary

$$-$$$ ✕ **Chayote.** Although it's slightly off the beaten path, this chic eatery—
★ all earthtones and contemporary Puerto Rican art—is definitely an "in" spot. The chef gives haute international dishes tropical panache. Starters include *sopa del día* (soup of the day) made with local produce, chayote stuffed with prosciutto, and corn tamales with shrimp in a coconut sauce. Half the entrées are seafood dishes, including an excellent pan-seared tuna with Asian ginger sauce. The ginger flan is a must for dessert. ⊠ *Hotel Olimpo Court, 603 Av. Miramar, Miramar,* ☎ *787/722–9385. AE, MC, V. Closed Sun. and Mon. No lunch Sat.*

$$-$$$ ✕ **Zabor Creative Cuisine.** In a restored plantation with a pastoral front yard, this inventive restaurant seems as if it's out on the island somewhere rather than on Avenida Ashford. One of the main pastimes here is grazing—that is, sharing such appetizers as breaded calamari in a tomato-basil sauce with your dinner companions. Of the notable main courses, try the veal chops stuffed with provolone, pancetta, and herbs and served with a garlic-merlot sauce or the catch of the day over yellow-raisin couscous in a mango-rosemary curry. ⊠ *14 Calle Candida, Condado,* ☎ *787/725–9494. AE, D, DC, MC, V. Closed Sun.–Mon. No lunch Tues.–Thurs. and Sat.*

$$ ✕ **Tangerine.** Tangerine spills onto a terrace fronting the Atlantic, whose steady breezes and distant roiling are as much a part of the dreamy scene as the muted orange-color lighting and cream walls. Asian-European fusion dishes appear under the provocative menu titles "Foreplay" (appetizers), "Loss of Innocence" (entrées), and "Sensuous Pleasures" (desserts). Appetizers such as Asiatic baby greens in a tangerine dressing or grilled scallops with mushrooms and noodles in a basil-cilantro sauce are seductive. Artful entrées include pork chops in tangerine vinaigrette with sage-potato puree and a pan-seared sea bass with sea-urchin butter sauce and mushroom couscous. ⊠ *Water Club, 2 Calle Tartak, Isla Verde,* ☎ *787/728–3666. AE, MC, V.*

Continental

$$-$$$$ ✕ **Augusto's Cuisine.** Austrian-born chef Augusto Schreiner, a graduate of the Salzburg Culinary School, regularly wins awards for his classic European cuisine. The menu changes seasonally; some of the dishes commonly served are veal carpaccio, steak au poivre, and seared tuna or shrimp in a mango curry. The bright dining room is made even cheerier

38

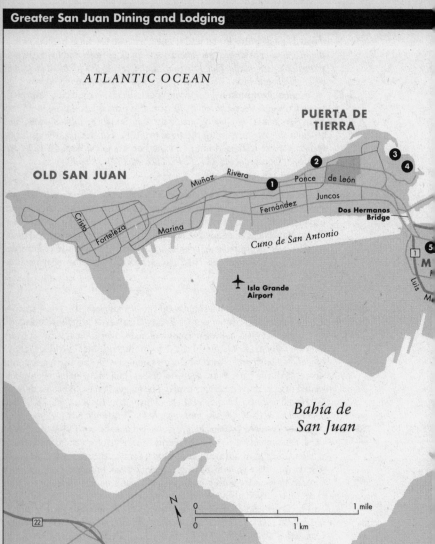

Dining

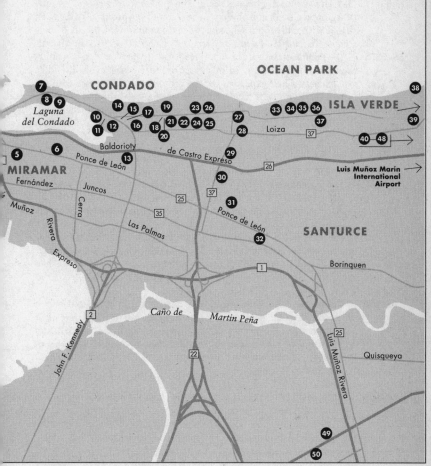

with floral prints and large bouquets. ⊠ *Hotel Excelsior, 801 Av. Ponce de León, Miramar,* ☎ *787/725–7700. AE, MC, V. Closed Sun.– Mon.*

$$–$$$$ ✕ **Dumas Restaurant.** The back porch of one of San Juan's few ocean-side restaurants overlooks the Atlantic crashing against the rugged Puerta de Tierra shore. There's usually a fine breeze, and sunsets behind the Old City skyline are breathtaking. The food is solid: seafood is a specialty, but the steak and poultry dishes are also rewarding. Try the roast sirloin with mushroom sauce or the seafood marinara. ⊠ *Av. Muñoz Rivera, Parada 7½, Puerta de Tierra,* ☎ *787/721–3550. AE, MC, V.*

$$–$$$$ ✕ **The Palm Restaurant.** The same great steak, seafood, and Italian dishes are served here as at the Palm's sister restaurant in New York; when you leave you half expect to see the Brooklyn Bridge rather than the beach. Caricatures of local and international celebrities hang on the walls. They and some glass dividers are the only light touches amid the dark wood of the bar and the booths. ⊠ *Wyndham El San Juan Hotel & Casino, 6063 Av. Isla Verde, Isla Verde,* ☎ *787/791–1000. AE, D, DC, MC, V. Closed Mon.*

Eclectic

$–$$$$ ✕ **The Greenhouse.** From 11:30 to 4:30, diners pour steadily into this casual Condado eatery. The late-night hours draw a lively crowd. A wide-ranging menu has such standards as burgers, French onion soup, grilled-chicken sandwiches, and omelets as well as more ambitious dishes like lobster tail or baked salmon. The desserts, from the rich chocolate cake to the light fruit sorbet, are divine. Everything is consistently well prepared—as well it should be given that the restaurant has had more than 20 years's worth of practice. ⊠ *1200 Av. Ashford, Condado,* ☎ *787/725–4036. AE, D, MC, V.*

$$–$$$ ✕ **Caribbean Grill Restaurant.** This restaurant in the Ritz-Carlton takes the elegance associated with the chain's name and gives it a Caribbean twist. The menu emphasizes a variety of grilled seafood; there's a mix of Caribbean and North American fare. Overall, it has some of the city's most consistently first-rate cuisine. ⊠ *Ritz-Carlton San Juan Hotel, Spa & Casino, Av. Las Gobernadores (Rte. 187), Isla Verde,* ☎ *787/253–1700. AE, D, DC, MC, V.*

$–$$$ ✕ **Pikayo.** Chef Wilo Benet artfully fuses classic French, Caribbean creole, and California nouvelle cuisine at this restaurant in the Museo de Arte de Puerto Rico. And, appropriately enough, dishes are a feast for the eye as well as the palate. The menu changes regularly, but a meal might consist of tostones stuffed with oven-dried tomatoes, followed by a hearty land-crab stew or mofongo topped with saffron shrimp. ⊠ *Museo de Arte de Puerto Rico, 300 Av. José de Diego, Santurce,* ☎ *787/721–6194. AE, MC, V. Closed Mon.*

Italian

$$–$$$$ ✕ **Martino.** Beneath a glass atrium on the top floor of the Black Diamond Hotel, Martino is a San Juan favorite for its classic northern Italian cuisine and its spectacular view of the Condado beach district. Start off with a hot seafood antipasto, followed by osso buco or one of the several fine pasta dishes, which are meals in themselves. Chef Martin Acosta's creations taste like they've come direct from the mother country to your table. ⊠ *55 Av. Condado, Condado,* ☎ *787/722–5356. AE, DC, MC, V. No lunch on weekends.*

$–$$ ✕ **Via Appia.** The food at this no-frills café is just as authentic and as tasty—from the pizza to the veal and peppers to house red wine—as its higher-priced *paisanos*. The outdoor seating area looks out on Condado's busy Ashford Avenue, which is usually filled with people coming from and going to the beach. Indoors there's air-conditioning but very little ambience. ⊠ *1350 Av. Ashford, Condado,* ☎ *787/725–8711. AE, MC, V.*

$ ✕ **La Buona Lasagne.** Don't let the elegance fool you. The prices are truly reasonable at this restaurant far from the well-trodden areas and in a restored art deco structure with tile floors, large picture windows, and pastel walls. There are about 30 pasta dishes, all freshly made with top-quality ingredients. The basic meat lasagne is just as good as the more elaborate penne with smoked salmon and a cream sauce. ⊠ *176 Calle Delbrey, corner of Baldorioty de Castro Expressway, Santurce,* ☎ *787/721–7488. AE, MC, V. Closed Sun. No dinner Mon.–Wed.*

Latin

$–$$$$ ✕ **Che's.** Juicy churrasco, lemon chicken, and grilled sweetbreads are specialties at this casual Argentine restaurant. The hamburgers are huge, and the french fries are fresh. The Chilean and Argentine wine list is also good. ⊠ *35 Calle Caoba, Punta Las Marías,* ☎ *787/726–7202. AE, D, DC, MC, V.*

$–$$ ✕ **Cielito Lindo.** There's a beach-shack quality to this Mexican establishment, but it serves a good mole, juicy flank steaks, and awesome enchiladas. There's also a wide selection of South of the Border brews, each one iced to perfection and served with a lime wedge. ⊠ *1108 Av. Magdalena, Condado,* ☎ *787/723–5597. AE, MC, V.*

$–$$ ✕ **La Vista Restaurant & Ocean Terrace.** You can choose from a wide-ranging menu while enjoying an ocean view at this 24-hour restaurant in the San Juan Marriott. There are Mexican, seafood, Puerto Rican, Caribbean, and Argentinian specials on different nights of the week. The regular menu includes such appetizers as crabcakes and *arepa* (a light flour biscuit often filled with seafood) salad. For an entrée, try the shrimp with garlic, papaya, and cilantro. ⊠ *San Juan Marriott Resort and Stellaris Casino, 1309 Av. Ashford, Condado,* ☎ *787/722–7000. AE, MC, V.*

Middle Eastern

$–$$ ✕ **Jerusalem.** You feel as if you're in an Arabian tent at one of San Juan's oldest Middle Eastern restaurants. Hypnotic music is piped in over the sound system, and belly dancers put on a great show. Although the environment may seem contrived, the food is straightforward and delicious. The *baba ghanoush* (eggplant puree with tahini, olive oil, lemon juice, and garlic) and tabbouleh make good starters; consider following them with grilled chicken kebabs or baked lamb. Entrées are served with Arabian rice, which is mixed with parsley and almonds, and a cucumber-and-tomato salad. For dessert, the baklava is unrivaled. ⊠ *G-1 Calle O'Neill, Hato Rey,* ☎ *787/764–3265. AE, D, MC, V.*

$–$$ ✕ **Tierra Santa.** San Juan's small community of Middle Eastern immigrants isn't large enough to explain the local affection for that region's cuisine—or the popularity of belly dancing (performers gyrate here on Friday and Saturday nights). You can contemplate these mysteries as you dine on such starters as hummus and falafel and entrées like roasted halibut in almond, lime, and garlic or lamb curry with oranges and onions. ⊠ *284 Av. Roosevelt, Hato Rey,* ☎ *787/754–6865. AE, MC, V.*

Seafood

$$–$$$$ ✕ **Marisquería Atlántica.** At this combination restaurant–retail store, the seafood is fresh and reasonably priced. Stop in for a cool drink at the bar and a side dish of calamari, served lightly breaded and in a spicy sauce. Specialties include fresh Maine lobster, grilled red snapper in a garlic sauce, and paella loaded with scallops, clams, shrimp, squid, and fish. ⊠ *2475 Calle Loíza, Punta Las Marías,* ☎ *787/728–5444. AE,*

MC, V. *Closed Sun.*; ⊠ *7 Calle Lugo Viñas, Puerta de Tierra,* ☎ *787/ 722–0890. AE, MC, V. Closed Mon.*

$–$$$ ✕ **Marisquería La Dorada.** This fine seafood establishment on Condado's restaurant row is surprisingly affordable. The grilled seafood platter is the specialty, but there are also excellent pastas and other fish dinners, including mahimahi in caper sauce and codfish in green sauce. The friendly waitstaff makes you feel genuinely welcome. ⊠ *1105 Av. Magdalena, Condado,* ☎ *787/722–9583. AE, D, MC, V.*

Spanish

$$–$$$$ ✕ **La Casona.** San Juan's moneyed class comes here for power lunches, but it's also a nice spot for a romantic dinner. The restored Spanish colonial residence has well-appointed rooms and blooming gardens. The menu is based solidly in Spain, but has many creative flourishes— start with the duck pâté or smoked salmon and move on to the duck breast in a raspberry sauce or the rack of lamb, which is first baked and then sautéed with brandy and fruit. ⊠ *609 Calle San Jorge, Santurce,* ☎ *787/727–2717. AE, D, DC, MC, V. Closed Sun.*

$$–$$$$ ✕ **Compostela.** Contemporary Spanish food and a 10,000-bottle wine cellar are the draws here. The dining room is pleasant, with bright colors and many plants, and the kitchen is honored yearly in local competitions for specialties such as mushroom pâté, port *pastelillo* (wild mushroom turnover), grouper fillet with scallops in salsa verde, rack of lamb, duck with orange and ginger sauce, and paella. ⊠ *106 Av. Condado, Santurce,* ☎ *787/724–6088. AE, DC, MC, V. No lunch Sat. Closed Sun.*

$$–$$$$ ✕ **Urdin.** The owners, who include Julián Gil, a well-known Puerto Rican model and actor, describe the menu here as Spanish with a Caribbean touch. The soup and seafood appetizers are particularly good, and a highly recommended entrée is *chillo urdin de lujo* (red snapper sautéed with clams, mussels, and shrimp in a tomato, herb, and wine sauce). The name of the restaurant comes from the Basque word for "blue," which is the dining room's dominant color. ⊠ *1105 Av. Magdalena, Condado,* ☎ *787/724–0420. AE, MC, V.*

$–$$$ ✕ **Miró Marisquería Catalana.** Like its namesake, the painter Joan Miró, this small restaurant beside the lobby of Hotel El Portal draws its inspiration from the Catalan region of Spain, where the cuisine is heavy on seafood and hearty tapas. Prints by the artist hang on the walls, and the overall design, dominated by bright hues and brass, is also influenced by Miró. Start off with braised chorizo and peppers or steamed clams with garlic. Main courses include lamb chops and grilled tuna or codfish in a red-pepper-and-eggplant sauce. ⊠ *76 Av. Condado, Condado,* ☎ *787/721–9593. AE, MC, V.*

$–$$$ ✕ **Ramiro's.** The smell of chef-owner Jesus Ramiro's imaginative
   ★   Castilian cooking fills the sea-green dining room. Ramiro is also known for his artistic presentation: flower-shape peppers filled with fish mousse, a mix of seafood caught under a vegetable net, roast duckling with sugarcane honey, and, if you can stand more, a kiwi dessert sculpted to resemble twin palms. ⊠ *1106 Av. Magdalena, Condado,* ☎ *787/721–9049. AE, DC, MC, V. No lunch Sat.*

LODGING

San Juan prides itself on its clean, comfortable, plentiful accommodations, and hoteliers, by and large, aim to please. Big hotels and resorts, several with casinos, and a few smaller establishments line the sandy strands along Condado and Isla Verde. Between these two neighborhoods, the Ocean Park area has homey inns as do the near-the-beach districts of Miramar and Santurce. Old San Juan has only a few noteworthy hotels, one of which has a casino.

The city's rooms aren't inexpensive: for a high-end beach-resort room, expect to pay at least $200–$300 for a double in high season—roughly mid-November through mid-April. For smaller inns and hotels, doubles start at $100–$150. As a rule, if your room is less than $50 in high season, then the quality of the hotel might be questionable. Although most hotels operate on the European plan (EP, no meals included), a few larger establishments offer other meal plans and/or all-inclusive packages.

Staying in a self-catering apartment or condo has advantages over a resort, especially for families. You can cook when and what you want, and you can enjoy considerable autonomy. Several companies represent such properties in San Juan. When booking, be sure ask about maid service, swimming pools, and any other amenities that are important to you. The small, government-sponsored inns, called *paradores* are primarily *en la isla* (out on the island) rather than in San Juan.

Small Inns of Puerto Rico (⊠ 954 Av. Ponce de León, Suite 702, Santurce 00907, ☎ 787/725–2901, FAX 787/725–2913, WEB www.prhta.com or www.prhtasmallhotels.com), a branch of the Puerto Rico Hotel and Tourism Association, is a marketing arm for some 25 small hotels island-wide. The organization occasionally has package deals including casino coupons and LeLoLai (a cultural show) tickets.

Michael Giessler of the **Caleta Guesthouse** (⊠ 11 Caleta de las Monjas, Old San Juan 00901, ☎ 787/725–5347, FAX 787/977–5642, WEB www.thecaleta.com) specializes in weekly and monthly rentals of furnished studios and apartments in Old San Juan. Investigate rates at high-end Isla Verde condominiums through **Condo World** (⊠ 4230 Orchard Lake Rd., Suite 5, Orchard Lake, MI 48323, ☎ 800/521–2980, FAX 248/683–5076). **Puerto Rico Vacation Apartments** (⊠ Calle Marbella del Caribe Oeste S-5, Isla Verde 00979, ☎ 787/727–1591 or 800/266–3639, FAX 787/268–3604, WEB www.sanjuanvacations.com) represents some 200 properties in Condado and Isla Verde.

CATEGORY	COST*
$$$$	over $225
$$$	$150–$225
$$	$75–$150
$	under $75

All prices are for a double room in high season, excluding 9% tax (11% for hotels with casinos, 7% for paradores) and 5%–12% service charge.

Old San Juan

$$$$ ★ 🏨 **El Convento Hotel.** Once a Carmelite convent, this 350-year-old building is a prime example of the right way to blend Old World gentility with modern luxury. Much of the original architecture is intact, including a colonial interior courtyard. Rooms have a Spanish-deco look, with dark woods, wrought-iron lamps, and ornate furniture. Complimentary wine and hors d'oeuvres are served before dinner, and there's an honor bar that's open until 4 AM. The courtyard's El Picoteo, street-side Café Bohemio, and the park-front tables of Agave Blue are among the dining choices. ⊠ *100 Calle Cristo, Old San Juan (Box 1048, 00902), ☎ 787/723–9020; 800/468–2779 direct to hotel, FAX 787/721–2877, WEB www.elconvento.com. 54 rooms, 4 suites. 3 restaurants, 2 bars, air-conditioning, in-room data ports, in-room safes, cable TV, in-room VCRs, no-smoking rooms, pool, gym, shops, library, dry cleaning, laundry service, con-*

cierge, business services, meeting room, parking (fee). AE, D, DC, MC, V. CP.

$$$$ 🏨 **Wyndham Old San Juan Hotel & Casino.** The gleaming Wyndham blends classic Spanish colonial lines with a modern, triangular shape that subtly echoes the cruise ships docked nearby. The lobby, adjacent to the casino, shines with multihue tiles and mahogany. Each standard room—with honey-color rugs, floral prints, and light woods—has a two-line phone, a coffeemaker, and a hair dryer. Spacious suites also have sitting rooms and extra TVs. On the ninth floor you'll find a small patio pool and whirlpool bath; the seventh-floor concierge level provides hassle-free check-ins, Continental breakfasts, and evening hors d'oeuvres. ⊠ *100 Calle Brumbaugh, Old San Juan 00901,* ☎ *787/721–5100 or 800/996–3426,* ℻ *787/721–1111,* ⓦⓔⓑ *www.wyndham.com. 185 rooms, 55 suites. Restaurant, 2 bars, air-conditioning, in-room data ports, in-room safes, cable TV, some minibars, no-smoking floors, room service, pool, hot tub, massage, gym, casino, dry cleaning, laundry service, concierge floor, business services, travel services, meeting rooms, parking (fee). AE, D, DC, MC, V. CP, EP.*

$$–$$$$ 🏨 **Gallery Inn.** Jan D'Esopo and Manuco Gandia transformed this rambling colonial house into an inn that's full of comforts and quirky details: winding, uneven stairs; a music room with a Steinway grand piano; courtyard gardens, where Jan's pet macaws and cockatoos hang out. Each room has a look all its own; several have whirlpool baths. From the rooftop deck there's a spectacular view of the forts and the Atlantic. The first-floor Galería San Juan displays artwork by Jan and others. There's no restaurant, but meals for groups can be prepared upon request. ⊠ *204–206 Calle Norzagaray, Old San Juan 00901,* ☎ *787/ 722–1808,* ℻ *787/724–7360,* ⓦⓔⓑ *www.thegalleryinn.com. 13 rooms, 10 suites. Dining room, air-conditioning, no-smoking rooms, some refrigerators, piano; no room TVs. AE, DC, MC, V. CP.*

$$ 🏨 **Hotel Milano.** This clean, affordable hotel is just steps from the old city's plazas, shops, and museums. Caribbean floral prints fill the guest rooms, many of which have two double beds. In Old San Juan noise is a way of life; for less clamor, opt for a room at the back. The rooftop restaurant, Panorama, provides expansive views of the city and the pier. ⊠ *307 Calle Fortaleza, Old San Juan 00901,* ☎ *787/729–9050 or 877/ 729–9050,* ℻ *787/722–3379,* ⓦⓔⓑ *home.coqui.net/hmilano. 30 rooms. Restaurant, bar, air-conditioning, cable TV, no-smoking rooms, some refrigerators. AE, MC, V. CP.*

$–$$ 🏨 **Caleta Guesthouse.** In a quiet area overlooking the Bahía de San Juan, this guest house gives you the sense of what it would be like to live in Old San Juan. Narrow stairs and hallways lead to the seven studios, each of which has its own character and can accommodate up to four people. Some suites have balconies; all have phones with answering machines. Returning guests often request the Sunshine Studio, with its warm light and outstanding views. Although proprietor Michael Giessler usually requires a two-night minimum stay, he can arrange daily rates with a month's notice. ⊠ *11 Caleta de las Monjas, Old San Juan 00901,* ☎ *787/725–5347,* ℻ *787/977–5642,* ⓦⓔⓑ *www.thecaleta.com. 7 rooms. Some air-conditioning, fans, cable TV in some rooms, kitchenettes, coin laundry, dry cleaning; no smoking. AE, MC, V. EP.*

San Juan

$$$$ 🏨 **Caribe Hilton San Juan.** In time for the new millennium, many amenities at the Caribe Hilton were refreshed so that you would be, too. The beach, the only private one in San Juan, has been expanded. The open-air lobby's sunken bar looks out over the gentle cascades of a tri-level pool, which is now adjacent to a wading pool and an area with whirlpool tubs. Rooms have ocean or lagoon views, and those on the executive floor include such services as private check-in and check-out and free Continental breakfasts and evening cocktails. Local businesspeople often frequent the on-site Morton's of Chicago restaurant. ✉ *Calle Los Rosales, San Gerónimo Grounds, Puerta de Tierra, 00901,* ☎ *787/721–0303 or 800/468–8585,* FAX *787/725–8849,* WEB *www.caribehilton.com. 602 rooms, 44 suites. 6 restaurants, bar, air-conditioning, in-room safes, cable TV, minibars, no-smoking floors, room service, pool, wading pool, hair salon, outdoor hot tub, massage, sauna, spa, steam room, 3 tennis courts, health club, beach, shops, children's programs, dry cleaning, laundry service, concierge, business services, meeting rooms, parking (fee). AE, D, DC, MC, V. CP, EP, MAP.*

$$$$ 🏨 **Condado Plaza Hotel and Casino.** The Atlantic and the Laguna del Condado border this high-rise, whose two wings—fittingly named Ocean and Lagoon—are connected by an enclosed, elevated walkway. Standard rooms have walk-in closets and dressing areas. There's a variety of suites, including those with oversize hot tubs. A stay on the Plaza Club floor entitles you to 24-hour concierge service, use of a private lounge, and complimentary Continental breakfasts and refreshments all day. Find your own place in the sun on the beach or beside one of four pools. Dining options include the poolside Tony Roma's as well as Max's Grill, which is open 24 hours. ✉ *999 Av. Ashford, Condado 00902,* ☎ *787/721–1000 or 800/468–8588; 800/624–0420 direct to hotel,* FAX *787/722–7955,* WEB *condadoplaza.com. 570 rooms, 62 suites. 7 restaurants, 2 bars, 2 lounges, air-conditioning, in-room data ports, in-room safes, some in-room hot tubs, cable TV, in-room VCRs, minibars, no-smoking rooms, room service, 3 pools, wading pool, 3 hot tubs, 2 tennis courts, health club, beach, dock, boating, casino, children's programs, dry cleaning, laundry service, concierge, concierge floor, business services, airport shuttle, parking (fee). AE, D, DC, MC, V. CP, EP, MAP.*

$$$$ 🏨 **Embassy Suites San Juan Hotel & Casino.** As the name implies, the guest quarters here are suites, and all have such amenities as irons and two-line phones with voice mail and call waiting. There are many plants throughout, and the hallways and glass elevators face an indoor garden. In the lobby, a pond and its waterfall help to buffer the sounds from the casino. Thanks to a location near Isla Verde Beach and a mere mile from the airport, the hotel is popular with people traveling for either business or pleasure. There's no business center, but the front desk allows guests to use a copier and a computer that has free Internet access. ✉ *8000 Calle Tartak, Isla Verde 00979,* ☎ *787/791–0505 or 800/ EMBASSY,* FAX *787/791–7776,* WEB *www.embassysuitessanjuan.com. 300 suites. 2 restaurants, bar, air-conditioning, in-room data ports, in-room safes, cable TV with video games, minibars, microwaves, no-smoking floors, refrigerators, room service, pool, hot tub, health club, shop, coin laundry, dry cleaning, laundry service, meeting rooms, travel services, parking (fee). AE, D, DC, MC, V. BP.*

$$$$ 🏨 **Inter-Continental San Juan Resort & Casino.** The spacious rooms in this 16-story hotel have pleasant views of the ocean, the San José Lagoon, or the city; suites overlook the pool. The jangling casino is just off the lobby, and on-site restaurants include the poolside Restaurant Ciao Mediterraneo; Ruth's Chris Steak House; and the Grand Market Café, with deli favorites you can eat on the spot or have packed up for a picnic on the beach. ✉ *187 Av. Isla Verde, Isla Verde 00914,* ☎ *787/791–6100 or 800/443–2009,* FAX *787/253–2510,* WEB *www.interconti.com. 381 rooms, 19 suites. 6 restaurants, 3 bars, air-conditioning, in-room safes, no-smoking rooms, pool, hot tub, spa, gym, beach, boating, shops, casino, nightclub, concierge, business services, meeting rooms. AE, D, MC, V. EP.*

$$$$ ☐ **Ritz-Carlton San Juan Hotel, Spa & Casino.** The Ritz's signature elegance won't undermine the feeling that this is a true beach getaway. The hotel's sandy stretch is lovely, as is the cruciform pool, which is surrounded by a garden overlooking the ocean. Works by Latin American artists adorn the lobby lounge and the hallways leading to the well-equipped business center. Rooms have a mix of traditional wooden furnishings and wicker pieces upholstered in soft greens. A full-service spa begs to pamper you with aloe body wraps and *parcha* (passion-fruit juice) massages. Though most room windows are sealed shut to muffle airport noise, many suites open onto terraces. ☒ *6961 Av. Los Gobernadores, Isla Verde 00979,* ☏ *787/253–1700 or 800/241–3333,* FAX *787/253–0700,* WEB *www.ritzcarlton.com. 403 rooms, 11 suites. 3 restaurants, 3 bars, sushi bar, air-conditioning, in-room data ports, cable TV, minibars, no-smoking floor, room service, pool, hair salon, hot tub, massage, sauna, spa, 2 tennis courts, aerobics, gym, casino, nightclub, baby-sitting, children's programs, dry cleaning, laundry service, concierge, concierge floor, business services, meeting rooms, parking (fee). AE, D, DC, MC, V. EP.*

$$$$ ☐ **San Juan Marriott Resort and Stellaris Casino.** The red neon sign atop the Marriott seems like a beacon, beckoning you to beautiful Condado beach. The hotel's soundproofed rooms have soothing pastel carpets, floral spreads, and attractive tropical art; balconies overlook the ocean, the pool, or both. Restaurants include the Tuscany, for northern Italian cuisine, and the casual La Vista, which is open 24 hours. On weekends, there's live entertainment in the enormous lobby, which, combined with the ringing of slot machines from the adjoining casino, makes the area noisy. A large pool area and a gorgeous beach are right outside. ☒ *1309 Av. Ashford, Condado 00907,* ☏ *787/722–7000 or 800/228–9290,* FAX *787/722–6800,* WEB *www.marriott.com. 512 rooms, 17 suites. 3 restaurants, 2 lounges, air-conditioning, in-room data ports, in-room safes, cable TV, minibars, no-smoking rooms, room service, pool, hair salon, hot tub, 2 tennis courts, health club, beach, casino, children's programs, dry cleaning, laundry service, concierge floor, business services, meeting rooms, travel services, parking (fee). AE, D, DC, MC, V. EP, FAP, MAP.*

$$$$ ☐ **The Water Club.** Every inch of this boutique hotel will soothe you.
★ Aromatherapy scents waft through corridors, candles light your way, and water runs inside the glass walls of elevators that glow with blue neon. They seem the proper ride for trips to the rooftop pool or to the rooms, all of which have ocean views and such contemporary amenities as CD players. Four suites are equipped with telescopes for stargazing or people-watching along Isla Verde beach. The Tangerine Restaurant is sensuous; and water is again a literal and a decorative element in the lobby's Liquid lounge and the rooftop's Wet bar. ☒ *2 Calle Tartak, Isla Verde 00979,* ☏ *787/728–3666 or 888/265–6699,* FAX *787/ 728–3610,* WEB *www.waterclubsanjuan.com. 84 rooms. Restaurant, 2 bars, air-conditioning, in-room data ports, in-room safes, cable TV, in-room VCRs, minibars, no-smoking floors, room service, pool, hot tub, massage, gym, beach, Internet, dry cleaning, laundry service, concierge, parking (fee). AE, D, DC, MC, V. EP.*

$$$$ ☐ **Wyndham El San Juan Hotel & Casino.** An immense antique chan-
★ delier illuminates the hand-carved mahogany paneling, Italian rose marble, and 250-year-old French tapestries in the huge lobby of this resort on the Isla Verde beach. You'll be hard pressed to decide whether you want a main tower suite with a whirlpool bath and a wet bar; a garden room with a whirlpool bath and a patio; or a casita with a sunken Roman bath. All guest quarters have such amenities as walk-in closets, irons, and CD players. Relax at the lobby's Cigar Bar or take dinner at the Ranch, a rooftop country-western bar and grill. ☒ *6063 Av.*

Isla Verde, Isla Verde 00902, ☎ 787/791–1000, 800/468–2818, or 800/ 996–3426, ⒻⒶⓍ 787/791–0390, ⓌⒺⒷ www.wyndham.com. 332 rooms, 57 suites. 8 restaurants, 14 bars, air-conditioning, in-room data ports, in-room safes, cable TV, in-room VCRs, minibars, no-smoking rooms, room service, 2 pools, wading pool, 5 hot tubs, 3 tennis courts, health club, beach, shops, casino, nightclub, children's programs, dry cleaning, laundry service, concierge, business services, meeting rooms, travel services, parking (fee). AE, DC, MC, V. EP, MAP.

$$$–$$$$ 🏨 **Radisson Ambassador Plaza Hotel & Casino.** The many on-site facilities and the location within walking distance of the beach are the draws here. Rooms and suites have such amenities as hair dryers and coffeemakers; some suites have microwaves. Business travelers often stay on the Ambassador Club floor, where the Continental breakfasts are free, and there's access to a rooftop lounge with a TV, a pool table, and complimentary snacks. The casino's energy seems to spill out into—if not overrun—the lobby. The second-floor restaurants, Café Mezzanine and La Scala, offer respite from the casino noise. ✉ *1369 Av. Ashford, Condado 00907, ☎ 787/721–7300 or 800/468–8512, ⒻⒶⓍ 787/723– 6151, ⓌⒺⒷ www.radisson.com/sanjuanpr_ambassador. 148 rooms, 88 suites. 2 restaurants, 2 bars, air-conditioning, in-room data ports, in-room safes, cable TV with movies, in-room VCRs, some minibars, no-smoking floors, room service, pool, hair salon, hot tubs, gym, casino, coin laundry, dry cleaning, laundry service, concierge, business services, travel services, meeting rooms, parking (fee). AE, MC, V. CP.*

$$–$$$$ 🏨 **Tu Casa.** *"Mi casa es su casa"* ("My house is your house") is the motto at this white-adobe lodging in a residential area just steps from Ocean Park beach. Proprietor Nancy Hernández has tastefully combined two houses to create rooms with kitchenettes and suites with full kitchens, living rooms, and dining areas. White-wicker furniture lends serenity, and gingham fabrics add touches of cheer. Common spaces, including a pool and bar area and plant-shaded patios, make it easy to unwind. At this writing, work was underway to expand to a third neighboring house and to add facilities to a fourth property across the street. ✉ *2071 Calle Cacique, Ocean Park 00911, ☎ 787/727–5100, ⒻⒶⓍ 787/982–3349, ⓌⒺⒷ www.tucasaguest.com. 20 rooms, 2 suites. Restaurant, bar, air-conditioning, some kitchenettes, some kitchens, no-smoking rooms, pool, beach. AE, MC, V. CP.*

$$–$$$ 🏨 **Hampton Inn & Suites San Juan Resort.** The Hampton Inn has a convenient location, a well-trained staff, and many facilities—all this, and rooms are almost half the price of those at luxury establishments. The hotel is within walking distance of Isla Verde beach and about a mile from the airport. Rooms count coffeemakers and irons among their amenities. The business center is open 24 hours, and free coffee and tea are available in the lobby around the clock as well. The Guacamayo Pool Bar & Grill has a basic menu of hamburgers, fries, and the like. ✉ *6530 Av. Isla Verde, Isla Verde 00979, ☎ 787/791–8777 or 800/HAMPTON, ⒻⒶⓍ 787/791–8757, ⓌⒺⒷ www.hamptoninn.com. 147 rooms, 54 suites. Restaurant, bar, air-conditioning, in-room data ports, in-room safes, some microwaves, cable TV, no-smoking floors, refrigerators, pool, gym, coin laundry, business services, meeting rooms, car rental, parking (fee). AE, MC, V. CP.*

$$–$$$ 🏨 **Howard Johnson Hotel.** Directly across from the access point to Isla Verde beach, this Howard Johnson seems more of a boutique hotel than a member of a franchise. Natural light fills the lobby, reflecting off the polished wood and marble and highlighting the colorful, Mexican-print upholstery. The on-site HoJo's restaurant not only serves that super-premium ice cream you remember from when you were a kid but also a surprising variety of international and Puerto Rican specialties. For finer dining accompanied by a panoramic view head to the rooftop

Fontana Di Roma restaurant. ✉ *4820 Isla Verde Av., Isla Verde 00979,* ☎ *787/728–1300,* 𝔽𝔸𝕏 *787/727–7150. 115 rooms. 2 restaurants, bar, air-conditioning, in-room data ports, cable TV, some microwaves, no-smoking floor, pool, gym, beach. AE, MC, V. EP.*

$$–$$$ 🏨 **Numero Uno.** Former New Yorker Esther Feliciano bought this three-story, red-roof guest house, spruced it up, and made it a very pleasant place to stay. It's in a quiet residential area, and its rooms are simple and clean; three have ocean views. Two apartments come with kitchenettes. A walled-in patio provides privacy for sunning or hanging out by the small pool, the bar, and Pamela's restaurant. Beyond the wall, the wide, sandy beach beckons; if you're a guest here you're provided with beach chairs and towels. ✉ *1 Calle Santa Ana, Ocean Park 00911,* ☎ *787/726–5010,* 𝔽𝔸𝕏 *787/727–5482. 11 rooms, 2 apartments. Restaurant, bar, air-conditioning, fans, pool, beach. AE, MC, V. CP.*

$$–$$$ 🏨 **Park Plaza Normandie.** One of the Caribbean's finest examples of art-deco architecture, this white and blue hotel hosted high-society types back in the 1930s. The couple who owned it was both glamorous and eccentric: the wife had a penchant for diving from the second floor into a central pool (now gone). Although the hotel doesn't have quite the same aura today, its French windows and doors, columns with Egyptian motifs, and other period details have been painstakenly restored. Guest rooms have mahogany beds; a stay in a room on the corporate floor gets you free Continental breakfast as well as access to business services and a private lounge. ✉ *Av. Muñoz Rivera at Parque de Tercer Milenio, Puerta de Tierra 00902,* ☎ *787/729–2929, 877/987–2929, or 800/44–UTELL,* 𝔽𝔸𝕏 *787/729–3083,* 𝕎𝔼𝔹 *www.normandiepr. com. 65 rooms, 118 suites. Restaurant, 2 bars, air-conditioning, cable TV, no-smoking floor, pool, hair salon, gym, beach, shop, baby-sitting, coin laundry, laundry service, business services, meeting rooms. AE, MC, V. CP, EP.*

$$ 🏨 **El Canario by the Sea.** This three-story, hunter-green hotel, wedged between blocky condo complexes, is near the beach, which is its main attraction. That said, the water fronting the property is too dangerous for swimming, but it's not far to a swath of sand with calmer waves. Rooms are comfortable (most of the furniture even matches) and have either two twin beds or one double. A simple Continental breakfast of fruit punch, coffee, and pastries is served in a small, enclosed patio. ✉ *4 Av. Condado, Condado 00907,* ☎ *787/722–8640 or 800/742–4276,* 𝔽𝔸𝕏 *787/725–4921,* 𝕎𝔼𝔹 *www.canariohotels.com. 25 rooms. Breakfast room, air-conditioning, cable TV, no-smoking rooms. AE, DC, MC, V. CP.*

$$ 🏨 **El Consulado.** On Condado's main drag, a couple of blocks from the sea, is this white, colonial-style building with a terra-cotta roof. It once housed the Spanish consulate; today it's a sedate, no-frills lodging, whose clean, comfortable guest quarters have dark-wood furnishings, paneling, and trim. Some rooms have small refrigerators; all have one queen or two double beds. Continental breakfast is served on a small brick patio beside the hotel, and numerous eateries are within walking distance. ✉ *1110 Av. Ashford, Condado 00907,* ☎ *787/289–9191 or 888/300–8002,* 𝔽𝔸𝕏 *787/723–8665,* 𝕎𝔼𝔹 *www.ihppr.com. 29 rooms. Air-conditioning, cable TV, some refrigerators. AE, D, DC, MC, V. CP.*

$$ 🏨 **Hotel La Playa.** Small, unassuming, and almost hidden, Hotel La Playa sits over the glistening green waters of Isla Verde beach. It bills itself as a quiet, gentle retreat and lives up to this claim. Throughout floors are tiled and clean. Rooms are simple, each with a single and a double bed or one double; those on the upper floors have water views. A plant-filled courtyard leads to a small bar; the restaurant, which is on a deck over the water, is famous for its burgers. ✉ *6 Calle Amap-*

ola, Isla Verde 00979, ☎ 787/791–1115 or 800/791–9626, FAX 787/791–4650, WEB *www.hotellaplaya.com. 15 rooms. Restaurant, bar, air-conditioning, cable TV, beach, free parking. AE, MC, V. CP.*

$–$$ ☐ **At Wind Chimes Inn.** So much about this villa invites you to relax: the spacious guest rooms, the patios shaded by bougainvillea and royal palms, the terra-cotta sundecks, the open terrace that's the perfect place to read, and the small pool with a built-in whirlpool bath. And there's the soft, ever-present jingling of wind chimes, reminding you that Condado beach and its sea breezes are just a block away. The Boat Bar, which is open only to guests, serves a light menu from 7 AM to 11 PM, and the staff is friendly and knowledgeable. ⊠ *1750 Av. McLeary, Condado 00911,* ☎ *787/727–4153 or 800/946–3244,* FAX *787/728–0671,* WEB *www.atwindchimesinn.com. 17 rooms, 5 suites. Bar, air-conditioning, pool, cable TV, some kitchenettes, no-smoking rooms, parking (fee). AE, D, MC, V. EP.*

$–$$ ☐ **Casa del Caribe.** Tucked discreetly off Ashford Avenue, just steps from the beach behind the Condado Marriott, this quiet guest house attracts sun-seekers—though restaurants, casinos, and shops are all nearby as well. The wraparound veranda is the perfect place for a siesta, accompanied by birdsong and the trickling of a fountain. Sarongs and beachwear are for sale at the front desk, and the hospitable staff will help you arrange island tours. Monthly rates are available. ⊠ *57 Calle Caribe, Condado 00907,* ☎ *787/722–7139 or 877/722–7139,* FAX *787/723–2575. 12 rooms, 1 suite. Air-conditioning, cable TV, some kitchenettes, no-smoking rooms, parking (fee), some pets allowed (fee). AE, D, MC, V. CP.*

$–$$ ☐ **L'Habitation Beach Guest House.** Alain Tasca—who is from Paris by way of Guadeloupe and Key West—has created a very relaxed and oh-so-French ambience at this guest house, which has a primarily gay clientele. Rooms are simple and comfortable; numbers 8 and 9 are the largest and have ocean views. A combined bar–snack bar sits in the corner of a palm-shaded patio between the guest house and the sands of Ocean Park. Beach chairs and towels are provided: get your gear together before having one of Alain's margaritas, which will knock your sandals off. ⊠ *1957 Calle Italia, Ocean Park 00911,* ☎ *787/727–2499,* FAX *787/727–2599. 10 rooms. Bar, snack bar, air-conditioning, fans, beach, free parking. AE, D, MC, V. CP.*

$–$$ ☐ **Hostería del Mar.** Condado's high-rises are far to the west of this
★ small, white inn on the beach in Ocean Park. Rooms are attractive and simple, with tropical prints and rattan furniture. Many rooms have ocean views, and four apartments have kitchenettes. The staff is courteous and helpful, and the ground-floor restaurant, which serves many vegetarian dishes as well as seafood and steaks, faces the trade winds and has fabulous beach views. ⊠ *1 Calle Tapia, Ocean Park 00911,* ☎ *787/727–3302 or 800/742–4276,* FAX *787/268–0772,* WEB *www.prhtasmallhotels.com. 8 rooms, 4 apartments, 1 suite. Restaurant, air-conditioning, some kitchenettes, beach, free parking; no smoking. AE, D, DC, MC, V. EP.*

$–$$ ☐ **Hotel Olimpo Court.** Personal attention is key at this quiet, family run hotel. It's something that owner Alexandra Rodríguez learned from her grandmother, and it has rewarded her with many repeat guests. Daily, weekly, and monthly rates are available for the single and double rooms, all of which are impeccably neat. Some have kitchenettes and small private balconies. You can take in ocean views from the sundeck, catch a flick at the nearby fine-arts movie theater, or wander over to the Laguna del Condado. The on-site restaurant, Chayote, is one of the city's best and most creative. ⊠ *603 Miramar Av., Miramar 00907,* ☎ *787/724–0600,* FAX *787/977–0655. 45 rooms. Restaurant, air-conditioning, cable TV, kitchenettes, no-smoking floors, free parking. AE, MC, V. EP.*

NIGHTLIFE AND THE ARTS

Several publications will tell you what's happening. *Qué Pasa,* the official visitor's guide, has current listings of events in the city and out on the island. For more up-to-the-minute information, pick up a copy of the English-language *San Juan Star,* the island's oldest daily. The Thursday edition's weekend section is especially useful. *Bienvenidos* and *Places,* both published by the Puerto Rico Hotel and Tourism Association, are also helpful. The English-language *San Juan City Magazine* has extensive calendars as well as restaurant reviews and cultural articles. The "Wikén" section of the Spanish-language newspaper *El Nuevo Dia* gives a weekly rundown that's also available on its Web site, www.endi.com.

Nightlife

From Thursday through Sunday, it's as if there's a celebration going on nearly everywhere in San Juan. Dress to party, particularly on Friday and Saturday nights. Puerto Ricans have flair, and both men and women love getting dressed up to go out. Bars are usually casual, but if you have on jeans, sneakers, and a T-shirt, you may be refused entry at nightclubs and discos.

Well-dressed visitors and locals alike often mingle in the lobby bars of large hotels, many of which have bands in the evening. Some hotels also have clubs with shows and/or dancing; admission starts at $10. Casino rules have been relaxed in recent years, injecting life into what was once a conservative hotel gaming scene. There are more games as well as such gambling perks as free drinks and live music.

In Old San Juan Calle San Sebastián is lined with bars and restaurants. Salsa music blaring from jukeboxes in cut-rate pool halls competes with mellow Latin jazz in top-flight night spots. The young and the beautiful often socialize in Plaza San José, and late January sees the Fiestas de la Calle San Sebastián, one of the Caribbean's best street parties.

Young professionals as well as a slightly older bohemian crowd fill Santurce, San Juan's historical downtown area, until the wee hours. The revitalized Plaza del Mercado (off Calle Canals between Ponce de León and Baldorioty de Castro) has structures—many painted in bright colors—dating from the 1930s or earlier. On weekend nights, the area's streets are closed to vehicular traffic. You can wander around with drinks, which are served in plastic cups, and sway to music that pours from countless open-air establishments and the marketplace's front plaza.

Bars

Atlantic Beach. The oceanfront deck bar of this hotel is famed for its early evening happy hours popular with the alternative-lifestyle crowd. But the pulsating tropical music, the wide selection of exotic drinks, and the ever-pleasant ocean breeze make it a hit regardless of sexual orientation. Good food is also served on deck. ⊠ *1 Calle Vendig, Condado,* ☎ *787/721–6100.*

El Batey. This wildly popular hole-in-the-wall bar, run by crusty New Yorker Davydd Gwilym Jones III, is like a military bunker. Pick up a pool cue for a game or grab a marker to add your own message to the graffiti-covered walls. The ceiling may leak, but the jukebox has the best selection of oldies in town. ⊠ *101 Calle Cristo, Old San Juan,* ☎ *787/725–1787.*

Borinquen Brewing Company. Behind glass at the back, sleek metal vats hold this microbrewery's lagers and stouts. The taps sprouting from the wooden bar are a rarity in Puerto Rico, where draft beer is virtually nonexistent. The music is good, and there's often sports on TV. The island art on the walls reaffirms that you're in the Caribbean and not a mainland suburb. ⊠ *4800 Av. Isla Verde, Isla Verde,* ☎ *787/268–1900. Closed Mon.*

Cigar Bar. The lobby bar of the Wyndham El San Juan Hotel & Casino, with its dark-wood interior and huge chandelier, is both lively and classy. Power brokers often indulge in fine smokes while mingling with local starlets and smartly attired visitors. ⊠ *6063 Av. Isla Verde, Isla Verde,* ☎ *787/791–1000.*

Liquid. In the lobby lounge of the Water Club hotel, glass walls filled with undulating water surround fashionable patrons seated on stools that seem carved from gigantic, pale seashells. If the wild drinks and pounding music are too much, head up to Wet, a romantic space on the penthouse floor. Relax at the bar or on a plush sitting-area chair, listen to R&B, and enjoy sushi under the stars. ⊠ *2 Calle Tartak, Isla Verde,* ☎ *787/725–4664 or 787/725–4675.*

Casinos

By law, all casinos are in hotels, and the government keeps a close eye on them. They're allowed to operate noon–4 AM, but within those parameters individual casinos set their own hours. In addition to slot machines, typical games include blackjack, roulette, craps, Caribbean stud poker (a five-card stud game), and *pai gow* poker (a combination of American poker and the ancient Chinese game of pai gow, which employs cards and dice). Dress for the larger casinos tends to be on the formal side, and the atmosphere is refined. That said, an easing of gaming regulations has set a more relaxed tone and made such perks as free drinks and live music more common. The range of available games has also greatly expanded. The minimum age is 18.

Condado Plaza Hotel and Casino. With its tentlike chandeliers and whirring slots, the Condado is popular with locals. A band performs at one on-site bar, and the TV is tuned into sports at another. ⊠ *999 Av. Ashford, Condado,* ☎ *787/721–1000.*

Inter-Continental San Juan Resort & Casino. You may feel as if you're in Las Vegas here, perhaps because this property was once a Sands. A torch singer warms up the crowd at a lounge-bar just outside the gaming room. Inside, a garish chandelier, dripping with strands of orange lights, runs the length of a mirrored ceiling. ⊠ *187 Av. Isla Verde, Isla Verde,* ☎ *787/791–6100.*

Ritz-Carlton San Juan Hotel, Spa & Casino. With its golden columns, turquoise and bronze walls, and muted lighting, the Ritz casino is refined by day or night. There's lots of activity, yet everything is hushed. ⊠ *Av. Las Gobernadores, Isla Verde,* ☎ *787/253–1700.*

San Juan Marriott Resort and Stellaris Casino. The crowd is casual, and the decor is tropical and bubbly at this spacious gaming room. A huge bar, in which a Latin-music act usually performs, and an adjacent café are right outside. ⊠ *1309 Av. Ashford, Condado,* ☎ *787/722–7000.*

Wyndham El San Juan Hotel & Casino. Slow-turning ceiling fans hang from a carved-wood ceiling, and neither the clangs of the slots nor the sounds of the salsa band disrupt the semblance of Old World. The polish continues in the adjacent lobby, with its huge chandelier, dark woods, and fine cigar bar. ⊠ *6063 Av. Isla Verde, Isla Verde,* ☎ *787/791–1000.*

Wyndham Old San Juan Hotel & Casino. It's hard to escape this ground-floor casino, the only place to gamble in Old San Juan. You can see it from the hotel's main stairway, from the balcony above, and from the lobby lounge. Light bounces off the Bahía de San Juan and pours through its many windows; passengers bound off their cruise ships and pour through its many glass doors. ⊠ *101 Calle Calle Brumbaugh, Old San Juan,* ☎ *787/721–5100.*

Dance Clubs

Asylum. San Juan's progressive youths favor this cavernous club, a warehouselike structure that's painted black on the outside and is almost as dark within. They come for the drum-and-bass, trance, rap, and electronic music. Performances are often live Thursday through Sunday. ⊠ *1420 Av. Ponce de León, Santurce,* ☎ *787/723–3416.*

Babylon. A long line of well-heeled patrons usually runs out the door of the club at the Wyndham El San Juan Hotel & Casino. Those with the staying power to make it inside step out of the Caribbean and into the ancient Middle East. Those who tire of waiting often head to El Chico Lounge, a small room with live entertainment right off the hotel lobby. ⊠ *6063 Av. Isla Verde, Isla Verde,* ☎ *787/791–1000.*

Club Lazer. This multilevel club has spots for quiet conversation, spaces for dancing to loud music, and a landscaped roof deck overlooking San Juan. The crowd is different every night; Saturday is ladies' night. ⊠ *251 Calle Cruz, Old San Juan,* ☎ *787/725–7581.*

Eros. The music is terrific at this club, which is popular with the gay community but is just as welcoming to heterosexuals. The lighting is dim, the dance floor is large, and the balcony bar overlooks all the drama. Most of the time DJs entertain, but bands have been known to perform here. ⊠ *1257 Av. Ponce de León, Santurce,* ☎ *787/722–1390.*

Martini's. An older, dressy crowd frequents this dance club—a one-time conference room—in the Inter-Continental hotel. It's known for its Las Vegas–style reviews; acts have included celebrity impersonators and flamenco music and dance troupes. Record parties and fashion shows are also held here from time to time. ⊠ *187 Av. Isla Verde, Isla Verde,* ☎ *787/791–6100 Ext. 356.*

Stanley's e-Net Club. The latest offering of a veteran San Juan disco owner gleams like a high-tech diner. Electronic music, rock, video-games, and Internet access are the draws. ⊠ *1515 Av. Ponce de León, Santurce,* ☎ *787/977–0770. Closed Mon.–Wed.*

The Stargate. This club is an established spot for dancing to either DJ selections or live music despite several name and theme changes. Right now, it's a space-age place. On Wednesday casual attire is the norm, but you better dress up to dance here Thursday through Saturday. There's a cigar bar upstairs. ⊠ *1 Av. Robert Todd, Santurce,* ☎ *787/725–4664 or 787/725–4675.*

Jazz Clubs

Café Bohemio. El Convento Hotel's streetside Latin restaurant turns into a live jazz club at 11 each night, when the kitchen closes. The music lasts 'til 2 AM; Thursday is the best night, with Latin jazz and crowds of pretty people who spill out onto a terrace. ⊠ *100 Calle Cristo, Old San Juan,* ☎ *787/723–9200.*

Unplugged Café. Near the Luis A. Ferré Performing Arts Center and the Puerto Rico Arts Museum, this club—opened by ex-members of Menudo, the Puerto Rican teen idol band of the '80s, and some local sports stars—has live jazz, rock, and blues. It's on the second floor of a restored art deco building and has balconies overlooking the action in downtown Santurce. ⊠ *365 Av. José de Diego, Santurce,* ☎ *787/723–1423. Closed Mon.*

Latin Music Clubs

El Balcón del Zumbador. A little off the beaten path, this venue has the city's best Afro-Caribbean music. Performers have included salsa great Roberto Roena, master percussionist Cachete Maldonado, and the legendary Cuban group Los Van Van. ⊠ *768 Av. Barbosa, Santurce,* ☎ *787/726–3082.*

La Fiesta Lounge. The lounge in the Condado Plaza Hotel and Casino sizzles with steamy Latin shows. An older crowd, many of them locals, frequently fills the long room, which has a wall of windows that open onto a handsome terrace overlooking the Atlantic. ⊠ *999 Av. Ashford, Condado,* ☎ *787/721–1000.*

Hijos de Borinquen. Famed artist Rafael Tufiño, who stops in once in a while and has a stool with his name on it, immortalized this beloved bar in one of his paintings. The audience often sings along with the Puerto Rican ballads; some people even play maracas, cow bells, or bongos. The pitch is fevered during Andrés Jiménez's revolutionary anthem "Despierta Borinquen." ⊠ *151 Calle San José, corner of Calle San Sebastián, Old San Juan,* ☎ *787/723–8126. Closed Mon.*

Nuyorican Café. There's something interesting happening here nearly every night, be it an early evening play, poetry reading, or talent show or a band playing Latin jazz, Cuban *son*, or Puerto Rican salsa later on. During breaks between performances the youthful, creative set converses in an alley outside the front door. ⊠ *312 Callejón de la Capellia, Old San Juan,* ☎ *787/977–1276. Closed Mon.*

Rumba. The air-conditioning blasts, works by local artists adorn the walls, and the crowd is hip. With a large dance and stage area and smokin' Afro-Cuban bands, it's one of the best parties in town. ⊠ *152 Calle San Sebastián, Old San Juan,* ☎ *787/725–4407.*

Night Bites

Carniceriáa Restaurant Díaz. Come here if you need a snack between dances. The *morcilla* sausage and roast pork go well with a drink. ⊠ *319 Calle Orbeta, Santurce,* ☎ *787/723–1903.*

Dunbar's. The crowd may be full of young professionals, but everyone is casual at this beachside bar. There's good food, sports on TV, a pool room, and live music Thursday through Saturday. ⊠ *1954 Calle McCleary, Ocean Park,* ☎ *787/728–2920.*

Hard Rock Café. Is it really a surprise to find a Hard Rock in Old San Juan? These days, they're almost as common as McDonald's. ⊠ *253 Recinto Sur, Old San Juan,* ☎ *787/724–7625.*

Krugger's. Old San Juan bar hoppers head to this fried-food emporium and adjacent bar when the late-night munchies hit. Codfish fritters, beef turnovers, crab and plantain rolls, and more are served until the wee hours. ⊠ *52 Calle San José, Old San Juan,* ☎ *787/723–2474. Closed Mon.*

Mango's Café. This Caribbean-style bar-restaurant near the beach has live jazz, Spanish pop, and reggae music every night that it's open. The menu has light, down-island fare. ⊠ *2421 Calle Laurel, Punta Las Marías,* ☎ *787/727–9328. Closed Sun.–Mon.*

El Patio de Sam. The clientele swears that this Old San Juan institution serves the island's best burgers. Potted plants and strategically placed canopies make the outdoor patio a fine place to eat in any weather. ⊠ *102 Calle San Sebastián, Old San Juan,* ☎ *787/723–1149.*

Restaurant Don Telfo. Photos of famous and not-so famous diners line the walls of this well-kept restaurant. You can head to the dining room for a sit-down meal or feast on the barbecued chicken, *pinchos* (pork kabobs), and *bacalaítos* (salt-cod fritters) that are served curbside. ⊠ *180 Calle Dos Hernmanos, Santurce,* ☎ *787/724–5752.*

The Arts

San Juan is the epicenter of Puerto Rico's lively arts scene, and on most nights there's likely to be a ballet, a play, or an art opening somewhere in town. Art galleries and museums abound throughout the city, particularly in Old San Juan. If you're in town on the first Tuesday of the month (September–December and February–May), take advantage of Old San Juan's **Gallery Night** (☎ 787/723–6286). Galleries and select museums open their doors after hours for viewings that are accompanied by refreshments and music. Afterward people head to bars and music clubs, and the area remains festive until well past midnight. The event is so popular that finding a parking space is difficult; it's best to take a cab.

Island Culture

LeLoLai (☎ 787/723–3135 weekdays; 787/791–1014 weekends and evenings) is a year-round festival that celebrates Puerto Rico's Indian, Spanish, and African heritage. Performances showcasing island music and folklore take place each week in different hotels. Because it's sponsored by the Puerto Rico Tourism Company and major San Juan hotels, passes to the festivities are included in some lodging packages. You can also purchase tickets to a weekly series of events for $15.

Performing Arts

Surrounded by lagoons and trees, the open-air **Amphiteatro Tito Puente** (✉ Luis Muñoz Marín Park, Hato Rey, ☎ 787/751–3353) is a great spot to hear hot Latin jazz, reggae, and Spanish pop music. It's named after the late, great musician who many credit with bringing salsa to the rest of the world. Shows usually take place Thursday through Sunday nights.

The **Centro de Bellas Artes Luis A. Ferré** (Luis A. Ferré Center for the Performing Arts; ✉ Av. José de Diego and Av. Ponce de León, Santurce, ☎ 787/725–7334) is the largest venue of its kind in the Caribbean. There's something going on nearly every night, from pop or jazz concerts to plays, opera, and ballet. It's also the home of the San Juan Symphony Orchestra. Luciano Pavoratti held his annual Operalia competition here in 1999, and Cuban musicians reunited as the Buena Vista Social Club played sold-out shows in 2000.

Named for Puerto Rican playwright Alejandro Tapia, **Teatro Tapia** (✉ La Fortaleza at Plaza Colón, Old San Juan, ☎ 787/722–0247) hosts theatrical and musical productions. Matinee performances with family entertainment are also held here, especially around the holidays.

OUTDOOR ACTIVITIES AND SPORTS

Many of San Juan's most enjoyable outdoor activities take place in and around the water. With miles of beach stretching across Isla Verde, Ocean Park, and Condado, there's a full range of water sports, including sailing, kayaking, windsurfing, kiteboarding, jet-skiing, deep-sea fishing, scuba diving, and snorkeling.

Options for land-based activities include tennis and walking or jogging at local parks. With a bit of effort—meaning a short drive out of the city—you'll find a world of championship golf courses and rainforest trails. Baseball is big in Puerto Rico, and the players are world class; many are recruited from local teams to play in the U.S. major leagues. The season runs October–February. Games are played in San Juan as well as other venues around the island.

Beaches

Balneario de Carolina. A government-maintained, gated beach, Balneario de Carolina is about 10 km (6 mi) east of Isla Verde on Avenida

Los Gobernadores (Route 187) and so close to the airport that the leaves rustle when planes take off. Its long stretch of sand is shaded by palms and almond trees and edged by surf that's often rough. There's plenty of room to spread out, though, and lots of amenities: lifeguards, bath-houses, picnic gazebos with tables and barbecue grills. The gates are open daily 8 AM–4:30 PM, and although there's plenty of parking ($2), city buses—including the B-40, which travels from Isla Verde and Río Piedras—stop here.

Balneario Escambrón. Just off Avenida Muñoz Rivera on the Puerta de Tierra stretch at the entrance to Old San Juan is the Parque de Ter-cer Milenio. In it you'll find the Balneario Escambrón, a patch of honey-color beach with shade provided by coconut palms and surf that's generally gentle. There are also lifeguards, showers, bathrooms, and restaurants. The park is open daily 7–7, and parking is $3. City buses A-9 and B-8 will drop you relatively close to this beach.

Playa del Condado. West of Old San Juan and east of Ocean Park and Isla Verde, this long, wide beach is often full of guests from the hotels and resorts that tower over it. Beach bars, water-sports outfitters, and chair-rental places abound, but there are no lifeguards. You can access the beach from several roads off Avenida Ashford, including calles Vendin, Earl, and Court; if you're driving, on-street parking is your only option. Adjacent to the Condado Plaza Hotel and just off Avenida Ashford is Playita Condado (its sign says CONDADO PUBLIC BEACH). Rocks in the waters off this tiny beach temper the waves, making it a great place for families with young children. There are also a few shade trees and, despite the gentle surf, lifeguards.

NEED A
BREAK?

Of Condado's many beach bars, one of the best is the terrace at **Piu Bello Gelato** (⌖ 1302 Av. Ashford, Condado, ☏ 787/977–2121), across the street from the Marriott hotel. It serves wraps, foccaccia-bread sandwiches, salads, and—best of all—homemade gelato.

Playa de Isla Verde. There aren't any lifeguards, but the sands are white, and the snorkeling is good at this beach east of Ocean Park. Like Con-dado, Isla Verde is bordered by high-rise hotels and has plenty of places to rent beach chairs and water-sports equipment or grab a bite to eat. The best entrance is from the dead-end Calle José M. Tartak off Avenida Isla Verde. Some street parking is available.

Playa de Ocean Park. A residential neighborhood just east of Condado and west of Isla Verde, is home to this wide, 1½-km-long (1-mi-long) stretch of golden sand. The waters are often choppy but still swimmable—take care, however, as there aren't any lifeguards are on duty. It's popular with college students, particularly on weekends, and it's also one of the two city beaches preferred by the gay community. (The other is in front of the Atlantic Beach Hotel.) There are public rest rooms, a playground, and a small police station at Parque Bar-bosa on the south side of Calle Park Boulevard. To get here by car, take Calle McLeary to Calle Soldado Serrano and Calle Park Boulevard. Parking spots line the roads.

NEED A
BREAK?

Surfer Alex García owns **Pinky's** (⌖ 51 Calle María Moczo, Ocean Park, ☏ 787/727–3347), a lively Ocean Park beach stand that serves fresh, delicious fruit shakes as well as sandwiches and salads. If you're really lazy, this place takes phone orders and will send a scooter-driving delivery guy right to your patch of sand. Note that Pinky's is closed on Monday, the day Alex prays that the waves will be high.

Participant Sports

Biking

Most streets don't have bike lanes, and auto traffic makes bike travel somewhat risky; further, all the fumes can be hard to take. That said, recreational bikers are increasingly donning their safety gear and wheeling through the streets, albeit with great care.

As a visitor, your best bet is to look into a bike tour offered by an outfitter. One popular 45-minute trip travels from Old San Juan's cobblestone streets to Condado. It passes El Capitolio and runs through either Parque del Tercer Milenio (ocean side) or Parque Luis Muñoz Rivera, taking you past the Caribe Hilton Hotel and over Puente Dos Hermanos (Dos Hermanos Bridge) onto Avenida Ashford. The truly ambitious can continue east to Ocean Park, Isla Verde, and right on out of town to the eastern community of Piñones and its beachside bike path.

Adrenalina (⊠ 4770 Av. Isla Verde, Isla Verde, ☎ 787/727–1233, WEB www.adrenalinapr.com) rents bikes and helmets by the hour ($10), half-day ($15), and full day ($25). **Hot Dog Cycling** (⊠ 5916 Av. Isla Verde, Isla Verde, ☎ 787/982–5344, WEB www.hotdogcycling.com) rents Cannondale bicycles for $30 a day and organizes group excursions to El Yunque and other places out on the island.

Golf

Puerto Rico is the birthplace of golf legend and raconteur Chi Chi Rodriguez—and he had to hone his craft somewhere. The island has more than a dozen courses, including some of championship caliber. Several make good day trips from San Juan. Be sure to call ahead for details on reserving tee times; hours vary and several hotel courses allow only guests to play or give preference to them. Greens fees start at $25 and go as high as $115.

There are four attractive Robert Trent Jones–designed 18-hole courses shared by the **Hyatt Dorado Beach Resort and the Hyatt Regency Cerromar Beach** (⊠ Rte. 693, Km 10.8 and Km 11.8, Dorado, ☎ 787/796–1234 Ext. 3238 or 3016) 27 km (17 mi) west of town.

Developed on what was once a coconut plantation, the public, 18-hole course at the **Bahía Beach Plantation** (⊠ Rte. 187, Km 4.2, Río Grande, ☎ 787/256–5600) is an old-time favorite that skirts the coast 35 km (21 mi) east of San Juan. Nonmembers can golf at **Berwind Country Club** (⊠ Rte. 187, Km 4.7, Río Grande, ☎ 787/876–3056) on weekdays. The 18-hole course, which is 35 km (21 mi) east of San Juan, is known for its tight fairways. With El Yunque rain forest as a backdrop, the two courses at the **Westin Río Mar Beach Resort and Country Club** (⊠ 6000 Río Mar Blvd., Río Grande, ☎ 787/888–6000), 35 mi (21 km) east of San Juan, are truly inspirational.

Hiking

Thirteen hiking trails loop past giant ferns, exotic orchids, sibilant streams and waterfalls, and broad trees reaching for the sun at **El Yunque** (⊠ Centro de Información El Portal, Rte. 191, Km 4.3, off Rte. 3, ☎ 787/888–1880, WEB www.southernregion.fs.fed.us/caribbean), about an hour's drive east of San Juan. The park, which is officially known as the Bosque Nacional del Caribe (Caribbean National Forest), has several information centers, but the best one is the Centro de Información El Portal. It's open daily 9–5; admission is $5.

Eco Action Tours (⊠ Condado Plaza Hotel, 999 Av. Ashford, Laguna Wing, Condado, ☎ 787/791–7509 or 787/640–7385) organizes a variety of hikes and excursions throughout the island.

Tennis

If you'd like to use the tennis courts at a property where you aren't a guest, call in advance for information about reservations and fees. There are two tennis courts at the **Condado Plaza Hotel and Casino** (✉ 999 Av. Ashford, Condado, ☎ 787/721–1000). Fees for nonguests range from $10 to $20 per hour. The four lighted courts of the **Isla Verde Tennis Club** (✉ Calles Ema and Delta Rodriguez, Isla Verde, ☎ 787/ 727–6490) are open for nonmember use at $4 per hour, daily 8 AM– 10 PM. The **Parque Central Municipo de San Juan** (✉ Calle Cerra, exit on Rte. 2, Santurce, ☎ 787/722–1646) has 17 lighted courts. Fees are $3 per hour 8 AM–6 PM and $4 per hour 6 PM–10 PM.

Water Sports

Many of the resort hotels on the Condado and Isla Verde strips either have their own water-sports centers or can refer you to reputable, free-standing outfitters on the beach. These establishments often rent gear, give lessons, and arrange trips for several water sports, including boating, sailing, fishing, scuba diving, and snorkeling.

The Normandie Hotel's **Caribe Aquatic Adventures** (✉ Av. Muñoz Rivera at Parque del Tercer Milenio, Puerta de Tierra, ☎ 787/724–1882 or 787/281–8858) has fishing, boating, and sailing trips of all kinds. It also rents snorkeling equipment and organizes group snorkeling excursions. **Castillo Watersports** (✉ San Juan Marriott Resort and Stellaris Casino, 1309 Av. Ashford, Condado, ☎ 787/728–2297 or 787/ 725–7970) rents gear and arranges fishing, boating, and sailing excursions. **Eco Action Tours** (✉ Condado Plaza Hotel, 999 Av. Ashford, Laguna Wing, Condado, ☎ 787/791–7509 or 787/640–7385) rents kayaks, Sunfish, hydrobikes, and jet skis; gives windsurfing lessons; and offers kayaking trips to other parts of the island. Its dive master, Peter Zervigón, arranges beginning and advanced beach or boat dives.

A good bet for a variety of water sports is the Wyndham El San Juan's **San Juan Water Fun** (✉ Wyndham El San Juan Hotel and Casino, 6063 Av. Isla Verde, Isla Verde, ☎ 787/643–4510). **Sun Riders Watersports** (✉ 999 Av. Ashford, Condado, ☎ 787/721–1000 Ext. 2699), in the Condado Plaza Hotel and Casino, rents gear for several types of water sports.

BOATING AND SAILING

The waves can be strong and the surf choppy, but the constant wind makes for good sailing, windsurfing, or kiteboarding (maneuvering a surfboard using a parachute-like kite), particularly in Ocean Park and Punta Las Marías (between Ocean Park and Isla Verde). The Laguna del Condado is popular for kayaking, especially on weekends. You can simply paddle around it or head out under the Puente Dos Hermanos to the San Gerónimo fort right behind the Caribe Hilton and across from the Condado Plaza.

In general, you can rent a small Sunfish for about $30 an hour, a Windsurfer for about $25 an hour (including a lesson), and kayaks for $25–$35 an hour. Jet skis go for about $45–$65 per half-hour and Wave Runners for $65 per half-hour.

Las Tortugas Adventures (✉ Cond. La Puntilla, 4 Calle La Puntilla, Apt. D1-12, Old San Juan, ☎ 787/725–5169) organizes group kayaking trips to the Reserva Natural Las Cabezas de San Juan and the Bahía Mosquito in eastern Puerto Rico. In the same location as the Velauno windsurfing center, **Real Kiteboarding** (✉ 2430 Calle Loíza, Punta Las Marías, ☎ 787/728–8716, WEB www.realkiteboarding.com) is a full-service kiteboarding center that offers lessons. You'll get the best windsurfing advice and equipment from Jaime Torres at **Velauno** (✉ 2430 Calle Loíza,

Punta Las Marías, ☎ 787/728–8716, 𝖂𝖤𝖡 www.velauno.com), the second-largest, full-service windsurfing center in the United States. It has rentals, repair services, and classes. It also sells new and used gear and serves as clearinghouse for information on windsurfing events throughout the island.

FISHING

Puerto Rico's waters are home to large game fish such as marlin, snook, wahoo, dorado, tuna, and barracuda; as many as 30 world records for catches have been set off the island's shores. Prices for fishing expeditions vary, but they tend to include all your bait and tackle, as well as refreshments, and start at $450 (for a boat with as many as six people) for a half-day trip to $750 for a full day. Other boats charge by the person, starting at $150 for a full day.

Half-day, full-day, split-charter, and big- and small-game fishing can be arranged through **Benitez Deep-Sea Fishing** (⊠ Club Náutico de San Juan, Miramar, ☎ 787/723–2292).

SCUBA DIVING AND SNORKELING

The waters off San Juan aren't the best places to scuba dive, but several outfitters conduct short excursions to where tropical fish, coral, and sea horses are visible at depths of 30 ft to 60 ft. Escorted half-day dives range $45–$95 for one or two tanks, including all equipment; in general, double those prices for night dives. Packages that include lunch and other extras start at $100; those that include accommodations are also available.

Snorkeling excursions, which include transportation equipment rental, and sometimes lunch, start at $50. Equipment rents at beaches for about $5–$7. (Caution: coral-reef waters and mangrove areas can be dangerous. Unless you're an expert or have an experienced guide, stay near the water-sports centers of hotels and avoid unsupervised areas.)

Mundo Submarino (⊠ Laguna Garden Shopping Center, Av. Baldorioty de Castro, Carolina, ☎ 787/791–5764) sells and rents snorkeling and diving equipment. **Ocean Sports** (⊠ 1035 Av. Ashford, Condado, ☎ 787/723–8513, 𝖂𝖤𝖡 www.osdivers.com) offers certified scuba dives; airtank fill-ups; and equipment repairs, sales and rentals. It also rents surfboards by the day.

SURFING

Although the west-coast beaches are considered *the* places to surf in Puerto Rico, San Juan was actually the place where the sport got its start on the island. In 1958 legendary surfers Gary Hoyt and José Rodríguez Reyes began surfing at the beach in front of Bus Stop 2½, facing El Capitolio. Although this spot is known for its big waves, the conditions must be nearly perfect to surf here. Today, many surfers head to Puerta de Tierra and a spot known as La Ocho (in front of Bus Stop 8 behind the Dumas Restaurant). Another, called the Pressure Point, is behind the Caribe Hilton Hotel.

In Condado, you can surf La Punta, a reef break behind the Presbyterian Hospital, or the Sheraton, a break named after the hotel (it's now a Marriott) with either surf or boogie boards. In Isla Verde, white water on the horizon means that the waves are good at the beach break near the Ritz-Carlton known as Pine Grove. East of the city, in Piñones, the Caballo has deep-to-shallow-water shelf waves that require a big-wave board known as a "gun." The surf culture frowns upon aficionados who divulge the best spots to outsiders. If you're lucky, though, maybe you'll make a few friends who'll let you in on where to find the best waves.

At Ocean Park beach, famous surfer Carlos Cabrero, proprietor of **Tres Palmas** (✉ 1911 Av. McLeary, Ocean Park, ☎ 787/728–3377), rents boards (daily rates are $25 for short boards and $30 for long boards), repairs equipment, and sells all sorts of hip beach and surfing gear. Near the Caribe Hilton hotel, you can rent boards by the day at **Wave Rider** (✉ 51 Calle Muñoz Rivera, Local #8, Puerta de Tierra, ☎ 787/722–7103, WEB www.waveriderpr.com). A short board will cost you $25; long boards are $30.

Spectator Sports

Baseball

Does the name Roberto Clemente ring a bell? The late, great star of the Pittsburgh Pirates, who died in a 1972 plane crash delivering supplies to Nicaraguan earthquake victims, was born near San Juan and got his start in the Puerto Rican pro leagues. Many other Puerto Rican stars have played in the U.S. major leagues, including the brothers Roberto Alomar and Sandy Alomar Jr.; their father, Sandy Alomar; and Hall of Fame inductees Tony Perez and Orlando Cepeda. The island's season runs October–February. Stadiums are in San Juan (Estadio Hiram Bithorn), Santurce, Ponce, Caguas, Arecibo, and Mayagüez; the teams also play once or twice in Aguadilla. General admission seats run about $5; the most expensive box seats cost $6–$7. Contact the tourist office for details on baseball games or call **Professional Baseball of Puerto Rico** (☎ 787/765–6285).

Horse Racing

Thoroughbred races are run year-round at **Hípodromo El Comandante,** a racetrack about 20 minutes east of San Juan. On race days the dining rooms open at 12:30 PM. Post time is 2:15 or 2:45 (depending on the season) Wednesday and Friday through Monday. ✉ *Av. 65th Infantry (Rte. 3), Km 15.3, Canóvanas,* ☎ *787/724–6060,* WEB *www. comandantepr.com.* ☉ *Wed. and Fri.–Mon. 1–7.*

SHOPPING

In Old San Juan—especially on Calles Fortaleza and San Francisco— you'll find everything from T-shirt emporiums to selective crafts stores, bookshops, art galleries, jewelry boutiques, and even shops that specialize in made-to-order Panama hats. Calle Cristo is lined with factory-outlet stores, including those for Coach, Dooney & Bourke, Polo-Ralph Lauren, Guess, and Tommy Hilfiger.

All the old city's stores are within walking distance of each other, and trolleys are at your beck and call. On weekends, artisans sell their wares at stalls around El Paseo de la Princesa. Caveat emptor: bargains (and, often, peace) are hard to find in Old San Juan, which is one of the Caribbean's most popular cruise-ship stops.

With many stores selling luxury items and designer fashions, the shopping spirit in Condado is reminiscent of that in Miami. Avenida Condado is a good bet for souvenirs and curios as well as art and upscale jewelry or togs. Avenida Ashford is considered the heart of San Juan's fashion district. There's also a growing fashion scene in the business district of Hato Rey. Thanks to Puerto Rico's vibrant art scene, more and more galleries and studios are opening, and many are doing so in neighborhoods outside the old city walls. If you prefer shopping in air-conditioned comfort, there are plenty of malls in and just outside San Juan.

Markets and Malls

Look for vendors selling crafts from kiosks at the **Artesanía Puertor-riqueña** (☎ 787/722–1709) in the tourism company's La Casita at Plaza Dársenas near Pier 1 in Old San Juan. Several vendors also set up shop to sell items such as belts, handbags, and toys along Calle San Justo in front of Plaza Dársenas.

In the suburb of Carolina, a few minutes east of San Juan on Route 3, you'll find a **Mercado Artesanal** (Artisans Market) and cultural fair every Sunday 1–5 at the Parque Julia de Burgos on Avenida Roberto Clemente (corner of Paseo de los Gigantes). In addition to craft and food booths, live bands perform, and there's often entertainment for the children.

For a mundane albeit complete shopping experience, head to **Plaza Las Américas** (✉ 525 Av. Franklin Delano Roosevelt, Hato Rey, ☎ 787/767–1525), which has 200 shops, including the world's largest JCPenney store, The Gap, Sears, Macy's, Godiva, and Armani Exchange, as well as restaurants and movie theaters.

Off Route 26 about 10 minutes east of San Juan you'll find **Plaza Carolina** (✉ Av. Fragosa, Carolina, ☎ 787/768–0514). About 30 minutes west of San Juan on Route 167 (off Route 22 and past the Buchanan toll), **Plaza del Sol** (✉ 725 West Main Av., Bayamón, ☎ 787/778–8724) includes Old Navy and Banana Republic, restaurants, and brand-new movie theaters. Off Avenida John F. Kennedy, about 15 minutes south of San Juan, **San Patricio Plaza** (✉ Av. San Patricio Av. at Av. Franklin Delano Roosevelt, Guaynabo, ☎ 787/792–1255) has a Boston Shoe and a Footaction USA, as well as restaurants and movie theaters.

Specialty Shops

Art

Many galleries and a few museums stay open late during Old San Juan's **Gallery Night** (☎ 787/723–6286). It's held from 6 to 9 on the first Tuesday of the month September to December and February to May.

Atlas Art (✉ 208 Calle Cristo, Old San Juan, ☎ 787/723–9987) carries contemporary paintings and prints as well as sculptures in glass and bronze. As one of the first galleries to set up shop outside of Old San Juan, **Galería Botello** (✉ 314 Av. Franklin Delano Roosevelt, Hato Rey, ☎ 787/250–8274, WEB www.botello.com) is something of a pioneer. It sells a broad range of works, from traditional *santos* (hand-carved figures of saints or religious scenes) to pieces by such up-and-coming Puerto Rican artists as María del Mater O'Neill, whose large formats and bold strokes and colors give familiar home-and-garden themes a twist. Botello also displays works by renowned artists Jorge Zeno, Arnaldo Morales, Charles Juhasz, Néstor Otero, Víctor Vázquez, Ada Bobonis, and Rosa Irigoyen.

Among those who have displayed their works at **Galería Petrus** (✉ 501 Av. Andalucía, Puerto Nuevo, ☎ 787/781–4115) are Dafne Elvira, whose surreal oils and acrylics tease and seduce (witness a woman emerging from a banana peel); Marta Pérez, another surrealist, whose bewitching paintings examine such themes as how life on a coffee plantation might have been; and Elizam Escobar, a former political prisoner whose oil paintings convey the often-intense realities of human experience. Petrus also sells the architectonic designs of Imel Sierra (who created the sculpture "Paloma" in Condado), which combine wood and metal elements.

Half a block from the Museo de Arte de Puerto Rico, **Galería Raíces** (✉ 314 Av. José de Diego, Santurce, ☎ 787/723–8909) is dedicated to showing work by such emerging Puerto Rican artists as Nayda Collazo Llorens, whose cerebral and sensitive multimedia installations examine connections and patterns in games, codes, and human memory. Raíces also displays the work of sculptors Annex Burgos and Julio Suárez. **Galería San Juan** (✉ Gallery Inn, 204–206 Calle Norzagaray, Old San Juan, ☎ 787/722–1808) shows sensuous sculptures of faces and bodies and watercolors of Old San Juan architecture by artist and innkeeper Jan D'Esopo.

Galería Tamara (✉ 210 Av. Chardón, Suite 104-A, Hato Rey, ☎ 787/764–6465) has abstract oil studies of the arc form by Wilfredo Chiesa (whose works also appear at the Peter Findlay Gallery in New York City) and oil paintings of placid home scenes by Carmelo Sobrino. **Galería Viota** (✉ 739 Av. San Patricio, Las Lomas, ☎ 787/782–1752 or 787/783–7230) features paintings and silkscreens by master Augusto Marín and large-format abstract expressionist works by the Paris-based Ricardo Ramírez.

José Alegría, who began amassing artworks at age 14 with a Dalí drawing, is as passionate about his gallery as he is about his personal collection. **OBRA** (✉ 301 Calle Tetuán, Old San Juan, ☎ 787/723–3206) is a visually pleasing space with museum-quality paintings, drawings, and sculptures by such Puerto Rican masters as Augusto Marín, Myrna Baez, and Rafael Tufiño as well as works by up-and-coming Cuban artists. Look also for the sea forms of world-famous glass artist Chihuly.

Books

A Condado classic, **Bell Book & Candle** (✉ 102 Av. José de Diego, Condado, ☎ 787/728–5000) caters to the local English-speaking community. **The Book Shop** (✉ 203 Calle Cruz, Old San Juan, ☎ 787/721–0617) sells books in English and Spanish. Its small, on-site café—with a large window facing Plaza de Armas—is a great place to read or people-watch. **Borders Books** (✉ Plaza Las Américas, 525 Av. Franklin Delano Roosevelt, Hato Rey, ☎ 787/777–0916), part of the U.S. superstore chain, fills 28,000 square ft in San Juan's biggest mall.

Among the city's finest bookshops is **Cronopios** (✉ 255 Calle San José, Old San Juan, ☎ 787/724–1815), which carries a full range of fiction and nonfiction in both English and Spanish, as well as music CDs. There are many small bookstores near the Universidad de Puerto Rico campus in Río Piedras. A local favorite is **Librería La Tertulia** (✉ Calle Amalia Marín and Calle González, Río Piedras, ☎ 787/765–1148, WEB www.latertulia.com). Although it specializes in books printed in Spanish, it also has English-language titles.

If you forgot to bring a book with you to Condado Beach, pick up a paperback at **Scriptum Books & Gallery** (✉ 1129 Av. Ashford, Condado, ☎ 787/724–1123), which is about midway between the Condado Plaza hotel and the Marriott. **Thekes** (✉ Plaza Las Américas, 525 Av. Franklin Delano Roosevelt, Hato Rey, ☎ 787/765–1539) sells contemporary fiction, magazines, and travel books in English and Spanish.

Cigars

The **Cigar House** (✉ 255 Calle Fortaleza, Old San Juan, ☎ 787/723–5223) has a small, eclectic selection of local and imported cigars. **Club Jibarito** (✉ 202 Calle Cristo, Old San Juan, ☎ 787/724–7797), with its large walk-in humidor, is *the* place for Puerto Rican and imported cigars, as well as such smoking paraphernalia as designer lighters, personal humidors, pipes, and pipe tobacco. Also on hand are silk ties, cuff links, and designer pens from Alfred Dunhill.

Clothing

ACCESSORIES

Louis Vuitton (⊠ 1054 Av. Ashford, Condado, ☎ 787/722–2543) carries designer luggage and leather items, as well as scarves and business accessories. Aficionados of the famous, lightweight Panama hat, made from delicately hand-woven straw, should stop at **Olé** (⊠ 105 Calle Fortaleza, Old San Juan, ☎ 787/724–2445). The shop sells top-of-the-line hats for as much as $1,000, as well as antiques, santos, sandals, and delicately crafted marionettes.

MEN'S CLOTHING

After many years of catering to a primarily local clientele, **Clubman** (⊠ 1351 Av. Ashford, Condado, ☎ 787/722–1867) is the classic choice for gentlemen's clothing. **Lazoff** (⊠ 356 Calle Teniente César González, Hato Rey, ☎ 787/766–6667) carries elegant men's formal and business attire. **Monsieur** (⊠ 1126 Av. Ashford, Condado, ☎ 787/722–0918) has casual, contemporary designs for men.

MEN'S AND WOMEN'S CLOTHING

For discounted clothing and home accessories, **Marshall's** (⊠ Plaza de Armas, Old San Juan, ☎ 787/722–0874) is charmingly integrated into the everyday life of many locals, some of whom consider it "The Temple." **Matahari** (⊠ 202 Calle San Justo, Old San Juan, ☎ 787/724–5869) sells unusual clothes for men and women as well as accessories, jewelry, and trinkets that proprietor Fernando Sosa collects during his trips around the world. **Nono Maldonado** (⊠ 1051 Av. Ashford, Condado, ☎ 787/721–0456) is well-known for his high-end, elegant linen designs for men and women.

WOMEN'S CLOTHING

E'Leonor (⊠ 1310 Av. Ashford, Condado, ☎ 787/725–3208) is a well-established store for bridal apparel, evening gowns, and cocktail dresses as well as more casual (yet still elegant) attire. Look for designs by Vera Wang and St. John. **La Femme** (⊠ 320 Av. Franklin Delano Roosevelt, Hato Rey, ☎ 787/753–0915) also sells attractive (and sexy) clothes and accessories. **Kation Boutique** (⊠ 1016 Av. Franklin Delano Roosevelt, Hato Rey, ☎ 787/749–0235) has designs by Fendi, Moschino, Gianni Versace, and Dolce and Gabbana.

Mademoiselle Boutique (⊠ 1504 Av. Ashford, Condado, ☎ 787/728–7440) sells only European apparel, including NewMan, Gerard Darel, and Ungaro Fever. The window displays at **Nativa Boutique** (⊠ 55 Calel Cervantes, Condado, ☎ 787/724–1396) are almost as daring as the clothes its sells. **Oui Boutique** (⊠ 348 Av. Franklin Delano Roosevelt, Hato Rey, ☎ 787/765–2424) sells local and international designer clothes and accessories.

Pasarela (⊠ 1302 Av. Ashford, Condado, ☎ 787/724–5444), which means "cat walk" in Spanish, seems a fitting name for a boutique offering designs by the likes of Nicole Miller, Luca Luca, La Perla, and Renato Nucci on sale. **Roma** (⊠ 241 Av. Eleanor Roosevelt, Hato Rey, ☎ 787/764–2120) is among the larger stores that sell designer items in the area. **Serenity** (⊠ 200 Calle San Justo, Old San Juan, ☎ 787/977–5744) imports attire from India and Morocco.

Furniture and Antiques

For almost two decades, Robert and Sharon Bartos of **El Alcázar** (⊠ 103 Calle San José, Old San Juan, ☎ 787/723–1229, WEB www.elalcazar.com) have been selling antiques and objets d'art from all over the world. **Dis-**

DESIGN LIONS

PUERTO RICO'S YOUNG fashion designers have opened many a boutique and atélier in metropolitan San Juan during the last few years. Their styles may differ, but these young lions all share an island heritage—complete with a tradition of true craftsmanship—and a level of sophistication acquired after studying and traveling abroad. The result is a fascinating assortment of original, exclusive, high-quality designs, often sold at reasonable prices.

With all the warmth and sun, it goes without saying that Puerto Rico's designers are most inspired when it comes to creations for the spring and summer seasons. Lacy, flowing creations and lightweight, if not sheer, fabrics dominate women's clothing. For men, the trend is toward updated linen classics in tropical whites and creams. Whatever you find will be one of a kind, with stylish—if not playful or downright sexy—lines.

Lisa Cappalli (✉ 151 Av. José de Diego, Condado, ☎ FAX 787/724–6575), a graduate of New York City's Parsons School of Design, opened her boutique and atélier in November 2000. She favors laces (lace-making is a family tradition) and soft, sensuous fabrics. All her creations seem to enhance the female form. She has custom-made and ready-to-wear collections and has also developed a line of children's clothing.

The neat-and-trim lines and forever-young styles by Fashion Institute of Technology graduate **Luis Antonio** (✉ 857 Av. Ponce de León, Miramar, ☎ 787/977–7816, WEB www.luisantonio.com) have been featured in *Cosmopolitan* and *Travel & Leisure* magazines. They're in great demand abroad and have earned him such celebrity clients as Jennifer López and Paulina Rubio. The energy is palpable in his 6,000-square-ft workshop, with its 12 sewing machines humming away. For men, Luis designs casual clothes; for women, exclusive evening gowns and prêt-à-porter dresses.

Prolific designer **David Antonio** (✉ 69 Av. Condado, Condado, ☎ 787/725–0600) inaugurated his Condado boutique in April 2001. It may be small, but it's full of surprises. His joyful creations range from updated versions of the men's classic *guayabera* shirt to fluid chiffon and silk tunics and dresses for women. For David, upbeat colors—bold reds and vibrant oranges—are important; so is movement, which he sees as a symbol of freedom.

Harry Robles (✉ 1752 Calle Loíza, Ocean Park, ☎ 787/727–3885, WEB www.harryrobles.com) has been established for a little longer than many of his peers. He specializes in gowns for women of all ages, and his draping designs are often dramatic but always elegant. Look for red or black-and-white creations in crepe, chiffon, or Dutchess satin.

Other young designers to watch include Stella Nolasco, Lisa Thon, and Gustavo Arango. To learn about all the design lions—and see their collections—consider visiting during one of the **San Juan Fashion Weeks** (contact Nono Maldonado, ☎ 787/721–0456) that take place in March and September. The weeks are full of shows and cocktail parties, all organized by the Puerto Rico Fashion Designers Group under the leadership of island fashion icons Nono Maldonado and Mirtha Rubio. For more information contact individual designers or Nono Maldonado.

— Isabel Abislaimán

eño Isleño (⊠ 258 Av. José de Diego, Puerto Nuevo, ☎ 787/707–7665, WEB www.disenoisleno.com) specializes in original, contemporary, Puerto Rican furniture and decorative items.

At **DMR Gallery** (⊠ 204 Calle Luna, Old San Juan, ☎ 787/722–4181) artist Nick Quijano sells classic Spanish colonial furniture and his own designs in a variety of Latin American woods. Near the Museo de Arte de Puerto Rico, **Trapiche** (⊠ 316 Av. José de Diego, Condado, ☎ 787/724–1469) purveys a fine selection of furniture and home accessories from Puerto Rico and the Dominican Republic.

Gifts

Exotic butterflies mounted in clear cases line the walls of **Butterfly People** (⊠ 152 Calle Fortaleza, Old San Juan, ☎ 787/732–2432); there's also a café and a gift shop featuring books on butterfly collecting. **Plastic Jungle Toystore** (⊠ 101 Calle Fortaleza, Old San Juan, ☎ 787/723–1076) sells creative toys, games, puzzles, and masks for children. You can find a world of unique spices and sauces from around the Caribbean, kitchen items, and cookbooks at **Spicy Caribbee** (⊠ 154 Calle Cristo, Old San Juan, ☎ 787/625–4690).

Handicrafts

For information about traditional handicrafts and local artisans, contact the Puerto Rico Tourism Company's **Asuntos Culturales** (Cultural Affairs Office, ☎ 787/723–0692). At the **Convento de los Dominicos** (⊠ 98 Calle Norzagaray, Old San Juan, ☎ 787/721–6866)—the Dominican Convent on the north side of the old city that houses the offices of the Instituto de Cultura Puertorriqueña—you'll find baskets, masks, the famous *cuatro* guitars, santos, books and tapes, and reproductions of Taíno artifacts.

The **Haitian Gallery** (⊠ 367 Calle Fortaleza, Old San Juan, ☎ 787/725–0986) carries Puerto Rican crafts as well as folksy, often inexpensive, paintings from around the Caribbean. The small shop at the **Museo de las Américas** (⊠ Cuartel de Ballajá, Old San Juan, ☎ 787/724–5052) sells authentic folk crafts from throughout Latin America. For one-of-a-kind santos, art, and festival masks, head for **Puerto Rican Arts & Crafts** (⊠ 204 Calle Fortaleza, Old San Juan, ☎ 787/725–5596).

Jewelry

In the Banco Popular building, the family-run **Abislaimán Joyeros** (⊠ Plaza Don Rafael, 206 Calle Tetuán, Old San Juan, ☎ 787/724–3890) sells fine jewelry designs by Sal Prashnik and Jose Hess, as well as watches by Baume & Mercier and Bertolucci. **Aetna Gold** (⊠ 111 Calle Gilberto Concepción de Gracia, Old San Juan, ☎ 787/721–4756), adjacent to the Wyndham Old San Juan Hotel, sells exquisite gold jewelry designed in Greece. For a wide array of watches and jewelry, visit the two floors of **Bared** (⊠ Calle Fortaleza and Calle San Justo, Old San Juan, ☎ 787/724–4811).

Diamonds and gold galore are found at **Joseph Manchini** (⊠ 101 Calle Fortaleza, Old San Juan, ☎ 787/722–7698). **Joyería Cátala** (⊠ Plaza de Armas, Old San Juan, ☎ 787/722–3231) is distinguished for its large selection of pearls. **Joyería Riviera** (⊠ 205 Cruz St., Old San Juan, ☎ 787/725–4000) sells fine jewelry by David Yurman and Rolex watches.

N. Barquet Joyeros (⊠ 201 Calle Fortaleza, Old San Juan, ☎ 787/721–3366), one of the bigger stores in Old San Juan, has Fabergé jewelry, pearls, and gold as well as crystal and watches. **Rheinhold Jewelers** (⊠ Plaza Las Américas, 525 Av. Franklin Delano Roosevelt, Hato Rey, ☎ 787/767–7837; ⊠ Wyndham El San Juan Hotel, 6063 Av. Isla Verde,

Isla Verde, ☎ 787/791–2521) sells exclusive designs by Stephen Dueck and Tiffany's.

SAN JUAN A TO Z

To research prices, get advice from other travelers, and book travel arrangements, visit www.fodors.com.

ADDRESSES
Letters addressed to San Juan should carry the recipient's name, the street number and name or post-office box, and "San Juan, PR," plus the five-digit U.S. Postal Service Zip code. San Juan consists of various neighborhoods, which aren't important to include on an envelope, but which may help you get around. From east to west, roughly, these include Old San Juan, Puerto da Tierra, Condado, Miramar, Ocean Park, Isla Verde, Santurce, and Hato Rey. The metropolitan area includes such suburbs as Cataño, Carolina, Guaynabo, and Bayamón.

AIR TRAVEL
CARRIERS
San Juan is the Caribbean hub for American Airlines, which handles some 70% of all air traffic from North America to the Caribbean. It operates nonstop flights from New York, Boston, Newark, Miami, and many other North American cities. Other airlines that serve the city from the mainland United States include Continental, Delta, and US Airways.

International carriers include Air Canada, Air France, British Airways, Canadian Airlines, LACSA, and Lufthansa's Condor. Connections between Caribbean islands can be made through American Eagle, LIAT, and others.

➤ MAJOR INTERNATIONAL CARRIERS: **Air Canada Vacations** (☎ 800/774–8993). **Air France** (☎ 800/237–2747). **British Airways** (☎ 787/723–4327). **Canadian Airlines** (☎ 800/426–7000). **Condor** (☎ 800/645–3880). **LACSA** (☎ 787/724–3444 or 800/225–2272).

➤ MAJOR U.S. CARRIERS: **American Airlines** (☎ 787/749–1747). **Continental** (☎ 787/793–7373). **Delta** (☎ 787/754–3333). **US Airways** (☎ 800/428–4322).

➤ SMALLER CARRIERS: **American Eagle** (☎ 787/749–1747). **LIAT** (☎ 787/791–0800).

AIRPORTS AND TRANSFERS
The Aeropuerto Internacional Luis Muñoz Marín is in Isla Verde, 18 km (11 mi) east of downtown. San Juan's other airport, the small Aeropuerto Fernando L. Rivas Dominici (also known as the Isla Grande Airport) near the city's Miramar neighborhood, serves flights to and from destinations on Puerto Rico and throughout the Caribbean. (Note that although the Dominici airport was still operating at this writing, its future was uncertain.)

➤ AIRPORT INFORMATION: **Aeropuerto Fernando L. Rivas Dominici** (☎ 787/729–8711). **Aeropuerto Internacional Luis Muñoz Marín** (☎ 787/791–4670).

AIRPORT TRANSFERS
Before arriving, check with your hotel about transfers: many area establishments provide transport from the airport, free or for a fee, to their guests. Otherwise, your best bets are *taxi turísticos* (tourist taxis) or an Airport Limousine Service minibus. Uniformed tourism company information officers at the airport can help you make arrangements.

Rates for both types of vehicles are based on your destination, though minibus prices vary depending on the time of day and the number of passengers. A taxi turístico to Isla Verde costs $8, a minibus about $2.50. To Condado the rates are $12 and $3, to Old San Juan, they're $16 and $3.50. For taxi turísticos, the officials will give you a slip with your zone written on it to hand to the driver. For minibuses, note that the driver may wait 'til he has a full load of passengers before leaving.

The Baldorioty de Castro Expressway (Route 26) runs from the airport into the city. Exits are clearly marked along the way, though you should check with your hotel to determine which one is best for you to take. With regular traffic, the drive from the airport all the way west to Old San Juan takes about 20 minutes, but you should plan on 40 minutes.

➤ Minibuses: **Airport Limousine Service** (☎ 787/791–4745).

BOAT AND FERRY TRAVEL
Cruise ships pull into the city piers on Calle Gilberto Concepción de Gracia in Old San Juan. The city bus terminal is next to Plaza de Colón in Old San Juan, and taxis line the street next to Pier 2. The ferry between the old city (Pier 2 on Calle Marina) and Cataño is operated by the Autoridad de los Puertos (Port Authority). It costs a mere 50¢ one-way and runs daily every 15 or 30 minutes from 5:45 AM until 10 PM.
➤ Boat and Ferry Information: The **Autoridad de los Puertos** (☎ 787/788–1155).

BUS TRAVEL
Guaguas (buses) run by the Autoridad Metropolitana de Autobuses (AMA, or Metropolitan Bus Authority) operate between 5 AM or 6 AM and 9 PM or 10 PM. They link Old San Juan with the business district, the beach neighborhoods, and the southern and western suburbs. Fares are 25¢ or 50¢, depending on the route, and *paradas* (bus stops) are clearly marked. Buses are comfortable—most are air-conditioned—but schedules are not always adhered to: plan to wait 15–30 minutes; longer on Sunday and holidays.

Covadonga and Plaza de Colón are the main Old San Juan stops. Destinations are indicated above the windshield. Bus B-21 runs through Condado all the way to Plaza Las Américas in Hato Rey. Bus A-5 runs from San Juan through Santurce and the beach area of Isla Verde. The A-3 covers Río Piedras and Hato Rey. To reach Santurce, hop the M-1. For more information on routes, contact the tourism company.

Island-wide bus service is less than comprehensive, so it's best to travel by *públicos* (public cars). These 17-passenger vans have yellow license plates ending in "P" or "PD." They stop in the main plazas of communities throughout the island and operate primarily during the day. Routes and fares are fixed, but schedules aren't. Call ahead for details. Línea Caborrojeña provides service to Cabo Rojo, Línea de Choferes Unidos de Ponce to Ponce, and Línea Sultana to Mayagüez.
➤ Contacts: **AMA** (☎ 787/767–7979). **Línea Caborrojeña** (✉ 956 Av. Las Palmas, Santurce, ☎ 787/723–9155). **Línea de Choferes Unidos de Ponce** (✉ Plaza Degetau, Plaza 18, Santurce, ☎ 787/722–3275). **Línea Sultana** (✉ 898 E. Calle González, Río Piedras, ☎ 787/767–5205 or 787/767–9377).

CAR RENTAL
Rates can start as low as $30 a day (plus insurance), most often with unlimited mileage. All the major U.S. agencies are represented in San

Juan. Local companies, sometimes less expensive, include Charlie Car Rental, L & M Car Rental, and Target.

➤ MAJOR AGENCIES: **Avis** (☎ 787/721–4499). **Budget** (☎ 787/791–3685). **Hertz** (☎ 787/791–0840). **National** (☎ 787/791–1805). **Thrifty** (☎ 787/253–2525).

➤ LOCAL AGENCIES: **Charlie Car Rental** (☎ 787/791–1101 or 800/289–1227). **L & M Car Rental** (☎ 787/791–1160 or 800/666–0807). **Target** (☎ 787/728–1447 or 800/934–6457).

CAR TRAVEL

The main highways into San Juan are Route 26 from the east (it becomes the Baldorioty de Castro Expressway after passing the airport), Route 22 (José de Diego Expressway) from the west, and Route 52 (Luis A. Ferré Expressway) from the south.

Avenidas Ashford and McLeary run along the coastal neighborhoods of Condado and Ocean Park. The main inland thoroughfares are avenidas Fernández Juncos, Ponce de León, and Luis Muñoz Rivera, which travel from Old San Juan, through Puerta de Tierra and Santurce, and on to Hato Rey. Running north–south are avenidas Franklin Delano Roosevelt and Central (also known as Piñeiro), which intersect Muñoz Rivera and Ponce de León. Avenida Kennedy runs mostly north–south and leads to the suburbs of Bayamón and Guaynabo.

EMERGENCY SERVICES

Central Towing provides island-wide 24-hour towing, lockout, flat-tire-change, and battery-booster services.

➤ CONTACTS: **Central Towing** (✉ Calle Santa Cecilia A-4, Caguas, ☎ 800/981–0087, 800/981–5050, or 787/744–5444).

GASOLINE

There aren't any stations in Old San Juan, but they're abundant elsewhere in the city. Some close at 11 PM or so; others are open 24 hours.

PARKING

There's some on-street parking, but meters are often broken. No-parking zones are indicated with yellow paint or signs, though rarely both. Just because a spot on the street is painted white (or not at all), doesn't mean it's a parking space. Fines for parking illegally range from $15 to $250.

In Old San Juan, park at La Puntilla, at the head of Paseo de la Princesa. It's an outdoor lot with the old city's cheapest rates (they start at 50¢ an hour). You could also try the Felisa Rincón de Gautier lot, also called Parking de Doña Fela, on Calle Gilberto Concepción de Gracia (also called Calle la Marina) or the Frank Santaella lot, also called the Covadonga lot, between Paseo de Covadonga and Calle Gilberto Concepción de Gracia, across from cruise-ship Pier 4. This is also the main bus terminus in Old San Juan, and the spot where the Old San Juan trolleys originate. Parking starts at $1.25 for the first hour. The lots open at 7 AM and close at 10 PM weekdays and as late as 2 AM on weekends.

ROAD CONDITIONS

City streets (the occasional pothole aside) and some highways are in great condition, but several of the older, heavily trafficked routes aren't very well maintained. People tend to ignore the law prohibiting jaywalking; watch out for pedestrians when driving in town.

RULES OF THE ROAD

Speed limits are posted in miles, distances in kilometers. In general city speed limits are 35 mph; on the highways they're 55–65 mph. Right turns on red lights are permitted. Seat belts are required; the fine for not using them is $50.

Traffic jams are common, particularly at rush hours (7 AM–9 AM and 3 PM–6 PM), throughout the metropolitan area. Several areas along main highways are undergoing repairs; be prepared for sudden slowdowns.

EMERGENCIES
➤ General Emergencies: **Ambulance, police, and fire** (☎ 911).
➤ Hospitals: **Ashford Presbyterian Memorial Community Hospital** (✉ 1451 Av. Ashford, Condado, ☎ 787/721–2160). **Clínica Las Américas** (✉ 400 Av. Franklin Delano Roosevelt, Hato Rey, ☎ 787/765–1919). **San Juan Health Centre** (✉ 200 Av. José de Diego, Condado, ☎ 787/725–0202).
➤ Police: **Turist Zone Police** (☎ 787/726–7020; 787/726–7015 for Condado; 787/728–4770 or 787/726–2981 for Isla Verde).
➤ Pharmacies: **Puerto Rico Drug Company** (✉ 157 Calle San Francisco, Old San Juan, ☎ 787/725–2202). **Walgreens** (✉ 1130 Av. Ashford, Condado, ☎ 787/725–1510).

ENGLISH-LANGUAGE MEDIA
The English-language daily, the *San Juan Star,* covers local and international news and local events. Radio Oso, WOSO 1030 on the AM dial, provides the local English-speaking community with up-to-the minute news.

GAY AND LESBIAN TRAVELERS
San Juan is a cosmopolitan and sophisticated city in which gays and lesbians will feel at home. There are many gay-friendly hotels and clubs, and the beach at Ocean Park tends to attract a gay crowd. Normal precautions regarding overt behavior stand, however; Puerto Ricans are often conservative about matters of sexuality and dress.

Frank Fournier of Connections Travel—which is a member of the International Gay and Lesbian Travel Association—is a reliable contact for gay and lesbian travelers. To find out about events, pick up a copy of the *Puerto Rico Breeze,* the island's gay and lesbian newspaper.
➤ Contacts: **Connections Travel** (✉ 257 Calle Tetuán, Old San Juan, ☎ 787/721–5550 or 787/721–7090).

HEALTH
Tap water is generally fine; just avoid drinking it after storms. Be sure to thoroughly wash or peel produce you buy in markets and grocery stores before eating it.

MAIL AND SHIPPING
San Juan post offices offer Express Mail next-day service to the U.S. mainland and to Puerto Rican destinations. Post offices are open weekdays 7:30–4:30 and Saturday 8–noon.
➤ Post Offices: **Old San Juan Branch** (✉ 153 Calle Fortaleza, Old San Juan, ☎ 787/723–1277). **San Juan Branch** (✉ 163 Av. Fernandez Juncos, Puerta de Tierra, ☎ 787/722–4134).

Most major courier services—Federal Express, UPS, Airborne Express—do business in Puerto Rico. You best bet is to let the staff at a Mail Boxes Etc. help you with your shipping. The company has are several branches in the metropolitan area.
➤ Major Services: **Mail Boxes Etc.** (✉ 202A Calle San Justo, Old San Juan, ☎ 787/722–0040; ✉ 2434 Calle Loíza, Punta Las Marías, Carolina, ☎ 787/268–1270 or 787/268–1090; ✉ 1357 Av. Ashford,

Condado, ☎ 787/724–8678; ⊠ 201–667 Av. Ponce de León, Miramar, ☎ 787/722–2755 or 787/722–3570).

MONEY MATTERS

Banks are generally open weekdays 8–4. The island's largest bank is Banco Popular de Puerto Rico, which has currency exchange services and branches and ATMs all over the island. Other banks include Banco Santander, Banco Bilbao Vizcaya, and Citibank.

➤ BANKS: **Banco Popular de Puerto Rico** (⊠ 206 Calle Tetuán, Old San Juan, ☎ 787/725–2636; ⊠ 1060 Av. Ashford, Condado, ☎ 787/725–4197; ⊠ Plaza Las Américas, 525 Av. Franklin Delano Roosevelt, Hato Rey, ☎ 787/753–4590 or 787/753–4511).

SAFETY

As you would in any other major city, use common sense. Guard your wallet or purse at all times, and avoid pulling out large wads of cash to make transactions. Don't wander along the beaches at night or leave anything unattended on the beach during the day. Lock all valuables in the hotel safe, and don't leave things out on the seat of your car.

WOMEN IN SAN JUAN

Carry only a handbag that closes completely and wear it bandolier style (across one shoulder and your chest). Open-style bags and those allowed to simply dangle from one shoulder are prime targets for pickpockets and purse snatchers. Avoid walking anywhere alone at night, and don't wear clothing that's skin tight or overly revealing.

TAXIS

The Puerto Rico Tourism Company oversees a well-organized taxi program. Taxi turísticos, which are painted white and have the *garita* (sentry box) logo, charge set rates based on zones; they run from the airport and the cruise-ship piers to Isla Verde, Condado, Ocean Park, and Old San Juan, with rates ranging $6–$16 per car. They also can be hailed in the same manner as metered cabs. City tours start at $30 per hour.

Metered cabs authorized by the Public Service Commission start at $1 and charge 10¢ for every additional ⅓ mi, 50¢ for every suitcase. Waiting time is 10¢ for each 45 seconds. The minimum charge is $3. Be sure the driver starts the meter.

Although you can hail cabs on the street, virtually every San Juan hotel has taxis waiting outside to transport guests; if there's none available, you or a hotel staffer can call one. Atlantic City Taxi and Major Taxicabs are reliable companies. Note that these radio taxis might charge an extra $1 for the pickup.

➤ CONTACT: **Public Service Commission** (☎ 787/751–5050).
➤ TAXI COMPANIES: **Atlantic City Taxi** (☎ 787/268–5050). **Major Taxicabs** (☎ 787/723–2460).

TELEPHONES

Puerto Rico's area code is 787, and you must dial it even when making local calls. (At this writing, the phone company was slated to introduce a new 939 area code.) Public phones are plentiful. Many use prepaid phone cards as well as coins.

TOURS

In Old San Juan, free trolleys can take you around, and the tourist board can provide you with a copy of *Qué Pasa,* which contains a self-guided walking tour. The Caribbean Carriage Company gives old city tours in horse-drawn carriages. It's a bit hokey, but it gets you off your feet.

Look for these buggies at Plaza Dársenas near Pier 1; the cost is $30–$60 per couple.

Wheelchair Getaway offers city sightseeing trips as well as wheelchair transport from airports and cruise-ship docks to San Juan hotels. Cordero Caribbean Tours runs tours in air-conditioned limousines for an hourly rate. The city has several reliable companies that can help you arrange tours in the city or out on the island, and most San Juan hotels also have tour desks.

➤ TOUR OPERATORS: **Caribbean Carriage Company** (☎ 787/797–8063). **Cordero Caribbean Tours** (☎ 787/786–9114; 787/780–2442 evenings). **Normandie Tours, Inc.** (☎ 787/722–6308). **Rico Suntours** (☎ 787/722–2080 or 787/722–6090). **Tropix Wellness Outings** (☎ 787/268–2173). **United Tour Guides** (☎ 787/725–7605 or 787/723–5578). **Wheelchair Getaway** (☎ 787/883–0131).

TRAVEL AGENCIES

➤ CONTACTS: **Agencias Bithorn** (✉ 1509 Calle López Landrón, Santurce, ☎ 787/725–7505). **Connections Travel** (✉ 257 Calle Tetuán, Old San Juan, ☎ 787/721–5550 or 787/721–7090). **Fred Imbert Travel** (✉ 150 Av. José de Diego, Condado, ☎ 787/724–0300).

TRAIN TRAVEL

San Juan plans to build a $1.6-billion elevated train system that will link it with its suburbs. The first phase is expected to connect Bayamón, Guaynabo, and Santurce. The second phase will connect Río Piedras to Carolina, and, later, to Luis Muñoz Marín International Airport. The system will eventually have 16 city stops.

VISITOR INFORMATION

You'll find Puerto Rico Tourism Company information officers (identified by their caps and shirts with the tourism company patch) near the baggage claim areas at Luis Muñoz Marín International Airport. There are also tourism offices at the American Airlines terminal and at terminals B and C. These are open daily 9 AM–10 PM in high season and daily 9 AM–8 PM in low season.

In San Juan, the tourism company's main office is at the old city jail, La Princesa, in Old San Juan. It operates a branch in a pretty pink colonial building called La Casita at Plaza Dársenas near Pier 1 in Old San Juan; it's open Monday–Wednesday 8:30–8, Thursday and Friday 8:30–5:30, and weekends 9–8. Be sure to pick up a free copy of *Qué Pasa,* the official visitors' guide. Information officers are posted around Old San Juan (look for them at the cruise-ship piers and at the Catedral de San Juan) during the day.

La Oficina de Turismo del Municipio de San Juan is affiliated with the city and has offices at the city hall, Alcaldía, in Old San Juan's Plaza de Armas, and at Playita Condado (in front of the Condado Plaza Hotel on Avenida Ashford). Both offices are open weekdays 8–4.

➤ TOURIST OFFICES: **Oficina de Turismo del Municipio de San Juan** (✉ Alcaldía, Plaza de Armas, Old San Juan, ☎ 787/724–7171 Ext. 2391; ✉ Av. Ashford, Condado, ☎ 787/740–9270). **Puerto Rico Tourism Company** (✉ Box 902-3960, Old San Juan Station, San Juan 00902-3960, ☎ 787/721–2400; ✉ Plaza Dársenas, near Pier 1, Old San Juan, ☎ 787/722–1709; ✉ Luis Muñoz Marín International Airport, ☎ 787/791–1014 or 787/791–2551).

3 EASTERN PUERTO RICO

To slide eastward out of metropolitan San
Juan is to enter a Puerto Rico of the past.
The region's cities are, of course, developed,
but the scenery between them is timeless.
Windswept bluffs, shallow surfless beaches,
and rain forest are among the delights.
Offshore are Vieques and Culebra, islets
whose solitary strands of powdery white
sand are lapped by crystalline—and, in
one case, bioluminescent—waters.

By Mary A.
Dempsey

T REE FROGS, RARE PARROTS, AND WILD HORSES only start the list of eastern Puerto Rico's offerings. The backdrops for encounters with an array of flora and fauna include the 28,000-acre El Yunque, the only tropical rain forest in the U.S. National Forest system; the seven ecosystems in the Reserva Natural Las Cabezas de San Juan; and Bahía Mosquito off Vieques, where tiny sea creatures appear to light up the waters.

The natural beauty and varied terrain continue in the area's towns as well. Loíza, with its strong African heritage, is tucked among coconut groves. Río Grande—which once attracted immigrants from Austria, Spain, and Italy—sits on the island's only navigable river. Naguabo overlooks what were once immense cane fields as well as Cayo Santiago, whose only residents are monkeys.

You can golf, ride horses, hike marked trails, and plunge into water sports throughout the region. In many places along the coast, green hills cascade down to the ocean. On the edge of the Atlantic, Fajardo serves as a jumping-off point for diving, fishing, and catamaran excursions. Luquillo is the site of a family beach so well equipped that there are even facilities enabling wheelchair users to enter the sea. Culebra's stunning beaches are isolated havens—for people and horses—rivaled only by those of nearby Vieques.

If you wish to get away from it all with a neatly packaged trip, eastern Puerto Rico has three of the island's top resorts: Wyndham El Conquistador, Westin Río Mar, and Candelero Resort at Palmas del Mar. The extensive facilities and luxury services at these large, self-contained complexes make the list of regional offerings more than complete.

Pleasures and Pastimes

Beaches
The Atlantic east coast is edged with sandy, palm-lined shores that are occasionally cut by rugged stretches. Some of these beaches are quiet, isolated escapes. Others—such as Luquillo and Seven Seas near Fajardo—are jammed with water-loving families, especially on weekends and during the Easter holidays. Many of Puerto Rico's most attractive strands are on Culebra and Vieques islands.

Dining
Puerto Ricans love sybaritic pleasures, and that includes fine dining—whether it be on Continental, Nueva Latina, or authentically native cuisine. In the east you'll find fine fare of all types. On the traditional side, look for the deep-fried snacks (often stuffed with meat or fish) known as *frituras* as well as numerous dishes laced with coconut. Plantains appear as the starring ingredient in the hearty *mofongo,* a seafood-stuffed dish, or as *tostones* (fried plantain chips). Fresh fish is commonly prepared with tomatoes, onions, garlic, or some combination of the three. Desserts explode with fruit flavors, including passion fruit, mango, guava, and tamarind. Note that some restaurants carry the tourist board's *"meson gastronómico"* designation. Such establishments specialize in typical island food.

CATEGORY	COST*
$$$$	over $35
$$$	$25–$35
$$	$15–$25
$	under $15

*per person for a main course at dinner

Golf

There's something to be said for facing a rolling, palm-tree-lined fairway with the distant ocean at your back. And then there are the ducks, iguanas, and pelicans that congregate in the mangroves near some holes. That's what golf in eastern Puerto Rico is all about. The Arthur Hills–designed course at El Conquistador Resort and Country Club is one of the island's best. The Flamboyán course, a Rees Jones creation at Candelero Resort at Palmas del Mar, consistently gets raves, as do the courses at the Westin Río Mar. An old-time favorite is the Bahía Beach Plantation course, which was developed on a former coconut plantation.

Lodging

The east coast has a couple of government-approved *paradores;* several large, lavish resorts; and a few "theme" properties, including an ecolodge. Like all of the Caribbean, Puerto Rico was slammed by the drop-off in tourism in late 2001. Several hotels closed—some for the off season, some completely. To entice visitors back, establishments began offering discounts; in some cases, rates were reduced by as much as 50%. At this writing, tourism was rebounding, although there were still deals to be found.

CATEGORY	COST*
$$$$	over $225
$$$	$150–$225
$$	$75–$150
$	under $75

All prices are for a double room in high season, excluding 9% tax (11% for hotels with casinos, 7% for paradores) and 5%–12% service charge.

Exploring Eastern Puerto Rico

As the ocean bends around the northeastern coast, it laps onto beaches of soft sand and palm trees, crashes against high bluffs, and almost magically creates an amazing roster of ecosystems. Beautiful beaches at Luquillo and the outer islands of Culebra and Vieques are complemented by more rugged southeastern shores. Inland, green hills roll down toward plains that once held expanses of coconut trees, such as those still surrounding the town of Loíza, or sugarcane, as evidenced by the surviving plantations near Naguabo and Humacao. Most notable, however, is the precipitation-fed landscape: green is the dominant color here.

Numbers in the text correspond to numbers in the margin and on the Eastern Puerto Rico and El Yunque maps.

Great Itineraries

IF YOU HAVE 3 DAYS

Combine a trip to **El Yunque** ⑤–⑧ with a swim at the beach in nearby 🏖 **Luquillo** ⑨ on your first day. Then head farther east to Reserva Natural Las Cabezas de San Juan, and check out the sands at Balneario Seven Seas outside of 🏖 **Fajardo** ⑩. Don't leave without a snack from one of the seafood kiosks near the beach. If there's no moon, sign up for a late-night excursion from Fajardo to the glow-in-the-dark **Bahía Mosquito** ⑫ at the outer island of **Vieques** ⑪–⑬. Use your third day for a snorkeling trip by catamaran to some coral reefs.

IF YOU HAVE 5 DAYS

Spend your first day hiking and picnicking in **El Yunque** ⑤–⑧; bring binoculars and watch for the rare Puerto Rican green parrot. On your second day, hit the sand and seas at 🏖 **Luquillo** ⑨, if you have children in tow, or Balneario Seven Seas near ⊞ **Fajardo** ⑩. On the third day, hop a ferry to ⊞ **Vieques** ⑪–⑬, lounge on a nearly deserted beach, and drink rum cocktails at sunset. In the evening, visit **Bahía Mosquito** ⑫ and swim with the sparkling dinoflagellates. On the fourth day, rent a bike and pedal around to the old Spanish fort, the shops, or the lighthouse. Then head to Bananas for a cold beer. Take the ferry back to Fajardo on your fifth day.

IF YOU HAVE 7 DAYS

Head straight to ⊞ **Fajardo** ⑩ and begin exploring the outer islands. On the first day, take the ferry to ⊞ **Vieques** ⑪–⑬ for an afternoon on the beach and an evening at **Bahía Mosquito** ⑫, with its glittery sea creatures. Use your second day to explore the island. Indulge in a savory meal at Café Blu followed by a snifter of aged Puerto Rican rum. On the third day, catch the ferry to **Culebra** ⑭ and visit stunning Playa Flamenco. On the fourth day, go snorkeling or scuba diving. Head back to Fajardo the next day; if there's time, visit the Reserva Natural Las Cabezas de San Juan. Use your sixth day to make an early trip to **El Yunque** ⑤–⑧, then drive farther south along the coast to **Naguabo** ⑮ and take the boat trip to Cayo Santiago—also known as Monkey Island. Afterward, grab a fresh-from-the-ocean snack facing Playa Húcares. Finish your trip at the posh Candelero Resort at Palmas del Mar outside ⊞ **Humacao** ⑯.

When to Tour

High season runs December 15 through April 15, but the east coast—preferred by those seeking abandoned beaches and nature reserves over casinos and urban glitz—tends to be less in demand than San Juan. The exception is Easter time, when Vieques, Culebra, and Luquillo become crowded with local sun lovers, merrymakers, and campers. Island festivals also draw crowds, but planning a trip around one of them will give you a true sense of the region's culture. Just be sure to make reservations well in advance if you're visiting during Easter or a fête. Although prices go down somewhat after high season, avoid visiting from June to October, when hurricanes are most likely to hit.

THE NORTHEAST AND EL YUNQUE

Just east of San Juan, at the community of Piñones, urban chaos is replaced with the peace of winding palm-lined roads that are interrupted at intervals by barefoot eateries and dramatic ocean views. The first major town you'll encounter is Loíza, where residents proudly claim their African heritage and where renowned mask-makers live. Farther southeast and inland is Río Grande, a community that grew by virtue of its location beside the island's only navigable river. The river rises within El Yunque, the local name for the Caribbean National Forest, a sprawling blanket of green covering a mountainous region south of Río Grande. Back on the coast, Balneario de Luquillo (Luquillo Beach) has snack kiosks, dressing rooms, showers, and facilities that enable wheelchair users to play in the ocean.

Southeast of Luquillo sits the Reserva Natural Las Cabezas de San Juan, with its restored lighthouse and variety of ecosystems. Anchoring the island's east coast is Fajardo, a lively port city with a large marina, ferry service to the outer islands, and a string of offshore cays. Catamarans based here sail to and from great snorkeling spots, yachts stop by to refuel or stock up on supplies, and local fishing craft chug in and out as part of a day's work.

Piñones

① *16 km (10 mi) east of San Juan.*

Funky Piñones is little more than a collection of open-air, seaside eateries. Sand floors, barefoot patrons, and tantalizing seafood—traditionally washed down with icy beer—have made it popular with locals, especially on weekend evenings. Traffic on the two-lane road in and out of the area is daunting on Friday and Saturday nights, when many places have merengue combos, Brazilian jazz trios, or reggae bands. You can rent a bike and follow the marked seaside trail that meanders for 11 km (7 mi). At this writing, plans were on the table to expand the bike path all the way to Isla Verde in San Juan.

Dining

$–$$$ ✕ **Pulpo Loco by the Sea.** Octopus, oysters, mussels, and crab lead the lineup here, though many locals come for a beer or a cocktail as much as for the food. If your thirst is greater than your hunger, you can opt for a lighter, seafood snack. ⊠ *Rte. 187, Km 4.5,* ☎ *787/791–8382. Reservations not accepted. AE, MC, V.*

$–$$$ ✕ **Soleil Beach Club and Bistro.** Slightly more refined than some of its neighbors, this restaurant sits on a wooden deck above the sand. Although seafood reigns, there are meat choices, too. There's also a bar, and bands playing Brazilian music or Latin jazz set the scene on weekend nights. ⊠ *Rte. 187, Km 4.5,* ☎ *787/253–1033 or 787/726–7614. Reservations not accepted. AE, MC, V.*

Outdoor Activities and Sports

As the beach is polluted, the area's big outdoor attraction is a bike path that follows the swaying coconut palms on a quiet, breezy stretch, sometimes crossing over the main roadway, but mostly running parallel to it. You can rent bikes for about $5 an hour from **Pulpo Loco By the Sea** (⊠ Rte. 187, Km 4.5, ☎ 787/791–8382).

Loíza

② *15 km (9 mi) east of Piñones.*

The drive from Piñones to Loíza, a coastal town of 30,000 steeped in African heritage, is along a curving road banked by palms and other foliage. The ocean pops into view from time to time, as do pastel wooden houses—sometimes elevated on stilts—and kiosks serving coconut drinks and fried snacks. Locals stroll along the road's shoulder carrying clusters of coconuts, a nod to the area's many groves.

Loíza is known for its colorful festivals and its respect for tradition. Early on the region in which it's set was largely undeveloped because the marshy land bred mosquitoes. It later became a haven for the descendants of slaves. Today the community is a center for the *bomba,* a dance traced to the Kongo people of West Africa. Sometimes wearing a flouncy white dress, the woman of a dancing couple moves in a relatively fixed pattern of steps while her partner improvises to the drumbeat. A lead singer and a choir perform a call-and-response song—recounting a local story or event—while percussionists play maracas, two *fuas* (wooden sticks that are smacked against a hard surface), two *buleadores* (low-timbre, barrel-shape drums), and a *subidor* (higher-pitched drum).

Bomba is key to the revelries at the annual Festival de Santiago Apóstol (St. James the Apostle Festival). During the celebration, which lasts for 10 days late in July, masked and costumed Loizanos combine religious processions—to a spot where a statue of the Virgin Mary is said to have been found under a tree many generations ago—with fireworks

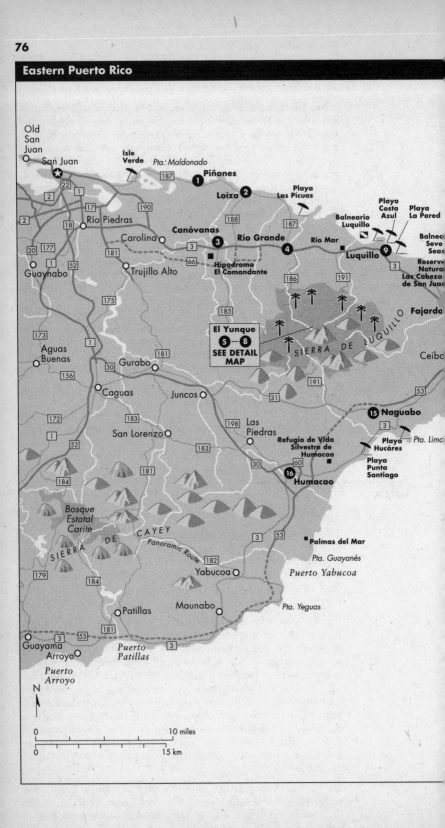

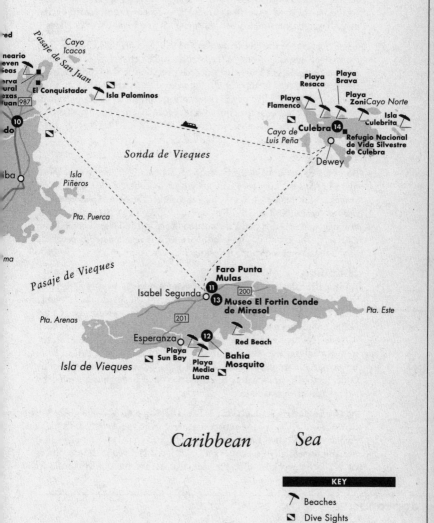

ATLANTIC OCEAN

Cayo
Icacos

Pasaje de San Juan

neario
even
eas

erva
ural
ezas
uan

El Conquistador

987

Isla Palominos

Playa
Resaca

Playa
Brava

Playa
Flamenco

Playa
Zoni

Cayo Norte

10

Cayo de
Luis Peña

Culebra

14

Isla
Culebrita

Sonda de Vieques

Dewey

Refugio Nacional
de Vida Silvestre
de Culebra

ba

Isla
Piñeros

Pta. Puerca

ma

Pasaje de Vieques

Faro Punta
Mulas

Isabel Segunda

11

200

13

Museo El Fortin Conde
de Mirasol

Pta. Este

Pta. Arenas

201

Esperanza

12

Red Beach

Playa
Sun Bay

Playa
Media
Luna

Bahía
Mosquito

Isla de Vieques

Caribbean   Sea

KEY

Beaches

Dive Sights

1 Exploring Sites

Ferry

Rain Forest

and other secular merrymaking. Each year, the family elected to "host" the festival erects an elaborate altar for the Mary statue and provides refreshments for the townspeople. Despite the festivities, St. James isn't Loíza's patron saint. St. Patrick holds that distinction, and the church is dedicated to him. Lively St. Patrick's Day festivities occur if the holiday falls on a weekend. Otherwise, residents save their energy for the bigger Santiago Apóstol fiesta.

Loíza's small downtown has been renovated and is pleasant; its citizens are proud of their town and welcome visitors. When it's not festival time, the area is worth a stop for the scenery and to see the crafts, including museum-quality festival masks made from coconut shells.

Some portions of the **Iglésia de San Patricio** (St. Patrick's Church) date from 1645, making it one of the island's oldest churches. It's home to a statue of the Virgin Mary that is worshipped during the Santiago Apóstol festivities. A side altar holds a statue of St. Patrick, the city's patron saint. If you'd like to see the interior without attending services, you can walk through the church just before or after Sunday mass. ⊠ *10 Calle Espíritu Santo, El Centro,* ☎ *787/876–2229.* ⊠ *Free.* ☉ *10 AM Sunday mass.*

The Arts
Bomba's renaissance dates from 1961, when a TV producer showed up in Loíza searching for residents who remembered the dance. In response, mask-maker Castor Ayala put together the **Ballet Folklórico Hermanos Ayala** (⊠ Rte. 187, Km 6.6, ☎ 787/876–1130), a folk music and dance troupe that performs around the island and elsewhere in Latin America. The group has no headquarters, but you can get its schedule at the mask-making shop, Artesanías Castor Ayala.

Shopping
Among the offerings at **Artesanías Castor Ayala** (⊠ Rte. 187, Km 6.6, ☎ 787/876–1130) are coconut-shell festival masks dubbed "Mona Lisas" because of their elongated smiles. Craftsman Raul Ayala Carrasquillo has been making these museum-quality pieces for more than 40 years, following in the footsteps of his late father, the esteemed craftsman for whom the store is named. Many of the masks, priced from $50 to $350, are used in Loíza's festivals. Others are snapped up by collectors. (Buyer beware: these masks have been much-copied by other craftspeople of late.)

At **Estúdio de Arte Samuel Lind** (⊠ Rte. 187, Km 6.6, ☎ 787/876–1494), down a short, dusty lane across the street from the Artesanías Castor Ayala, artist Samuel Lind sculpts, paints, and silk-screens images that are quintessentially Loizano. Lind's work is displayed in the two floors of his latticework studio. Of special note are his colorful folk-art posters.

Canóvanas

❸ *8 km (5 mi) southwest of Loíza; 22 km (14 mi) east of San Juan.*

Most people pass right through this town, but it has two superlative draws. Canóvanas is home to the Caribbean's largest thoroughbred horse-racing track and Puerto Rico's biggest factory-outlet mall.

Outdoor Activities and Sports
Try your luck with the exactas and quinielas at **Hípodromo El Comandante** (⊠ Rte. 3, Km 15.3, ☎ 787/724–6060, 🕸 www.comandantepr.com), Canóvanas's large thoroughbred race track. Post time is 2:15 or 2:45 (depending on the season) Wednesday and Friday through Monday. There's a restaurant here as well as an air-conditioned clubhouse,

and after Friday's first race, there's dancing to the music of a Latin band in the Winners Sports Bar. Parking and admission to the grandstand are free; clubhouse admission is $3.

Shopping

Right off the highway in Canóvanas, the **Belz Factory Outlet World** (⊠ Rte. 3, Km 18.4, ☎ 787/256–7040, WEB www.belz.com) has more than 75 stores, including Nike, Guess, Mikasa, The Gap, Levi's, Liz Claiborne, and Tommy Hilfiger. There's also a large food court.

Río Grande

❹ *5 km (3 mi) east of Canóvanas; 13 km (8 mi) southeast of Loíza; 35 km (21 mi) southeast of San Juan.*

This urban cluster of about 50,000 residents proudly calls itself "The City of El Yunque," as it's the closest community to the rain forest, and most of the reserve falls within its district borders. Two images of the rare green parrot, which makes its home in El Yunque, are found on the city's coat of arms; another parrot peeks out at you from the town's flag. The city is also near the posh Westin Río Mar resort, known for its seaside golf courses, lovely beach, and first-class restaurants.

The Río Espíritu Santo, which runs through Río Grande, begins in El Yunque's highest elevations and is the island's only navigable river. Thus it was once used to transport lumber, sugar, and coffee from plantations. Immigrants flocked to the region to take advantage of the employment opportunities; many of today's residents can trace their families to Spain, Austria, and Italy.

El Museo del Cartel is devoted to posters, a tradition on the island, and the artists who design them. The collection dates from the 1950s and includes many posters created for island festivals and art exhibits. The facility also offers classes in such arts as silk-screening. ⊠ *37 Calle Pimentel, El Centro,* ☎ *787/889–5820 or 787/887–2133.* ☞ *Free.* ☉ *Tues.–Sun. 9–5.*

The family-run **Hacienda Carabali** is a good place to see Puerto Rico's Paso Fino horses in action. You can even jump in the saddle yourself. Riding excursions ($45 an hour) include a one-hour jaunt along Río Mameyes and the edge of El Yunque and a two-hour ride along Balneario de Luquillo. Outdoor concerts are sometimes held at the ranch, and staffers can also help you arrange shuttle transportation to and from San Juan. ⊠ *Rte. 992, Km 4, at Mameyes River Bridge, Barrio Mameyes,* ☎ *787/889–5820 or 787/889–4954.* ☉ *Daily 9:30–5.*

Beach

Playa Las Picúas is northeast of Río Grande on a bay close to where the Río Espíritu Santo meets the Atlantic. There are no facilities, but the water is fine.

Dining and Lodging

$$–$$$$ ✕ **Palio.** Executive chef Marcus Rodriguez enlivens his northern Italian dishes with aromatic spices at this beautifully decorated restaurant, with its black-and-white checkerboard floor and its shiny, dark wood accents. The seafood selections are particularly noteworthy. ⊠ *Westin Río Mar, 6000 Bul. Río Mar, Rte. 968, Km 1.4, Barrio Palmer,* ☎ *787/888–6000 Ext. 4808. AE, MC, V. No lunch.*

$$–$$$ ✕ **Chef Wayne.** For his own establishment, chef Wayne Michaelson, a veteran of the island's top kitchens, has devised an eclectic menu with such entrées as Cajun-style chicken breast, grilled Caribbean lobster, and filet mignon. Set in a large white house surrounded by rain forest, the main dining room has a Western theme. You can also eat on

the front balcony, with its ocean views, or on the back balcony, facing the forest. As this place is off the main route on a winding, unmarked road, you might want to call ahead for directions. ⊠ *Off Rte. 992,* ☎ *787/889–1962 or 787/889–2911. MC, V. Closed Tues. No lunch Fri.*

$–$$ ✕ **Las Vegas.** At this meson gastronómico the chicken is marinated in local spices and served with rice and *gandules* (pigeon peas). There's also a selection of delicious seafood dishes. The atmosphere is casual thanks to the many hikers that drop in on their way to or from El Yunque rain forest. ⊠ *Rte. 191, Km 1.3,* ☎ *787/887–2526. AE, MC, V.*

$–$$ ✕ **Shimas.** "Asian" is the word at this casual bistro. The sushi bar is a big draw, and Thai curries join Szechuan dishes and Japanese teriyaki on the tempting cross-cultural menu. ⊠ *Westin Río Mar, 6000 Bul. Río Mar, Rte. 968, Km 1.4, Barrio Palmer,* ☎ *787/888–6000 Ext. 4821. AE, MC, V.*

$–$$ ✕ **Villa Pesquera.** The view of the Río Espíritu may initially draw diners into this restaurant, but it's the savory seafood that keeps them coming back. Try the catch of the day—whatever it is, it's always a winner. This is also a sweet spot for a sunset cocktail. ⊠ *Rte. 877, Km 6.6,* ☎ *787/887–0140. MC, V.*

$$$$ 🏨 **Westin Río Mar Beach Resort.** Golf, biking, tennis, and playing in the waters off a mile-long beach are just some of the attractions at this top-notch resort. Every room in the seven-story hotel, which anchors the complex, has a balcony that faces the sea or the golf courses and mountains. There are also one- and two-bedroom villas for guests who want more space and privacy. Tropical color schemes are used throughout as are such luxurious touches as natural woods, Italian tile, and marble accents. ⊠ *6000 Bul. Río Mar, Rte. 968, Km 1.4, Barrio Palmer, (Box 2006, 00721),* ☎ *787/888–6000,* FAX *787/888–6204,* WEB *www.westinriomar.com. 600 rooms, 72 suites, 59 villas. 7 restaurants, 4 lounges, air-conditioning, in-room data ports, in-room safes, cable TV with movies and video games, in-room VCRs, no-smoking rooms, 3 pools, spa, 2 18-hole golf courses, 13 tennis courts, health club, beach, dive shop, windsurfing, boating, fishing, bicycles, shop, casino, dance club, children's programs, dry cleaning, laundry service, concierge, business services, meeting rooms, car rental, airport shuttle, free parking. AE, MC, V. FAP.*

$$–$$$$ 🏨 **Rio Grande Plantation Eco Resort.** Walking paths pass flowers and wind around fruit trees at this peaceful resort in the foothills of El Yunque. It's on a portion of what was, in the late 1700s, a 200-acre sugarcane plantation and is often used for corporate retreats. Accommodations are primarily two-story villas, which have such amenities as Jacuzzis and kitchenettes. The staff members pride themselves on being attentive to their guests. Note that there's no on-site restaurant, and the closest eatery is a 15-minute drive. ⊠ *Rte. 956, Km 4, Barrio Guzman Abajo (Box 6526, Loíza Station, Santurce, San Juan 00914),* ☎ *787/887–2779,* FAX *787/888–3239,* WEB *www.riograndeplantation.com. 19 villas, 4 rooms, 1 cottage. Air-conditioning, in-room VCRs, kitchenettes, microwaves, pool, hot tub, basketball, meeting rooms, free parking. AE, MC, V. EP.*

Nightlife

Pick a game—Caribbean stud poker, blackjack, slot machines—and then head to the Las Vegas–style **Westin Río Mar Resort Casino** (⊠ 6000 Bul. Río Mar, Rte. 968, Km 1.4, Barrio Palmer, ☎ 787/888–6000). If all that betting gives you a thirst, step into the Players Bar, which is connected to the gaming room.

Outdoor Activities and Sports

You can rent windsurfing equipment ($25 an hour), sea kayaks ($15 an hour), and bikes ($20 a day) from **Iguana Watersports** (⊠ 6000

Bul. Río Mar, Rte. 968, Km 1.4, Barrio Palmer, ☎ 787/888–6000) at the Westin Río Mar. Staffers can also direct you to the resort's catamaran excursions desk.

GOLF

The 18-hole **Bahia Beach Plantation Course** (⊠ Rte. 187, Km 4.2, ☎ 787/256–5600, WEB www.golfbahia.com) skirts the north-coast beaches. A public course, it was carved out of a long-abandoned coconut grove. Greens fees are $30–$50, depending on day of the week and the time of day.

The **Berwind Country Club** (⊠ Rte. 187, Km 4.7, ☎ 787/876–3056) has an 18-hole course known for its tight fairways and demanding greens. For $50, nonmembers can golf here Monday through Friday.

Part of the Westin Río Mar Beach Resort, the **Westin Río Mar Country Club** (⊠ 6000 Bul. Río Mar, Rte. 968, Km 1.4, Barrio Palmer, ☎ 787/888–1401 for golf information or 787/888–7066 for tennis information) has two 18-hole courses offering vistas of El Yunque and the Atlantic. The River Course, designed by Greg Norman, has challenging fairways and bunkers. The Ocean Course has slightly wider fairways than its sister; ducks, iguanas, and pelicans congregate in the mangroves near its fourth hole. If you're not a resort guest, be sure to reserve tee times at least 24 hours in advance. Greens fees are $90. The club also has 13 tennis courts, four of which are lighted. You can play here for $19 an hour.

Shopping

Puerto Rican pottery, with some designs inspired by the Taíno Indians, fill the shelves of **Cerámicas Los Bohíos** (⊠ Av. 65th Infantry, Km 21.7, ☎ 787/887–2620). The picturesque **Treehouse Studio** (⊠ unmarked road off Rte. 3, ☎ 787/888–8062), not far from the rain forest, sells vibrant watercolors by Monica Laird, who also gives workshops. Call for an appointment and directions.

El Yunque

★ ⑤–⑧ *11 km (7 mi) southeast of Río Grande; 43 km (26 mi) southeast of San Juan.*

Between Río Grande and Luquillo, on Route 191, are the 28,000 acres of verdant foliage and often-rare wildlife that make up El Yunque, the only rain forest within the U.S. National Forest system. Formally known as the Bosque Nacional del Caribe (Caribbean National Forest), El Yunque's colloquial name is believed to be derived from the Taíno word, *yukiyu* (good spirit), although some people say it comes directly from *yunque,* the Spanish word for "anvil," because some of the forest's peaks have snub shapes.

Rising to 3,500 ft above sea level, this protected area didn't gain its "rain forest" designation for nothing: more than 100 billion gallons of precipitation fall over it annually, spawning rushing streams and cascades, 240 tree species, and oversized impatiens and ferns. In the evening, millions of inch-long *coquís* (tree frogs) begin their calls. El Yunque is also home to the *cotorra,* Puerto Rico's endangered green parrot, as well as 67 other types of birds.

The forest's 13 hiking trails are well maintained; many of them are easy to walk and less than a mile long. If you prefer to see the sights from a car, follow Route 191. Several trailheads, observation points, and other highlights are along this touring road, which is the park's main thoroughfare. Las Cabezas observation point is at Km 7.8; La Coca Falls, one of two waterfalls where you can take a refreshing dip (the other,

La Mina Falls, is to the south), lies just past Km 8.1; and the Torre Yokahu observation point sits at Km 8.9. When hurricanes and mud slides haven't caused portions of the road to be closed, you can drive straight from the entrance to Km 13, the base of El Yunque Peak.

Arrive early and plan to stay the entire day. You'll be charged an admission fee for El Portal Information Center, which has interactive exhibits, but entrance to the rest of the park and the other information centers is free. Although camping isn't permitted, there are picnic areas with sheltered tables and bathrooms. (The recreation areas are open from 7:30 AM to 6 PM daily.) Bring binoculars, a camera, water, and sunscreen; wear a hat or visor, good walking shoes, and comfortable clothes. Although daytime temperatures rise as high as 80°F (27°C), wear long pants as some plants can cause skin irritations. There are no poisonous snakes in the forest (or on the island as a whole), but bugs can be ferocious, so repellent is a must. And remember: this is a rain forest, so be prepared for showers.

★ **❺** A lizard's tongue darts across three video screens, a forest erupts in flames, a tiny seedling pushes up from the ground and flourishes. Before you begin exploring El Yunque, check out the high-tech, interactive displays—explaining forests in general and El Yunque in particular—at **Centro de Información El Portal,** the information center near the northern entrance. Test your sense of smell at an exhibit on forest products, listen to actor Jimmy Smits (who is part Puerto Rican) narrate a movie on El Yunque, and inquire about the day's ranger-led activities. This is also a good place to pick up trail maps, souvenirs, film, water, and snacks. All exhibits and publications are in English and Spanish. ⊠ *Rte. 191, Km 4.3 (off Rte. 3),* ☎ *787/888–1880,* WEB *www.southernregion.fs.fed.us/caribbean.* 🖾 *$3.* ☉ *Daily 9–5.*

❻ The **Torre Yokahu** (Yokahu Observation Tower), which resembles a castle turret, rises from a little roadside hill. A peek through the windows of its circular stairway gives you a hint of the vistas awaiting you at the top: 1,000-year-old trees, exotic flowers in brilliant hues, birds in flight. Postcards and books on El Yunque are sold in the small kiosk at the tower's base. The parking lot beside the tower has rest rooms. ⊠ *Rte. 191, Km 8.9,* ☎ *no phone.* 🖾 *Free.* ☉ *Daily 7:30–6.*

❼ Just beyond the forest's halfway point along Route 191, the **Centro de Información Sierra Palm** is a great place to stop for trail updates. El Yunque's steep slopes, unstable wet soil, heavy rainfall, and exuberant plant life result in the need for intensive trail maintenance; some trails must be cleared and cleaned at least twice a year. Rangers at the office here have information on closures, conditions of open trails, what flora and fauna to look for, and any activities planned that day. There are rest rooms and water fountains by the parking lot. ⊠ *Rte. 191, Km 11.6,* ☎ *no phone,* WEB *www.southernregion.fs.fed.us/caribbean.* 🖾 *Free.* ☉ *Daily 7:30–6.*

❽ Palo Colorado, the red-barked tree in which the endangered cotorra nests, dominates the forest surrounding the **Centro de Información Palo Colorado.** The center—which is home to Forest Adventure Tours and its two-hour, ranger-led hikes (reservations are required)—is the gateway for several walks. The easy Baño del Oro Trail starts at a concrete pool built in the 1930s (swimming isn't permitted) and loops 2 km (1 mi) through an area dubbed the Palm Forest. The even shorter El Caimitillo Trail starts at the same place and runs for about 1 km (½ mi). Although it begins as asphalt, the challenging El Yunque/Mt. Britton Trail turns to gravel as it climbs El Yunque Peak. Just beyond the trailhead

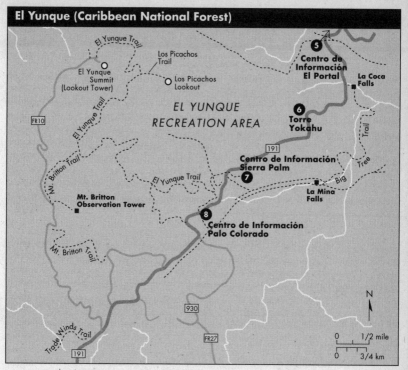

El Yunque (Caribbean National Forest)

is the Palo Colorado Stream, followed by the detour to the Baño del Oro and Caimitillo trails. At a higher elevation you can follow the Mt. Britton spur to an observation tower built in the 1930s. Without detours onto any of the side trails, El Yunque Trail takes about three hours round-trip and includes some mild ascents. Signs clearly mark each turnoff, so it's hard to get lost if you stay on the path. All the trails here are edged by giant ferns, bamboo, and oversize impatiens. There are rest rooms and parking at the center and a picnic area nearby. ⊠ *Rte. 191, Km 11.9,* ☎ *787/888–5646,* WEB *www.southernregion.fs.fed.us/caribbean.* ☞ *Free; guided hikes $5.* ☉ *Daily 8–5.*

Shopping

While in the Centro de Información El Portal, buy a recording of the tree frog's song or a video about the endangered green parrot, pick up a coffee-table book about the rain forest, try on El Yunque T-shirts, and check out the books for ecominded children at the large **Caribbean National Forest Gift Shop** (⊠ Rte. 191, Km 4.3, ☎ 787/888–1880). Tucked among the rain-forest gifts are other Puerto Rican items, including note cards, maps, soaps, jams, and coffee.

En Route Puerto Ricans rarely drive from El Yunque or Río Grande to Luquillo without a stop at the *friquitines* (seafood kiosks) that line Route 3 west of the beach turnoff. They're busy all day, serving passing truckers, area businesspeople, and sand-covered families en route to or from the beach in Luquillo. Although some kiosks have larger seating areas than others, they all offer much the same fare, including cold drinks, plates of fried fish (head and tail still attached), conch salad, and fritters (usually codfish or corn).

144 PARROTS AND COUNTING

THE TAÍNO INDIANS CALLED IT the *iguaca*, Spanish speakers refer to it as the *cotorra*, and scientists know it as *Amazona vittata*. Whatever moniker it takes, the Puerto Rican green parrot—the only one native to the island—is one of the world's 10 rarest birds. It nests primarily in the upper levels of El Yunque and in the nearby Sierra de Luquillo. The bird is almost entirely green, though there are touches of blue on its wings, white rings around its eyes, and a red band just above its beak. It's only about 12 inches long, and its raucous squawk doesn't match its delicate appearance. The parrots mate for life. In February (the rain forest's driest season), they build nests within tree hollows and lay three to four eggs. Both parents feed the young.

When the Spanish arrived, the parrot population was an estimated 1 million on the main island, Vieques, and Culebra. But colonization meant deforestation, and by the mid-19th century, there was already a recorded decline in the number of birds. The decrease was even more rapid after the Spanish-American War, when the United States began clearing forest lands. Hurricanes and parasites have also affected the population, and parrot hunting was common until being outlawed in 1940. By 1967, there were only 19 birds; in a 1975 count, the total was only 13.

A program to increase the number of parrots has shown marked success. In late May 2001, 16 parrots bred in rain forest aviaries were successfully released into El Yunque. Although such releases are annual events, this was the largest one to date. Radio tracking has shown that the birds are dispersing throughout more of El Yunque. Officials are optimistic that their numbers will continue to grow. At this writing, there were an estimated 44 green parrots in the wild and another 100 in captivity. If you're very observant (and very lucky), you might just spot one.

Luquillo

9 *13 km (8 mi) northeast of Río Grande; 45 km (28 mi) east of San Juan.*

Known as the "Sun Capital" of Puerto Rico, Luquillo has one of the island's best-equipped family beaches. It's also a community where fishing traditions are respected. On the east end of Balneario de Luquillo, past the guarded swimming area, fishermen launch small boats and drop nets in open stretches between coral reefs.

Like many other Puerto Rican towns, Luquillo has its signature festival, in this case the Festival de Platos Típicos (Festival of Typical Dishes), a late November culinary event that revolves around one ingredient: coconut. During the festivities, many of the community's 18,000 residents gather at the main square to sample treats rich with coconut or coconut milk. There's also plenty of free entertainment, including folk shows, troubadour contests, and salsa bands.

Beaches

Just off Route 3, gentle, shallow waters lap the edges of **Balneario de Luquillo,** a palm-lined beach that's a magnet for families. It's well equipped with dressing and rest rooms, lifeguards, guarded parking, food stands, picnic areas, and even cocktail kiosks. It's most distinctive facility, though, is the Mar Sin Barreras (Sea Without Barriers), a low-sloped ramp leading into the water that allows wheelchair users to take a dip. The beach is open every day but Monday from 9 to 5. Admission is $2 per car.

Waving palm trees and fishing boats add charm to the small **Playa Costa Azul,** although the ugly residential buildings along the beach make an unattractive backdrop. The water here is good for swimming, and the crowds are thinner than elsewhere, but there are no facilities.

Playa La Pared, literally "The Wall Beach," is a surfer haunt. Numerous local competitions are held here throughout the year, and several surfing shops are close by just in case you need a wet suit or a wax for your board. The waves here are medium-range.

Dining and Lodging

$–$$ ✕ **Brass Cactus Bar & Grill.** The ribs and burgers melt in your mouth, and the helpings of crispy fries are generous. Buffalo wings, poppers (stuffed hot peppers), chicken, and steak are also mainstays. Nearly every dish—Southwestern or otherwise—is washed down with beer. Televisions broadcast the latest sporting events, and on the weekend bands often replace the jukebox. ⊠ *Rte. 3, Complejo Turistico Condominio,* ☎ 787/889–5735. *AE, MC, V.*

$–$$ ✕ **Lolita's.** Burritos—washed down with oversize margaritas, of course— are the specialties of this casual Mexican restaurant. Combo plates let you taste a bit of everything, from tacos to enchiladas. Those who eschew tequila can try the yummy house sangria. ⊠ *Rte. 3, Barrio Juan Martín,* ☎ 787/889–5770. *Reservations not accepted. AE, MC, V.*

$–$$ ✕ **Victor's Place.** In a small blue building on downtown's main plaza, this local institution has been serving up Puerto Rican specialties for more than six decades. Traditionally prepared seafood and steaks come with large servings of beans, rice, and tostones. The atmosphere is casual. ⊠ *2 Calle Jesús T. Piñero,* ☎ 787/889–5705. *Reservations not accepted. MC, V. Closed Tues.*

$$ ▥ **Luquillo Beach Inn.** This five-story, white-and-pink hotel is within walking distance of the public beach and caters to families—children stay free with their parents. The one- or two-bedroom suites have sofa beds, kitchenettes, and living rooms equipped with TVs and stereos; the largest sleep up to six people. It's a good jumping off point for visits to El Yunque. Transportation (about $45) can be arranged from San Juan. ⊠ *701 Ocean Dr., 00773,* ☎ *787/889–1063 or 787/889–3333,* ℻ *787/889–1966,* ⬛ *home.coqui.net/jcdiaz. 36 suites. Bar, air-conditioning, fans, cable TV with movies, in-room VCRs, kitchenettes, microwaves, room service, pool, outdoor hot tub, dry cleaning, laundry service, business services, free parking. AE, MC, V. FAP.*

Outdoor Activities and Sports

Divers' Outlet (⊠ 38 Calle Fernández Garcia, ☎ 787/889–5721 or 888/ 746–3483) is a full-service dive shop. It offers PADI certification, rents equipment, and can arrange scuba outings. **La Selva Surf** (⊠ 250 Calle Fernández Garcia, ☎ 787/889–6205, ⬛ www.rainforestsafari.com/ selva), near Playa La Pared, has anything a surfer could need, including news about current conditions. It also sells sunglasses, T-shirts, skateboards, sandals, watches, bathing suits, and other beach necessities.

Fajardo

🔟 *11 km (7 mi) southeast of Luquillo; 55 km (34 mi) southeast of San Juan.*

Fajardo, founded in 1772, has historical notoriety as a port where pirates stocked up on supplies. It later developed into a fishing community and an area where sugarcane flourished. (There are still cane fields on the city's fringes.) Today it's a hub for the yachts that use its marinas; the divers who head to its good offshore sites; and for the day-trippers who travel by catamaran, ferry, or plane to the off-islands of Culebra and Vieques. With the most significant docking facilities on the island's eastern side, Fajardo is a bustling city of 37,000—so bustling, in fact, that its unremarkable downtown is often congested and difficult to navigate.

Puerto del Rey Marina, home to 750 ships, is one of the Caribbean's largest marinas. It's the place to hook up with a scuba-diving group, arrange an excursion to Vieques's Bioluminescent Bay, or charter a fishing boat. The marina also has several restaurants and boating-supply stores. ⊠ *Rte. 3, Km 51.2,* ☎ *787/860–1000,* WEB *www.marinapuertodelrey.com.*

The 316-acre **Reserva Natural Las Cabezas de San Juan,** on a headland north of Fajardo, is owned by the nonprofit Conservation Trust of Puerto Rico. You ride in open-air trolleys and wander down boardwalks through seven ecosystems, including lagoons, mangrove swamps, and dry-forest areas. Green iguanas skitter across paths, and guides identify other endangered species. A half-hour hike down a wooden walkway brings you to the mangrove-lined Laguna Grande, where bioluminescent microorganisms glow at night. The restored Fajardo lighthouse is the final stop on the reserve's mandatory tour (reservations required). Its Spanish colonial tower has been in operation since 1882, making it Puerto Rico's second-oldest lighthouse. The first floor houses ecological displays; a winding staircase leads to an observation deck. A few miles past the reserve is the fishing area known as Las Croabas, where seafood snacks are sold along the waterfront. ⊠ *Rte. 987 near Las Croabas,* ☎ *787/722–5882 or 787/860–2560,* WEB *www. fideicomiso.org.* ▣ *$5.* ⊙ *Fri.–Sun.; groups only Wed.–Thurs. Guided tours are required; English tours at 2.*

Beach
Balneario Seven Seas, on Route 987 near the Reserva Natural Las Cabezas de San Juan, is a long stretch of powdery sand with a smattering of shade. Facilities include a few refreshment kiosks, picnic and camping areas, changing rooms, bathrooms, and showers. On weekends, the beach attracts crowds keen on its calm, clear waters—perfect for swimming and other water sports. It's closed on Monday.

Dining and Lodging
$$$ ✕ **Blossom's.** Teppanyaki creations join Hunan and Szechuan specialties at this restaurant. The sushi bar gets rave reviews. Note that diners tend to dress up here, and there's an overall sense of romance. ⊠ *Rte. 987, Km 3.4,* ☎ *787/863–1000 Ext. 7048. Reservations essential. AE, MC, V. No lunch Mon.–Sat.*

$$–$$$ ✕ **Ristorante Otello.** You can dine inside, enveloped in soft, romantic light, or slide outside to the terrace for a breezy meal under the stars at this northern Italian restaurant, one of the many eateries at the Wyndham El Conquistador Resort and Country Club. Start with the minestrone—it's a guaranteed winner—and follow it with one of the pasta or risotti dishes. ⊠ *Rte. 987, Km 3.4,* ☎ *787/860–0555. AE, MC, V. No lunch.*

$–$$$ ✕ **A La Banda.** At this friendly, waterside eatery you can sit in a dining room with nautical details or on a terrace overlooking the marina. Steaks and poultry figure on the menu, but the kitchen truly excels at Puerto Rican and seafood dishes, including fresh lobster. ⊠ *Puerto del Rey Marina, Rte. 3, Km 51.2,* ☎ *787/860–9162. MC, V.*

$–$$ ✕ **Anchor's Inn.** Seafood is the specialty at this meson gastronómico. Clever maritime decor and superb cooking have made it a local favorite;

the convenient location down the road from El Conquistador Resort lures visitors. Try the *chillo entero* (fried whole red snapper) or the paella. ⊠ *Rte. 987, Km 2.7, Villas Las Croabas,* ☎ *787/863–7200. Reservations not accepted. AE, MC, V. Closed Tues.*

$–$$ ✕ **Rosa's Sea Food.** Despite its name, this a good spot for steak and chicken as well as seafood. As this is meson gastronómico, the preparations for many dishes are authentically Puerto Rican. ⊠ *Rte. 195, Tablazo 536, Playa Punta Real,* ☎ *787/863–0213. Reservations not accepted. AE, MC, V. Closed Wed.*

$ ✕ **Sardinera Seven Seas.** If you've worked up a hunger at Seven Seas Beach walk across the sand and over a grassy hill to this no-frills, down-home landmark. You know the seafood here is fresh: fishermen fillet their catches on tables outside the restaurant. Choices include crab stew, grilled red snapper, and a rich selection of *pastelitos* (deep-fried turnovers stuffed with crab, shrimp, or lobster). The place closes at around 7 PM daily. ⊠ *Calle Croabas, Km 5.5, Las Croabas,* ☎ *787/ 863–0320. Reservations not accepted. No credit cards.*

$$$$ 🏨 **Wyndham El Conquistador Resort and Country Club.** What many
★ consider Puerto Rico's loveliest resort is on a bluff above the ocean. The colossal hotel and the villas in Las Casitas Village and Las Olas Village have Moorish and Spanish colonial architectural details. Cobblestone streets and fountain-filled plazas enhance the feeling that this place is more like a community than a complex. The resort's beach is on Palomino Island just offshore; a free shuttle boat takes you there and back. The staff prides itself on its attentive service. If the place seems familiar, it may be because the James Bond movie *Goldfinger* was filmed here. ⊠ *1000 Av. El Conquistador (Box 70001, 00738),* ☎ *787/863– 1000, 800/996–3426, or 800/468–5228,* 𝔽𝔸𝕏 *787/253–0178,* 𝕎𝔼𝔹 *www.wyndham.com. 715 rooms, 16 suites. 11 restaurants, 4 bars, air-conditioning, cable TV with movies and video games, minibars, 5 pools, spa, 18-hole golf course, 8 tennis courts, health club, beach, dive shop, snorkeling, windsurfing, boating, jet skiing, marina, shop, casino, nightclub, children's programs, dry cleaning, laundry service, meeting rooms, airport shuttle. AE, MC, V. FAP.*

$$ 🏨 **Fajardo Inn.** This 4-acre hilltop property has a hotel and a B&B. The views—of the Atlantic and El Yunque against a backdrop of gardens—are lovely from either. It's a breezy, comfortable inn with reasonable prices. ⊠ *Rte. 195, 52 Parcelas, Beltran Sector, 00740,* ☎ *787/ 860–6000,* 𝔽𝔸𝕏 *787/860–5063,* 𝕎𝔼𝔹 *www.fajardoinn.com. 54 rooms. Restaurant, breakfast room, sports bar, air-conditioning, pool, meeting room, free parking. AE, MC, V. EP.*

$–$$ 🏨 **Parador La Familia.** From the white wooden guest house—the property's centerpiece—the view is right out to the ocean. It's a convenient spot to land for the night, and it's on the list of government-approved paradores. The restaurant serves decent breakfasts and light lunches. ⊠ *Rte. 987, Km 4.1, Las Croabas, 00648,* ☎ *787/863–1193,* 𝔽𝔸𝕏 *787/ 860–5354,* 𝕎𝔼𝔹 *www.hotellafamilia.com. 35 rooms. Restaurant, bar, pool, shop, meeting rooms, free parking. AE, DC, MC, V. FAP.*

Nightlife

Although most of the evening action takes place in the El Conquistador's lounges, there are a few neighborhood bars where locals drink beer. You can play slots, blackjack, roulette, and video poker at **El Conquistador Casino** (⊠ 1000 Av. El Conquistador, ☎ 787/863–1000), a typical hotel gambling facility within the resort's lavish grounds.

Outdoor Activities and Sports

GOLF

The 18-hole Arthur Hills–designed course at **El Conquistador Country Club** (⊠ 1000 Av. El Conquistador, ☎ 787/863–6784) is famous for its 200-ft changes in elevation. The trade winds make every shot challenging.

WATER SPORTS

At **East Winds Excursions** (⊠ Puerto del Rey Marina, Rte. 3, Km 51.4, ☎ 787/863–3434, WEB www.eastwindcats.com) a 62-ft catamaran takes you offshore for diving and snorkeling. The outing features stops at isolated beaches and a lunch buffet. **Palomino Divers** (⊠ 1000 Av. El Conquistador, ☎ 787/863–1000 Ext. 7917), at El Conquistador Resort, focuses its scuba and snorkeling activity on the islets of Palominos, Lobos, and Diablo. At **Sea Ventures Pro Dive Center** (⊠ Puerto del Rey Marina, Rte. 3, Km 51.4, ☎ 787/863–3483 or 800/739–3483, WEB www.divepuertorico.com) you can get PADI certified, arrange dive trips to 20 offshore sites, or organize boating and sailing excursions.

Shopping

At El Conquistador Resort, Maria Elba Torres runs the **Galería Arrecife** (⊠ 1000 Av. El Conquistador, ☎ 787/863–3972), which shows only works by artists living in the Caribbean. Look for ceramics by Rafael de Olmo and jewelry made from fish scales. Chocolate-loving Laurie Humphrey had trouble finding a supplier for her sweet tooth, so she opened the **Paradise Store** (⊠ Rte. 194, Km 0.4, ☎ 787/863–8182). Lindt and other gourmet chocolates jam the shop, which also sells flowers and such gift items as Puerto Rican–made soaps.

VIEQUES AND CULEBRA

A hop west from Fajardo across the water are the two islands where Puerto Ricans go when they want to escape from civilization: Vieques and Culebra. The beauty of both is readily apparent, whether you approach by sea or air. Banana-shape Vieques floats atop azure water; smaller Culebra is edged by white sands and encircled by islets.

These sleepy outposts are—for now, anyway—bereft of traffic lights, casinos, fast-food chains, movie houses, and other modern trappings. Temperatures hover around 80 degrees, the stunning white beaches are devoid of crowds, and "barefoot" is often part of the dress code. The many open-air restaurants and simple guest houses rely on overhead fans and trade winds to keep you comfortable.

Both islands—sometimes dubbed the "Spanish Virgin Islands"—are accessible from the main island via 90-minute ferry trips and 10-minute puddle-jumper flights that leave Fajardo daily. There's also air service from San Juan. Note that during the Easter holidays, mainlanders flock here for camping and partying on the beach. If you're planning a trip during Holy Week, make reservations as far in advance as possible and don't expect to find tranquility.

Vieques

⑪–⑬ *13 km (8 mi) southeast of Fajardo by sea.*

Local lore has it that Captain Kidd once visited Vieques when it was a pirate haven. Through the early 1900s, sugarcane dominated the economy. Later in the century, the United States commandeered the island for use as a naval training ground. The military still controls two-thirds of it, including some of the best beaches, and although Puerto Ricans have staged protests aimed at ousting the military from Vieques, they've made little headway. The 2001 terrorist attacks and the heightened concern over national security and military preparedness decreased the likelihood that the military will cease exercises in the near future.

ISLAND IRE

FOR NEARLY SIX DECADES, the U.S. Navy has set the course of Vieques's development. It owns the island's eastern and western sections, and the civilian area is sandwiched in between. Fishermen have protested the live-fire maneuvers here for years. But when an off-target bomb killed a civilian on navy land in April of 1999, opposition began to transform the island's placid beaches into political hotbeds.

In late 1999, Puerto Rico's governor called for a vote on whether the navy should stay or go by 2003. A nonbinding referendum in July 2001 found that 68% of Vieques's voters wanted the navy to leave immediately. Governor Sila Calderon, who took office that year, fueled the opposition by voicing her own opinion that the military must leave.

For much of 2000 and 2001, protests became so commonplace that there were encampments of opponents. Songs with such titles as "Paz Pa' Vieques" ("Peace for Vieques") began to surface, as did bumper-stickers and T-shirts with protest slogans. Environmental lawyer Robert F. Kennedy Jr. (who gave a baby daughter the middle name "Vieques"), the wife of Reverend Jesse Jackson, and Reverend Al Sharpton were arrested for trespassing on a bombing range. Latin pop celebrities added to the fanfare when they joined the activities.

In early 2002 a U.S. District Court judge dismissed Governor Calderon's federal lawsuit aimed at halting the shelling exercises. In it, the governor had charged that they caused health problems. The military argued that the exercises were essential. At the same time, many of the protestors vowed to no longer invade navy lands; they made the promise to show solidarity with the dozens of Puerto Ricans killed in the World Trade Center attack.

Still, in April 2002, after a six-month hiatus, passions flared anew when navy planes began exercises at a contested firing range. The military action came under a compromise arrangement in which the navy will practice only 90 days a year—down from 180—and ammunition will be limited to inert bombs.

Although President George W. Bush has expressed his support for the navy's removal in 2003, U.S. lawmakers have taken an increasingly pro-military position in the brouhaha citing the events of September 11, 2001. They have even gone so far as to bar the navy from closing the range until it finds another suitable location—a position that may well keep controversy alive for years to come.

Some say the navy's presence has both helped to keep the island pristine—there's little land on which to develop megaresorts—and provided it with a good infrastructure, including roadways, water service, and an airport that's better maintained than you might expect on an island this size. And, in truth, the bombing sounds like distant thunder.

Some 9,300 civilians call Vieques home, many of them expatriate artists and guest-house or vacation-villa owners from the mainland United States. Other islanders fish for a living or work in tourism-related fields. All were drawn here by the same thing that lures visitors: quiet days, small-town friendliness, and natural beauty. Only 6 km (4 mi) across at its widest point, the 34-km-long (21-mi-long) island is packed with stunning beaches (so many that some aren't even named) and marvelous scuba and snorkeling opportunities.

Just because Vieques is sleepy doesn't mean there's nothing to do besides hit the beach. It has two communities—Isabel Segunda, where the ferries dock, and the smaller Esperanza. It's also home to the astonishing Bahía Mosquito, a fort built by the early Spanish governors, and several good restaurants.

⓫ **Faro Punta Mulas,** a Spanish-built lighthouse beside a ferry dock, dates from the late 1800s. In 1992 it was carefully restored and now houses a maritime museum that traces much of the island's history, including the visit by South American liberation leader Simón Bolívar. ⌂ *At end of Rte. 200,* ☎ *787/741–0060.* ⌷ *Free.* ☉ *Wed.–Sun. 10–4.*

★ ⓬ **Bahía Mosquito** (Mosquito Bay, also known as Bioluminescent Bay or Phosphorescent Bay) is one of the world's best spots to have a glow-in-the-dark experience with undersea dinoflagellates. Tour operators offer kayak trips or excursions on nonpolluting boats to see the bay's tiny microorganisms that appear to light up when their water is agitated. Dive into the bay and you'll emerge covered in sparkling water. Look behind your boat, and you'll see a twinkling wake. Even the fish that jump from the water will bear an eerie glow. The high concentration of dinoflagellates sets the bay apart from the other spots (including others in Puerto Rico) that are home to these tiny organisms. The bay is at its best when there is little or no moonlight; rainy nights are beautiful, too, because the raindrops splashing in the water produce ricochet sparkles. Some of the best excursions to the bay are offered by Sharon Grasso of Island Adventures. ⌂ *South central side of island, on unpaved roads off Rte. 997,* ☎ *no phone.* ⌷ *Free.* ☉ *Daily.*

⓭ The **Museo El Fortín Conde de Mirasol** (Count of Mirasol Fort Museum) is housed in what was the last military structure begun by the Spaniards in the New World. It was erected on Vieques's northern coast in 1840 at the order of Count Mirasol, then governor of Puerto Rico. The museum has changing exhibits of local art and displays of items that chronicle Vieques's past: Taíno Indian relics, flags of the European powers that hoped to lay claim to the island, a collection of early maps, and a bust of Simón Bolívar. ⌂ *471 Calle Magnolia, Isabel Segunda,* ☎ *787/741–1717,* ⓦ *www.enchanted-isle.com/elfortin.* ⌷ *$1.* ☉ *Wed.–Sun. 10–4.*

Beaches

Of Vieques's more than three dozen beaches, **Playa Sun Bay** on Route 997 is one of the most popular. Its white sands skirt a mile-long, crescent-shape bay. You'll find food kiosks, picnic tables, camping areas, and a bathhouse; on weekdays, when the crowds are thin, you might also find wild horses grazing among the palm trees in the shady area facing the sea. Admission to the beach is $2 a day on weekends; it's free on weekdays.

An unpaved road east of Playa Sun Bay and off Route 997 leads to **Playa Media Luna,** a pretty little beach that's ideal for families because the water is calm and below your knees for yards out. This is a good spot to try your hand at snorkeling. Take note, though, that there are no facilities.

Within the navy's territory, **Red Beach** is a primo sunbathing spot. The water is crystal clear, but the surf is strong, making swimming here difficult. There are no facilities, so bring snacks and plenty of drinking water. You get here only after traveling a series of unpaved, unnamed roads, so ask for directions from a hotel staffer; while you're at it, ask whether the beach is even open as the military sometimes restricts access to it.

Dining and Lodging

$$-$$$ ✕ **Café Blu.** The island's most elegant restaurant is beside the posh Inn
★ on the Blue Horizon, right on the coast. Start with a drink at the bar, then move to a table for an unforgettable meal of pan-blackened tuna, fresh trout marinated with tropical spices, or Asian barbecued lamb. If you're a cigar smoker, seek out the "Cigar Tree," a tree surrounded by chairs where stogie lovers congregate to light one up and savor a snifter of port. ⊠ *Rte. 966, Km. 4.2,* ☎ *787/741–3318. AE, MC, V. No lunch. Closed Mon.–Wed.*

$$-$$$ ✕ **Café Media Luna.** Tucked into an old building in Isabel Segunda, this eatery is a local favorite. You'll have a hard time figuring out what type of food it specializes in, though; the menu runs the gamut from Vietnamese spring rolls to tandoori chicken to seafood cooked in wine. All of the options are good. ⊠ *351 Calle Antonio G. Mellado, Isabel Segunda,* ☎ *787/741–2594. AE, MC, V. No lunch. Closed Mon.– Tues.*

$-$$ ✕ **Trapper John's.** This restaurant at the Crow's Nest guest house is popular for its happy hour (5–7 with free appetizers) and its theme nights. On Friday and Saturday, for example, prime rib is the special. But the real treats are the Caribbean lobster and the veal scallopini. ⊠ *Rte. 201, Km 1.6, Barrio Florida,* ☎ *787/741–0033. AE, MC, V.*

$$$-$$$$ 🏨 **Inn on the Blue Horizon.** The island's most expensive hotel consists
★ of six Mediterranean-style villas and a main house near the sea on what used to be a plantation. You truly feel away from it all at this gorgeous 20-acre complex. None of the rooms has a phone, and even air-conditioning is rare (only two rooms have it), but with the breezy location you won't notice the absence. ⊠ *Rte. 996, Km 4.2, outside Esperanza (Box 1556, 00765),* ☎ *787/741–3318,* FAX *787/741–0522,* WEB *www.innont.thebluehorizon.com. 9 rooms. Restaurant, bar, no air-conditioning in some rooms, fans, no room TVs, pool, massage, bicycles, free parking; no kids under 14. AE, MC, V. BP.*

$$$ 🏨 **Casa Cielo.** The fact that it has no physical address is an indication of just how much of a getaway this sprawling great house—atop a windswept hill 13 km (8 mi) from Vieques's east coast—really is. Seven of its rooms face the ocean (some the Atlantic, some the Caribbean) and have private balconies; two face the garden patio. The inn prides itself on providing such sumptuous extras as all-cotton sheets and massages. ⊠ *Box 310, 00765,* ☎ FAX *787/741–2403,* WEB *www.enchanted-isle.com/ casacielo. 9 rooms. No air-conditioning in some rooms, fans, pool, massage, meeting rooms; no kids, no smoking. MC, V. BP.*

$$-$$$ 🏨 **Crow's Nest.** This quiet guest house has 5 acres and an outdoor deck with a marvelous view. Although it's not on the water, it's just a few minutes' drive from Esperanza and its restaurants and is an easy jumping-off point for visits to beaches on either coast. ⊠ *Rte. 201, Km 1.6, Barrio Florida, 00765,* ☎ *787/741–8525,* FAX *787/741–1294,* WEB *www.*

crownestvieques.com. 15 rooms. Restaurant, breakfast room, air-conditioning, fans, kitchenettes, pool. AE, MC, V. BP.

$$–$$$ ⊠ **Hacienda Tamarindo.** Interior designer Linda Vail and her husband
★ Burr are the charming hosts at this hilltop guest house, which is named
after the venerable tamarind tree that rises three stories in the lobby.
The panoramic views include grounds landscaped with coconut palms
and mahogany trees as well as tropical flowers. Half the guest rooms—
which have terra-cotta floors, light pastel color schemes, and antiques—are air-conditioned. The rest are cooled by overhead fans and
trade winds. A full breakfast is served on the second-floor terrace. ⊠
Rte. 996, Km 4.5, outside Esperanza (Box 1569, 00765), ☎ *787/741–
8525,* FAX *787/741–3215,* WEB *www.enchanted-isle.com/tamarindo. 16
rooms. Breakfast room, no air-conditioning in some rooms, fans, pool;
no kids under 15. AE, MC, V. BP.*

Nightlife

Amapola Tavern (⊠ 144 Calle Flamboyán, Esperanza, ☎ 787/741–
1382) has salsa music coming from its sound system, the island's
biggest TV screen (making this *the* place to be on sports nights), and
a bartender who turns out exquisite tropical concoctions. **Bananas** (⊠
142 Calle Flamboyán, Esperanza, ☎ 787/741–8700) equals burgers
and booze—not to mention enthusiastic crowds. There's sometimes live
music and dancing.

Outdoor Activities and Sports

BOATING

Aqua Frenzy Kayaks (⊠ at dock area below Calle Flamboyán, Esperanza, ☎ 787/741–0913) rents kayaks and arranges kayak tours of
Bahía Mosquito. Reservations for the excursions, which cost $20,
must be made at least 24 hours in advance. Former schoolteacher
Sharon Grasso's **Island Adventures** (⊠ Rte. 996, Esperanza, ☎ 787/
741–0720) will take you to the glowing Bahía Mosquito aboard nonpolluting, electrically powered pontoon boats. The cost is about $20
per person.

SCUBA DIVING AND SNORKELING

Blue Caribe Dive Center (⊠ Calle Flamboyán, Esperanza, ☎ 787/741–
2522, WEB www.enchanted-isle.com/bluecaribe) offers scuba excursions to several sites; night dives in Bahía Mosquito can also be arranged.
Environmentalist Richard Barone's **Get Snorkeled! with Captain Richard**
(⊠ no office; trips are launched from the shore at Esperanza, ☎ 787/
741–1980) is a program of shallow-water, from-the-shore snorkeling
expeditions geared toward children. As you snorkel, he stops to point
out the habits of sea creatures.

Shopping

Artists show and sell their work at **Casa Vieja Gallery** (⊠ Rte. 996 outside Esperanza, ☎ 787/741–3078), in a Caribbean-style building at the
entrance to the grounds of Inn on the Blue Horizon. For swimsuits and
sun dresses, try **The Mall** (⊠ Rte. 996, Esperanza, ☎ 787/741–3751),
which isn't a mall in the conventional sense, but rather a bright boutique.

Culebra

⑭ *28 km (17 mi) east of Fajardo by sea.*

There's archaeological evidence that small groups of pre-Columbian
people lived on Culebra, and certainly pirates landed here from time
to time. But Puerto Rico's Spanish rulers didn't bother laying claim to
it until 1886; its dearth of freshwater made it unattractive for settlement. Although it now has modern conveniences, its pace seems little
changed from a century ago.

Twelve kilometers (seven miles) long, five kilometers (three miles) wide, and mostly unspoiled, Culebra is actually more of an islet than an island. At one point it was controlled, like its neighbor Vieques, by the U.S. Navy. When the military withdrew, it turned much of the land into a wildlife reserve. There's only one town, Dewey, named after U.S. Admiral George Dewey.

The whole island operates like a small town: people know each other, people respect each other, and no one wants noise or drama. When the sun goes down, Culebra winds down as well. But during the day it's a delightful place to stake out a spot on the beach and read, swim, or search for shells. So what causes stress on the island? Nothing.

Commissioned by President Theodore Roosevelt in 1909, **Refugio Nacional de Vida Silvestre de Culebra** is one of the nation's oldest wildlife refuges. Some 1,500 acres of the island make up a protected area. It's a lure for hikers and bird-watchers: Culebra teems with seabirds, from laughing gulls and roseate terns to red-billed tropic birds and sooty terns. Maps and trails of the refuge are hard to come by, but you can stop by the U.S. Fish and Wildlife Service office near the airport (and close to the cemetery) to find out about trail conditions and determine whether you're headed to an area that requires a permit. The office also can tell you whether the leatherback turtles are nesting. From mid-April to mid-July, volunteers help to monitor and tag these creatures, which nest on Culebra's beaches, especially Playa Resaca and Playa Brava. If you'd like to volunteer, you must agree to help out for at least three nights. ⊠ *Between Rte. 250 and Rte. 251, near Monte Resaca, north of Dewey,* ☎ *787/742–0115 or 787/254–3456 for information about leatherback monitoring.* ✆ *Free.* ☉ *Daily.*

Beaches

Take a dive boat or water taxi to Culebra's offshore islet, Culebrita, where you'll find **Playa Culebrita** and its fabulous coral reef. The beach is gorgeous, and there's a series of rocks that form natural pools. Snuggling into one of them is like taking a warm bath. This is a superb spot for snorkeling right from the shore. You can also visit an old lighthouse.

Off Route 250 on Culebra's north coast, **Playa Flamenco** is an amazingly long stretch of white sand. During the week it's pleasantly uncrowded; on the weekend, though, it fills up. As you stroll along it, don't be surprised if you come upon a rusting tank or two—they're left over from when the area was used by the U.S. Navy. (To get here, you should ask for directions from a local; the nearest roads are unnamed and unnumbered.)

As you head down rugged roads at the end of Route 250 to **Playa Zoni,** you'll wonder whether it's worth the tortuous journey. It is. On the island's northeastern end, about 11 km (7 mi) northeast of Dewey, this beach is far more isolated—precisely because of the hassle getting here—than Playa Flamenco, and many believe it's just as beautiful. It's also a good spot for snorkeling.

Dining and Lodging

$–$$ ✕ **Dinghy Dock.** Dinghy Dock is a pulse point for Dewey. Culebra's version of heavy traffic—including the arrival and departure of the thatch-covered water taxi, *Muff the Magic Fun Boat*—takes place around the dock where this restaurant sits. The long menu includes vegetarian specialties as well as T-bone steaks. Daily specials often concentrate on the restaurant's forte: creole-style seafood, including grilled native grouper and yellowtail. ⊠ *Carretera Fulladoza, Dewey,* ☎ *787/742–0581. Reservations not accepted. MC, V.*

$-$$　✕🏠 **Mamacitas.** On a breezy dock overlooking a canal, the restaurant ($-$$) here is the kind of place where you start up a conversation with the folks at the plastic table next to yours and end up making lasting friendships. Begin with a tropical drink and then move on to well-made pasta dishes or seafood fresh from the ocean. The adjoining guest house has only three rooms, but each is charming and has a balcony; one also has a kitchenette. ✉ 66 *Calle Castelar, Dewey 00775,* ☎ 787/742–0090. *3 rooms. Restaurant, air-conditioning, fans, dock. AE, MC, V. FAP.*

$$　🏠 **Club Seaborne.** Overlooking Fulladoza Bay and a 10-minute drive from Dewey, this pretty pink complex consists of communal rooms and two guest rooms in a main house, eight villas, a two-bedroom cottage, and a small efficiency apartment dubbed the Crow's Nest. The cottage has kitchen facilities and is popular with families. Gardens form the backdrop. ✉ *Carretera Fulladoza, Km 1.5 (Box 357, 00775),* ☎ 787/742–3169, ℻ 787/742–3176. *3 rooms, 8 villas, 1 cottage with kitchen. Restaurant, bar, pool, library. AE, MC, V. BP.*

$-$$　🏠 **Posada La Hamaca.** Functional rather than cozy, this little guest house is in a concrete building at the edge of Dewey. It's within walking distance of restaurants, shops, and grocery stores. Ice, coolers, and towels for the beach are provided free of charge. You can hang out at the back dock, which is on a canal that separates Culebra's harbor from the Caribbean. ✉ 68 *Calle Castelar (Box 388), Dewey 00775,* ☎ 787/742–3516, ℻ 787–742–0181, 🌐 *www.posada.com. 8 rooms, 3 apartments. Air-conditioning, fans, some kitchenettes, dock. MC, V. EP.*

Outdoor Activities and Sports

BIKING

Biking is a good way to explore the island on your own. You can rent bikes for $20 a day at **Culebra Bike Shop** (✉ 138 Calle Escudero, Dewey, ☎ 787/742–2209).

BOATING

At **Flamenco Resort & Fishing Club** (✉ 10 Pedro Nárquez, Playa Flamenco, ☎ 787/742–3144) you can charter sailboats for offshore exploring. **Reef Link Divers** (✉ Carretera Fulladoza, inside Dinghy Dock restaurant, Dewey, ☎ 787/742–0581) rents kayaks for about $8 an hour.

SCUBA DIVING AND SNORKELING

Travelers have recounted that dives with **Culebra Dive Shop** (✉ 317 Calle Escudero, Dewey, ☎ 787/742–3335, 🌐 www.culebradiveshop.com) are spectacular. A one-tank dive runs about $45. For about the same price, the shop also offers day-long snorkeling trips. **Reef Link Divers** (✉ Carretera Fulladoza, inside Dinghy Dock restaurant, Dewey, ☎ 787/742–0581) caters to everyone—from beginners to experts—and specializes in coral-reef sites near Culebra. A day package starts at $75; a full-week package that includes a night dive runs about $350. Full-day snorkeling trips cost about $45 per person, including lunch.

Shopping

Loma Gift Shop (✉ Calle Escudero at the canal, Dewey, ☎ 787/742–3565) is a good spot for T-shirts, jewelry, island photographs and watercolors, and other souvenirs. The tiny gift shop at **Mamacitas** (✉ 66 Calle Castelar, Dewey, ☎ 787/742–0090) guest house has exceptional hand-painted T-shirts and other original-design gifts.

THE SOUTHEASTERN COAST

From Fajardo, a good way to explore the southeast is to travel along the old coastal Route 3 as it weaves on and off the shoreline and passes through small towns. The route takes a while to travel but offers terrific beach and mountain scenery.

Naguabo

⑮ *18 km (11 mi) southwest of Fajardo.*

In this fast-growing municipality's downtown, pastel buildings give the main plaza the look of a child's nursery: a golden-yellow church on one side faces a bright-yellow city hall, and a pink-and-blue amphitheater anchors one corner. It's a good spot for people-watching until the heat drives you to the beach.

Offshore, Cayo Santiago—also known as Monkey Island—is the site of some of the world's most important rhesus monkey research. A small colony of monkeys was introduced to the island in the late 1930s, and since then scientists have been studying their habits and health, especially as they pertain to the study of diabetes and arthritis. You can't land at Cayo Santiago, but Captain Frank Lopez sails a small tour boat—*La Paseadora Naguabeña*—around it.

Beach

Off Route 3 just outside Naguabo, **Playa Húcares** is *the* place to be. Casual outdoor eateries and funky shops vie with the water for your attention. Two Victorian-style houses anchor one end of the waterfront promenade; a dock with excursion boats anchors the other.

Dining and Lodging

$–$$ ✕ **Chumar.** Like the other food kiosks on Playa Húcares, you order at the counter and then grab a seat at one of the plastic tables that line the sidewalk. Paper plates and plastic cutlery accompany the yummy, down-home seafood. ⊠ *Rte. 3, Km 66.5,* ☎ *no phone. Reservations not accepted. MC, V.*

$ ✕ **El Bobby.** This outdoor eatery is one of many in a cluster—the local version of a food court—on Playa Húcares. The fare is unpretentious: fish dishes, deep-fried meat- or seafood-stuffed snacks, and well-chilled beer. On weekends, this place is packed. ⊠ *Rte. 3, Km 66.5,* ☎ *no phone. Reservations not accepted. MC, V.*

$–$$ ⊞ **Casa Cubuy Ecolodge.** El Yunque's southern edge is the setting for this hotel. If you're up for a hike, trails from the lodge lead to a waterfall. If you'd rather relax, hammocks await you on the tiled veranda. Guest rooms are simple—no phones or TVs—but comfortable, with tile floors, rattan furniture, white bedspreads, a wall of windows, and sliding glass doors that open onto balconies. (Note that you must climb many stairs to reach the upper rooms; if this a problem request a room on the lower level.) The proprietor, who believes that healthful eating translates into healthful living, serves meals that are both tasty and wholesome. ⊠ *Rte. 191, Km 22, Barrio Río Blanco, 00744,* ☎ *787/874–6221,* WEB *www.casacubuy.com. 8 rooms. Dining room, no air-conditioning, fans, hiking, free parking. AE, MC, V. FAP.*

Outdoor Activities and Sports

Captain Frank Lopez will sail you around Cayo Santiago aboard *La Paseadora Naguabeña* (⊠ Playa Húcares dock, Rte. 3, Km 66.6, ☎ 787/850–7881). Lopez, a charming, well-informed guide, gears the outings to the group. In an hour or 90 minutes, you can motor around the island and watch the monkeys. You can also make arrangements in advance for snorkeling stops or for him to drop you off at another islet and pick you up later.

En Route Between Naguabo and Humacao are stretches of beach and swaths of undeveloped land, including the swamps, lagoons, and forested areas of the **Refugio de Vida Silvestre de Humacao.** This nature reserve has recreational areas, an information office, rest rooms, children's activities, and camping sites. Fishing and hiking are allowed in some parts, but you should check to see what permits are required. ⊠ *Rte. 3, Km 74.3,* ☎ *787/852–6088 or 787/724–2500.* ⊡ *Free.* ☉ *Weekdays 7:30–3:30.*

Humacao

⑯ *15 km (9 mi) southwest of Naguabo; 55 km (34 mi) southeast of San Juan.*

Humacao, a city of 52,000, is a southeastern powerhouse. It's an educational center and has a growing industrial sector that's slowly replacing the agriculture-based economy. Although it's not considered a tourist destination in and of itself, it's the city associated with the sprawling Candelero Resort at Palmas del Mar, which is outside town. Downtown Humacao, with its narrow, heavily trafficked streets, contains some interesting neocolonial architecture.

Museo Casa Roig, the former residence of sugarcane plantation owner and banker Antonio Roig Torruellas, was built in 1919. Czech architect Antonio Nechodoma designed the facade, unusual for its wide eaves, mosaic work, and stained-glass windows with geometric patterns. This was Puerto Rico's first 20th-century building to go on the register of National Historic Monuments. The Roig family lived in the home until 1956, and it was then abandoned before being turned over to the University of Puerto Rico in 1977. It's currently a museum and cultural center, with historical photos, furniture, and rotating exhibits of works by contemporary island artists. ⊠ *66 Calle Antonio López,* ☎ *787/852–8380.* ⊡ *Free.* ☉ *Wed.–Fri. and Sun. 10–4.*

Plaza de Humacao, downtown's broad square, is anchored by the pale pink Catedral Dulce Nombre de Jesús (Sweet Name of Jesus Cathedral), which dates from 1869. It has a castlelike facade, and even when its grille door is locked, you can peek through to see the sleek altar, polished floors, and stained-glass windows dominated by blues. Across the plaza, four fountains splash under the shade of old trees. People pass through feeding the pigeons, children race down the promenade, and retirees congregate on benches to chat. Look for the little monument with the globe on top; it's a tribute to city sons who died in wars. ⊠ *Av. Font Martel at Calle Ulises Martinez.*

Beach

Right beside the Refugio de Vida Silvestre de Humacao, north of the city on Route 3, is **Playa Punta Santiago,** a long strand with closely planted palm trees that are perfect for stringing up hammocks. The beach has changing facilities and bathrooms, and, at this writing, plans for food kiosks and lifeguard stations are on the table. Until everything's in place, access to the beach is free of charge.

Dining and Lodging

$$–$$$ ✕ **Hermés Creative Cuisine.** The menu at this elegant restaurant in the Palmas del Mar Country Club is distinctive. Chef Hermés Vargas, from the Condado restaurant that also bears his name, likes to experiment with game, including wild boar and venison. You can eat yours alfresco on the terrace or by candlelight in the dining room. ⊠ *Rte. 906, Km 86.4, Palmas del Mar,* ☎ *787/285–2277 or 787/285–2266. Reservations essential. AE, MC, V. No dinner Mon.*

$–$$$ ✕ **Chez Daniel.** The dockside setting and casual atmosphere belie the elegance of Chef Daniel Vasse's meals. His French country–style dishes are noteworthy, and the Catalan-style *bouillinade,* full of fresh fish and bursting with the flavor of a white garlic sauce, is exceptional. When the stars are out and the candles are lit, this spot is 100% romantic. ⊠ *Rte. 906, Palmas del Mar,* ☎ *787/852–6000. Reservations essential. AE, MC, V. Closed Tues.*

$–$$ ✕ **La Pesqueria.** It's difficult to find this rustic waterside restaurant: it has no sign, so be on the lookout for a busy parking lot and picnic tables. The day's fresh catch comes from the kitchen whole; if it's available, the red snapper is especially good as are any of the menu's snacks. ⊠ *Off Rte. 906, near Palmas del Mar Marina,* ☎ *no phone. Reservations not accepted. No credit cards.*

$$$$ ☐ **Candelero Resort at Palmas del Mar.** Shuttle buses scoot you around, and parking attendants and other personnel are good about giving directions. You need such assistance: with 3,000 acres, the grounds are seemingly endless. Accommodations include a 100-room hotel with 110 villas. There are also 85 privately owned condos, a 106-unit time-share complex, myriad bars and restaurants, and a casino. The hotel's rooms and public spaces are open and airy; many have balconies. If you want more space, inquire about the villas, which can be rented by the day, the week, or longer. There's no shortage of activity, from water sports to tennis and golf. ⊠ *Rte. 906 (Box 2020, 00792),* ☎ *787/852–6000,* FAX *787/852–6320,* WEB *www.palmasdelmar.com. 100 rooms, 110 villas. 13 restaurants, 15 bars, air-conditioning, cable TV with movies, minibars, room service, pool, 2 18-hole golf courses, 20 tennis courts, health club, horseback riding, beach, dive shop, dock, snorkeling, windsurfing, fishing, shop, casino, children's programs, airport shuttle. AE, MC, V. MAP.*

Nightlife

The **Palmas del Mar Casino** (⊠ Rte. 906, ☎ 787/852–6000) offers everything from blackjack to slot machines. The action is liveliest on weekends.

Outdoor Activities and Sports

Candelero Resort at Palmas del Mar (⊠ Rte. 906, ☎ 787/285–2256) has two courses: the Rees Jones–designed Flamboyán course is named for the nearly six dozen flamboyant trees that pepper its fairway. The course winds around a lake, over a river, and to the sea before turning toward sand dunes and wetlands. The older, Gary Player–designed Palmas course has a challenging par 5 that scoots around wetlands. Greens fees are $70–$100. **Shiraz Charters** (⊠ Rte. 906, Candelero Resort at Palmas del Mar, Site 6, ☎ 787/285–5718, WEB www.charternet. com/fishers/shiraz) specializes in deep-sea fishing charters in search of tuna. Eight-hour trips start about $150 per person, including equipment and snacks.

EASTERN PUERTO RICO A TO Z

To research prices, get advice from other travelers, and book travel arrangements, visit www.fodors.com.

AIR TRAVEL

In peak season, Vieques Air Link and Isla Nena Air Service offer four flights daily from San Juan to Vieques and two flights daily to Culebra; trips last about 30 minutes and cost $60–$115 one way. There are also daily flights (about 15 minutes long) between San Juan and Fajardo. Both carriers also make the 10-minute flight to the outer islands from Fajardo.

➤ CARRIERS: **Isla Nena Air Service** (☎ 787/741–6362). **Vieques Air Link** (☎ 787/722–3736 or 888/901–9247).

AIRPORTS

Travelers from outside Puerto Rico generally fly into San Juan's Aeropuerto Internacional Luis Muñoz Marín and then transfer to Aeropuerto Fernando L. Rivas Dominici (also known as the Isla Grande Airport) for flights elsewhere on the island. Fajardo is served by the small Aeropuerto Diego Jiménez Torres, which is just southwest of the city on Route 976. The tiny Aeropuerto Antonio Rivera Rodríguez is on Vieques's northwest coast, less than a 15-minute cab ride from Isabel Segunda. Culebra's Aeropuerto Benjamin Rivera Noriega is at the north end of Calle Escudero, which runs right into downtown Dewey. The landing field at Aeropuerto Regional de Humacao is used mostly by private planes.

➤ AIRPORT INFORMATION: **Aeropuerto Antonio Rivera Rodríguez** (☎ 787/741–8358). **Aeropuerto Benjamin Rivera Noriega** (☎ 787/742–0022). **Aeropuerto Diego Jiménez Torres** (☎ 787/860–3110). **Aeropuerto Fernando L. Rivas Dominici** (☎ 787/729–8790). **Aeropuerto Internacional Luis Muñoz Marín** (☎ 787/791–4670). **Aeropuerto Regional de Humacao** (☎ 787/852–8188).

BUS TRAVEL

Puerto Rico's bus system is inefficient and difficult to use if you don't know the island well and/or don't speak Spanish fluently. There are two basic services: the *públicos* (minivans run by transportation cooperatives) and local, city buses. Públicos travel between San Juan and Fajardo (with a stop at the ferry terminal) Monday through Saturday from 4 AM to 6 PM. The full journey can take up to two hours; fares run up to $5, depending on where you board and where you are dropped off, and you pay the driver directly (it's not necessary to tip). There are no central terminals and no information numbers: you simply flag públicos down anywhere along the route (most of which is Route 3).

Within cities and towns, local buses pick up and discharge at marked stops and cost 35¢–50¢. You enter and pay (the exact fair is required) at the front of the bus and exit at the front or the back. Vieques and Culebra are served by their own inexpensive públicos, whose drivers often speak English. Just flag them down. Rates vary depending on your destination, but are usually under $1.

CAR RENTAL

Fajardo and other eastern cities, as well as many resorts, have well-known U.S. rental agencies that offer a range of sizes and makes. (Note that most agencies require drivers to be at least 25 years old.) On Vieques and Culebra, by contrast, you'll find primarily local agencies, including several that specialize in sports-utility vehicles. Rates generally start about $25 a day.

➤ AGENCIES: **Acevedo's Car Rental** (⊠ Rte. 201, Km 1.0, Vieques, ☎ 787/741–4380). **Carlos Jeep Rental Rental** (⊠ Culebra, ☎ 787/742–3514). **Culebra Car Rental** (⊠ Benjamin Rivera Noriega Airport, ☎ 787/742–3277). **L & M** (⊠ Rte. 3 Marginal, Km 43.8, Fajardo, ☎ 787/860–6868, WEB www.lmcarrental.com). **Leaseway of Puerto Rico** (⊠ Rte. 3, Km 44.4, Fajardo, ☎ 787/860–5000). **Martineau Car Rental** (⊠ Rte. 200, Km 3.4, Vieques, ☎ 787/636–7071, WEB www.enchanted-isle.com/martineaucar). **Prestige Car Rental** (⊠ Benjamin Rivera Noriega Airport, ☎ 787/742–3242). **Thrifty** (⊠ Puerto del Rey Marina, ☎ Fajardo, ☎ 787/860–2030, WEB www.thrifty.com).

CAR TRAVEL

From San Juan, the east coast is accessible via Route 3 or Route 187 if you want to visit Loíza. At Fajardo, the road intersects with Route 53, a fast toll road that continues down the coast. Route 3 however also continues along the coast and provides a more scenic, if slower, trip. Although Puerto Ricans are good about giving directions, be sure to get good maps before you set out.

EMERGENCY SERVICES

Rental car agencies usually give customers emergency road service numbers to call. There's no AAA service on Puerto Rico.

GASOLINE

Gas stations are found along major roads and within cities and towns. Gasoline is sold in liters, not gallons, and at this writing the prices were just under 32¢ a liter. Although few eastern stations have round-the-clock hours, many are open until midnight and most are open seven days a week. Note that gas is rarely self-service; an attendant usually pumps it.

PARKING

Although parking can be a nightmare (a pricey one at that) in San Juan, it's no problem out on the island except during festivals. Some mid-size cities have metered on-street parking as well as lots; in smaller communities street parking is the norm, and it's generally free.

ROAD CONDITIONS

The main roads are in good shape, but many highway exit and other signs have been blown down by hurricanes and may or may not have been replaced. When it rains, be alert for flash flooding, even on the major highways.

EMERGENCIES

➤ EMERGENCY NUMBERS: **General** (☎ 911). **Medical** (☎ 787/876–2042 or 787/876–2429 in Loíza; 787/823–2550 or 787/887–2020 in Río Grande; 787/889–2620 or 787/889–2020 in Luquillo; 787/863–2550 or 787/863–2020 in Fajardo; 787/874–7440 or 787/874–2020 in Naguabo). **Police** (☎ 787/876–2042 or 787/876–2429 in Loíza; 787/823–2550 or 787/887–2020 in Río Grande; 787/889–2620 or 787/889–2020 in Luquillo; 787/863–2550 or 787/863–2020 in Fajardo; 787/874–7440 or 787/874–2020 in Naguabo).

➤ HOSPITALS: **Hospital Dr. Dominguez** (✉ 300 Font Martello, Humacao, ☎ 787/852–0505). **Hospital Gubern** (✉ 110 Antonio R. Barcelo, Fajardo, ☎ 787/863–0294). **Hospital San Pablo del Este** (✉ General Valero, Km 2.4, Fajardo, ☎ 787/863–0505). **Ryder Memorial Hospital** (✉ Salida Humacao-Las Piedras, Humacao, ☎ 787/852–0768).

➤ PHARMACIES: **Farmacia Mediania** (✉ Rte. 187, Km 7.0, Loíza, ☎ 787/876–1927). **Walgreens** (✉ Fajardo Plaza, Fajardo, ☎ 787/860–1060; ✉ Oriental Plaza, Humacao, ☎ 787/852–1868).

ENGLISH-LANGUAGE MEDIA

Puerto Rico has one English-language daily newspaper, the *San Juan Star,* which is circulated all over the island and on the off islands. English-language magazines and books are readily available in shopping malls and in hotel shops on the island's eastern side, although proper bookstores are in short supply outside of metropolitan San Juan.

FERRY TRAVEL

The Puerto Rico Ports Authority runs passenger ferries from Fajardo to Culebra and Vieques. Service is from a terminal in the Fajardo port zone at the end of Route 195, about a 90-minute drive from San Juan. The terminal office is open daily 8 to 11 and 1 to 3; a municipal parking lot next to the ferry costs $5 a day. On Culebra, the ferry pulls right into downtown Dewey. The Vieques ferry dock is within walking distance of downtown Isabel Segunda.

FARES AND SCHEDULES

The ferry from Fajardo to Vieques runs three times a day, seven days a week; the one from Fajardo to Culebra operates twice a day, seven days a week. Although there's a published schedule, it's always best to phone and confirm the departure times. The Vieques trip costs $2 one way; for Culebra it's $2.25. The ferry takes about 45 minutes to Vieques, just under 90 minutes to Culebra.

➤ FERRY INFORMATION: **Culebra ferry terminal** (☎ 787/742–3161). **Fajardo Autoridad de los Puertos** (Fajardo Port Authority; ☎ 787/863–0705, 787/863–0852, or 800/981–2005). **Vieques ferry terminal** (☎ 787/741–4761).

HEALTH

Tap water is generally fine on the island; just avoid drinking it after storms (when the drinking-water supply might become mixed with sewage). Thoroughly wash or peel produce you buy in markets and at grocery stores before eating it.

Sunstroke and sunburn are always concerns. Drink plenty of fluids, and use sunscreen with a high SPF factor. Mosquitoes carrying dengue fever aren't uncommon; wear repellent if you notice mosquitoes or are traveling during the rainy season. Wear trousers and long-sleeved shirts while hiking in wildlife reserves. And don't swim in water where you see signs indicating unsafe conditions (because of either undertow or pollution).

MAIL AND SHIPPING

Puerto Rico is part of the U.S. postal system, and most communities of any size have multiple branches of the post office. Some aren't, however, open on Saturday. Big hotels and resorts also have postal drop boxes.

➤ POST OFFICES: **Fajardo main post office** (✉ 102 Calle Garrido Morales E, Fajardo, ☎ 787/863–0802). **Naguabo main post office** (✉ 100 Rte. 31, Naguabo, ☎ 787/874–3115). **Vieques main post office** (✉ 97 Calle Muñoz Rivera, Suite 103, Isabel Segunda, ☎ 787/741–3891).

OVERNIGHT SERVICES

Puerto Rico has express overnight mail delivery through the U.S. Postal Service as well as Federal Express, which usually operates through office supply stores or other commercial outlets. (Note that FedEx doesn't offer Saturday pickup on the island.)

➤ MAJOR SERVICES: **Candelero Resort at Palmas del Mar** (✉ Rte. 906, Humacao, ☎ 800/463–3339). **Office Max** (✉ Rte. 3, Fajardo, ☎ 800/463–3339). **Post Net** (✉ Rte. 3, Río Grande, ☎ 800/463–3339; ✉ 118 Av. Ortiz Estela, Humacao, ☎ 800/463–3339).

MONEY MATTERS

Banks and ATMs (or ATHs, as they're known here) are plentiful. Banks usually open weekdays 9 to 5; very few have hours on Saturday and those that do are open only 'til noon. Foreign currency exchange is available at banks; as part of the United States, Puerto Rico uses U.S. currency.

➤ BANKS AND EXCHANGE SERVICES: **Banco Popular** (✉ 115 Muñoz Rivera, Isabel Segunda, Vieques, ☎ 787/741–2071; ✉ Rte. 3, Km 42.4, Fajardo, ☎ 787/860–1570). **Banco Roig** (✉ 55 Calle Antonio Lopez, Humacao, ☎ 787/852–8601). **Citibank** (✉ 15 Calle Pedro Marquez, Dewey, Culebra, ☎ 787/742–0220). **Westernbank** (✉ Calderón Mujica at L.M. Rivera, Canóvanas, ☎ 787/876–3745).

SAFETY

Although crime isn't as high in the island's eastern areas as it is in San Juan, use prudence. Avoid bringing valuables with you to the beach; if you must do so, be sure not to leave them in view in your car. Carjacking used to be a problem in metropolitan San Juan, but such crimes have dropped dramatically. Still, it's best to keep your car locked while driving. Avoid out-of-the way beaches after sunset.

LOCAL SCAMS

If in doubt about another motorist's behavior (or you suspect a fender bender is part of a scam), drive to a populated area, a gas station, or highway toll booth rather than stopping. Such scams aren't common, but they happen from time to time.

TAXIS

You can flag cabs down on the street, but it's faster and safer to have your hotel call one for you. Either way, make sure the driver is clear on whether he or she will charge a flat rate or use a meter to determine the fare. In most places, the cabs are metered.

➤ CAB COMPANIES: **Fajardo Taxi Service** (☎ 787/860–1112). **Humacao Taxi** (☎ 787/852–6880). **Lolo Felix Tours** (Vieques; ☎ 787/485–5447). **Ruben's Taxi** (Culebra; ☎ 787/405–1209).

TELEPHONES

Puerto Rico's main area code is 787; a new, 939 area code is being introduced gradually. Public phones are abundant throughout the island. They operate with phone cards, credit cards, and coins (25¢ for a local call). You need to dial the area code, even for local calls, but not the "1" prefix unless it's a long-distance number.

TOURS

Captain James Smith's Blackbeard West Indies Charter offers fishing and dive-boat excursions out of Fajardo; prices start at about $45 for half-day dive trips. East Wind has sailing, snorkeling, and beachcombing excursions aboard a 62-ft catamaran; a packaged half-day trip costs about $55. Culebra Divers is one of that island's best-known operators for diving and snorkeling; prices vary depending on whether classes are involved and the duration of the trip. A three-hour snorkeling excursion, for example, starts at about $30. Vieques Nature Tours arranges educational snorkeling trips on glass-bottom boats; these trips are popular with children. Rates depend on group size. (Note that this operator has no office; you must call to arrange tours.)

➤ TOUR OPERATORS: **Blackbeard West Indies Charter** (✉ HC-01 Box 13025, Río Grande 00745, ☎ 787/887–4818). **Culebra Divers** (✉ 4 Calle Pedro Marquez, Dewey, Culebra, ☎ 787/742–0803, WEB www.culebradivers.com). **East Wind** (✉ Puerto del Rey Marina, Rte. 3, Km 51.4, Fajardo, ☎ 787/860–3434). **Vieques Nature Tours** (☎ 787/741–1980).

TRAVEL AGENCIES

➤ CONTACTS: **Condado Travel** (✉ 50 Av. Carrera, Humacao, ☎ 787/852–4200). **Coupi Travel Service** (✉ 23 Av. Baldorioty, Naguabo, ☎ 787/874–3075). **Good Travel and Tours** (✉ 21 Calle Pimentel, Barrio Las Flores, Río Grande, ☎ 787/887–6150).

VISITOR INFORMATION

The island's tourism offices are hit and miss when it comes to helpful material. The cities usually offer information through offices connected to city hall, and most are open only during business hours on weekdays. The tourism desk in Isabel Segunda's city hall has information on bike rental, maps and brochures, and details on how to reach all Vieques's beaches.

➤ TOURIST INFORMATION: **Culebra Tourism Office** (✉ 250 Calle Pedro Marquez, Dewey, ☎ 787/742–3521). **Fajardo Tourism Office** (✉ 6 Av. Muñz Rivera, ☎ 787/863–4013 Ext. 274). **Luquillo Tourism Office** (✉ 154 Calle 14 de Julio St., ☎ 787/889–2225). **Naguabo Tourism Office** (✉ Rte. 3, Km 66.6, Playa Húcares, ☎ 787/874–0389). **Río Grande Office of Tourism and Culture** (✉ Calle San José, Plaza de Recreo, ☎ 787/887–2370). **Vieques Tourism Office** (✉ 449 Calle Carlos Lebrón, Isabel Segunda, ☎ 787/741–5000 Ext. 26).

4 SOUTHERN PUERTO RICO

The Maunabo Lighthouse in the east and the Cabo Rojo Lighthouse in the west serve as bookends to Puerto Rico's "other side," the less visited area south of the Cordillera Central. Here you can lunch on a balcony overlooking verdant inland valleys, sun and swim on uninhabited cays, stroll through city plazas rich with Spanish colonial architecture, or hike in a rare dry tropical forest.

By Delinda
Karle

G OVERNORS, PATRIOTS, AND POETS have hailed from south-ern Puerto Rico, and this rich history is a source of pride for present-day residents. Throughout the region you'll find meticulously maintained historic homes as well as museums large and small.

While colonial San Juan evolved into a fortified center of Spanish military power during the 18th and 19th centuries, enterprising planters found the rich soil to the south perfect for cultivating sugarcane. But agriculture wasn't the south's only attraction: isolated coves and cays gave safe harbor to pirates and smugglers. San Germán, Puerto Rico's second-oldest city, became an enclave of both planters and outlaws. Today it retains a boisterous spirit. Called the "Pearl of the South," Ponce, the region's largest city, has long been a trade and agricultural hub. In the 1990s, many of the distinctive older buildings of Ponce Centro, the downtown district, were renovated, creating a charming old town. Ponce is also home to an exceptional art museum and a riotous pre-Lenten festival.

Tucked among the mountains in the south-central region are such towns as Aibonito and Barranquitas, with steep streets and great views. Coamo is another of the colonial centers that have retained their historical charm. The southern beaches attract casual, fun-loving crowds. Cabo Rojo and La Parguera are especially popular, particularly with local families looking for a break from urban stress. Teeming underwater life draws divers from around the world, and forest reserves entice hikers down shaded paths to waterfalls and lakes.

When traveling the south's usually well-maintained network of roads, it's wise to carry a good map—but don't hesitate to ask for directions from the locals. As often as not you'll get a history lesson thrown into the bargain.

Pleasures and Pastimes

Beaches
You'll find surfing beaches, like Inches near Patillas, and calm bays for swimming, such as Boquerón Beach in Cabo Rojo. Ballena Bay, near Guánica, has oft-deserted sandy stretches. Boat operators make trips to such uninhabited cays as Gilligan Island off the coast of Guánica and Caja de Muertos off Ponce.

Dining
Open-air dining and traditional Puerto Rican cuisine are the norm south of the cordillera. Some of more ambitious restaurants are experimenting, which means you might find chicken or pork with tamarind or guava sauce or fish in a plantain crust. The southern coast—especially the city of Salinas and the Joyuda area in Cabo Rojo—is known for seafood. Along Route 184, near Cayey, look for *lechoneras,* restaurants serving slow-roasted *lechón* (pork), a local delicacy cooked outdoors over coals.

Reservations are usually optional, but you might want to make them on weekends in the more touristy areas. A 15%–20% tip is customary; most restaurants won't include it in the bill, but it's wise to check.

CATEGORY	COST*
$$$$	over $35
$$$	$25–$35
$$	$15–$25
$	under $15

per person for a main course at dinner

Hiking

Vegetation in the region's two reserves is dramatically different: the Bosque Estatal Carite between Cayey and Patillas is a tropical rain forest; outside Guánica is a rare dry tropical forest. Both provide excellent bird-watching. Guides take you on tours through Cañon de San Cristóbal near Aibonito, the island's deepest gorge. The walk to the Cabo Rojo Lighthouse along the rugged cliffs at the southwesternmost tip of the island is beautiful especially at sunset. There are good trails throughout the area, but printed guides to routes outside the reserves are rare. Ask locals for directions to their favorite paths.

Lodging

Modest, family-oriented establishments near beaches or in small towns are the most typical accommodations. Because the southeast is so popular with islanders, some hotels consider summer their high season and lower their rates in winter, contrary to the norm. Southern Puerto Rico doesn't have the abundance of luxury hotels and resorts found to the north and east; however, the Hilton Ponce & Casino and the Copamarina Beach Resort in Guánica are self-contained complexes with the breadth of facilities and services.

CATEGORY	COST*
$$$$	over $225
$$$	$150–$225
$$	$75–$150
$	under $75

All prices are for a double room in high season, excluding 9% tax (11% for hotels with casinos, 7% for paradores) and 5%–12% service charge.

Scuba Diving and Snorkeling

Southern Puerto Rico is an undiscovered dive destination, which means unspoiled reefs and lots of fish. You can arrange for dive boats at Caribe Playa Beach Resort in the southeast, Ponce's La Guancha, and the Hotel Copamarina in the southwest. Shore diving and snorkeling are best around islands or cays or along the western coast between Ponce and Cabo Rojo.

Exploring Southern Puerto Rico

Less than an hour's drive south from San Juan on the Luis A. Ferré Expressway (Route 52) brings you to an elevation of almost 3,000 ft as you cross the Cordillera Central (central mountain range) into southern Puerto Rico. Towns such as Cayey, Aibonito, and Barranquitas are cooler than those on the coastal plain and in winter, overnight temperatures can drop into the 40s when it's in the 60s or 70s on the coast. Elsewhere, southern Puerto Rico is drier and hotter than the north or east. Although El Yunque in the east gets an average of 200 inches or rain yearly, the southwestern town of Guánica averages 30 inches.

The southeastern part of the island—which includes a section of the scenic Ruta Panorámica (Panoramic Route)—has a rugged shoreline where cliffs drop right into the water. Covered with dry vegetation, the southwest's ragged coast has wonderful inlets and bays and jagged peninsulas that make for breathtaking views.

Numbers in the text correspond to numbers in the margin and on the Southern Puerto Rico, Ponce Centro, Greater Ponce, and San Germán maps.

Great Itineraries

IF YOU HAVE 3 DAYS

Head south from San Juan to ▥ **Ponce** ⑨–㉑ via Route 52, stopping for a seafood lunch in **Salinas** ⑦ before touring Ponce's historical center. On the following day, visit some of the other attractions in and around the city, perhaps the Museo de Arte de Ponce, the Castillo Serrallés, or the Centro Ceremonial Indígena de Tibes. Dedicate your final day to ▥ **Guánica** ㉒, where you'll find wonderful beaches and the Bosque Estatal de Guánica.

IF YOU HAVE 5 DAYS

Make a leisurely trip south from San Juan on Route 52, spending a night in one of the mountain towns. You can take the thermal waters of ▥ **Coamo** ⑧, thought by some to be Ponce de León's Fountain of Youth. If you're a serious hiker, seek out El Cañon de San Cristóbal. Continue to ▥ **Ponce** ⑨–㉑ for two days of exploring. Travel west along the coast and settle at a waterfront hotel near either ▥ **Guánica** ㉒ or ▥ **Cabo Rojo** ㊱. For your last two days, stretch out an a beach or hike the Bosque Estatal de Guánica.

IF YOU HAVE 7 DAYS

Travel to ▥ **Cabo Rojo** ㊱, making it your base for four days of sunbathing, snorkeling the reefs, hiking in the Bosque Estatal de Guánica, and exploring colonial **San Germán** ㉕–㉟. Set aside a night for dinner at one of the many fine seafood restaurants in nearby Joyuda and if your trip falls during a new moon, take a nighttime excursion to the Bahía Fosforescente to see the shining dinoflagellates. Finish up with three days of sightseeing in **Ponce** ⑨–㉑.

When to Tour

The temperate climate of the mountainous central zone makes it a pleasure to visit year-round. Locals especially like to head up to this area in summer, when Aibonito holds its Flower Festival (late June or July), and Barranquitas hosts its Artisans Fair (July). The resort towns of Cabo Rojo, Guánica, and La Parguera are also popular with residents over Easter weekend and in summer, when children are out of school. Ponce's spirited pre-Lenten Carnival, held the week before Ash Wednesday, draws many visitors. Note that during busy times, some *paradores* and hotels require a minimum two- or three-night stay on weekends.

CENTRAL SOUTHERN PUERTO RICO

In this mountainous region on the southern side of the Cordillera Central, church steeples rise above villages, trees arch over winding roads that also serve as cattle crossings. In spring, *flamboyáns* (flamboyant trees) transform green hills into a vermilion conflagration. By the time the Luis A. Ferré Expressway (Route 52) hits the city of Cayey, known for the views from its hillside restaurants, you truly feel *"en la isla"* ("out on the island"). At about 2,000 ft above sea level, Aibonito is the island's highest town. It's called "The Queen of Flowers" because of the abundant flora that thrive there. Barranquitas is more remote, nevertheless history claims it as a cradle of intellectuals. This quaint town is revered as the home of patriot Luis Muñoz Rivera.

Leaving the Cordillera Central, the scenery becomes drier and more rugged. The Caribbean sparkles in the distance, and the plain between the sea and the mountains, once the heart of the sugarcane industry, is now the domain of cattle. Tucked into the foothills, Coamo, an important center in Spanish times and a popular thermal springs resort since the early 1900s, has many historical buildings. The strip malls and shopping centers lining the route into Ponce, "The Pearl of the South," belie its charming colonial center.

Cayey

❶ *50 km (30 mi) south of San Juan.*

Since it was founded in 1773, Cayey has attracted both visitors and settlers. Early on the Spanish realized that the valley surrounding it was perfect for growing coffee and tobacco. Later, people were simply drawn by the refreshing breezes. Today its population of 51,000 swells—particularly on weekends—with *sanjuaneros* (residents of San Juan) who shop in the strip malls on its outskirts, dine in its hillside restaurants, or picnic in the nearby Bosque Estatal Carite.

In the 7,000-acre **Bosque Estatal Carite,** 40 km (25 mi) of trails run through stands of palms, Honduras mahogany, and Spanish cedars—many of which host orchids. One trail leads to Charco Azul (Blue Pond), whose cool waters appeal to overheated hikers. Before setting out, get hiking information at the park manager's office near the entrance on Route 184. If you'd like a space in one of the two campgrounds, be sure to get a permit in advance from the Puerto Rico Department of Natural Resources in San Juan. Picnic tables are scattered throughout the forest, and bath room facilities are available near the campgrounds. ⊠ *Rte. 184, Km 20, Guavate Sector,* ☎ *787/747–4545; 787/724–3724; or 787/724–3724 for camping permits.* 🖼 *Free.* ☉ *Manager's office open weekdays 9–5.*

NEED A BREAK?

Mouthwatering marinated lechón, slow-roasted over open pits, is offered at a string of **lechoneras** along Route 184 just before the entrance to the Bosque Estatal Carite. They also serve slow-roasted chicken and a variety of compatible side dishes.

Dining and Lodging

$ ✕ **Martin's BBQ.** Locals come here for a quick fix of traditional slow-roasted chicken with all the trimmings—rice and beans, *tostones* (fried plaintains), and yucca. You order your food at the counter, choosing precisely how much chicken and which side dishes you want. There are picnic tables outside, tables inside, and takeout service. ⊠ *Rte. 1 at Cayey exit off Rte. 52,* ☎ *787/738–1144. MC, V.*

$$ ✕▥ **Sand and the Sea.** In the open-air dining room ($$, closed Mon-
★ day–Thursday), the south-coast views are breathtaking, and the evening breezes are cool enough that you might find the fireplace ablaze. Nightly piano performances of show tunes and Puerto Rican ballads take away any remaining chill, especially when they become singalongs. Grilled steak and seafood dominate the menu, which changes so much that it's posted on a blackboard. Try the Russian tostones (with sour cream and caviar). For overnight stays, four rooms—decorated like those in a New England bed-and-breakfast—are available. Be sure to make room reservations at least a week in advance. ⊠ *Rte. 714, Km 5.2, Cercadillo Sector, 00736,* ☎ *787/738–9086. 4 rooms. Restaurant. AE, D, MC, V. CP.*

Aibonito

❷ *20 km (12 mi) northwest of Cayey.*

Legend has it that Aibonito got its name when a Spaniard exclaimed *"¡Ay, que bonito!"* ("Oh, how pretty!") upon seeing the valley where the town now stands. At 1,896 ft above sea level, it's Puerto Rico's highest city. Aibonito is known as "The Queen of Flowers" because

ATLANTIC OCEAN

Pta. Borinquén
Isabela
Mora [2]
Camuy Hatillo
Arecibo
Barceloneta

Bahía de Aguadilla Aguadilla
Quebradillas [22] [2]
Man

Aguada
Moca [111]
Bajadero [10]
[140]

Rincón [115]
San Sebastián [109]
[119]
Bosque Estatal de Río Abajo
Florid

[111]
[146]

Bahía de Añasco
Añasco
Lares
[140]
Utuado [141]

Las Marías [108]
[111]
Jayuya [14]

Mayagüez
Panoramic Route
Maricao [128]
Collores
Adjuntas *CORDILLER Reserva F Toro N.*

Pta. Guanajibo
Las Vegas
[120]
[143]

San Germán 25—35 SEE DETAIL MAP
Reserva Forestal Maricao
CORDILLERA CENTRAL
Panoramic Route
Villal

Hormigueros
[139]

Joyuda
[120]
Sabana Grande
[10]

Playa Joyuda
36 Cabo Rojo
[100]
[102]
[128]
Peñuelas
Coto Laurel

Buyé
Lajas
[101]
[2]
Yauco 23
Guayanilla
[132]
[14]
Calzac

Boquerón

Balneario Boquerón
■ **Refugio de Vida Silvestre La Parguera** [116]
Palomas
Ponce 9—21 SEE DETAIL MAPS
La Guancha

El Combate
24
Guánica 22
Bosque Estatal de Guánica ■
El Tuque

La Playuela
Ensenada
Pta. Brea
Gilligan Island
Bahía Ballena

Bosque Estatal de Boquerón
Playita Rosada
Bahía Fosforescente
Punta Jacinto

Playa Santa
Balneario Caña Gorda

N

0 — 10 miles
0 — 15 km

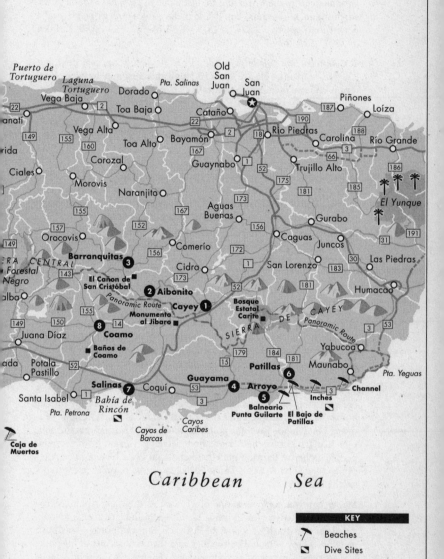

Caribbean Sea

KEY	
⚓	Beaches
◣	Dive Sites
①	Exploring Sights
– – –	Panoramic Route
🌴	Rain Forest

flowering plants thrive in its temperate climate. The city hosts a flower festival every year, usually in late June or July, and gives awards for blossoms and garden design. Live music and craft stalls add to the festivities. A double-steepled cathedral graces the charming town square, which is surrounded by shops and restaurants. Local guides organize outings to nearby El Cañon de San Cristóbal.

🌀 **Mirador Piedra Degetau** (Degetau Lookout Rock) is a scenic point near Aibonito. From the tower, use the telescope to get a closer look at the surrounding mountains. You'll find picnic tables under gazebos and a playground nearby. ⊠ *Rte. 7718, Km 0.7*, ☎ *787/735–3880*. 🎫 *Free*. ☉ *Wed.–Sun. 9–6.*

★ **El Cañon de San Cristóbal** is difficult to find without local help, but it's well worth the effort. Trails of tropical, but somewhat dry, vegetation lead to a breathtaking waterfall. Félix Rivera, a local guide, heads expeditions to the island's deepest gorge, starting from La Piedra restaurant. The fee is $20 per person; call for reservations. ☎ *787/735–5188 or 787/612–0338; 787/735–8721 to arrange trips with Felix Rivera.*

Dining

$–$$ ✕ **La Piedra.** Ingredients straight from the garden liven up the menu at this restaurant on the outskirts of Aibonito. If you're in the area on Sunday, try the excellent buffet of Puerto Rican food—*arroz con pollo* (rice with chicken), lechón, tostones, yucca, and rice and *gandules* (pigeon peas). ⊠ *Rte. 7718, Km 0.8*, ☎ *787/735–1034*. D, MC, V. No dinner Mon.–Tues.

Barranquitas

❸ *15 km (9 mi) northwest of Aibonito.*

Founded in 1804, the small mountain town of Barranquitas appears to have changed little over the years. Its steep streets and quaint plaza seem light-years away from the frenetic energy of Puerto Rico's larger cities. Its tranquillity has made Barranquitas a popular location for summer homes. One of the most beautiful, El Cortijo (on Route 162 at Km 9.9), was built in 1938 and is said to be haunted by a former servant. Although it's closed to the public, consider stopping to admire the sprawling white structure from the road. You *can* visit the former home and the mausoleum of two of Barranquitas' most famous residents: Luis Muñoz Rivera, a politician and newspaperman, and his son, Luis Muñoz Marín, the island's first elected governor. In July, craftspeople gather in Barranquitas for the annual Feria Nacional de Artesanías (National Artisans Fair), one of the most popular such events on the island.

Museo Luis Muñoz Rivera, one block west of the main square, occupies the house where Luis Muñoz Rivera—a politician, poet, and journalist famous for his support of Puerto Rican autonomy—was born in 1859. Many personal belongings and the manuscripts of his political writings and poems are housed here. There's also a friend's car—a 1912 Pierce Arrow—which transported Muñoz to political events. The small wooden house is considered a superb example of 19th-century rural architecture. It's wise to call in advance; the museum doesn't always stick to its posted hours. ⊠ *10 Calle Muñoz Rivera*, ☎ *787/857-0230*. 🎫 *Free*. ☉ *Mon.–Sat. 8:30–5.*

Steps away from Luis Muñoz Rivera's birthplace you'll find the **Mausoleo de la Familia Muñoz** (⊠ *Calle Padre Berríos*, two blocks west of main plaza), where Muñoz Rivera and his son, Luis Muñoz Marín, are buried with other members of their family. There's a small, parklike area and a memorial to the two island politicians.

Dining and Lodging

$–$$ ✗ **Casa Bavaria.** Enjoy a bit of Germany at this out-of-the-way eatery outside the town of Orocovis, about 16 km (10 mi) northwest of Barranquitas. Owned by Mike López, whose mother is German, and Mike's German-born wife, Martina Bolik, Casa Bavaria is a kitschy blend of a biergarten and a casual country restaurant. Choose bratwurst and sauerkraut or chicken and rice and beans. On weekends, patrons spend a good part of the day enjoying the view from the terrace, singing along with the jukebox, and joking with the waiters, many of whom speak German as well as English and Spanish. ⊠ *Rte. 155, Km 38.3,* ☎ *787/862–7818. AE, MC, V. Closed Mon.–Wed.*

$$ ✗▦ **Hacienda Margarita.** This secluded hotel just north of Barranquitas is known for its sweeping mountain views. Seventeen modern rooms—each with a balcony—are in a concrete building. Smaller wooden buildings house 10 more rustic rooms that have two beds and can accommodate up to four people. Watch the sun go down from the outdoor terrace or dine in the restaurant ($–$$), well known for its Puerto Rican cuisine. It's open Friday for dinner and Saturday and Sunday for lunch and dinner. ⊠ *Rte. 152, Km. 1.7 (Box 100, PMB 583, 00794),* ☎ *787/857–0414,* ℻ *787/857–1265. 27 rooms. Restaurant, cable TV, pool, meeting rooms. MC, V. EP.*

Guayama

❹ *28 km (17 mi) southeast of Cayey; 49 km (31 mi) southeast of Barranquitas.*

Guayama was founded in 1736, but was destroyed by fire in the early 1800s. In the 19th century it recovered when the sugarcane industry grew and construction exploded. Examples of colonial and creole buildings can be seen throughout the city. One of the finest 19th-century creole homes is the Casa Cautiño on the main plaza, now a museum.

Guayama's 44,000 residents are proud of the claim that their city is the cleanest on the island. On Sunday, trolley tours of town start at the Casa Cautiño museum, often with the mayor at the wheel. The nearby countryside is home to Paso Fino horses. Each March at the Marcelino Blondet Stadium you can watch these high-stepping show horses strut their stuff during the Feria Dulce Sueño, a fair named after one of the island's most famous Paso Finos. Folk music and crafts are part of the festivities. At this writing, golf legend Chi Chi Rodríguez had just announced plans to build an 18-hole golf course and golf school on Route 173 on the outskirts of town.

★ **Casa Cautiño** is an elegant home built in 1887 for sugar, cattle, and coffee baron Genaro Cautiño Vázquez and his wife, Genoveva Insúa. A balcony with ornate grillwork graces the exterior. You'll be swept back in time walking through the home's rooms, which are filled with Victorian and art deco furniture. Don't miss the modern-for-its-time bathroom, complete with a standing shower. ⊠ *1 Calle Palmer, at Calle Vicente Palé Matos,* ☎ *787/864–9083.* ▣ *$1.* ✸ *Tues.–Sat. 9– 4, Sun. 10–5.*

Dining and Lodging

$ ✗ **Rex Cream.** The natural, tropical-fruit ice cream at this small shop in the center of town is hard to pass up. Flavors vary, depending on what's in season, but often include lime, pineapple, tamarind, and *guanábana* (soursop). You can also get milk shakes—the mango shake is outstanding. ⊠ *24 Calle Derkes,* ☎ *no phone. No credit cards.*

$ ✕ **El Suarito.** You're surrounded by history at this restaurant in a building that dates from 1862. The site has seen life as a repair shop for horse-drawn buggies, a gas station, and, since the mid-1900s, a restaurant. The place is always hopping with townspeople who stop by at all hours for a meal or a drink. You can get eggs and toast for breakfast, sandwiches throughout the day, and roasted chicken or pork chops for dinner. ⊠ *6 Calle Derkes, at Calle Hostos,* ☎ *787/864–1820. MC, V. Closed Sun.*

$$ ✕🏨 **Molino Inn.** This tidy hotel is on the outskirts of Guayama, near the ruins of a Spanish *molino* (sugar mill). Nine acres of grounds—including flower beds and a large pool—surround its two buildings. Join the local business crowd for the international and Caribbean cuisines at the Molinito restaurant ($–$$). There's often live music on weekends. ⊠ *Av. Albizu Campos at Rte. 54 (Box 2393, 00785–2393),* ☎ *787/866–1515,* 𝖥𝖠𝖷 *787/866–1510. 20 rooms. Restaurant, lounge, cable TV, pool, tennis court, basketball, laundry service. AE, MC, V. EP.*

Outdoor Activities and Sports

For $22, golfers can get in nine holes at the **Aguirre Golf Club** (⊠ Rte. 705, Km 3, Aguirre, ☎ 787/853–4025), built in 1925 for the executives of a sugar mill. Open daily, it's known as a short but tough course.

Arroyo

❺ *6 km (4 mi) east of Guayama.*

Arroyo is popular for its nearby beaches, especially Punta Guilarte, and its many fiestas. Its patron saint festival honoring the Virgin of Carmen, patron saint of fishermen, is held every July, and its fish festival is in October. Most of the festivities take place on the boardwalk along the *malecón* (sea wall), officially known as Paseo de Las Américas.

In 1855, Arroyo was a small but bustling port surrounded by cane fields. Today, remnants of its past are scattered throughout the town. The old customs house is now a museum, and a refurbished sugarcane train, which runs on weekends and holidays, is one of the main attractions. Arroyo also contributed to the development of modern communications. Samuel F. B. Morse installed a telegraph machine in his son-in-law's farm on the outskirts of town in 1858 and connected it to another in the center of town, creating what is believed to be the Caribbean's first telegraph line. The main street is named after Morse, and there's a monument to the inventor in the main plaza. A trolley makes a scenic tour of the town with stops along the way.

Housed in an ornate pink building next to the city hall, the **Museo Antigua Aduana de Arroyo** (Museum of the Old Customs House of Arroyo) traces the history of the town and some of its well-known inhabitants, including Samuel F. B. Morse. It also has a small display of Indian artifacts and revolving exhibits of contemporary works by local artists. ⊠ *65 Calle Morse,* ☎ *787/839–8096.* 🎟 *Free.* 🕐 *Wed.–Fri. 9–noon and 1–4:30, weekends 9–4:30.*

🔄 **El Tren del Sur** (*The Train of the South*) takes passengers for one-hour trips along an old rail line between Arroyo and Guayama. The train carried cane from the fields to the mills from 1915 to 1958; today it's one of the island's few working trains. Call in advance; service is frequently disrupted. ⊠ *Rte. 3, Km. 130.9,* ☎ *787/271–1574.* 🎟 *$3.* 🕐 *Trains run hourly on weekends and holidays 9:30–4:30.*

Beach

Balneario Punta Guilarte, east of Arroyo's city center, is one of the south coast's most popular beaches. There are palm trees for shade, changing facilities, picnic tables, and barbecue grills. In summer it's crowded with locals, especially on weekends and holidays; in winter it's almost deserted.

Dining and Lodging

$–$$ ✕ **La Llave del Mar.** This casual, air-conditioned restaurant is across from Arroyo's malecón. It's popular with townsfolk for its wide variety of seafood. The menu also includes grilled steaks. ✉ *Paseo de Las Américas,* ☎ 787/839–6395. *AE, MC, V. Closed Mon.–Tues.*

$–$$ 🏨 **Centro Vacacional Punta Guilarte.** Geared primarily to Puerto Rican families, this government-run vacation center is great if you're looking for no-frills beachside accommodations. Cabins and villas have refrigerators and stoves, but you need to bring bed linen and kitchen utensils. (In a pinch you can find inexpensive supplies at the Wal-Mart 15 minutes west on Route 3 at the Guayama exit.) Some pillows and blankets are available, but you should make arrangements for them when you make your reservation. Also state in advance the number of beds you need. ✉ *Balneario Punta Guilarte, Rte. 3, Km 128.5, 00714,* ☎ 787/722–1771 or 787/839–3565, 📠 787/722–0090. *28 cabins, 32 villas. No air-conditioning in some rooms, some fans, refrigerators, 2 pools, beach. MC, V. EP.*

Patillas

❻ *6 km (4 mi) northeast of Arroyo.*

Patillas, "Emerald of the South," is a tranquil city of about 22,000, with a small plaza and steep, narrow streets. The best sightseeing is along the coast east of town, where Route 3 skirts the Caribbean. This stretch passes rugged cliffs and beautiful beaches, many of which have not yet been discovered by visitors.

Dining and Lodging

$–$$ ✕ **El Mar de la Tranquilidad.** Get a table on the deck at the edge of the Caribbean. You'll find good Puerto Rican cuisine and lots of seafood, including lobster, red snapper and *mofongo* (mashed plantains with seafood). Be sure to sample one of the restaurant's daiquiris—there's a huge list from which to choose. ✉ *Rte. 3, Km 118.9,* ☎ 787/839–6469. *AE, V, MC. No dinner Mon.–Wed.*

$$ ✕🏨 **Caribe Playa Beach Resort.** The resort is a good base from which
★ to explore the southeast coast. Comfortable rooms have a patio or a balcony and border a crescent-shape beach (it's a little rocky, but it's still good for a refreshing dip). Unwind by the pool, in a hammock tied between coconut trees, or in the informal library. You can arrange for boat trips, fishing and scuba diving excursions, and massages. The Seaview Terrace ($–$$) is open for breakfast, lunch, cocktails, and dinner; reservations are required for dinner. ✉ *Rte. 3, Km 112.1 (HC 764, Box 8490, 00723),* ☎ 787/839–7719 or 787/839–6339, 📠 787/839–1817. 🌐 *www.caribeplaya.com. 32 rooms. Restaurant, no air-conditioning in some rooms, no TV in some rooms, pool, beach, playground, some pets allowed. AE, MC, V. EP.*

Beaches

El Bajo de Patillas, on Route 3 south of Patillas, offers tranquil sunning and good swimming. **Channel,** in front of the Caribe Playa resort, is good for bodysurfing and swimming, although the bottom can be rocky. **Inches,** a few miles east of Patillas, is known as a surfing beach.

OFF THE
BEATEN PATH

FARO DE MAUNABO – Route 3 going eastward intersects with Route 901, the eastern portion of the cross-island Ruta Panorámica. Along the way you'll pass animals grazing in fields and cliffs that drop straight down to the ocean. If you turn off on Route 760 and take it to the end, you'll be rewarded by a dramatic view of the Faro de Maunabo (Maunabo Lighthouse, not open to the public) at Punta Tuna.

Salinas

➐ *29 km (18 mi) west of Guayama; 35 km (22 mi) west of Patillas.*

Most visitors are familiar with this town only from seeing its name on an exit sign along Route 52. Islanders, however, know that the road to it off the expressway leads to some of Puerto Rico's best seafood restaurants. Most of them are along the seafront in the Playa de Salinas area, reached by heading south on Route 701.

Dining

$–$$ ✕ **Puerta la Bahía.** The spacious, air-conditioned dining area has huge windows overlooking the water and an extensive seafood menu. For a lighter meal, try one of the fish soups or the croquettes stuffed with crab. Heartier dishes include salmon fillets, grouper, lobster, and mofongo. You can also get chicken or beef dishes. ⊠ *End of Calle Principal, Sector Playita Final,* ☎ *787/824–7117. AE, MC, V.*

Coamo

➑ *33 km (20 mi) southwest of Cayey; 20 km (13 mi) northwest of Salinas.*

Founded by the Spanish in 1579, Coamo was the third city established in Puerto Rico. It dominated the south of the island until the mid-1880s, when political power shifted to Ponce. Coamo town, however, remained an important outpost; several decisive battles were fought here during the Spanish-American War in 1898.

The thermal springs outside Coamo are said to be the Fountain of Youth for which Ponce de León was searching. In the mid-1800s a fashionable resort was built nearby, and people have been coming for a soak in the waters ever since. Coamo is also famous for the San Blas Half-Marathon, which brings competitors and spectators from around the world. The race, held in early February, covers 18 km (13 mi) of the city's hilly streets.

The city's spiritual heart is an 18th-century church on the central plaza. Other buildings dating from the 19th century line Coamo's steep streets, and today you'll find car mechanics, hair salons, and pharmacies operating out of them.

Off the main square, the **Museo Histórico de Coamo** is appropriately housed in the former residence of one of the city's illustrious citizens, Clotilde Santiago, a wealthy farmer and merchant born in 1826. The museum is on the second floor of this sprawling, tangerine-color building that dates from 1863. Several rooms are decorated with colonial-style furnishings, and photographs of the town and the Santiago family line the walls. ⊠ *29 Calle José I. Quintón,* ☎ *787/825–1150 Ext. 206.* ☒ *Free.* ☉ *Weekdays 8–noon and 1–4:30, weekends by reservation.*

Outside Coamo on Route 546, you can take a dip at the famous **Baños de Coamo,** thermal springs that are said to have curative powers. The on-site parador allows day-trippers to bathe in its warm pool for $5 (parador guests enjoy it on the house). There's also a free public bathing area at the end of a path behind the parador. ⊠ *Rte. 546, Km 1,* ☎ *787/825–2186 to springs.* ☉ *Daily 10–5:30.*

Dining and Lodging

$–$$ ✕ **Chicken Burger.** Don't let the name fool you. Although it's known for its grilled chicken, this popular spot's menu also features steaks, hamburgers, fish, mofongo, and more. Eat indoors with air-conditioning or outside on a patio. ✉ *Rte. 153,* ☎ *787/825–4761. MC, V.*

$$ ✕🏨 **Parador Baños de Coamo.** On weekends musicians play in the in-
★ terior patio of this rustic country inn, portions of which date from the 19th century. Rooms—in four modern two-story buildings—open onto latticed wooden verandas and have a cozy, lodgelike feel. Thermal water flows from sulfur springs into a swimming pool a few steps away from a cool-water pool, where you can still see walls dating from 1843. In the dining room ($–$$), portions of delicious *churrasco* (bar-becued meats) with rice and beans are generous. ✉ *Rte. 546, Km 1 (Box 540, 99769),* ☎ *787/825–2186 or 787/825–2239,* ℻ *787/825–4739. 48 rooms. Restaurant, bar, cable TV, 2 pools, video game room. AE, D, MC, V. EP.*

Outdoor Activities and Sports

The **Coamo Springs Golf Course** (✉ Rte. 546 just before Baños de Coamo parador, ☎ 787/825–1370) is popular due to its rugged beauty. When it's raining in the capital, sanjuaneros drive down here for a day of play. The 18-hole course, designed by Ferdinand Garbin, is open daily; greens fees are $50.

PONCE

❾–㉑ *34 km (21 mi) southwest of Coamo.*

Puerto Rico's second-largest city (population 194,000) extends from the Caribbean to the foothills of the Cordillera Central. It evolved into a center of international commerce during the 19th century, luring im-migrants from around the world with the promise of jobs. Trade brought money, which was lavished on its architecture: elegant homes and public buildings are a striking contrast to the fortresslike struc-tures of the military-minded Old San Juan.

Many of the 19th-century buildings in Ponce Centro (Downtown Ponce) have been renovated, and the Museo de Arte de Ponce—endowed by native son and former governor Luis A. Ferré—is considered one of the Caribbean's finest art museums. Just as famous as the museum is Ponce's pre-Lenten carnival. The colorful costumes and *vejigante* (mis-chief maker) masks worn during the festivities are famous throughout the world. The best dining in Ponce is just west of town. Seafood restau-rants line the highway in an area known as Las Cucharas, named for the spoon-shape bay you'll overlook as you dine.

You can catch a free, city-run trolley or *"chu chu"* train from Plaza las Delicias, the main square, to the major attractions. On weekends there are free horse-and-carriage rides around the plaza. Ponceños are proud of their city, the "Pearl of the South," and offer all visitors a warm welcome.

Ponce Centro

At the heart of Ponce Centro is the Plaza las Delicias (Plaza of Delights) with trees, benches, and the famous Lion fountain. Several interesting buildings are on this square or the adjacent streets, making the area perfect for a leisurely morning or afternoon stroll.

A Good Walk

Start on the tree-lined Plaza las Delicias. (You'll find parking nearby on Calle Marina, Calle Isabel, and Calle Reina.) Dominating it is the

Catedral Nuestra Señora de Guadalupe ⑨, dating from 1835. Across the street is the **Casa Armstrong-Poventud** ⑩, home of the institute of culture's Ponce branch. Leaving Armstrong-Poventud, cross back to the plaza, circle south by the Alcaldía (City Hall), and continue to the plaza's east side to visit the red-and-black striped fire station, **Parque de Bombas** ⑪.

From the intersection of Calles Marina and Cristina, take Calle Cristina a block east to one of the city's first restoration projects, **Teatro La Perla** ⑫, at the corner of Cristina and Mayor. One block north of the theater, at Calles Mayor and Isabel, is a former home that's now the **Museo de la Historia de Ponce** ⑬. A block east, at the corner of Calles Salud and Isabel, is the **Museo de la Música Puertorriqueña** ⑭. Four blocks west (you will go by Plaza las Delicias again, and Calle Isabel will turn into Calle Reina) is the 1911 architectural masterpiece **Casa Wiechers-Villaronga** ⑮. For more early 20th-century architecture, continue west on Calle Reina, where you'll see examples of *casas criollas,* wooden homes with the spacious front balconies that were popular in the Caribbean during the early 1900s.

TIMING

Although it's possible to see Ponce Centro in one morning or afternoon, it's best to devote a full day and evening to it. Explore the streets and museums during daylight, then head for the plaza at night when the Lion fountain and street lamps are lighted and townspeople stroll the plaza.

Sights to See

⑩ **Casa Armstrong-Poventud.** Banker and industrialist Carlos Armstrong and his wife, Eulalia Pou, moved into this neoclassical house designed and built for them in 1901 by Manuel V. Domenech. The house is known for its ornate facade, which is chock-full of columns, statues, and intricate moldings. It now houses the Ponce offices of the Institute of Puerto Rican Culture, but you can walk through several rooms decorated with colonial furniture. Note the high, pressed-tin ceilings and the decorative glass doors in the foyer. ⊠ *Calle Union, across from Catedral, Ponce Centro,* ☎ *787/844–2540 or 787/840–7667.* ▣ *Free.* ⊙ *Weekdays 8–4:30.*

⑮ **Casa Wiechers-Villaronga.** Alfredo B. Wiechers returned to Ponce after studying architecture in Paris to become one of the city's premier architects. He designed this house, built in 1911, for himself. In 1918, he sold it to the Villaronga-Mercado family. Arches and columns found throughout the interior are typical of Wiechers' designs. The facade has a chamferred corner, common on Ponce's early 20th-century buildings. Check out the stained-glass windows and the rooftop gazebo. Inside, you'll find original furnishings and exhibits on Wiechers and other Ponce architects of his era. ⊠ *Calle Reina and Calle Meléndez Vigo, Ponce Centro,* ☎ *787/843–3363.* ▣ *$1.* ⊙ *Wed.–Sun. 8:30–4:30.*

⑨ **Catedral Nuestra Señora de Guadalupe.** This cathedral dedicated to the Virgin of Guadalupe is built on the site of a 1670 chapel destroyed by earthquakes. Part of the current structure, where mass is still held, dates from 1835. After another earthquake in 1918, new steeples and a roof were put on and neoclassical embellishments were added to the facade. Inside you'll see stained-glass windows, chandeliers, and two alabaster altars. ⊠ *Plaza las Delicias, Ponce Centro,* ☎ *787/842–0134.* ⊙ *Services daily 6 AM and 11 AM.*

⑬ **Museo de la Historia de Ponce.** Housed in two adjoining, neoclassical buildings, this museum has 10 exhibition halls covering Ponce's development from the Taíno Indians to the present. Guided tours in English and Spanish last 50 minutes and give an overview of Ponce's past.

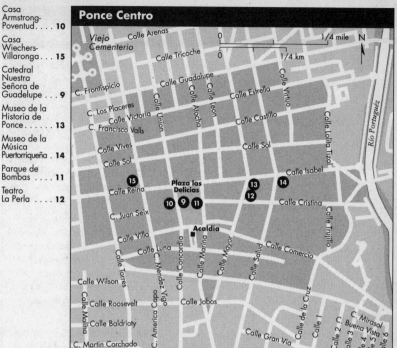

Ponce Centro

✉ *51–53 Calle Isabel, Ponce Centro,* ☎ *787/844–7071 or 787/843–4322.* ✈ *$3.* ◷ *Wed.–Mon. 9–5.*

⑭ Museo de la Música Puertorriqueña. At this museum you'll learn how Puerto Rican music has been influenced by African, Spanish, and Native American cultures. On display are instruments, such as the *triple* (a small string instrument resembling a banjo), and memorabilia of local composers and musicians. The small museum takes up several rooms in a neoclassical former residence. ✉ *Calle Isabel and Calle Salud, Ponce Centro,* ☎ *787/848–7016.* ✈ *$1.* ◷ *Wed.–Sun. 8:30–4:30.*

⑪ Parque de Bombas. Built in 1882 as a pavilion for an agricultural fair and then used as a firehouse, this distinctive red-and-black striped building is now a fire-fighting museum, complete with antique trucks. Half-hour tours in English and Spanish are given on the half hour. ✉ *Plaza las Delicias, Ponce Centro,* ☎ *787/284–4141 Ext. 342.* ✈ *Free.* ◷ *Wed.–Mon. 9:30–6.*

NEED A BREAK? An institution for more than 40 years, **King's** (✉ 9223 Calle Marina, ☎ 787/843–8520), across from Plaza las Delicias, is *the* place for ice cream in Ponce. It serves 12 varieties, from tamarind and passion-fruit to classic chocolate and vanilla. A bench in the tiny storefront seats three, but most folks take their cups and cones across the street and stake out shady plaza benches. King's is open daily from 8 AM to midnight.

⑫ Teatro La Perla. This theater was restored in 1941 after an earthquake and fire damaged the original 1864 structure. The striking interior contains seats for 1,047 and has excellent acoustics. It's generally open for a quick look on weekdays. ✉ *Calle Mayor and Calle Cristina, Ponce Centro,* ☎ *787/843–4322 information; 787/843–4080 ticket office.* ✈ *Free.* ◷ *Weekdays 8–4:30.*

Close-Up

MASKED MISCHIEF

A **WEEK BEFORE** Ash Wednesday, *vejigantes* (pronounced veh-hee-GAN-tays), wearing long, colorful robes and brightly painted horned masks, turn the normally placid city of Ponce into a hotbed of rowdiness. Gangs of these masked mischief makers prowl the city streets for a week, scaring anyone in their path. Some historians date this tradition to a Spanish one of the 1600s that targeted lapsed Christians. Men in long robes and grotesque masks waved cow bladders, or *vejigas*, on long sticks at passersby, attempting to frighten them back into churches for Lent. Today, items such as balloons and plastic bottles have replaced organic vejigas, and the playful masks present the face of Ponce's exquisite folk art to the world.

Unlike carnival masks from other parts of the island, which are made of coconut shells (Loíza) or fine metallic screening (Hatillo), Ponce masks are made of papier-mâché. Many have African and Native American elements; it's even possible to detect influences from ancient Greece and Rome. The minimum number of horns permitted is two, but most masks have several protruding from the forehead, chin, and nose. Antique masks with more than 100 horns sprouting in every direction have been documented.

Masks created at the beginning of the 20th century were usually painted red with yellow dots or vice versa. Today you'll also see every color and pattern imaginable during Ponce's carnival and throughout the year in museums here and abroad. You'll also find them for sale at crafts stores and arts festivals. Small, simple masks start at around $20 or $30. Larger ones by well-known makers—whose techniques have often been passed down through generations of their families—cost as much as $100. One of the best-known mask-making families today is the Caraballo family from the Playa de Ponce area.

Greater Ponce

The greater Ponce area has some of Puerto Rico's most notable cultural attractions, including one of the island's finest art museums and its most important archaeological site.

A Good Tour

The **Museo de Arte de Ponce** ⑯ is on Avenida Las Américas, south of Plaza las Delicias and not far from the Luis A. Ferré Expressway (Route 52). Anyone with a taste for art can happily while away many hours in its galleries. East of the museum you can pick up Route 14 south to the Caribbean and **La Guancha** ⑰, a boardwalk with food kiosks, a playground, and a child-friendly public beach. It's a good place to relax and let the younger generation work off energy. From here, if you retrace your path north past downtown you'll be heading to Calle Bertoly and El Vigía (Vigía Hill), where the **Cruceta El Vigía** ⑱ towers over the city and the **Castillo Serrallés** ⑲, a former sugar baron's villa, is a popular attraction.

Farther north on Route 503 is the **Centro Ceremonial Indígena de Tibes** ⑳, which displays native artifacts dating back more than 1,500 years. You'll have to backtrack to reach Route 10, then head north to **Hacienda Buena Vista** ㉑, a former coffee plantation that's been restored by the Puerto Rican Conservation Trust. (Call ahead to arrange a tour.)

You can drive to all these sights or hop on the free trolleys or *chu chu* trains that run from Plaza las Delicias to the museum, La Guancha, and El Vigía. You'll need a car or a cab to reach Tibes and Hacienda Buena Vista.

TIMING

To follow the full tour above, you should plan to spend at least 1½ or 2 days. If you don't want to devote that much time, choose the sights you find most appealing.

Sights to See

★ ⑲ **Castillo Serrallés.** Now a museum, this lovely Spanish-style villa overlooking the city and the sea was built in the 1930s for Ponce's wealthiest family, the makers of Don Q rum. Guided tours give you a glimpse of the lifestyle of the sugar barons and explain the area's sugar production history. ⊠ *17 El Vigía El Vigía,* ☎ *787/259–1774,* WEB *www.castilloserralles.com.* ⊡ *$3.* ⊙ *Tues.–Thurs. 9:30–5, Fri.–Sun. 10–5:30.*

⑳ **Centro Ceremonial Indígena de Tibes.** The Tibes Indian Ceremonial Center, discovered after flooding from a tropical storm in 1975, is a very important archaeological site. The pre-Taíno ruins and burial grounds date from AD 300 to AD 700. Be sure to visit the small museum before taking a walking tour of the site, which includes ceremonial playing fields used for a ritual ball game that some think was similar to soccer. The fields are bordered by smooth stones, some engraved with petroglyphs that researchers believe might have ceremonial or astronomical significance. A village with several thatch huts has been reconstructed in an original setting. ⊠ *Rte. 503, Km 2.2, Barrio Tibes,* ☎ *787/840–2255 or 787/840–5685,* WEB *http://ponce.inter.edu/tibes/tibes.html.* ⊡ *$2.* ⊙ *Tues.–Sun. 9–4.*

⑱ **Cruceta El Vigía.** At the top of Vigía Hill is a colossal cross where the Spanish once watched for ships, including those of marauding pirates. You can climb the stairs or take an elevator to the top of the 100-ft cross for a panoramic view of the city and beyond. ⊠ *Across from Castillo Serrallés, El Vigía,* ☎ *787/259–3816,* WEB *www.castilloserralles. net.* ⊡ *$1.* ⊙ *Tues.–Sun. 9:30–5:30.*

🖐 ⑰ **La Guancha.** Encircling the cove of a working harbor, the seaside boardwalk features kiosks where vendors sell local food and drink. The adjacent park has a large children's area filled with playground equipment and on weekends, live music. The nearby public beach has rest rooms, changing areas, a medical post, and plenty of free parking. ⊠ *End of Rte. 14, La Guancha,* ☎ *787/844–3995.*

★ ㉑ **Hacienda Buena Vista.** Built as a fruit farm in 1838 by Salvador Vives, Hacienda Buena Vista later became a corn-flour mill and finally a coffee plantation. In 1987 the plantation house was restored by the Puerto Rican Conservation Trust, which also preserved the original waterwheel, hydraulic systems, and additional machinery. Inside the two-story house, furniture, documents, and other memorabilia give a sense of what it was like to live on a coffee plantation nearly 150 years ago. The two-hour tour, given four times a day (once in English), is by reservation only. (Allow yourself half an hour to travel the winding Route 10 from Ponce.) Afterward, you can buy coffee beans and souvenirs at the gift shop. ⊠ *Rte. 10, Km 16.8, Sector Corral Viejo,* ☎ *787/722–5882 weekdays; 787/284–7020 weekends,* WEB *www.fideicomiso.org/hacienda.htm.* ⊡ *$5.* ⊙ *Wed.–Sun. (tour groups only Wed.–Thurs.).*

★ ⑯ **Museo de Arte de Ponce.** The lovely building designed by Edward Durrell Stone, who was also an architect for New York's Museum of Mod-

Greater Ponce

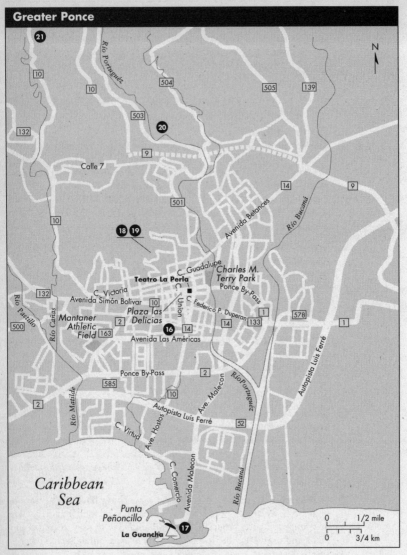

ern Art, contains more than 1,500 paintings, sculptures, and prints. You'll find the work of Puerto Rican artists such as Francisco Oller; Latin American painters such as Bartolome Murillo; and Europeans such as Peter Paul Rubens, Auguste Rodin, and Thomas Gainsborough. The highlight of the European collection is the pre-Raphaelite paintings, particularly *Flaming June,* by Frederick Leighton, which has become the museum's unofficial symbol. Watch for special exhibits and occasional concerts. ⊠ *2325 Av. Las Américas, Sector Santa María,* ☎ *787/848–0505,* WEB *www.museoarteponce.org.* ☞ *$4.* ☉ *Daily 10–5.*

Beaches

Caja de Muertos (Coffin Island) has the best beaches in the Ponce area. The public beach by **La Guancha,** at the end of Route 14 is small, but the shallow water makes it nice for children. There's some shade under thatched umbrellas, but bring sunscreen. About 5 km (3 mi) west on Route 2, **El Tuque** has a swimming area and picnic tables.

Dining and Lodging

$$–$$$$ ✕ **Mark's at the Meliá.** One of the island's best restaurants is tucked
★ off the lobby of the Meliá hotel. Chef Mark French has won praise from the Caribbean Chefs Association, and his dishes live up to that honor. The menu here changes often, but you'll always find a long list of appetizers that could include a three-cheese onion soup or a bacon, lettuce, and tomato salad. The restaurant has drawn raves for creations such as plantain-crusted dorado with congri, and the chocolate truffle cake has drawn people from as far away as San Juan. ⊠ *75 Calle Cristina, La Guancha, Ponce,* ☎ *787/284–6275. AE, MC, V. Closed Mon.–Tues.*

$$–$$$ ✕ **La Cava.** Dark-wood paneling and low lighting set a romantic tone
★ at this intimate restaurant in the Hilton Ponce & Casino. It's known for an award-winning wine list and a menu that gracefully melds international cuisines. Try the goulash of venison, the ostrich medallions on a mango chutney tart, or the lamb chops. The appetizer list includes sushi and selections from an oyster bar. ⊠ *1150 Av. Caribe, La Guancha,* ☎ *787/259–7676. Reservations essential. AE, D, MC, V.*

$–$$$ ✕ **El Ancla.** Families favor this restaurant at the edge of the sea. The kitchen serves generous and affordable plates of fish, crab, and other fresh seafood with tostones, *papas fritas* (french fries), and garlic bread. Try the shrimp in garlic sauce, the salmon fillet with capers, or the delectable mofongo. The piña coladas—with or without rum—and the flan are exceptional. There are two dining rooms—one for those who smoke and another for those who don't. ⊠ *9 Av. Hostos Final, Ponce Playa,* ☎ *787/840–2450. AE, MC, V.*

$–$$ ✕ **Lupita's.** Knock-your-socks-off margaritas are the perfect accompaniment to the heaping portions of highly seasoned Mexican-American food at this downtown restaurant. You can eat indoors or in the courtyard. There's live music Tuesday through Saturday after 11 PM. ⊠ *60 Calle Isabel, Ponce Centro,* ☎ *787/848–8808. MC, V.*

$–$$ ✕ **Pito's.** Dine indoors or on a waterfront balcony at this restaurant in Las Cucharas. In addition to a wide selection of seafood, you can also order chicken and steak dishes. To indulge, try the shrimp wrapped in bacon, a specialty here. There's live music on Friday and Saturday nights. ⊠ *Rte. 2, Sector Las Cucharas,* ☎ *787/841–4977. AE, MC, V.*

$ ✕ **Café Tompy.** The prices are right at this no-frills cafeteria, which draws a big lunch crowd. You can sample such down-home Puerto Rican cuisine as chicken, lechón, rice and beans, and yucca; order a sandwich; or simply re-energize with a strong cup of coffee. It's open daily for lunch and dinner; breakfast is served Monday through Saturday. ⊠ *56 Calle Isabel, Ponce Centro,* ☎ *787/840–1965. MC, V.*

\$\$\$\$ 🏨 **Hilton Ponce & Casino.** A black-sand beach borders the south coast's
★   biggest resort, a cream-and-turquoise complex on 80 acres 6 km (4 mi)
outside of Ponce. With a large corporate clientele, the open-air lobby
has an efficient, business-like feel. The mood lightens up in other parts
of the hotel, such as the casual La Terraza (\$\$–\$\$\$) restaurant, whose
staff serves breakfast, lunch, and dinner to diners seated at tables in
an atrium surrounded by a gigantic waterfall. Guest rooms are bright
and have lots of floral patterns. If the shopping arcade and casino don't
keep you busy, the many outdoor activities will. At this writing, plans
for two golf courses were on the table. ✉ *1150 Av. Caribe, La Guancha (Box 7419, 00732),* ☎ *787/259–7676 or 800/445–8667; 800/981–
3232 direct to hotel,* 📠 *787/259–7674,* 🌐 *www.ponce-hilton.com.
148 rooms, 5 suites. 2 restaurants, 3 bars, in-room safes, cable TV with
movies and video games, minibars, pool, hot tub, sauna, spa, driving
range, 4 tennis courts, exercise equipment, basketball, Ping-Pong, volleyball, beach, bicycles, shops, casino, dance club, video game room,
baby-sitting, children's programs, playground, business services, meeting rooms, parking (fee). AE, DC, MC, V. EP.*

\$\$ 🏨 **Holiday Inn Ponce.** The *trío* music that fills the lobby bar nightly
and the dance beat that pulsates from the disco lend considerable
Latin flair to this Holiday Inn on the outskirts of Ponce. Adding to the
energy is the sound of slots ringing each evening at the Tropical Casino.
The Tanama (\$–\$\$\$) restaurant serves Spanish, Puerto Rican, and
nouvelle cuisine; there are also several seafood restaurants in the nearby
Las Cucharas area. Rooms are spacious, and each has its own balcony.
✉ *3315 Ponce Bypass, El Tuque, 00731,* ☎ *787/844–1200 or 800/
465–4329,* 📠 *787/841–8683,* 🌐 *www.hidpr.com/ponce.htm or
www.sixcontinentshotels.com/holiday-inn. 116 rooms. Restaurant, 2
bars, cable TV, refrigerators, 2 pools, gym, casino, dance club, Internet, video game room, meeting rooms. AE, MC, V. EP.*

\$\$ 🏨 **Hotel Meliá.** In the heart of Ponce, near Plaza las Delicias, this fam-
★   ily-owned hotel is a good, low-key base for exploring downtown's landmark buildings and museums. The lobby, with its high ceilings and
blue-and-beige tile floors, is well-worn but charming. Rooms have a
somewhat dated European feel. Breakfast is served on the rooftop terrace, which overlooks the city and mountains. Six suites have balconies
with terrific views of Ponce's historic district. ✉ *75 Calle Cristina, Ponce
Centro (Box 1431, 00733),* ☎ *787/842–0260 or 800/742–4276,* 📠
787/841–3602, 🌐 *home.coqui.net/melia. 75 rooms. Restaurant, bar,
cable TV, parking (fee). AE, MC, V. CP.*

\$ 🏨 **Hotel Bélgica.** Right off Plaza las Delicias, this hotel is both com-
fortable and economical. A stairway off the large lobby inside the colonial building leads to clean rooms with dark-wood furniture and pastel
walls. Guest quarters vary in size (Room 3 is one of the largest); many
have a table or a desk, and some have a balcony overlooking the
street. The hotel has no restaurant or bar, but there are plenty of options in the neighborhood. ✉ *122 Calle Villa, Ponce Centro, 00731,*
☎ *787/844–3255,* 📠 *787/844–6149. 20 rooms. Some pets allowed.
MC, V. EP.*

Nightlife and the Arts

Nightlife

In downtown Ponce, people embrace the Spanish tradition of the
paseo, an evening stroll with family and friends around Plaza las Delicias, which is spectacular at night when its old-fashioned street lamps
glow and the fountain is lit. The boardwalk at La Guancha is also a
lively scene with ponceños out for a stroll and a bite to eat. Live bands
often play on weekends.

The **Hilton Ponce & Casino** (⊠ Rte. 14, 1150 Av. Caribe, La Guancha, ☎ 787/259–7676) has several options for nightlife: the casino stays open nightly until 4 AM; on Thursday, Friday, and Saturday you can dance at the Pavilion disco; and on Friday and Saturday merengue and salsa fill La Bohemia lounge. The **Holiday Inn Ponce** (⊠ 3315 Ponce Bypass, El Tuque, ☎ 787/844–1200) features *trío* music nightly in its Caribbean Lobby Bar and live dance music Friday and Saturday nights at Holly's disco. The casino is open nightly until 4 AM.

Hollywood Café (⊠ Bul. Miguel Pou, Km 5.5, Ponce Centro, ☎ 787/ 843–6703) has occasional live music and draws a college-age crowd. **Lupita's** (⊠ 60 Calle Isabel, Ponce Centro, ☎ 787/848–8008) often has live music, ranging from guitar to blues and rock and roll, Tuesday through Saturday. **Olé Plena** (⊠ 57 Calle Isabel, Ponce Centro, ☎ 787/841–6162) schedules live music, often jazz, many weeknights and some Saturdays.

The Arts

Check for theater productions and concerts at the **Teatro La Perla** (⊠ Calle Mayor and Calle Cristina, Ponce Centro, ☎ 87/843–4322 information; 787/843–4080 ticket office). The **Museo de Arte de Ponce** (⊠ 2325 Av. Las Américas, Sector Santa María, ☎ 787/848–0505) occasionally sponsors chamber music concerts and recitals by members of the Puerto Rico Symphony Orchestra.

Outdoor Activities and Sports

You'll see many varieties of coral, parrotfish, angelfish, and grouper in the reefs around the island of Caja de Muertos. **Marine Sports and Dive Shop** (⊠ 1244 Av. Muñoz Rivera, Villa Grillasca, ☎ 787/844– 6175) rents equipment and arranges tours. **Rafy Vega's Island Venture** (☎ 787/842–8546) offers two-tank dive excursions as well as snorkeling trips. The company also takes day-trippers from La Guancha to Caja de Muertos—a 45-minute boat ride—for a day of relaxing on the beach. The trips cost $20 per person and include a light lunch.

Shopping

On holidays and during festivals, artisans sell wares from booths in the Plaza las Delicias. Souvenir and gift shops are plentiful in the area around the plaza, and Paseo Atocha, a pedestrian mall with shops geared to residents, runs north of it. Carnival masks, hammocks, Puerto Rican coffee, and rum fill the shelves of **Mi Coqui** (⊠ 9227 Calle Marina, Ponce Centro, ☎ 787/841–0216). Just outside town, **Plaza del Caribe Mall** (⊠ Rte. 2, Km 227.9, ☎ 787/259–8989), one of the island's largest malls, has stores such as Sears, JCPenney, and Gap. **Utopia** (⊠ 78 Calle Isabel, Ponce Centro, ☎ 787/848–8742) sells carnival masks and crafts.

SOUTHWEST PUERTO RICO

With sandy coves and palm-lined beaches tucked in the coastline's curves, southwestern Puerto Rico fulfills everyone's fantasy of a tropical paradise. The area is popular with local vacationers on weekends and holidays, but many beaches are nearly deserted on weekdays. Villages along the coast are picturesque places where oysters and fresh fish are sold at roadside stands. On the southwesternmost peninsula, the rugged stretch leading to the Cabo Rojo Lighthouse has pink-sand beaches.

Guánica

㉒ *24 mi (38 km) west of Ponce.*

Juan Ponce de León first explored this area in 1508 when searching for the elusive Fountain of Youth. Nearly 400 years later, U.S. troops landed first at Guánica during the Spanish-American War in 1898. The event is commemorated with an engraved marker on the city's malecón. Sugarcane dominated the landscape through much of the 1900s, and the ruins of the old Guánica Central sugar mill, closed in 1980, loom over the town's western area, known as Ensenada. Today most of the action takes place at the beaches and in the forests outside of Guánica.

The 9,200-acre **Bosque Estatal de Guánica** (Guánica State Forest), a United Nations Biosphere Reserve, is a great place for hikes and bird-watching expeditions. It's an outstanding example of a tropical dry coastal forest, with some 700 species of plants and more than 100 types of birds. There are 12 major trails through the sun-bleached hills, from which you'll see towering cacti as well as *guayacán* and gumbo limbo trees. There are also several caves to explore. You can enter on Route 333, which skirts the forest's southwestern portion, or at the end of Route 334, where there's a parks office. ✉ *Rte. 333 or 334,* ☎ *787/821–5706.* 🎟 *Free.* ☉ *Daily 9–5.*

Beaches

At the end of Route 333, U-shaped **Bahía Ballena** combines a beautiful beach with calm water. The gentle water at **Balneario Caña Gorda,** on Route 333, washes onto a wide swath of sand fringed with palm trees. There are picnic tables, bathrooms, showers, and changing facilities. You can rent jet skis, kayaks, and pedal boats at **Playa Santa,** which is at the end of Route 325 in the Ensenada district. Rugged cliffs make a dramatic backdrop for the beach at **Punta Jacinto,** on Route 333, but the water can be rough.

Gilligan Island is a cay surrounded by coral reefs and skirted by gorgeous beaches. There are picnic tables and rest rooms, but no other signs of civilization. Boats leave the San Jacinto dock, stopping for passengers at nearby hotels, during the week every hour, on the hour, from 10 to 5; on weekends boats leave every half hour from 8:30 to 5. Round-trip passage is $4. (To reach San Jacinto, take the first right after the Copamarina Beach Resort on Route 333 and go less than ¼ mi.) The island is often busy on weekends and around holidays, but during the week it's usually quiet. On Monday it's closed for cleaning.

Dining and Lodging

$–$$ ✕ **La Concha.** A tourist board–designated *meson gastronómico* (restaurant that serves traditional island dishes), this family favorite specializes in seafood. Mofongo leaves the kitchen filled with shrimp, lobster, or conch. The hearty *asopao* (gumbo-like soup) is made with seafood or chicken. There's also fried chicken with rice and beans, filet mignon in onion sauce, and churrasco covered with mushrooms. ✉ *C-4 Calle Principal, Playa Santa, Ensenada,* ☎ *787/821–5522. AE, MC, V.*

$$$–$$$$ ✕▥ **Copamarina Beach Resort.** To one side of the Copamarina's 16 acres of flowers and fruit trees is the Caribbean; to the other, is dry tropical forest. If the resort's beach is too crowded with other guests and their children, several equally beautiful stretches are minutes away. Rooms are basic but spacious; all have balconies or patios and at least partial ocean views. The red snapper is a must at the Coastal Cuisine restaurant ($$–$$$), but you'll need to rent a car for outings to other area eateries and nightspots. ✉ *Rte. 333, Km 6.5 (Box 805, 00653),* ☎ *787/821–0505 or 800/468–4553,* 🖷 *787/821–0070,* 🕸

www.copamarina.com. 106 rooms, 2 villas. Restaurant, bar, cable TV, refrigerators, 2 pools, 2 wading pools, 2 hot tubs, spa, massage, 2 tennis courts, gym, volleyball, beach, dive shop, snorkeling, windsurfing, boating, playground, meeting rooms. AE, MC, V. CP, MAP, EP.

$$
★
🏨 **Mary Lee's by the Sea.** This meandering complex of apartments and suites looks out on the water from quiet grounds full of bright flowers. The distinctive layout is the result of a hodgepodge of additions to the original building. Seven units have a sea view; in the eighth you'll catch a glimpse of the ocean as well as of the Bosque Estatal de Guánica. Maid service is provided weekly; daily service can be arranged for an additional fee. You can rent kayaks or hop a boat to Gilligan Island. ⊠ *Rte. 333, Km 6.7, San Jacinto Sector (Box 394, 00635),* ☎ *787/821–3600,* ℻ *787/821–0744,* ⓌⒺⒷ *www.maryleesbythesea.com. 8 units. Kitchenettes, boating, some pets allowed; no room phones, no room TVs. MC, V. EP.*

$$
🏨 **Paul Julien's Caribbean Vacation Villa.** No need to bring your own sports gear—it's included in the price of a room. The villa consists of three efficiency apartments and a two-bedroom apartment on a small swimming beach. The facility's sporting equipment includes beginner and racing kayaks, windsurfers, mountain bikes, and snorkeling and scuba gear. Windsurfing and kayaking lessons are available for an extra charge. ⊠ *Rte. 333, #15, San Jacinto Sector (Box 432, 00653),* ☎ *787/821–5364,* ℻ *787/821–0681,* ⓌⒺⒷ *www.caribbeanvacationvilla. com. 4 units. Cable TV, kitchens, dive shop, windsurfing, boating, bicycles; no room phones. No credit cards. EP.*

Outdoor Activities and Sports

HIKING

The Bosque Estatal de Guánica has 12 major trails for which the forest office on Route 334 has maps. **Paul Julien's Caribbean Vacation Villa** (⊠ Rte. 333, #15, San Jacinto Sector, ☎ 787/821–5364) arranges guided hikes and rents gear, such as lighted helmets for cave exploration.

WATER SPORTS

Dramatic walls created by the continental shelf provide great diving off the Guánica coast. There are also shallow gardens around Gilligan Island and Cayo de Caña Gorda (off Balneario Caña Gorda) that attract both snorkelers and divers. **Dive Copamarina** (⊠ Rte. 333, Km 6.5, ☎ 787/821–6009 Ext. 771 or 719) at the Copamarina Beach Resort offers instruction and trips. **Paul Julien's Caribbean Vacation Villa** (⊠ Rte. 333, #15, San Jacinto Sector, ☎ 787/821–5364) rents scuba gear and windsurfing equipment.

Yauco

㉓ *8 km (5 mi) north of Guánica.*

The picturesque town of Yauco in the southern foothills of the Cordillera Central is known for its coffee and the February festival celebrating the end of the bean harvest. It's rumored to be the birthplace of *chuletas can can* (twice-cooked pork chops), called "can can" because of the resemblance the pork chop's edges have to dancers' skirts.

Dining

$–$$
✕ **La Guardarraya.** In an old-fashioned country-style house, with windows that look out on gardens, you'll find some of the best chuletas can can anywhere. Other traditional dishes include stewed rice and pork, steak with onions, and fried chicken. Save room for the vanilla flan. ⊠ *Rte. 127, Km 6.0,* ☎ *787/856–4222. MC, V. Closed Mon.*

Outdoor Activities and Sports

Campo Allegre (✉ Rte. 127, Km 5.1, ☎ 787/856–2609) is a 204-acre horse ranch that conducts ½-hour, 1-hour, and 2-hour rides through the hills surrounding Yauco. There are also pony rides for children. The on-site restaurant serves Yauco's specialty: chuletas can can.

La Parguera

㉔ *13 km (8 mi) west of Guánica; 24 km (15 mi) southwest of Yauco.*

La Parguera is famous for its bioluminescent bay, which may not be as spectacular as that near Vieques island but which is still a beautiful sight on a moonless night. Glass-bottom boats leave for 45-minute bay trips from a pedestrian walkway that has a Coney Island feeling, with booths selling candy and tropical drinks. The town bursts with Puerto Rican vacationers on long holiday weekends and in summer. From February through April, keep your eyes open for roadside vendors selling the area's famous pineapples. There's good diving and fishing in the area, and swimmers can take boats to cays or head to beaches in nearby Guánica or Cabo Rojo.

At night, boats line up along the pedestrian mall in La Parguera to take visitors out to view the **Bahía Fosforescente.** Microscopic dinoflagellates glow bright on moonless nights when disturbed by movement. ✉ *On pedestrian mall.* 🎫 *Boat ride $5.* ☼ *Nightly 7:30–midnight.*

Beaches

The small **Playita Rosada,** at the end of Calle 7, doesn't compare to some of the long beaches on the southwestern coast, but it's convenient for a quick swim and a picnic. For about $5 per person boats will transport you to and from **Isla Mata de la Gata** for a day of swimming and snorkeling. You can take a boat to and from **Cayo Caracoles** for $5 per person. This island has mangroves to explore as well as plenty of places to swim and snorkel.

Dining and Lodging

$–$$ ✗ **La Casita.** The decor is simple, but generous portions of seafood make this family-run restaurant one of the town's favorites. Try the asopao served with lobster or shrimp or one of several surf-and-turf dishes. ✉ *Calle Principal at western edge of town,* ☎ *787/899–1681. MC, V. Closed Mon.*

$–$$ ✗ **Parguera Blues Café.** Off La Parguera's main street, this publike restaurant serves its own special Blues Burgers (made with blue cheese), filet mignon, chicken or shrimp with pasta, and the fish of the day. There's live music Friday and Saturday nights. ✉ *Centro Commercial El Muelle, Av. Los Pescadores,* ☎ *787/899–4742. MC, V.*

$$ ✗🏨 **Parador Villa Parguera.** Each large, colorful room in this parador
★ on the Bahía Fosforescente has a balcony or terrace, and throughout the complex you'll see bright tropical flowers. A spacious dining room ($–$$), overlooking the pool and the bay beyond, serves excellent native and international dishes. On Saturday night there's live music and a floor show in the dance club. ✉ *Rte. 304, Km 3.3 (Box 273, Lajas, 00667),* ☎ *787/899–7777 or 787/899–3975,* 🖷 *787/899–6040,* 🌐 *www.villaparguera.com. 70 rooms. Restaurant, lounge, cable TV, pool, dance club, video game room, meeting rooms. AE, D, DC, MC, V. EP.*

$$ 🏨 **Parador Villa del Mar.** "Peaceful" best describes this parador on a hill overlooking La Parguera. Rooms are comfortable and clean, but they don't have spectacular views. You'll find a small lounge by the reception area and a small pool tucked between the administrative building and the guest rooms. An open-air restaurant serves breakfast to guests for an additional $5 per person. ✉ *3 Calle Albizu Campos (Box*

1297, San Germán, 00683), ☎ 787/899–4265, FAX 787/899–4832, WEB
*www.pinacolada.net/villadelmar. 25 rooms. Breakfast room, cable TV,
pool; no room phones. AE, MC, V. EP.*

Nightlife and the Arts

Action at the pedestrian mall heats up at sunset, when people stroll
near the sea. The live floor show at **Parador Villa Parguera** (⊠ Rte.
304, Km 2.3, ☎ 787/899–7777 or 787/899–3975) starts at 7 on Saturday and includes a buffet. The show changes every three months;
performances have included a comedy revue and folkloric dancing. The
cost is $35, including the dinner. On Friday and Saturday, **Parguera
Blues Café** (⊠ 3 Calle Albizu Campos, ☎ 787/899–4265) has a rock
or blues band starting at 9 or 10 PM.

Outdoor Activities and Sports

FISHING

You can spend a day or half-day fishing for blue marlin, tuna, or reef
fish with Captain Mickey Amador at **Parguera Fishing Charters** (⊠
Rte. 304, Km 3.8, ☎ 787/382–4698 or 787/899–4698).

SCUBA DIVING AND SNORKELING

There are more than 50 shore-dive sites off La Parguera. Some of the
most popular are Fallen Rock, Old Buoy, Black Wall, the Aquarium,
and the Pinnacles. **Paradise Scuba** (⊠ Rte. 304, Km 1.3, ☎ 787/899–
7611) has classes and trips, including night snorkeling excursions in
phosphorescent waters. **Parguera Divers** (⊠ Posada Porlamar, Rte. 304,
Km 3.3, ☎ 787/899–4171) offers scuba and snorkeling expeditions
and basic instruction.

Shopping

Outdoor stands near Bahía Fosforescente sell all kinds of souvenirs,
from T-shirts to beaded necklaces. In La Parguera's center, there are
several small souvenir shops, including **Nautilus** (⊠ Rte. 304, ☎ 787/
899–4565), that sell T-shirts, posters, mugs, and trinkets made from
shells.

San Germán

㉕–㉟ *10 km (6 mi) north of La Parguera; 166 km (104 mi) southwest of
San Juan.*

During its early years, San Germán was a city on the move. Although
debate rages about the first settlement's exact founding date and location, the town is believed to have been established in 1510 near
Guánica. Plagued by mosquitoes, the settlers moved north along the
west coast, where they encountered French pirates and smugglers. In
the 1570s they fled inland to the current location, but they were still
harassed. Determined and creative, they dug tunnels and moved beneath the city (the tunnels are now part of the water system.) Today
San Germán has a population of 39,000, and its intellectual and political activity is anything but underground. Students and professors
from the Inter-American University often fill the town's bars and cafés.

Around San Germán's two main squares—Plazuela Santo Domingo and
Plaza Francisco Mariano Quiñones (named for an abolitionist)—are
buildings done in every conceivable style of architecture found on the
island including mission, Victorian, creole, and Spanish colonial. The
city's tourist office offers a free guided trolley tour. Most of the buildings are private homes; two of them—the Capilla de Porta Coeli and
the Museo de Arte y Casa de Estudio—are museums. The historical
center is surrounded by strip malls, and the town is hemmed to the
south and west by busy seaside resorts.

128

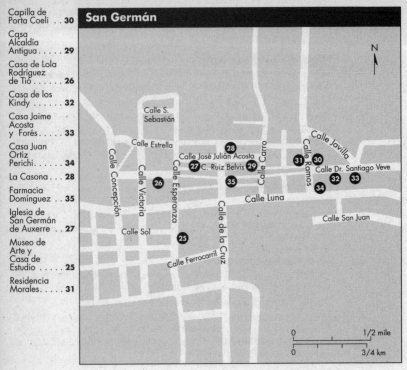

San Germán

The **Museo de Arte y Casa de Estudio,** at the city's southern edge, is a yellow, early 20th-century home with neoclassical influences that has been turned into a museum. Displays include colonial furnishings, religious art, and Taíno artifacts; there are also changing art exhibits by local painters. ⊠ *7 Calle Esperanza,* ☎ *787/892–8870.* ☜ *Free.* ☉ *Wed.–Sun. 10–noon and 1–3.*

The **Casa de Lola Rodríguez de Tió** (circa 1870) is on the National Registry of Historic Places and bears the name of poet and independence activist Lola Rodríguez de Tió. A plaque claims she lived in this light green creole-style house, though town officials say it belonged to her sister. Rodríguez, whose mother was a descendent of Ponce de León, was deported several times by Spanish authorities here for her revolutionary ideas. She lived in Venezuela and then in Cuba, where she died in 1924. The museum, which contains Rodríguez's desk and papers, isn't regularly open to the public; check with the tourist office. ⊠ *13 Calle Dr. Santiago Veve,* ☎ *787/892–3500 to arrange a visit.* ☜ *Free.*

The central Plaza Francisco Mariano Quiñones is dominated by the **Iglesia de San Germán de Auxerre.** This yellow-and-white neoclassical church dates from 1739 and was built atop its predecessor. Be sure to look up at the carved wood ceiling in the nave. The impressive crystal chandelier was added in 1860. ⊠ *Plaza Francisco Mariano Quiñones,* ☎ *787/892–1027.* ☉ *Mass Mon.–Sat. at 7 AM and 7:30 PM and Sun. at 7, 8:30, and 10 AM and 7:30 PM.*

On the north side of Plaza Francisco Mariano Quiñones, at Calle José Julien Acosta and Calle Cruz, is the two-story, yellow **La Casona.** It was built in 1871 for Tomás Agrait, who made it his home and a center of cultural activities in San Germán. It was later owned by the Bahr family and is also known as La Casona de Bahr. Inside it is a shop, Casa Vieja (☎ 787/264–3954), that carries Caribbean antiques.

㉙ The **Casa Alcaldía Antigua** (Old Municipal Building) is at the eastern end of Plaza Francisco Mariano Quiñones. From 1844 to 1950 it served as the city hall and municipal prison. At this writing the Spanish-colonial style building was being renovated.

★ **㉚** One of the oldest Christian religious structures in the Americas, the **Capilla de Porta Coeli** (Heaven's Gate Chapel), overlooks the long, rectangular Plazuela de Santo Domingo. The original complex, which included a convent, was built in 1606; much of it was demolished in 1866, leaving only the chapel and a vestige of the convent's front wall. The mission-style chapel was restored and reopened for services in 1878. Now it functions as a museum of religious art, displaying painted wooden statuary by Latin American and Spanish artists. ⊠ *Plazuela Santo Domingo,* ☎ *787/892–5845.* ☞ *$1.* ☉ *Wed.–Sun. 9–4:45.*

㉛ The **Residencia Morales** (⊠ 38 Calle Ramos), across the street from the Capilla de Porta Coeli on the Plazuela de Santo Domingo, is a private home designed in 1913 by architect Pedro Vivoni for his brother, Tomás Vivoni. The white, Victorian building takes up an entire city block and has numerous towers and gables. The current owners have kept it in mint condition.

㉜ **Casa de los Kindy** (⊠ 64 Calle Dr. Santiago Veve), east of the Plazuela de Santo Domingo, is a 19th-century home known for its eclectic architecture, which includes neoclassical and creole elements. Note the stained-glass windows and the latticework on the balcony. It's now a private residence and not open to the public.

㉝ Down the street from Casa de los Kindy is **Casa Jaime Acosta y Forés** (⊠ 70 Calle Dr. Santiago Veve), a beautiful yellow-and-white wooden house built in 1918. Inside, the walls are covered floor to ceiling with stenciling, and over the door is attractive fretwork. The house isn't open to the public.

㉞ You'll find an excellent example of Puerto Rican ornamental architecture in the **Casa Juan Ortiz Perichi** (⊠ 94 Calle Luna), a block southeast of the Plazuela de Santo Domingo. This gigantic white home with a wraparound balcony was built in 1920. Note the stained-glass windows and wood trim around the doors. It's not open to the public.

㉟ Constructed in 1877, the dark-orange, Spanish colonial **Farmacia Domínguez** (⊠ Calles Cruz and Dr. Santiago Veve) started out as a pharmacy and then became a restaurant. (At this writing, it was closed to the public and up for sale.)

Dining and Lodging

$–$$$ ✗ **Cilantro's.** In a 120-year-old mansion called Casa Real, chef Carlos Rosario serves new Puerto Rican cuisine in an intimate, second-floor dining room (reservations are a good idea). Surrounded by arched walls, stained-glass windows and decorative Spanish tiles, you can try dorado with a black bean sauce or squid stuffed with sausage and lobster. There are also vegetarian dishes, and on Tuesday nights sushi is added to the menu. The restaurant offers changing lunch specials. ⊠ *85 Calle Luna,* ☎ *787/264–2735. D, MC, V. Closed Wed.*

$–$$ ✗ **Del Mar y Algo Mas.** Chef Eric John has made paella the signature dish of his restaurant near the Capilla de Porta Coeli. The menu includes a variety of Puerto Rican dishes, with an emphasis on seafood. ⊠ *Plazuela Santo Domingo, at Calle Carro,* ☎ *787/636–4265. MC, V.*

$ ✗🛏 **Oasis.** San Germán's only hotel is in a melon-color, Spanish colonial mansion near the center of town. It's far from luxurious, but

Close-Up

LIVES OF THE SANTOS

WHEN THEY ARRIVED on Puerto Rico, the Spanish missionaries spread the word of God and fostered a spirited folk art. As many of their parishioners couldn't read, the missionaries often commissioned local artisans to create pictures and statues depicting Bible stories and saints or *santos*. These figures—fashioned of wood, clay, stone, or even gold—are still given a place of honor in homes throughout the island.

Early *santeros* (carvers) were influenced by the Spanish baroque style. As time went on, however, they came into their own. Later figures are simple and small, averaging about 8 inches tall. They're also made of such natural materials as vegetable dyes and real hair. The craft has been passed along within families or communities, and most of today's santeros have no formal art training. San Germán has been associated with santos-making since the origins of the art form, and central Puerto Rico's Rivera family has been known for its carvings for more than 150 years.

Each santo has a traditional characteristic or two that makes it recognizable. You can spot the Virgin by her blue robes, St. Francis by the birds and animals with him, St. Barbara by her tower, and the Holy Spirit by its hovering dove. St. John, the island's patron saint, is an ever-popular subject, as is the Nativity, which might be rendered with just the Holy Family, or the family with an entire supporting cast of herald angels, shepherds, and barnyard animals.

Carvings of Los Santos Reyes (The Three Kings) are also popular. Their feast day, January 6, is important on Puerto Rico. Celebrations often continue for days before or after the actual holiday, when it's difficult to find a home without these regal characters. Although the three riders are often depicted carrying their traditional gifts of gold, frankincense, and myrrh, you may see a magi strumming the *cuatro*, an island guitar.

— Karen English

there's a small pool and a helpful staff. Rooms are small and dark; those in a newer annex are better maintained than those in the original mansion. The restaurant ($–$$) serves generous portions of Puerto Rican food. ✉ *72 Calle Luna (Box 1063, 00683),* ☎ *787/892–1175 or 800-942–8086,* FAX *787/892–4546. 52 rooms. Restaurant, bar, cable TV, pool. AE, D, DC, MC V. EP.*

Cabo Rojo

36 *11 km (7 mi) west of San Germán.*

Named for the pinkish cliffs that surround it, Cabo Rojo was founded in 1771 as a port for merchant vessels—and for the smugglers and pirates who inevitably accompanied ocean-going trade. Today it's known as a family resort destination, and many small, inexpensive hotels line its shores. Seaside settlements such as Puerto Real and Joyuda—the latter has a strip of more than 30 seafood restaurants overlooking the water—are found along the coast. Although you can hike in wildlife refuges at the outskirts of town, there aren't any area outfitters, so be sure to bring along water, sunscreen, and all other necessary supplies.

★ The **Bosque Estatal de Boquerón** (Boquerón National Forest) encompasses three tracts of land at the island's southern tip. You can hike along a rugged peninsula to the 1881 Cabo Rojo Lighthouse at the end of Route 301. (Note: it's not open to the public.) The forest also includes the Refugio de Aves, a bird sanctuary on Route 301 at Km 1.2, and an interpretive center on Route 101 in the village of Boquerón. ⊠ *Rte. 301 and Rte. 101,* ☎ *787/851–7260 interpretive center.* 🎫 *Free.* ⊘ *Bird sanctuary and interpretive center weekdays 7–3:30.*

Refugio de Vida Silvestre, run by the U.S. Fish and Wildlife Service, has an interpretive center with exhibits of live freshwater fish and sea turtles. You see as many as 100 species of birds along the trails, even the elusive yellow-shouldered blackbird. ⊠ *Rte. 301, Km 5.1,* ☎ *787/ 851–7258.* 🎫 *Free.* ⊘ *Weekdays 7–3:30.*

Beaches

The long stretch of sand at **Balneario Boquerón,** off Route 101 is a favorite with islanders, especially during Easter weekend. You'll find changing facilities, cabins, showers, rest rooms, and picnic tables; it costs $2 to enter with a car. The white-sand **Buyé,** at Km 4.8 on Route 307, has palm trees and crystal-clear waters. At the end of Route 3301 is **El Combate,** which draws college students to its rustic waterfront eateries. You can rent small boats and kayaks here, and in summer there are often concerts and festivals. Palms dot **Playa Joyuda,** a good swimming beach that runs alongside Route 102. Crescent-shape **La Playuela** is the most secluded of the area's beaches. It's on Route 301 near the salt flats.

Dining and Lodging

$–$$$ ✕ **El Bohío.** Watch tarpon play in the water while you dine on the enclosed deck at this informal restaurant. The long list of seafood is prepared in a variety of ways: shrimp comes breaded, stewed, or in a salad; conch is served as a salad or cooked in a butter and garlic sauce. ⊠ *Rte. 102, Km 9.7, Joyuda,* ☎ *787/851–2755. AE, DC, MC, V.*

$–$$ ✕ **Annie's.** A dining room with windows facing the ocean is a fitting place to try some of the southwest coast's best seafood. You can snack on *empanadillas* (deep-fried fritters) stuffed with seafood or feast on red snapper with rice and beans. This place is casual and friendly. ⊠ *Calle 3, El Combate,* ☎ *787/254–0021. AE, MC, V. Closed Mon.–Wed.*

$–$$ ✕ **Galloway's.** From a porch overlooking Bahía Boquerón, catch the sunset while enjoying seafood—caught fresh from local waters and often prepared in traditional ways. The menu also has a few international choices, including some Italian dishes. There's a lively happy hour and occasional live music. ⊠ *12 Calle José de Diego, Balneario Boquerón,* ☎ *787/254–3302. MC, V. Closed Wed.*

$ ✕ **Cafetería Los Chapines.** This rustic seaside shack sells cold drinks, snacks, and fish and chicken dishes. Be sure to try one of the specialty sandwiches, which are made with deep-fried plantains instead of bread. ⊠ *Calle 3, El Combate,* ☎ *787/254–4005. MC, V.*

$$ ✕🏨 **Bahía Salinas Beach Hotel.** The Cabo Rojo Lighthouse is this resortlike parador's closest neighbor. You can wander along the boardwalk or the garden paths, bask in the sun on a deck or terrace, or relax in a Jacuzzi that's filled with therapeutic salt crystals from the nearby salt flats. Rooms are spacious and have reproduction Puerto Rican antiques. The Agua al Cuello restaurant ($–$$$) serves seafood; don't overlook the giant tostones. ⊠ *End of Rte. 301 (HC-01 Box 2356, 00622),* ☎ *787/254–1212 or 877/205–7507,* 🖷 *787/254–1215,* 🕸 *www.bahiasalinas.net. 24 rooms. Restaurant, bar, lounge, cable TV, pool, hot tub, gym, playground; no room phones. MC, V. BP, CP, EP, MAP.*

$–$$ ✕⬚ **Combate Beach Hotel.** Just a few steps from El Combate, this hotel has large guest rooms as well as six apartments with full kitchens. The Puerto Angelino restaurant ($–$$) serves seafood and Puerto Rican fare. Other restaurants and night spots are within walking distance along shore. ⊠ *Rte. 3301, El Combate (Box 1138, 00622),* ☎ *787/254–7053 or 787/254–2358,* FAX *787/254–2358. 20 units. Restaurant, bar, cable TV, refrigerators, pool; no room phones. MC, V. EP.*

$ ✕⬚ **Parador Boquemar.** You can walk to Balneario Boquerón from this parador. Guest quarters are decorated with tropical prints and rattan furniture; ask for a third-floor room with a balcony overlooking the water. La Cascada restaurant ($–$$) offers Puerto Rican cuisine. On weekends the lounge is filled with live music. ⊠ *Calle Gill Buyé (Box 133, 00622),* ☎ *787/851–2158 or 888/634–4343,* FAX *787/851–7600,* WEB *www.boquemar.com. 75 rooms. Restaurant, lounge, cable TV, refrigerators, pool, meeting rooms. AE, D, DC, MC, V. EP.*

$–$$ ⬚ **Parador Joyuda Beach.** Right on the shore, near Joyuda's restau-
★   rant row, this friendly parador has a large lobby and spacious rooms. Ask for one of the sunset suites, which have ocean views. You'll find drinks and a snack bar by the pool. ⊠ *Rte. 102, Km 11.7, Joyuda (HC 01 Box 18410, 00623),* ☎ *787/851–5650 or 800/981–5464,* FAX *787/ 255–3750,* WEB *www.joyudabeach.com. 41 rooms. Snack bar, cable TV, pool, beach. AE, MC, V. EP.*

Nightlife

The **Bahía Salinas Beach Hotel** (⊠ End of Rte. 301, ☎ 787/254–1212) often has live music shows. In Boquerón, **Galloway's** (☎ 787/254–3302) draws an interesting crowd to its bar and has occasional live music. Check with **Tropicoro Sports Bar** (☎ 787/254–2466), a lively El Combate bar with billiard tables, to see whether there's a band playing.

Outdoor Activities and Sports

GOLF

Get in nine holes at the **Club Deportivo del Oeste** (⊠ Rte. 102, Km 15.4, Joyuda Sector, ☎ 787/254–3748 or 787/851–1880). Jack Bender incorporated the hills in his design to provide golfers with panoramic views while they play. The course is open daily; greens fees are $30.

WATER SPORTS

Several reef-bordered cays lie off the Cabo Rojo area near walls that drop to 100 ft. A mile-long reef along Las Coronas, better known as Cayo Ron, has a variety of hard and soft coral, reef fish, and lobster. You can arrange snorkeling and scuba trips with **Tour Marine** (⊠ Rte. 101, Km 14.1, Joyuda Sector, Puerto Real, ☎ 787/851–9259). The company will also take anglers out to waters off Cabo Rojo's coast.

SOUTHERN PUERTO RICO A TO Z

To research prices, get advice from other travelers, and book travel arrangements, visit www.fodors.com.

AIR TRAVEL

Aeropuerto Mercedita is about 8 km (5 mi) east of Ponce's downtown. It accommodates private planes and Cape Air flights from San Juan. Taxis at the airport operate under a meter system; it costs about $6 to get downtown. Some hotels have shuttles from the airport, but you must make arrangements in advance.

➤ AIRPORT INFORMATION: **Aeropuerto Mercedita** (⊠ Rte. 506 off Rte. 52, ☎ 787/842–6292).

➤ CARRIER: **Cape Air** (☎ 787/844–2099 in Ponce; 787/253–1121 in San Juan; 800/352–0714 in the U.S., WEB www.flycapeair.com).

BUS TRAVEL

There's no easy network of buses linking the towns in southern Puerto Rico with the capital of San Juan or with each other. Some municipalities and private companies operate buses or *públicos* (usually large vans) that make many stops. Call ahead; although reservations aren't usually required, you'll need to check on schedules, which change frequently. The cost of a público from Ponce to San Juan is about $15 to $20; agree on a price before you start your journey.

➤ BUS INFORMATION: **Choferes Unidos de Ponce** (✉ Terminal de Carros Públicos, Calle Vives and Calle Mendéz Vigo, Ponce, Ponce Centro, ☎ 787/764–0540). **Línea Caborrojeña** (✉ Rte. 103 in center of town, Cabo Rojo, ☎ 787/723–9155). **Línea San Germeña** (✉ Terminal de Carros Públicos, Calle Luna at entrance to town, San Germán, ☎ 787/722–3392 or 787/892–1076).

CAR RENTAL

You can rent cars at the Luis Muñoz Marín International Airport and other San Juan locations. There are also car rental agencies in some of the larger cities along the south coast. Rates run about $35–$45 a day, depending on the car. You may get a better deal if you rent a car for a week or more. Test your vehicle before heading out to be sure it runs properly.

➤ AGENCIES: **Avis** (✉ Mercedita Airport, Ponce, ☎ 787/842–6154). **Dollar** (✉ Av. Los Caobos and Calle Acacia, Ponce, ☎ 787/843–6940). **International Car Rental** (✉ Rte. 100, Km 6.0, Cabo Rojo, ☎ 787/254–0384). **Leaseway of Puerto Rico** (✉ Rte. 3, Km 140.1, Guayama, ☎ 787/864–8149).

CAR TRAVEL

A road map is essential in southern Puerto Rico. So is patience: allow extra time for twisting mountain roads and wrong turns. Some roads, especially in rural areas, aren't plainly marked. The fastest route through the region is the Luis Ferré Expressway (Route 52), a toll road that runs from San Juan to Ponce, crossing the island's central mountain range.

EMERGENCY SERVICES

There's no AAA service in Puerto Rico, but independent tow trucks regularly scout the Luis A. Ferré Expressway (Route 52) looking for disabled vehicles. Police also patrol the expressway. A number of towing companies will send trucks on request.

➤ CONTACTS: **Alfredo Towing Service** (☎ 787/251–6750). **Dennis Towing** (☎ 787/504–5724).

GASOLINE

Gas stations are plentiful, particularly near expressway exits and at town entrances on secondary roads. Some stations are open 24 hours, but many close at around midnight or 1 AM. At this writing, regular gas cost about 32¢ a liter.

PARKING

You can find free on-street parking in most southern cities; metered parking is rare. Larger communities have lots in their downtown areas. Prices are usually less than $1 an hour.

ROAD CONDITIONS

Major highways in southern Puerto Rico are well maintained. Watch out for potholes on secondary roads, especially after heavy rains.

EMERGENCIES

➤ EMERGENCY NUMBER: **General** (☎ 911).

➤ HOSPITALS: **Hospital de Area Alejandro Buitrago** (✉ Av. Central and Calle Principal, Guayama, ☎ 787/864–4300 or 787/892–1860). **Hos-**

pital de la Concepción (✉ 41 Calle Luna, San Germán, ☎ 787/892–
1860). **Hospital Damas** (✉ 2213 Ponce Bypass Rd., Villa Grillasca,
Ponce, ☎ 787/840–8686).

➤ PHARMACIES: **El Amal** (✉ Valle Real Shopping Center, Rte. 2 Ur-
banización Valle Real, Ponce, ☎ 787/844–5555). **Walgreens** (✉ 1
Calle Marginal, Guayama, ☎ 787/864–5355; ✉ 13 Av. Fagot, Ponce
Centro, Ponce, ☎ 787/841–2135; ✉ 64 Calle Luna, San Germán, ☎
787/892–1170).

ENGLISH-LANGUAGE MEDIA

Publications in English are harder to find in southern Puerto Rico than
in San Juan. Look for the English-language edition of the *San Juan Star*
on newsstands and in drug stores and gas stations. Some hotel gift shops
have a small selection of English-language books and newspapers.
Your best bet is Isabel II Books & Magazine in Ponce, which has a large
selection of books, magazines, and mainland papers, although the
newspapers are normally delivered a day or two late.

➤ BOOKSTORES: **Isabel II Books & Magazine** (✉ 66 Calle Isabel, Ponce
Centro, Ponce, ☎ 787/848–5019).

HEALTH

The island's tap water is generally safe to drink. Fruits should be well
washed before being eaten if bought from a roadside stand or in a market. Remember that the sun is strong and shines most of the time on
the south coast, so be sure to have sunscreen and drinking water with
you.

MAIL AND SHIPPING

There are branches of the U.S. Post Office throughout the region. You
can buy stamps in Pueblo Supermarkets and in many gift shops.

➤ POST OFFICES: **Cabo Rojo** (✉ 64 Calle Carbonell, ☎ 787/851–
1095). **Guayaman** (✉ 151 Calle Ashford, ☎ 787/864–1150). **Ponce**
(✉ 94 Calle Atocha, Ponce Centro, ☎ 787/842–2997).

OVERNIGHT SERVICES

Express delivery services are available at the U.S. Post Office. Some
shops are authorized to handle Federal Express (FedEx) packages, and
there are FedEx stations in Ponce and Guayama. Note that there's no
Saturday pick-up service in the area. You can drop off packages and
U.S. mail at area PostNet stores, which also sell envelopes and boxes.

➤ MAJOR SERVICES: **FedEx** (✉ Plaza Guayama, Rte. 3 Km 134.9,
Guayama, ☎ 877/838–7834; ✉ Mercedita Airport, Ponce, ☎ 877/838–
7834). **PostNet** (✉ Calle 3, Urbanization Borinquen, Cabo Rojo, ☎
787/254–0384).

MONEY MATTERS

You'll find plenty of banks in the region, and many supermarkets, drug
stores, and gas stations have ATMs. Banks are normally open weekdays 9 AM to 3 PM or 4 PM. Some banks—such as the Scotiabank
branch in Ponce—are also open until noon on Saturday. You can exchange foreign currency in Banco Popular branches; Scotiabank exchanges Canadian currency. Western Union service is available at
Pueblo Supermarkets.

➤ BANKS AND EXCHANGE SERVICES: **Banco Popular** (✉ Plaza Guayama,
Rte. 3, Km 134.9, Guayama, ☎ 787/866–0180; ✉ Plaza las Delicias,
Ponce Centro, Ponce, ☎ 787/843–8000 or 787/848–2410). **Scotiabank**
(✉ Plaza las Delicias, Ponce Centro, Ponce, ☎ 787/259–8535).

SAFETY

Like anywhere else, you need to take caution against crime in southwestern Puerto Rico. Don't leave valuables unattended at the beach

or out in plain sight inside your car. Use caution when walking in cities, especially at night.

TAXIS

In Ponce, you can hail taxis in tourist areas and outside hotels. In smaller towns, it's best to call a taxi. You can also hire a car service (make arrangements through your hotel); often you can negotiate a rate that's lower than what you would pay for a taxi.

➤ CAB COMPANIES: **Borinquen Taxi** (☎ 787/843–6000 or 787/843–6100 in Ponce). **Ojeda Taxi** (☎ 787/259–7676 in San Germán). **Ponce Taxi Association** (☎ 787/842–3370).

➤ LIMOUSINE COMPANIES: **Ponce Limousine Service** (☎ 787/848–0469).

TELEPHONES

Puerto Rico's main area code is 787; a new, 939 area code is being introduced gradually. You must dial the area code and the 7-digit number on any call you make in Puerto Rico. Dial 1 before the area code when calling from one municipality to another. Public phones are readily available throughout the southern part of the island, but you may have to try two or three phones before you find one that works. A local call costs 25¢, and you can pay with credit cards, phone cards, or coins.

TOURS

Call the Museo de la Historia de Ponce to arrange for a tour of Ponce's historical sights. Tours, which vary in length, start at $5 per person. Alelí Tours and Encantos Ecotours Southwest in La Parguera offer ecological tours of the southwestern area, including two- or three-hour kayak trips that cost about $25. San Juan tour operators also offer trips to the Bosque Estatal de Guánica, Ponce, and elsewhere. Prices start at around $45 per person and include transportation from San Juan hotels.

➤ TOUR OPERATORS: **Alelí Tours** (✉ Rte. 304, Km 3.2, La Parguera, ☎ 787/899–6086). **Encantos Ecotours Southwest** (✉ El Muelle Shopping Center, Av. Pescadores, La Parguera, ☎ 787/808–0005). **Museo de la Historia de Ponce** (✉ 51–53 Calle Isabel, Ponce Centro, Ponce, ☎ 787/844–7071). **Sunshine Tours** (✉ Normandie Hotel, Av. Muñoz Rivera at Parque de Tercer Milenio, Puerta de Tierra, San Juan, ☎ 787/729–2929).

TRAVEL AGENCIES

➤ CONTACTS: **Boquerón Travel** (✉ 60 Muñoz Rivera, Cabo Rojo, ☎ 787/851–4751). **Coco Travel** (✉ 1-N Calle Calimano, Guayama, ☎ 787/864–1683). **Trade Winds Travel Agents** (✉ 42 Calle Comercio, Ponce Centro, Ponce, ☎ 787/844–0420).

TROLLEY AND TRAIN TRAVEL

Ponce offers free transportation to its major attractions on trolleys and tourist trains. They run daily from 9 AM to about 9:30 PM, and leave from Plaza las Delicias. On Sunday, Guayama has a free trolley that runs to many sights. Arroyo's free trolley operations on Saturday and Sunday, and a trolley tour of San Germán is available by appointment.

➤ CONTACTS: **Arroyo Trolley** (✉ Acaldía de Arroyo, 64 Calle Morse, Arroyo, ☎ 787/721–1574). **Guayama Trolley** (✉ Acaldía de Guayama, Calle Vicente Pales, Guayama, ☎ 787/864–7765). **Ponce Trolley and Chu Chu** (✉ Ponce Municipal Tourism Office, Plaza las Delicias, Ponce Centro, Ponce, ☎ 787/841–8160). **San Germán Trolley** (✉ Acaldía de San Germán, 136 Calle Luna, San Germán, ☎ 787/892–3500).

VISITOR INFORMATION

In Ponce, the municipal tourist office is open weekdays 8–4:30, and the Puerto Rico Tourism Company has hours weekdays 8–5. The Cabo Rojo branch is open Monday through Saturday 8–4:30. Smaller cities generally have a tourism office in the city hall that's open weekdays 8–noon and 1–4.

➤ CONTACTS: **Ponce Municipal Tourist Office** (✉ 2nd floor of Citibank, Plaza las Delicias, Ponce Centro, Ponce [Box 1709, 00733], ☎ 787/841–8160 or 787/841–8044). **Puerto Rico Tourism Company** (✉ Rte. 101, Km 13.7, Cabo Riojo, ☎ 787/851–7070; ✉ 291 Av. Los Caobos, Sector Vallas Torres, Ponce, ☎ 787/843–0465).

5 NORTHWESTERN PUERTO RICO

You can find everything from underground rivers to high mountain peaks in northwestern Puerto Rico. The area also has world-class surfing and swimming beaches; championship golf courses; and, inland, some of the Caribbean's best mountain scenery.

Updated by
Caryn Nesmith

L ESS THAN A CENTURY AGO, northwestern Puerto Rico was over-
whelmingly rural. Some large fruit plantations dotted the coast, while
farther inland coffee was grown on hillside *fincas* (farms). Regardless, a few ports, notably the west-coast city of Mayagüez, took
on a somewhat cosmopolitan air and drew immigrants from around
the world.

The generally slow pace of the area began to change during the mid-
20th century. The government's Operation Bootstrap program drew
more manufacturing into the area, new roads brought once-isolated
towns into the mainstream, and tourists began to discover the gold sand
of the Atlantic coast and the mighty waves near the town of Rincón.

On the Atlantic coast, Dorado was one of the first areas to develop
luxury resorts, and it now offers top-notch hotels, golf courses, and
almost every kind of water sport imaginable. Inland the more remote
mountain areas still produce coffee; they also lure more adventurous
travelers to their narrow, winding roads. Just past Arecibo begin the
rolling hills of karst country, terrain built up by limestone deposits in
which erosion has produced fissures, sinkholes, underground streams,
and caverns. It's here, in several large forest reserves and around the
Río Camuy cave network, that Puerto Rico has its greatest ecotourism
potential—though you'll still find yourself far from crowds.

On the west coast, the waves around Aguadilla and Rincón are as popular as ever. Visitors of all kinds come here to surf or just enjoy the
beaches and sunsets. Many have decided not to return home.

Pleasures and Pastimes

Dining

Throughout northwestern Puerto Rico you'll find wonderful *criollo* cuisine, interspersed with international restaurants ranging from French
to Japanese. You can enjoy five-course meals in elegant surroundings
at night, then sip morning coffee on an outdoor balcony the next
morning.

Tips, normally 15%–20%, are usually not included in the bill, but it's
always wise to double-check.

CATEGORY	COST*
$$$$	over $35
$$$	$25–$35
$$	$15–$25
$	under $15

per person for a main course at dinner

Hiking

Northwestern Puerto Rico has a number of forest reserves that rival
the better-known El Yunque in beauty. The Bosque Estatal de Río Abajo
has trails in the island's "karst country." The cloud-covered Bosque
Estatal de Toro Negro has waterfalls, natural pools, and the island's
tallest mountain peak, Cerro de Punta, which rises to 4,398 ft. The
drier Bosque Estatal de Maricao is known for its numerous species of
birds, including many on the endangered list. For the truly adventurous, the uninhabited Mona Island 31 km (50 mi) off the western coast,
has hiking, camping, fishing, and diving.

Lodging

Lodging in the area runs the gamut from posh resorts offering windsurfing lessons and championship golf courses to rustic cabins in the

middle of a forest reserve. The Dorado area has a concentration of sleek resorts; the western part of the island near Rincón has a variety of hotels, from furnished apartments geared toward families to colorful small hotels. In the central mountains, a few old plantation homes have been turned into wonderful country inns that transport you back to slower and quieter times.

CATEGORY	COST*
$$$$	over $225
$$$	$150–$225
$$	$75–$150
$	under $75

All prices are for a double room in high season, excluding 9% tax (11% for hotels with casinos, 7% for paradores) and 5%–12% service charge.

Surfing

Rincón hosted the World Surfing Championship in 1968, and its beaches have some of the best waves in the world, especially in winter. Other areas on the north coast, such as Aguadilla and Isabela, have impressive waves as well.

Exploring Northwestern Puerto Rico

Highway 22 heads west from San Juan and swings around the northwestern part of the island, skirting the beaches of the northern coast. A short 45 minutes from the capital is the resort town of Dorado. Farther west, at Arecibo, the island's limestone karst country begins, filled with strangely shaped hills, cliffs, and sinkholes. You can delve into the area by taking Route 10 south, which leads to the Río Abajo Forest Reserve and the mountain town of Utuado, or by taking Route 129, which leads to the karst country's premier attraction, Las Cavernas del Río Camuy.

Numerous small, narrow roads traverse the rugged Cordillera Central, the island's central mountain range. Much of the Ruta Panorámica, a network of small roads running horizontally across the island, passes through this area.

After Arecibo, Highway 22 turns into Highway 2 and continues down the west coast, where the ragged shoreline holds some of the island's best surfing beaches—as well as calmer swimming beaches—and a steady contingent of surfers gives the area a laid-back atmosphere.

Numbers in the text correspond to numbers in the margin and on the Northwestern Puerto Rico map.

Great Itineraries

IF YOU HAVE 3 DAYS

If you feel like indulging yourself, spend three days at one of the 🏨 **Dorado** ① resorts. Set aside a day to visit one of Puerto Rico's greatest natural wonders, Parque de las Cavernas del Río Camuy, and one of its greatest man-made ones, Observatorio de Arecibo.

If you want a more relaxed, secluded environment, try 🏨 **Isabela** ③, a quiet town with a gorgeous shoreline and get-away-from-it-all inns. Spend your first day on the beach, capping it off with a sunset horseback ride along the shore. On the second day, head to Parque de las Cavernas del Río Camuy and Observatorio de Arecibo, and on day three visit the friendly beachfront town of **Rincón** ⑩.

IF YOU HAVE 5 DAYS

For the first three days use one of the converted coffee plantations near 🏨 **Utuado** ④ as your base camp and explore the area's sights, such as

Parque de las Cavernas del Río Camuy, Observatorio de Arecibo, Bosque Estatal de Toro Negro, Parque Ceremonial Indígena de Caguana, and Lago Dos Bocas. Then make your way to the west coast and ⊞ **Rincón** ⑩ for two days of great waves, beautiful sunsets, and laid-back good times.

IF YOU HAVE 7 DAYS

Start out with two days at a ⊞ **Dorado** ① resort, spend three days exploring the inlands and staying at a former coffee plantation in the mountains near ⊞ **Utuado** ④ or ⊞ **Jayuya** ⑤, and finish up with two days in ⊞ **Rincón** ⑩ on the west coast. Or . . . forget about variety and dedicate your entire week to one of those three locations—just make sure you don't miss Parque de las Cavernas del Río Camuy, a highlight of any trip to this region.

When to Tour

In winter the weather is at its best, but you'll have to compete with other visitors for hotel rooms; book well in advance. Winter is also the height of the surfing season on the west coast. In summer, many family-oriented hotels fill up with *sanjuaneros* escaping the city for the weekend—some hotels require a two-night stay. Larger resorts normally drop their rates in summer by at least 10%. The weather gets hot, especially in August and September, but the beaches help keep everyone cool.

THE NORTH COAST

West of San Juan, large tracts of coconut palms silhouette Dorado and its environs, the scenic remnants of large coconut and fruit plantations. Farther west, near Arecibo, the island's limestone karst country is distinguished by haystack-shape hills (called *mogotes* by locals) and underground rivers and caves. One of the island's most fascinating geological wonders is the Río Camuy cave system, one of the largest such systems in the western hemisphere. Nearby, science takes center stage at the Arecibo Observatory, the largest radar–radio telescope in the world.

Dorado

❶ *27 km (17 mi) west of San Juan.*

This small and tidy town has a definite festive air about it, even though more and more it's turning into a suburb for San Juan's workers. It's one of the oldest vacation spots on the island, having gotten a boost in 1955 when Laurance Rockefeller bought the pineapple, coconut, and grapefruit plantation of Dr. Alfred Livingston and his daughter, Clara, and built a resort on the property. Today, the former plantation is the site of the Hyatt Regency Cerromar Hotel and the Hyatt Dorado Beach Resort & Country Club, two top luxury resorts that include four of the best-known golf courses in Puerto Rico. The town of Dorado itself is fun to visit; its winding road leads across a bridge to a main square, and there are small delis, restaurants, and shops nearby. Most visitors, however, don't stray too far from the beach or their hotel.

Beaches

At the end of Route 697, Dorado's **Playa Sardinera** is suitable for swimming and has shade trees, changing rooms, and rest rooms. **Playa Breñas,** between the two Hyatt resorts in Dorado, is known for its surfing; adventurous swimmers also enjoy the waves. The 2,500-ft-long **Playa Cerro Gordo,** at the end of Route 690, is lined with cliffs. It's very popular and can get crowded on weekends. **Playa Los Tubos,** on Route 687 in Vega Baja, is popular for both swimming and surfing. It holds a summer festival with merengue and salsa groups and water-sports competitions, normally the first week of July.

Dining and Lodging

$$ ✕ **El Ladrillo.** This cozy spot with brick floors and walls (*el ladrillo* means "the brick") is known for its grilled steaks, including T-bones and filet mignon. It also has a wide selection of seafood—try the *zarzuela*, a combination of lobster, squid, octopus, clams, and more. ✉ *Calle Méndez Vigo 334,* ☎ *787/796–2120. AE, MC, V.*

$–$$ ✕ **A La Brasa Steakhouse.** The black tables and chairs of this Argentine steakhouse are offset by red and green walls. Meat is served with a *chimichuri* sauce (parsley garlic, vinegar, and oregano). A delicious dessert selection is the *panqueque de dulce de leche,* a caramel crêpe. ✉ *Rte. 693, Km 8.5,* ☎ *787/796–4477. AE, D, MC, V.*

$–$$ ✕ **Mangére.** You'll find a long menu of Italian cuisine and 86 wines at this spacious restaurant decorated in pastel colors. Entrées include veal medallions with Portabello and porcini mushrooms, smoked Norwegian salmon with capers, and linguine carbonara. ✉ *Rte. 693, Km 8.5,* ☎ *787/796–4444. AE, D, MC, V.*

$$$$ ✕⊡ **Hyatt Dorado Beach Resort & Country Club.** Sprawling over 1,000 acres on a secluded white-sand beach, the Hyatt Dorado is a former plantation. Most rooms have four-poster beds, patios or balconies, and marble baths. For the requisite romantic dinner, ask for a table on the balcony at Su Casa ($$$–$$$$), òne of the resort's five restaurants. Its creative Puerto Rican cuisine includes such dishes as pork chops with *achiote adobe* (a tamarind, pepper, and paprika sauce). Free trolleys take you to the Dorado's sister property, the Regency Cerromar Beach, where you have access to all the facilities. Note that MAP is compulsory from December 15 through the end of February. ✉ *Rte. 693, Km 10.8, 00646,* ☎ *787/796–1234 or 800/233–1234,* ℻ *787/796–2022,* ⎍⎐⎐ *www.doradobeach.hyatt.com. 298 rooms. 5 restaurants, 2 pools, spa, 2 18-hole golf courses, 7 tennis courts, jogging, beach, bicycles, children's program. AE, D, DC, MC, V. EP, MAP.*

$$$$ ✕⊡ **Hyatt Regency Cerromar Beach Resort & Casino.** Of the twin Hyatt resorts, this hotel is more lively, both night and day. The complex is very sports- and family-oriented, and its famous river pool is one of the longest in the world, flowing some 1,776 ft under bridges and over waterfalls and waterslides. Most rooms have balconies with ocean views. The casino and Club Bacchus disco are centers of nightlife. At the Steak Co. ($$$–$$$$), try the pan-seared swordfish; the Zen Garden serves Japanese and Chinese cuisine and has a sushi bar. A trolley takes you next door to the Dorado Beach Resort. ✉ *Rte. 693, Km 11.8, 00646,* ☎ *787/796–1234 or 800/233–1234,* ℻ *787/796–4647,* ⎍⎐⎐ *www.cerromarbeach.hyatt.com. 506 rooms. 4 restaurants, 4 bars, 3 pools, spa, 2 18-hole golf courses, 10 tennis courts, jogging, beach, bicycles, casino, children's program. AE, D, DC, MC, V. EP.*

Nightlife

Nights are normally quiet in Dorado, but if you're looking for some action, the **Hyatt Regency Cerromar Beach Resort & Casino** (✉ Rte. 693, Km 11.8, ☎ 787/796–1234) is the place to go. The casino is busy at night and sometimes has live music. The mythology-theme Club Bacchus disco is open Thursday through Sunday starting at 8 PM, and the Flamingo Bar, overlooking the ocean and the resort's distinctive river pool, has live music in the evenings Wednesday through Sunday.

Outdoor Activities and Sports

FISHING

Dorado Marine Center (✉ 271 Calle Méndez Vigo, ☎ 787/796–4645) has equipment and packages for deep-sea and light-tackle fishing.

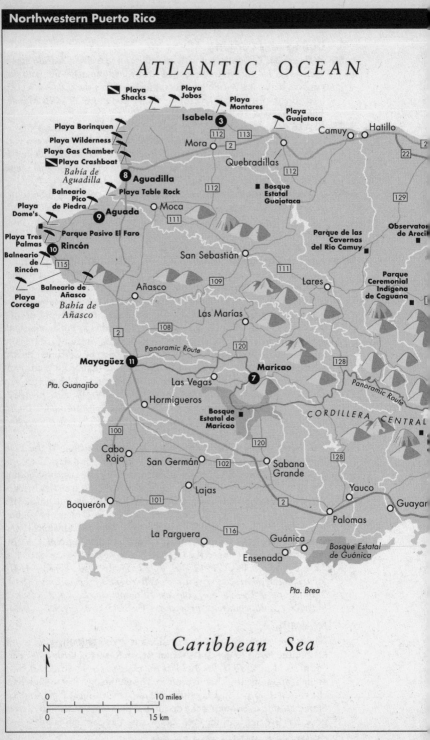

ATLANTIC OCEAN

Playa Shacks
Playa Jobos
Playa Montares
Isabela 3
Playa Guajataca
Camuy
Hatillo
Playa Borinquen
Playa Wilderness
Playa Gas Chamber
Playa Crashboat
Bahía de Aguadilla
Mora
112
113
2
Quebradillas
112
Bosque Estatal Guajataca
129
8 Aguadilla
Playa Table Rock
112
Balneario Pico de Piedra
Moca
111
Parque de las Cavernas del Río Camuy
Observator de Areci
Playa Dome's
9 Aguada
Parque Pasivo El Faro
San Sebastián
Parque Ceremonial Indígena de Caguana
Playa Tres Palmas
10 Rincón
Balneario de Rincón
115
Añasco
109
Lares
111
Playa Corcega
Balneario de Añasco
Bahía de Añasco
Las Marías
2
108
120
Panoramic Route
128
Mayagüez 11
Las Vegas
Maricao 7
Panoramic Route
Pta. Guanajibo
Hormigueros
Bosque Estatal de Maricao
CORDILLERA CENTRAL
100
120
Cabo Rojo
San Germán
102
Sabana Grande
128
Boquerón
Lajas
2
Yauco
Guayar
101
La Parguera
116
Guánica
Palomas
Bosque Estatal de Guánica
Ensenada

Pta. Brea

Caribbean Sea

N

0   10 miles
0   15 km

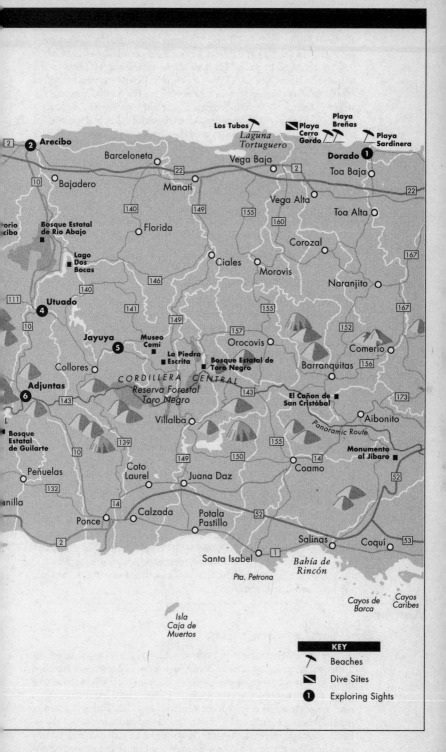

GOLF

The four golf courses at Dorado's twin **Hyatt Resorts** (⊠ Rte. 693, Km 10.8 and Km 11.8, ☎ 787/796–1234) were all designed by Robert Trent Jones, Sr. The 4th hole at the Dorado Beach Resort's 18-hole **East Course** has been ranked by Jack Nicklaus as one of the top 10 holes in the world. The Dorado Beach's **West Course** is buffeted by constant breezes off the Atlantic, making it tough to negotiate. The **South Course** at the Regency Cerromar has challenging winds and lagoons. The Regency's **North Course** has a links-style design; the beautiful 7th hole is surrounded by flowering plants and has a view of the ocean and the resort. All Hyatt courses are open to the public. Prices vary from $95 to $145 for guests and nonguests alike; the North and South Courses are less expensive.

The 7,100-yard **Dorado Del Mar** golf course (⊠ Rte. 693, west of Dorado city center, ☎ 787/796–3065) is a Chi Chi Rodríguez signature course with narrow fairways that can be a challenge to hit when the wind picks up. Green fees are $90 in the morning and $40 after 1 PM.

HORSEBACK RIDING

Tropical Paradise Horse Back Riding (⊠ off Rte. 690, west of Hyatt Regency Cerromar, ☎ 787/720–5454) arranges rides along Cibuko Beach on beautiful Paso Fino horses.

SNORKELING AND SCUBA DIVING

The north coast has several good areas for snorkeling and diving, including an underwater "aquarium" full of tropical fish and coral, a few yards from the shore of Cerro Gordo Beach. For trips, call **Dorado Marine Center** (⊠ 271 Calle Méndez Vigo, ☎ 787/796–4645).

WINDSURFING

Lisa Penfield, a former windsurfing competitor, gives beginner lessons at the **Watersports Center at the Dorado Beach Resort & Country Club** (⊠ Rte. 693, Km 10.8, ☎ 787/796–2188).

Shopping

For arts and crafts, try **Jorge Cancio Arte y Artesanias** (⊠ Rte. 693, Km 10.8, ☎ 787/796–4025) at the Hyatt Regency Cerromar Beach, where you'll find ceramics, jewelry, spices, jams, and the rare *mundillo* lace (also called bobbin lace), once commonly made by the women of the northwest coast.

About 20 minutes from Dorado via Highway 22 at Exit 55 is Puerto Rico's first factory outlet mall. **Prime Outlets Puerto Rico** (⊠ Hwy. 2, Km 54.8, Barceloneta, ☎ 787/846–9011) is a pastel village of more than 40 stores selling discounted merchandise from such familiar names as Liz Claiborne, Polo, Calvin Klein, Brooks Brothers, the Gap, Reebok, and Tommy Hilfiger.

Arecibo

❷ *60 km (38 mi) west of Dorado.*

As you approach Arecibo on Highway 22, you see its white buildings glistening in the sun against an ocean backdrop. The town was founded in 1515 and is known as the "Villa of Captain Correa" because of a battle fought here by Captain Antonio Correa and a handful of Spanish soldiers to repel a British sea invasion in 1702. Today it's a busy manufacturing center, and serves as a link for visits to two of the island's most fascinating sights—the Parque de las Cavernas del Río Camuy and the Observatorio de Arecibo, both south of the city—and for heading deeper into the central mountain region. For one of the best ocean drives on the island, get off the main road at Barceloneta and take Route 681 into Arecibo's waterfront district.

★ The 268-acre **Parque de las Cavernas del Río Camuy** contains one of the world's largest cave networks and the third-longest underground river in the world. A tram takes you down a mountain covered with bamboo and banana trees to the entrance of Cueva Clara de Empalme. Hour-long guided tours in English and Spanish lead you on foot through the 180-ft-high cave, which has large stalactites and stalagmites and blind fish found only in the region's caves. The visit ends with a tram ride to Tres Pueblos sinkhole, where you can see the river passing from one cave to another, 400 ft below. Tours are first-come, first-served; plan to arrive early on holidays and weekends, when local families join the tourists. There's a picnic area; camping is possible. ⊠ *Rte. 129, Km 18.9,* ☎ *787/898–3100.* ⊠ *$10.* ⊙ *Wed.–Sun. 8–4, last tour at 3:45.*

★ Hidden among fields and hills is **Observatorio de Arecibo,** the world's largest radar–radio telescope, operated by the National Astronomy and Ionosphere Center of Cornell University. A 20-acre dish, with a 600-ton suspended platform hovering eerily over it, lies in a 563-ft-deep sinkhole in the karst landscape. The observatory has been used to search for extraterrestrial life, and if it looks familiar it may be because scenes from the movie *Contact* were filmed here. You can walk around the platform and view the huge dish, and tour the visitor center, which has two levels of interactive exhibits on planetary systems, meteors, and weather phenomena. ⊠ *Rte. 625, Km 3.0,* ☎ *787/878–2612,* WEB *www.naic.edu.* ⊠ *$4.* ⊙ *Wed.–Fri. noon–4, weekends 9–4.*

The **Faro de Arecibo** (Arecibo Lighthouse) has a museum and scaled down replicas of Christopher Columbus's *Niña, Pinta,* and *Santa María* ships that you can explore. There are also model huts and *bateyes,* or gathering places, used by the island's original inhabitants, the Taíno Indians. Guides discuss the island's history, and, on weekends, groups in traditional masks fill the air with music; there's a bar with a sitting area from where you can watch the revelry. Follow the signs from Highway 2. ⊠ *End of Rte. 655, Km 0.5,* ☎ *787/817–1936.* ⊠ *$5.* ⊙ *Mon.–Thurs. 9–6, Fri.–Sun. 9–9.*

OFF THE BEATEN PATH
LARES – Follow Route 129 south to Route 111 and you'll arrive at the small town of Lares, known for a national uprising that took place there in 1868. A rebellious group declared a Republic of Puerto Rico, but the insurgency, now known as "El Grito de Lares," was quickly put down by the Spanish. Today, *independentistas* flock to the town's square, Plaza de la Revolución, each September 23 to honor the anniversary of the brief cry for independence. Across from the square, Heladería de Lares has been making a more modest nationalistic statement for more than 30 years by serving up ice cream in such flavors as rice, bean, and plantain.

Dining and Lodging

$-$$ ✕ **El Buen Café.** Between Arecibo and the neighboring town of Hatillo, this diner attached to a parador is a local favorite and is often packed on the weekends. Favorites dishes include *carne mechada* (stuffed pot roast), chicken and rice soup, and seafood. Breakfast is also served starting at 5 AM. ⊠ *381 Hwy. 2, Km 84, Hatillo,* ☎ *787/898–3495. AE, MC, V.*

$ ✕ **El Nuevo Olímpico.** A convenient stop when heading west from Arecibo on Highway 22, this restaurant offers fast food Puerto Rican style. You can get snacks such as *empanadillas* (deep-fried turnovers) or full meals such as *mofongo* (mashed plantains filled with meat or seafood). Breakfast consists primarily of egg dishes and sandwiches. There's a small, air-conditioned seating area, or you can join the locals outside at picnic tables on the balcony. The restaurant is open weekdays from 7 AM to midnight and stays open even later on weekends. ⊠ *Hwy. 2, Km 93.3, Camuy,* ☎ *787/898–4545. MC, V.*

$$ 🏨 **Hotel Villa Real.** The Villa Real is at the main entrance to Arecibo, making it a good spot for an overnight stay if you're heading to the cave park or observatory or are en route to the central mountains or the west coast. The rooms are clean and spacious; some have refrigerators, and others have fully equipped kitchens. A separate building has 13 larger apartments. Its restaurant serves criollo food. ⊠ *Hwy. 2, Km 67.2 (Box 344, 00613),* ☎ *787/881–4134,* 𝕱𝕬𝕏 *787/881–1992. 40 rooms, 4 villas, and 13 apartments. Restaurant, some kitchens, some refrigerators, pool. AE, MC, V.*

Outdoor Activities and Sports
KAYAKING AND RAFTING

Locura Arecibeña/Río Grande de Arecibo Kayak Rentals (☎ 787/878–1809) offers weekend kayaking, including bird-watching trips, that go to Caño Tiburones Channel between Barceloneta and Arecibo, the Río Grande south of Arecibo, and the Río Manatí near Ciales. Weekend rafting trips are also available, mainly in winter when the rapids are at their best, and mainly on Río Manatí. Reservations must be made three days in advance. (Ask for Jenaro Colón.)

Isabela

3 *36 km (23 mi) west of Arecibo.*

Founded in 1819 and named for Spain's Queen Isabella, this small, whitewashed town on the northwesternmost part of the island skirts tall cliffs that overlook the rocky shoreline. Locals have long known of the area's natural beauty, and lately more and more off-shore tourists have begun coming to this niche, which offers secluded hotels, fantastic beaches, and, just inland, hiking through one of the island's forest reserves.

Explore karst topography and subtropical vegetation at the 2,357-acre **Bosque Estatal Guajataca** (Guajataca State Forest) between the towns of Quebradillas and Isabela. There are more than 46 walking trails on which to see 186 species of trees, including the royal palm and ironwood, and 45 species of birds—watch for red-tailed hawks and Puerto Rican woodpeckers. Bring a flashlight and descend into the Cueva del Viento to find stalagmites, stalactites, and other strange formations. At the Route 446 entrance to the forest there's an information office where you can pick up a hiking map. A little farther down the road is a recreational area with picnic tables and an observation tower. ⊠ *Rte. 446, Galateo Alto Sector,* ☎ *787/872–1045.* 🎫 *Free.* ☉ *Information office open weekdays 8–5.*

Beaches
Playa Shacks, on Route 4466 at Route 466, is known for its snorkeling and surfing. Along Route 466, **Playa Jobos** is famous for surfing but can have dangerous breaks. Not far from Playa Jobos on Route 466, **Playa Montones** is a beautiful beach for swimming and frolicking in the sand and has a natural protected pool where children can splash. Toward Quebradillas and off Route 113, **Playa Guajataca** stretches by what is called El Tunel, part of an old tunnel used by a passenger and cargo train that ran from San Juan to Ponce from the early to mid-1900s. Today, kiosks selling local snacks and souvenirs surround the area with live music playing on weekends. Just before El Tunel, off Highway 2, is **El Merendero de Guajataca,** a picnic area with cliffside trails for a spectacular view of the coastline.

THE ABOMINABLE CHUPACABRA

THE HIMALAYAS have their Yeti, Britain has its crop circles, New Jersey has its legendary Jersey Devil . . . and Puerto Rico has its Chupacabra. This "goat sucker" (as its name translates) has been credited with strange attacks on goats, sheep, rabbits, horses, and chickens since the mid-'70s. The attacks happen mostly at night, leaving the animals devoid of blood, with oddly vampirelike punctures in their necks.

Though the phenomenon began in the 1970s, there seemed little activity until a surge of attacks was reported in Puerto Rico in the 1990s. In the mid-'90s a mayor in the town of Canóvanas received international attention and support from local police for his weekly search parties equipped with a caged goat as bait. The police stopped short of fulfilling the mayor's request for a special unit devoted to the creature's capture.

Sightings offer widely differing versions of the Chupacabra; it has gray, scraggly hair and resembles a kangaroo or wolf, or walks upright on three-toed feet. Some swear it hops from tree branch to tree branch, and even flies, leaving behind, in the tradition of old Lucifer, the acrid stench of sulphur. It peers through large, oval, sometimes red eyes, and "smells like a wet dog" as its reptilian tongue flicks the night air. It has, according to some, attacked humans, ripped through screen windows, and jumped family dogs at picnics.

Anthropologists note that legends of blood-sucking creatures permeate history, from the werewolves of France to the vampires of eastern Europe. Even the ancient Mayans included a vampire deity in their pantheon. And legendary blood-lusters are legion throughout the history of South America and the Caribbean. According to a 1995 article in the *San Juan Star,* island lore abounds with monsters predating the Chupacabra. The *comecogollo* was a version of bigfoot— but smaller and a vegetarian. It was particularly sweet on *cogollo,* a baby plantain that springs up near its parent plant. In the early 1970s, the Moca vampire also attacked small animals, but opinion differed on whether it was alien, animal, or really a vampire. The *garadiablo,* a swamp creature that emerged from the ooze at night to wreak havoc on the populace also struck fear in the early '70s. This "sea demon" was described as having the face of a bat, the skin of a shark, and a humanlike body.

Though the Chupacabra is mainly attributed to Puerto Rico, it has also been active in other spots with large Hispanic communities—Mexico, southern Texas, and Miami—and its scope is pretty wide. The list of reported sightings on elchupacabra.com includes such unlikely locales as Maine and Missouri. And the Chupa's coverage on the Web isn't limited to sci-fi fan sites: Princeton University maintains a Web site meant to be a clearinghouse for Chupa information, and the beast's story appears on the Learning Channel's site at tlc.com.

What to make of Chupa? Above the clamor of the fringe elements that believe Chupacabra to be Beelzebub incarnate or part of an advanced team of alien invaders, and among those who simply believe in the possibility of weird and yet-undiscovered terrestrial life forms, one hears the more skeptical voice of reason. Zoologists have suggested that the alleged condition of some Chupacabra victims may actually be the result of exaggerated retelling of the work of less mysterious animals, such as a tropical species of bat known to feed on the blood of small mammals. Even some bird species are known to eat warm-blooded animals. Skeletal remains of an alleged Chupacabra found in Chile were determined to be those of a wild dog. This, however, doesn't explain the sightings of the hairy, ravenous beast. Then again, there's no accounting for the Loch Ness Monster either.

— Karl Luntta

Dining and Lodging

$–$$ ✕ **Happy Belly's on the Beach.** If you're in the mood for a hamburger or fajita, this laid-back restaurant with outdoor seating on the beach is a good stop after a day of fun in the sun. ⊠ *Playa Jobos, Rte. 4466, Km 7.5,* ☎ *787/872–6566. AE, MC, V.*

$$$–$$$$ ✕⊡ **Villa Montaña.** This secluded cluster of buildings near the border of Isabela and Aguadilla feels like a community unto itself. The airy one-, two-, and three-bedroom suites have mahogany furniture and canopied beds; some have kitchenettes and laundry facilities. The grounds abut Playa Shacks, and the open-air Eclipse restaurant and bar ($$–$$$) serves Caribbean-Asian fusion cuisine highlighting local seafood. ⊠ *Rte. 446, Km 1.2 (Box 530, 00662),* ☎ *787/872–9554 or 888/780–9195,* FAX *787/872–9553,* WEB *www.villamontana.com. 26 rooms. Restaurant, some kitchenettes, 2 pools, 2 tennis courts, gym. AE, D, MC, V. EP.*

$$ ✕⊡ **Villas del Mar Hau.** The hub of the Villas del Mar Hau is a fanci-
★ ful row of pastel one-, two-, and three-bedroom cottages overlooking Playa Montones. They aren't luxurious, but if you're looking for comfort and seclusion in an unpretentious atmosphere, you'll have a hard time doing better. There are also 16 suites, some with kitchens. The popular restaurant, Olas y Arena ($–$$), is known for fish and shellfish; the paella is especially good. ⊠ *Rte. 4466, Km 8.3 (Box 510, 00662),* ☎ *787/872–2045 or 787/872–2627,* FAX *787/872–0273,* WEB *www.villahau. com. 40 rooms. Restaurant, fans, some kitchens, pool, tennis court, basketball, horseback riding, laundry facilities; no air-conditioning in some rooms, no TV in some rooms. AE, MC, V. Restaurant closed Mon. EP.*

$$ ⊡ **Parador El Guajataca.** Perched on a small bluff overlooking the Atlantic, this small inn between Quebradillas and Isabela, makes the most of its fabulous location. Its rooms are modest, but have extraordinary ocean views. The palm-lined swimming pool overlooks the ocean as well and paths lead to Guajataca Beach. ⊠ *Hwy. 2, Km 103.8, Quebradillas (Box 1558, 00678),* ☎ *787/895–3070,* FAX *787/895–2204,* WEB *www.elguajataca.com. 38 rooms. Restaurant, pool, 2 tennis courts, basketball, beach, playground. AE, MC, V. EP.*

Outdoor Activities and Sports

HORSEBACK RIDING

Tropical Trail Rides (⊠ Rte. 4466, Km 1.9, ☎ 787/872–9256) has two-hour morning and afternoon rides along the beach and through a forest of almond trees. Groups leave from Playa Shacks. The **Villas del Mar Hau** (⊠ Rte. 466, Km 8.3, ☎ 787/872–2045) will make horseback riding arrangements for guests only.

SNORKELING AND SCUBA DIVING

Beginning and advanced divers can explore the underground caves off of Playa Shacks through **La Cueva Submarina Dive Shop** (⊠ Rte. 466, Km 6.3, ☎ 787/872–1390, WEB www.lacuevasubmarina.com). It also offers certification courses and snorkeling trips.

OFF THE
BEATEN PATH
PALACETE LOS MOREAU – In the fields south of Isabela toward the town of Moca, a French family settled on a coffee and sugar plantation in the 1800s. The grand two-story house, trimmed with gables, columns, and stained-glass windows, was immortalized in the novel *La Llamarada,* written in 1935 by Puerto Rican novelist Enrique A. Laguerre. In Laguerre's novel about conditions in the sugarcane industry, the house belonged to his fictional family, the Moreaus. While it doesn't have many furnishings, you can walk through the house and also visit Laguerre's personal library in the mansion's basement. The home is open free of charge weekdays from 8 to 11 and from 1 to 3:30. ⊠ *Hwy. 2 to Rte. 464, then turn left at Ruben's Supermarket,* ☎ *787/830–2540.*

WEST-CENTRAL INLANDS

Spanning unruly karst terrain and parts of the Puerto Rico's rugged central mountain range, the west-central inlands is a beautiful mixture of limestone cliffs, man-made lakes, and sprawling forest reserves. It's here, in the Bosque Estatal de Toro Negro, that the island's highest peak, Cerro de Punta, rises 4,398 ft above sea level.

Coffee was once a dominant crop along hillsides between Utuado and Maricao, and it can still be seen growing in small plots today. A few of the old plantation homes have been turned into quaint country inns, all of them stocked with plenty of blankets for cool evenings when temperatures—especially in higher elevations—can drop into the 40s.

Sans large resorts, glitzy casinos, and beaches, this area of Puerto Rico is for those who like to get off the well-traveled roads and spend time exploring small towns, rural areas, and unspoiled nature. Driving here takes patience; some of the roads aren't clearly marked, and others twist and turn for what seems an eternity. But the area's natural beauty has attracted people for centuries, including pre-Columbian Indians, who have left behind remnants of earlier civilizations.

Utuado

4 *32 km (20 mi) south of Arecibo; 104 km (65 mi) from San Juan.*

Utuado was named after a local Indian chief, Otoao. Surrounded by mountains and dotted with blue lakes, the town of Utuado sits in the middle of lush natural beauty. Just driving on Route 10 between Arecibo and Utuado is an experience—imposing brown limestone cliffs flank the road, and clouds often hover around the tops of the surrounding hills. The town's narrow and sometimes busy streets lead to a double-steepled church on the main plaza. The best sights, however, are outside town along winding side roads.

In the middle of karst country, the **Bosque Estatal de Río Abajo** (Río Abajo State Forest) spans some 5,000 acres and includes huge bamboo stands and native silk-cotton trees. It also has several plantations of Asian teaks, Dominican and Honduran mahogany, and Australian pines, which are part of a government tree management program that supplies wood for the local economy (primarily for artisans and fence building). Walking trails wind through the forest, which is one of the habitats of the rare Puerto Rican parrot. An information office is near the entrance, and a recreation area with picnic tables is farther down the road. ⊠ *Rte. 621, Km 4.4,* ☎ *787/817–0984.* ⊠ *Free.* ☉ *Daily.*

East of Bosque Estatal de Río Abajo is **Lago Dos Bocas,** one of several man-made lakes near Utuado. Government-operated boats take you around the U-shape lake from a dock, called El Embarcadero, near the intersection of Routes 123 and 146. Although the boats are used primarily as a means of public transit for residents, the 45-minute ride around the lake is pleasant and scenic, and gets you to four shoreline restaurants known for criollo cuisine and seafood. The boats are free and leave daily at 7 AM, 8:30 AM, and every hour on the hour between 10 and 5. Note: trips after 3 are for residents and returning passengers only. The lake is stocked with sunfish, bass, and catfish and you can fish from the shore. ⊠ *Off Rte. 10, accessed via Rtes. 621, 123, 146, and 612,* ☎ *787/879–1838, El Embarcadero.* ⊠ *Free.* ☉ *Daily.*

The 13 acres of **Parque Ceremonial Indígena de Caguana** were used more than 800 years ago by the Taíno tribes for worship and recreation, including a game—thought to have religious significance—that

MODERN DAY TAÍNOS?

PUERTO RICO'S FIRST INHABITANTS—today known as Arcaicos (Archaics)—appear to have traveled on rafts from Florida around AD 500. They were hunter-gatherers, who lived near the shore and subsisted on fish and fruit. Evidence suggests that by AD 1000 the Arawak Indians, who came from South America by canoe, were replacing the Arcaicos. The agrarian Taíno (a subgroup of the Arawak) established thatched villages on the island, which they called Boriquén.

In his journal Columbus describes the Taíno as "beautiful and tall, with a gentle, laughing language." Although this language was unwritten, it still echoes in some island place names and in everyday items, such as *casabe* (a kind of bread). Many Taíno folktales have also survived as have some art and artifacts. These peaceful rain-forest dwellers were adept at wood, shell, and stone carving, and the small figures they made of people and animals had great significance. Known as *cemí* (or *zemí*), the diminutive statues were believed to have the power to protect villages and families. And maybe they've done just that.

Studies by the University of Puerto Rico suggest that there are still islanders with Taíno genes. Researchers visited isolated communities in the mountains of Maricao and found that around 70% of subjects with such characteristics as dark skin and straight black hair had traces of Amerindian DNA. Another study in Mayagüez found that 50% of the subjects had such traces. Although it has long been held that the Taíno were virtually wiped out within two decades of their 1493 encounter with Columbus, these findings may mean that the Taínos survived much longer or were more numerous than previously thought.

— Karen English and John Marino

resembled modern-day soccer. Today you can see 10 *bateyes* (courts) of various sizes, large stone monoliths (some with petroglyphs), and recreations of Taíno gardens. ☒ *Rte. 111, Km 12.3,* ☎ *787/894–7325.* ☞ *$2.* ☼ *Daily 8:30–4.*

Dining and Lodging

$–$$ ✕ **El Fogón de Abuela.** This rustic restaurant on the edge of Dos Bocas Lake would make any Puerto Rican grandmother envious. The menu features stews, red snapper (whole or filleted), and fricassees, including pork chop, goat, and rabbit. You arrive either by taking the public boat from El Embarcadero on Route 612, by calling the restaurant from the dock and requesting a boat be sent to pick you up (free of charge), or by driving to the south side of the lake. From Utuado, take Route 111 to Route 140 to Route 612 and follow that to its end. ☒ *Lago Dos Bocas,* ☎ *787/894–0470. MC, V. Closed Mon.–Thurs.*

$$ ✕▥ **Hotel La Casa Grande.** It's not hard to imagine Tarzan swinging in
★ for dinner at this quaint inn. The main house contains a restaurant, bar, and reception area. The other five wooden buildings hold 20 guest rooms. There are no TVs, phones, or radios in the rooms, but a chorus of tiny tree frogs provides symphonies at night. Dining is on an outdoor patio at Jungle Jane's restaurant ($–$$); the menu features lemon-garlic chicken breast, and Puerto Rican specialties such as *asopao* (stew) with shrimp. ☒ *Rte. 612, Km 0.3 (Box 1499, 00641),* ☎ *787/894–3939 or*

800/343–2272, FAX *787/894–3900,* WEB *www.hotelcasagrande.com. 20 rooms. Restaurant, fans, pool; no air-conditioning. AE, MC, V. EP.*

Outdoor Activities and Sports

HIKING

Expediciones Tanamá (⊠ Rte 111, Km 14.5, Barrio Angeles, ☎ 787/894–7685, WEB http://home.coqui.net/albite/albite/index.html) leads half-day ($59) or full-day ($95) excursions into the Río Tanamá underground cave system. Guides speak limited English, but are friendly and eager. Lunch is included. There's a free camping site adjacent to the office, which provides electricity and bathrooms.

HORSEBACK RIDING

Rancho de Caballos de Utuado (⊠ Rte. 612, across from Hotel La Casa Grande, ☎ 787/894–0240) offers three- to four-hour horse rides along a river, lake, and through mountain forests.

KAYAKING

Jenaro Colón at **Locura Arecibeña/Río Grande de Arecibo Kayak Rentals** (☎ 787/878–1809) can arrange for rentals and weekend guided tours. Kayaks are available for rent at **Rancho Marina** (⊠ Rte. 612, Lago Dos Bocas, ☎ 787/894–8035).

Jayuya

⑤ *24 km (15 mi) southeast of Utuado.*

This small town of 15,000 is in the foothills of the Cordillera Central, Puerto Rico's tallest mountain chain. Cerro de Punta, the island's highest peak, looms to the south of the town center. Named after the Indian chief Hauyua, Jayuya is known for preserving its Indian heritage and draws people from all over the island for its yearly Indigenous Festival in November, which features crafts, exhibits, parades, music, and dancing. Coffee is still grown in the area—look for the locally produced Tres Picachos.

★ The main attraction of the 7,000-acre **Bosque Estatal de Toro Negro** (Toro Negro State Forest) is the 4,398-ft Cerro de Punta. It has the island's highest lake, Lago Guineo; natural ponds; waterfalls (including the 200-ft Doña Juana Falls); and gigantic bamboo, royal palms, and oak trees. The Doña Juana Recreational Area off Route 143 has picnic tables and a campground. Take one of the many hiking trails branching out from the recreational area to watch for exotic birds such as the Guadalupe woodpecker, or drive to a trail on the western edge of the forest that leads to the top of Cerro de Punta (a 30- to 45-minute hike). The reserve also contains a huge but often out-of-service swimming pool built into the side of a mountain. If you're going to camp, be sure to bring blankets, as it can get cold here at night. Camping permits must be obtained at the Department of **Natural and Environmental Resources** (☎ 787/724–3724) on Avenida Fernández Juncos in San Juan, next to the Club Náutico. Permits must be requested at least 15 days in advance. ⊠ *Rte. 143, Km 31.8,* ☎ *787/867–3040.* 🎟 *Free.* ☉ *Daily.*

The tiny **Museo Cemí** (Cemí Museum) is named for its shape, which is like that of a *cemí,* a Taíno artifact believed to have religious significance. On display is a collection of Taíno pottery and religious and ceremonial objects found on the island. ⊠ *Rte. 144, Km 9.3,* ☎ *787/828–1241.* 🎟 *Free.* ☉ *Weekdays 8–4:30, weekends 10–3:30.*

⑭ **La Piedra Escrita** (Written Rock) is a huge boulder with several highly visible Taíno petroglyphs, located in a stream among several other large rocks. It's somewhat hard to find—watch for a sign along the road, then pull over and look for an old stairway that takes you down to

COFFEE—PUERTO RICO'S BLACK GOLD

WHEN THE LATE ISLAND POET Tomás Blanco wrote that coffee should be "black as the devil, hot as hell, and sweet as sin," he may well have had Puerto Rican brews in mind. Cultivated at high altitudes in a swirl of cool, moist air and mineral-rich soil, the island's beans are like gold—the black and aromatic sort.

Introduced in the mid-18th century with shrubs imported from nearby Martinique (after being brought by French farmers to that island from France), coffee started its life in Puerto Rico as a minor cash crop, cultivated mainly for consumption. But by the end of the 1700s, Puerto Rico was producing more than a million pounds of coffee a year, and by the late 19th century, the island was the world's seventh largest producer of coffee.

Puerto Rican coffee had benefited from the labors and experimentation of immigrants experienced in coffee production, and it was highly respected by connoisseurs in Europe and the Americas. Its status grew, yet Puerto Rican coffee suffered after Spain ceded the island to the United States in 1898, and after several major hurricanes all but wiped out the crop. Today, with chichi coffee bars opening daily throughout the United States and in major urban centers worldwide, Puerto Rican beans have once again taken their place next to the Jamaica Blue Mountain and Hawaiian Kona varieties as one of the world's premium coffees.

The secret is in the coffee bean itself (called "cherry"). The island's dominant bean is the *arabica*; it has a more delicate and lower-yielding cherry and produces half the caffeine of the prolific *robusta* bean found on the mega-plantations of Central and South America. The arabica cherry, in the proper conditions, is known as the richest and most flavorful among the coffee varieties. Cloud cover, tree shade, soil composition, and the altitude at which the coffee bushes are grown—higher than 3,000 ft above sea level—combine to produce a slow-ripening bean that stays on the bush at least two months longer than at lower elevations. This lengthy ripening process acts as a sort of "pre-brew," imbuing the bean with a rich flavor and a slightly sweet aftertaste.

As the beans ripen, they turn from green to yellow to red and the trees produce a white flower with a pleasant aroma similar to jasmine. Coffee picking season starts in August and continues through February. The process is slow and delicate because workers pick through bushes manually to collect only the cherries that are fully ripe. Small, family-run pulperies are the norm in Puerto Rico. In them the ripened beans are pulped (shelled) to remove the outer covering, then fermented to remove a thin layer that covers the bean, called the "mucilago." The beans are then dried, roasted, and packed. The main coffee-growing areas of the island lie in the wet, mountainous regions of Yauco, Lares, and Las Marís, where the limited suitable terrain makes large-scale production impossible, and thus makes the coffee all the more precious a commodity.

Throughout Puerto Rico look for local brands: Yauco Selecto, Rioja, Yaucono, Cafe Rico, Crema, Adjuntas, Coqui, and Alto Grande Super Premium. Alto Grande has gained the most fame off the island and is guaranteed to have been grown at high altitudes. It's best consumed straight up as espresso, though many prefer to cut it with hot milk, the traditional *café con leche*, a local equivalent of café au lait. It also makes a great gift to carry home.

— Karl Luntta

the stream. This is also a nice, secluded spot for a picnic lunch. ⊠ *Off Rte. 144, near Museo Cemí.* ☜ *Free.*

Dining and Lodging

$$ ✕🏠 **Parador Hacienda Gripiñas.** Built on the grounds of a coffee plan-
★ tation, this elegant inn is surrounded by gardens and mountain peaks.
Rooms have balconies overlooking lush scenery. The restaurant ($–$$)
serves steaks, lobster, shrimp, and criollo fare such as chicken with rice
and beans. For dessert, try the *tembleque*—a custard made from coconut milk and sugar. Across from the house are a bar and a swimming pool filled with cool mountain water. One hiking trail near the
property leads to Cerro de Punta, about a 2½-hour climb. ⊠ *Rte. 527,
Km 2.7 (Box 387, 00664),* ☎ *787/828–1717,* 𝔽𝔸𝕏 *787/828–1718,* 𝕎𝔼𝔹
*www.haciendagripinas.com. 19 rooms. Restaurant, pool, hiking. AE,
MC, V. MAP.*

Adjuntas

❻ *27 km (17 mi) southwest of Jayuya.*

The coffee-growing town of Adjuntas sits north of Puerto Rico's Ruta
Panorámica. While known for its coffee, it's also the world's leading
producer of citron, a fruit whose rind is processed here and then
shipped for use in sweets, especially fruitcakes. Few tourists do more
than drive through the town itself, but it has a quaint central plaza and
a sporadic trolley used mostly by locals and school children.

Hiking trails, surrounded by wild-growing impatiens, lead up to the
3,900-ft Pico Guilarte and into other areas of **Bosque Estatal de Guilarte**
(Guilarte State Forest). Bird watchers have 26 different species to look
for, including the carpenter bird. Or if your interest is botany, you can
find a variety of trees, including candlewood, trumpet, Honduran mahogany, and Honduran pine. There's a pleasant picnic area near a eu-
calyptus grove. ⊠ *Rte. 518 at Rte. 131,* ☎ *787/829–7804.* ☜ *Free.*
☉ *Daily.*

Dining and Lodging

$$–$$$ ✕🏠 **Villas de Sotomayor.** Covering 14⅓ acres, this complex of cabins
has a summer-camp atmosphere. The focus is on horseback riding, and
there are stables on the premises. You can also take horse-and-carriage
rides around the grounds. Rooms are in separate, modern cabins and
range from one bedroom with refrigerators only to two bedrooms with
kitchenettes. The on-site restaurant ($$–$$$) is open daily and serves
international and criollo cuisine—it is known for its *mofongo relleno*
(stuffed mashed plantains). ⊠ *Rte. 123, Km 36.8 (Box 28, 00601),* ☎
787/829–1717, 𝔽𝔸𝕏 *787/829–1774,* 𝕎𝔼𝔹 *www.villassotomayor.com. 34
rooms. Restaurant, some kitchenettes, refrigerators, 2 pools, 2 tennis
courts, badminton, basketball, horseback riding. AE, D, MC, V. EP.*

Maricao

❼ *59 km (37 mi) west of Adjuntas; 43 km (27 mi) east of Mayagüez.*

Puerto Rico's smallest municipality (pop. 6,200), Maricao is part of
the island's coffee country and hosts a well-known Coffee Harvest Festival each February. Although not far from Mayagüez—the third-
largest urban area on the island—Maricao has an isolated feeling;
driving in the area is more akin to being deep in the central mountain
region.

Drier than other forest reserves found near the central mountains,
★ **Bosque Estatal de Maricao** (Maricao State Forest) is known as a bird-
watcher's paradise. The 60 species found here—29 of which are en-

dangered—include the Puerto Rican vireos and the elfin woods warbler. Part of the reserve is the Maricao Fish Hatchery on Route 410 at Km 1.7, which contains a collection of ponds and tanks where fish are raised to stock island lakes. You'll find an information center and a stone observation tower about half a mile beyond the forest entrance. The Centro Vacacional Monte de Estado has rustic cabins for rent. ⊠ *Rte. 120 at Rte. 366, ☎ 787/319–4128 or 787/838–3710 for hatchery tours.* 🎫 *Free.* ☉ *Park: Daily. Hatchery: Wed.–Sun. 8:30–11:30 and 1–3:30.*

Dining and Lodging

$$ ✕🖼 **Parador La Hacienda Juanita.** Part of a coffee plantation in the
★   1800s, this is surrounded by forest and exudes the slower pace of days gone by. Rooms are in four separate buildings, and some have four-poster beds and antiques from the coffee industry's heyday. La Casona de Juanita restaurant ($$) serves up criollo cuisine, including *sancocho,* a hearty soup made with meat and root vegetables. Meals are served on a sweeping balcony where you can reach up and pull fruit off the trees. ⊠ *Rte. 105, Km 23.5 (Box 777, 00606), ☎ 787/838–2550,* 𝔽𝔸𝕏 *787/838–2551,* 𝕎𝔼𝔹 *www.haciendajuanita.com. 21 rooms. Restaurant, fans, pool, tennis court, hiking; no air-conditioning. AE, MC, V. MAP.*

THE WEST COAST

Adventurers since the time of Christopher Columbus have been drawn to the jagged coastline of northwestern Puerto Rico. Columbus made his first stop here on his second voyage to the Americas in 1493. His exact landing point is the subject of ongoing dispute—both Aguadilla on the northernmost tip of the coast and Aguada just to Aguadilla's south claim the historic landing, and both have monuments honoring the explorer.

Five centuries later, people are still discovering the area, lured primarily by the numerous beaches. The town of Rincón, which gained notoriety by hosting the World Surfing Championship in 1968, draws surfers from around the globe, especially in winter when the waves are at their best. Numerous calmer beaches nearby fit the bill if you just want to catch some rays, have a swim, and relax. From December through February, if you keep your eyes on the ocean you may spot humpback whales.

About halfway down the coast is Mayagüez, the island's third-largest urban area, where you'll find an interesting mix of Spanish colonial and eclectic 20th-century architecture. The city makes for an enjoyable day trip, but come nightfall you'll want to make your way back to the shore, where you can view some of the island's most spectacular sunsets.

Aguadilla

❽   *20 km (13 mi) southwest of Isabela; 130 km (81 mi) west of San Juan.*

Weathered but lovely, the faded facades of many of Aguadilla's buildings seem indicative of its long and somewhat turbulent past. Officially incorporated as a town in 1775, Aguadilla subsequently suffered a series of catastrophes, including a devastating earthquake in 1918 and strong hurricanes in 1928 and 1932. Determined to survive, the town rebuilt after each disaster, and by World War II it became known for the huge U.S. Air Force base north of it, originally called Borinquen Field and renamed Ramey Air Force Base. The base was an important link in the U.S. defense system throughout World War II and the Cold

War. Ramey ceased to be an active base in 1973, and today comprises an airport, a golf course, and some small businesses, although many structures stand empty.

Downtown Aguadilla has many small wooden homes, and resembles a fishing village. The natural spring where Columbus is said to have gotten water during his stop is now part of the somewhat rundown El Parterre Parque on Avenida Muñoz Rivera. Residents mingle in Parque Colón (Columbus Park) at the end of Calle Comercio, but the biggest attractions are swimming, surfing, snorkeling, and diving off Aguadilla's beaches. Modest hotels near town attract budget-conscious travelers; those looking for more luxurious accommodations usually stay in the nearby towns of Isabela or Rincón.

Along Route 107—an unmarked road crossing through a golf course—you'll find the ruins of **La Ponderosa,** an old Spanish lighthouse, as well as its replacement Punta Borinquen at Puerto Rico's northwest point. The original was built in 1889, and later destroyed by an earthquake in 1918. The U.S. Coast guard rebuilt the structure in 1920.

Las Cascadas Aquatic Park (⊠ Hwy. 2, Km 126.5, ☎ 787/819–1030; ⊠ $12.95) has a large wave pool, giant slides, and the "Crazy River," a long, free-flowing river pool. The park is closed October–November.

Beaches

★ Aguadilla's **Playa Crashboat,** off Route 458, is famous throughout the island for the colorful fishing boats docked on its shores, its long, beautiful stretch of sand, and its clear water, which often looks like glass. Named after rescue boats that used to be docked here when Ramey Air Force Base was in operation, the beach is good for swimming and snorkeling when waters are calm, and has picnic huts, showers, and rest rooms. It often hosts music festivals, especially in summer. One Route 107, **Playa Borinquen** is calmer than the surfing beaches to the south. **Playa Wilderness and Playa Gas Chambers,** north of Playa Crashboat via Route 107, are often frequented by surfers. (Wilderness is recommended only for experienced surfers, as it can have dangerous breaks.)

Dining and Lodging

$$ ✕🏨 **Hotel Cielomar.** Almost every room at this beachfront property has an ocean view and most rooms have balconies as well. The specialty of the open-air restaurant El Bohío ($–$$) is seafood. There's often live music on the weekends. ⊠ 84 Av. Montemar, 00605, ☎ 787/882–5959 or 787/882–5961, FAX 787/882–5577, WEB www.cielomar.com. 52 rooms. Restaurant, bar, cable TV, pool, video game room, playground. AE, MC, V. EP.

$$ ✕🏨 **Parador El Faro.** This family-owned inn has modern, roomy, simply decorated rooms. The property isn't exactly beachfront, but Crashboat and other beaches are 2.4 km (1½ mi) away, as is a golf course. There are two restaurants on the premises, including the popular Three Amigos ($–$$), which features a combination of Italian, Mexican, and criollo cuisines. ⊠ Rte. 107, Km 2.1 (Box 5148, 00605), ☎ 787/882–8000 or 888/300–8002, FAX 787/882–1030, WEB www.ihppr.com. 70 rooms, 5 suites. 2 restaurants, cable TV, pool, tennis court, basketball. AE, D, DC, MC, V. EP.

Outdoor Activities and Sports

GOLF

The 18-hole **Punta Borinquen Golf Course** (⊠ Rte. 107, Km 2, ☎ 787/890–2987), on the former Ramey Air Force Base, was built in 1940 for use by the military and is said to have been played by U.S. presidents, including Dwight D. Eisenhower. Now a public course, it's known for its tough sand traps and strong cross winds. Prices are approximately $20 per person and $20 to rent a cart. It's open daily.

SCUBA DIVING AND SNORKELING

Aquatica Underwater Adventures, at the former Ramey Air Force Base (⊠ Rte. 110, Km 10, Gate 5, ☎ 787/890–6071), offers scuba diving certification courses and dives off Aguadilla and Isabela beaches. You can also arrange snorkeling trips and rent snorkeling equipment. It's open Monday–Saturday 9–5 and Sunday 9–3.

Aguada

❾ *8 km (5 mi) south of Aguadilla.*

The town of Aguada (pop. 36,000) gleams with modern concrete buildings and has the bustling feel of a large city. It shares with Aguadilla the claim that Christopher Columbus first set foot in Puerto Rico in its vicinity, and it has a statue of the explorer in its main plaza. Regardless of where Columbus actually landed, Aguada seems to be the sentimental favorite; on November 19, crowds descend on the town to celebrate Discovery Day with parades, food, and music. The rest of the year, Puerto Ricans and off-shore visitors find tranquillity on Aguada's beaches.

Beaches

Balneario Pico de Piedra, also called the Aguada Public Beach, is a nice swimming beach frequented by families. It's at the end of Route 441, and it has parking facilities, changing rooms, and rest rooms. **Playa Table Rock,** north of Balneario Pico de Piedra on Route 441, is known for its snorkeling and surfing.

Dining and Lodging

$-$$ ✕ **El Plátano Loco.** You'll never think of the plantain as only a side dish again. "The Crazy Plantain" finds new uses for the fruit, using it as "bread" to surround burgers and sandwiches, turning it into soups and french fries, adding it to mofongo, pizza, and flan. The restaurant, which consists mostly of an open-air pavillion, sits on a bluff and can be hard to find, but the locals will be glad to point you in the right direction. From Aguada's central plaza, take Route 115 to Route 441. Turn right at a bar called Parada 5 and follow the signs. ⊠ *Rte. 441, Jagüey Bajío,* ☎ *787/868–0241,* WEB *www.platanoloco.com. Closed Mon.–Wed.*

$$ ▥ **JB Hidden Village.** This whitewashed hotel in a rural area is part of the government's parador program and is known for being family-friendly. The modern rooms and suites all have balconies, some overlook the countryside, others the pool. Two larger suites have Jacuzzis. There's a restaurant on the premises, and fine beaches are close by—Aguada Public Beach is 10 minutes away, and it's a 20-minute drive to Rincón. ⊠ *Rte. 416, Km 9.5 (Box 937, 00602),* ☎ *787/868–8686,* FAX *787/868–8701. 45 rooms. Restaurant, cable TV, pool. MC, V. EP.*

Rincón

❿ *9.5 km (6 mi) southwest of Aguada.*

Jutting out into the ocean along the rugged western coast, Rincón, meaning "corner" in Spanish, may have gotten its name because of how it is nestled in a corner of the coastline. Some, however, trace the town's name to Gonzalo Rincón, a 16th-century landowner who let poor families live on his land. Whatever the history, the name suits the town, which is like a little world unto itself.

Rincón remains laid-back and unpretentious even though it jumped into the surfing spotlight after hosting the World Surfing Championship in 1968. It has also become known worldwide for the Horned Dorset Primavera, the only Relais & Chateaux property in Puerto Rico and one of only a handful in the Caribbean. The town caters to all sorts of travelers, from budget-conscious surfers to families to those looking for a romantic getaway. It has long been known for its small hotels and cottages, but recently large, concrete condominiums and larger hotels have begun to spring up, including the 102-room Rincón Del Mar, which is scheduled to open in September 2002 on Route 115 next to Corcega Beach.

The beat picks up from October through April, when the waves are the best, but tourists can be found here year-round, and many American mainlanders have settled here. If you visit between December and February, you might get a glimpse of the humpback whales that winter off the coast.

Because of its unusual setting, Rincón's layout can be a little disconcerting. The main road, Route 413, loops around the coast, and many beaches and sights are on dirt roads intersecting with it. Most hotels and restaurants hand out detailed maps of the area.

Surrounding the Punta Higuera Lighthouse, **Parque Pasivo El Faro** features small kiosks at the water's edge with telescopes you can use to look for whales. (Have patience, though, even during the "season," from December through February; it could take days to spot one.) You can also glimpse the rusting dome of the defunct Bonus Thermonuclear Energy Plant from here; it has been closed since 1974 but could be resurrected as a nuclear-energy museum. The park is a nice place to take in sunsets, and there are also benches, a shop, and a refreshment stand on the grounds. The lighthouse is closed to the public, but it's hard to walk away without taking a photo of the stately white structure. ⊠ *Calle El Farooff Rte. 413.* 🖾 *Free.* ☉ *Daily 8 AM–midnight.*

Beaches

Dome's (named for the nuclear power plant's nearby dome), **Maria's**, and **Steps** (named for a concrete set of steps sitting mysteriously at water's edge) are lined up in a row off Route 413 going north toward the lighthouse. Surfers swear by the waves at **Playa Tres Palmas,** where the snorkeling is also good. It's on Route 413. Swimmers can enjoy the tranquil waters of the **Balneario de Rincón,** on Route 115 just before it intersects with Route 413. It has parking facilities and rest rooms. The long stretch of yellow sand at **Playa Corcega,** in front of Parador Villa Antonio and Hotel Villa Cofresí, is considered one of the best swimming beaches in Rincón.

Dining and Lodging

$$ ✕ **The Landing.** This spacious restaurant has a large, beautiful wooden bar that's often filled with a mix of people, from surfers to retirees. You can dine on pasta, steaks, and burgers inside or on a back terrace overlooking the ocean. There's also a children's menu with junior burgers and chicken fingers. On weekend nights when live bands play, the place often fills with a younger crowd. ⊠ *Rte. 413, Km 4.7,* ☎ *787/823–3112. AE, MC, V.*

$–$$ ✕ **Larry B's.** Tucked next to the bar at Beside the Point Inn is a wooden patio where you can watch the surf crash against the beach while dining on generous helpings of simply prepared steaks, shrimp, pasta, salads, and fresh fish. Larry himself serves up the food, and he's happy to regale you with tales of his wave-seeking exploits. ⊠ *Rte. 413, Barrio Puntas,* ☎ *787/823–3210. MC, V. Closed Mon.–Wed.*

$–$$ ✕ **El Molino del Quijote.** Spanish and Puerto Rican cuisine are served here in a charming thatch-roof building. Additional tables in the garden overlook the water. The paella, mofongo, and sangría are superb, and so is the service. ⊠ *Rte. 429, Km 3.3,* ☎ *787/823–4010. AE, MC, V. Closed Mon.–Thurs.*

$–$$ ✕ **Sandy Beach.** On top of a hill overlooking the beach with the same name, this restaurant offers rooftop dining for the best view of the coast. Specialties include fresh fish, steaks, pasta, and salads, with signature desserts like the chocolate marquise, a rich chocolate pudding. ⊠ *Rte. 413, Km 4.3,* ☎ *787/823–1034,* WEB *www.sandybeachinn.com. No credit cards.*

$$$$ ✕🏨 **Horned Dorset Primavera.** Each room at this secluded hotel is
★   uniquely furnished with antiques, including four-poster beds. Some rooms have private plunge pools. There are no radios, TVs, or phones in the rooms, and no facilities for children. The main house has elegant West Indian plantation–style furniture and glistening chandeliers. The newer Casa Escondida is designed to resemble a turn-of-the-20th-century Puerto Rican hacienda. Dinner has tropical touches and a heavy Cordon Bleu influence. The menu changes daily but might include crab salad with cilantro and mango, and roasted duck with black cherries. Dress is formal by island standards—no shorts allowed. Breakfast and lunch are more casual. ⊠ *Rte. 429, Km 3 (Box 1132, 00677),* ☎ *787/ 823–4030, 787/823–4050, or 800/633–1857,* FAX *787/725–6068,* WEB *www.horneddorset.com. 31 rooms. Restaurant, fans, 2 pools, croquet, gym, beach, library. Restaurant reservations required. AE, MC, V. CP, EP, MAP.*

$$ ✕🏨 **Hotel Villa Cofresi.** With large balconies, an outdoor restaurant, and a beachfront bar, the Hotel Villa Cofresí gives you plenty of ways to enjoy the ocean view. The restaurant's menu ($$) includes steaks, seafood and Puerto Rican cuisine. Some rooms have kitchen facilities. There's also a souvenir shop, and the hotel can arrange a host of water sports. ⊠ *Rte. 115. Km 12.0, 00677,* ☎ *787/823–2450,* FAX *787/823– 1770,* WEB *www.villacofresi.com. 51 rooms. Restaurant, bar, some kitchenettes, pool. AE, D, MC, V. CP.*

$$ ✕🏨 **Lazy Parrot.** This fanciful hotel built on a mountainside offers rooms decorated in different tropical themes, such as whale and fish motifs. A honeymoon suite includes a waterbed and private Jacuzzi. The inn's restaurant ($$) is popular with surfers and features conch fritters, chicken wings, snapper breaded with almonds and cornflakes, coconut shrimp, and Thai chicken. ⊠ *Rte. 413, Km 4.1, 00677,* ☎ *787823– 5654 or 800/294–1752,* FAX *787/823–0224,* WEB *www.lazyparrot.com. 11 rooms. Restaurant, 2 bars, refrigerators, pool, hot tub. AE, D, MC, V. CP.*

$$–$$$ 🏨 **Lemontree Waterfront Cottages.** These large, sparkling-clean apartments sit right on the beach. Each unit is decorated with a bright tropical colors and local artwork and has a deck with a wet bar and grill. Choose from one three-bedroom unit with two baths, one two-bedroom unit, two one-bedroom units, or two newer studios with kitchenettes. Maid service can be arranged. The beach here is small, but larger ones are nearby. ⊠ *Rte. 429, Km 4.1 (Box 200, 00677),* ☎ *787/823– 6452,* FAX *787/823–5821,* WEB *www.lemontreepr.com. 6 apartments. Cable TV, kitchenettes. AE, MC, V. EP.*

Nightlife

On weekends, **Calypso** (⊠ Rte. 413 at Maria's Beach, ☎ 787/823– 4151) often has live Latin or rock 'n' roll bands. **The Landing** (⊠ Rte. 413, Km 4.7, ☎ 787/823–3112) is a popular spot for live music on weekends. For a romantic drink after dinner, try the second-floor dining room of the **Sandy Beach Surf Club** (⊠ Rte. 413 near Sandy Beach, ☎ 787/823–1146), which has a fantastic view of the town's lights.

Outdoor Activities and Sports

WATER SPORTS

Marlin, dorado, wahoo, and kingfish can be hooked in the waters off Rincón. For divers, **Desecheo Island,** about 20 km (13 mi) off the coast of Rincón, has abundant reef and fish life. A rocky bottom sloping to 120 ft rims the island; one formation known as Yellow Reef is distinguished by long tunnels and caverns covered with purple hydrocoral. There are other sites with plentiful fish and coral in the shallower water just off Rincón's shores.

Desecheo Dive Shop (⊠ Rte. 413, Km 2.5, ☎ 787/823–0390) rents surfing and snorkeling equipment, and organizes fishing charters and diving trips. Scuba certification courses are available. Along with organizing a fishing charter or whale-watching trip, **Moondog Charters** (⊠ Black Eagle Marina off Rte. 413, ☎ 787/823–7168) will take a minimum of four people on a trip to Desecheo Island to snorkel or scuba dive. Prices are from $45 to $95. **Taíno Divers** (⊠ Black Eagle Marina off Rte. 413 [Box 164, 00677]; ☎ 787/823–6429, FAX 787/823–7243, WEB www.tainodivers.com) has daily fishing trips, dive charters to Desecheo Island, excursions to Mona Island, and whale-watching rides. They also have scuba PADI certification courses.

Shopping

Eco-Logic-Co (⊠ Parque Pasivo El Faro, Calle El Faro, ☎ 787/823–1252) has fun and ecologically oriented souvenirs. **HotWavz** (⊠ Rte. 413 at Maria's Beach, ☎ 787/823–3942) rents surfboards and sells beach gear. Pick up new and used surfboards, body boards, kayaks, and snorkeling equipment, or rent equipment, at **West Coast Surf Shop** (⊠ 2E Calle Muñoz Rivera, ☎ 787/823–3935).

Mayagüez

⑪ *24 km (15 mi) southeast of Rincón.*

Known as the "Sultan of the West," Mayagüez was founded in 1760 and is said to have gotten its name from a local Taíno chief called Mayagez, whose name means "place of great waters." The city was a busy port under Spanish rule and was rebuilt after several natural disasters, including a fire in 1841 that devastated the downtown area. Evidence of the influence of diverse immigrants and constant rebuilding is seen in the variety of the city's structures, which run the gamut from neoclassical to Victorian to Baroque.

With some 100,000 residents, Mayagüez is now the third-largest urban area on the island, after San Juan and Ponce. Small wooden houses dot the landscape, lending a working-class feel to this port city that became known for its tuna-canning industry in the 20th century. While not a tourist mecca, Mayagüez is nevertheless fun to explore on a morning or afternoon outing. Its pleasant main square, Plaza Colón with lots of shade trees and benches, is dominated by a large statue of Christopher Columbus. One block away on McKinley Street is the city's most noteworthy building, the domed Teatro Yagüez, which dates from 1902. Just outside the city center, the U.S. Department of Agriculture runs a research station with acres of botanical gardens near the University of Puerto Rico's Mayagüez campus.

Puerto Rico's only (and modest) zoo, **Zoológico Dr. Juan A. Rivero,** is about 24 km (15 mi) outside the city. Zebras, rhinoceros, giraffes, tigers, camels, and hippopotami make up an African savana exhibit. Future plans include an aviary and invertebrate and butterfly exhibits. ⊠ *Rte. 108, north of Rte. 65,* ☎ *787/834–8110.* ☞ *$3–$6.* ☉ *Wed.–Sun. 8:30–4; Tue.–Sun. in summer.*

Founded in 1901 on a 235-acre farm on the outskirts of Mayagüez, the **Estación Experimental de Agricultura Tropical** (Tropical Agriculture Research Station) is run by the U.S. Department of Agriculture and contains a tropical plant collection that has been nurtured for more than half a century. More than 2,000 plant species from all over the tropical world are found here, including teak, mahogany, cinnamon, nutmeg, rubber, and numerous exotic flowers. Free maps are available for self-guided tours. ⊠ *Hwy. 2 and Rte. 108,* ☎ *787/831–3435.* ⌨ *Free.* ☉ *Weekdays 7–4.*

The **Teatro Yagüez** is an extravagant beige-and-white theater dating from 1902 that's famed throughout the island for its lavish, columned facade and dome roof. The structure is still the main venue for theater in Mayagüez. If there aren't rehearsals going on, you can step in for a view of the enormous stage. ⊠ *Calle McKinley at Calle Dr. Basóra,* ☎ *787/ 834–0523.* ⌨ *Free.* ☉ *Daily except when rehearsals are scheduled.*

OFF THE
BEATEN PATH

MONA ISLAND – Known as the Galapagos of the Caribbean, Mona Island, about 50 mi off the coast of Mayagüez, has long been an adventurers' outpost. It's said to have been settled by the Taíno and visited by both Christopher Columbus and Juan Ponce de León. Pirates were known to use the small island as a hideout, and legend has it that there is still buried treasure to be found here. Today, however, Mona's biggest lures are its natural beauty and distinctive ecosystem. The island has 200-ft cliffs filled with caves and is home to a number of endangered species, such as the Mona iguana and leatherback sea turtle. A number of seabirds, including red-footed boobies, also inhabit the island. Off its coast are reefs filled with tropical fish, black coral, and underwater caverns. The island is uninhabited except for transient campers and personnel from the Department of Natural and Environmental Resources. Travelers must get there by boat—planes aren't permitted to land. Several tour operators offer overnight camping and diving trips to the island. The best time to visit is between July and October, but note that reservations must be made well in advance.

Beach

Mayagüez isn't famous for its beaches—you'll find better stretches in Rincón, about 25 minutes north—but the **Balneario de Añasco,** also called Tres Hermanos Beach, is 10 minutes north of town via Highway 2 and Routes 115 and 401. The beach, dotted with palm trees, is nice for swimming and has changing facilities and rest rooms.

Dining and Lodging

$$–$$$ ✕ **El Estoril.** Splurge in the elegant tiled dining room or have a more relaxed meal at the wood-and-brick bar area. Seafood is the specialty: order a traditional paella or try the lobster *al Estoril* (wrapped in mozzarella and bacon and flambéed). There are also meat and pasta dishes. ⊠ *100 Calle Méndez Vigo,* ☎ *787/834–2288. Closed Sun. AE, MC, V.*

$ ✕ **Ricomini Bakery.** This popular bakery is open daily from 6 AM to midnight and is a good spot to try one of Mayagüez's trademark delicacies, a Brazo Gitano (literally "Gypsy Arm")—a gigantic jellyroll filled with anything from guava to lemon to sweet cheese. You can also find another famous local product here, Fido's Sangría, made from the closely guarded secret recipe of Mayagüez resident Wilfredo Aponte Hernández. There are also other pastries, sandwiches, and freshly baked bread. ⊠ *202 Calle Méndez Vigo, next to cathedral,* ☎ *787/ 832–0565. AE, MC, V.*

$$$–$$$$ ✕⌂ **Mayagüez Resort & Casino.** Despite the presence of the casino, the hotel has an elegant yesteryear air, especially at the Veranda Terrace Bar, a long, sweeping terrace where you can sip a cocktail while watching large plants sway in the breeze and guests frolic in the pool. Outside of downtown, off Highway 2, the resort draws a mix leisure travelers and businesspeople. Some rooms have private balconies. The restaurant, El Castillo ($$–$$$), specializes in seafood. The Añasco Public Beach is 10 minutes away. ⌧ *Rte. 104, Km 0.3, off Hwy. 2 (Box 3781, 00681),* ☎ *787/832–3030 or 888/689–3030,* FAX *787/265–1430,* WEB *www.mayaguezresort.com. 140 rooms. Restaurant, bar, lounge, pool, 3 tennis courts, gym, casino, playground. AE, D, MC, V. EP.*

$–$$$ ✕☎ **Holiday Inn Mayagüez and Tropical Casino.** Here you'll find all the comforts associated with the Holiday Inn name and an easy-to-reach location close to the downtown historic district and 5 minutes from the airport. Golf, beaches, and shopping are nearby. The Holly Cafe ($$–$$$) serves a mixture of Caribbean and international cuisine with a Sunday "South American nights" brunch. The hotel bar and the Holly Disco are packed with locals on weekends. ⌧ *2701 Hwy. 2, Km 149.9, 00681,* ☎ *787/833–1100,* FAX *787/833–1300,* WEB *www.holiday-inn. com/mayaguezpri.com. 142 rooms. Restaurant, bar, lounge, pool, exercise equipment, casino, dance club, shop, business services. AE, D, MC, V. CP.*

$$ ☎ **Hotel El Sol.** In the heart of downtown Mayagüez, this small inn, part of the government's parador program, offers clean and modern rooms with rattan furnishings. The lobby area feels somewhat cramped, but the rooms are spacious, and the hotel also has a bar, restaurant, and small swimming pool. ⌧ *9 Calle Santiago Riera Palmer, 00680,* ☎ *787/834–0303 or 866/765–0303,* FAX *787/265–7567,* WEB *www. hotelelsol.com. 52 rooms. Restaurant, bar, pool. AE, D, MC, V. CP.*

Nightlife and the Arts

Dom Pepe Italian Restaurant & Gallery Bar (⌧ 56 Calle Méndez Vigo, ☎ 787/834–4941) is a block from Plaza Colón and has live eclectic music upstairs on Thursday night. **Holiday Inn Mayagüez** (⌧ Hwy. 2, Km 149.9, ☎ 787/834–0303) has a busy casino, and its disco is a popular spot for the younger crowd on Friday and Saturday nights. The casino at the **Mayagüez Resort & Casino** (⌧ Rte. 104, Km 0.3, ☎ 787/ 832–3030) is popular with both residents and tourists. **Teatro Yagüez** (⌧ Calle McKinley at Calle Dr. Basora, ☎ 787/834–0523) often features plays and comedy revues, mostly in Spanish.

Shopping

Small stores and pharmacies dot downtown Mayagüez. For heavy-duty shopping, the **Mayagüez Mall** (⌧ Hwy. 2, Km 159.4, ☎ 787/834–2760) has local stores, a food court, and stateside chains such as JCPenney.

NORTHWESTERN PUERTO RICO A TO Z

To research prices, get advice from other travelers, and book travel arrangements, visit www.fodors.com.

AIR TRAVEL

Continental Airlines generally runs flights Tuesday, Thursday, Saturday, and Sunday from Newark, New Jersey to Aguadilla, but frequently changes depending on the season. American Eagle services three flights daily between San Juan and Mayagüez. American Eagle also offers a daily flight out of Mayagüez to and from Santo Domingo. A former charter airline, North American Airlines, runs flights between New York's JFK airport and Aguadilla on Monday and Saturday.

➤ AIRLINES: **American Eagle** (☎ 787/749–1747, WEB www.aa.com). **Continental** (☎ 800/433–7300, WEB www.continental.com). **North American Airlines** (☎ 718/322–1300, WEB www.northamair.com).

AIRPORTS

Aguadilla's Rafael Hernández Airport is on the old Ramey Air Force Base. The Eugenio María de Hostos Airport is just north of Mayagüez on Highway 2.

▶ AIRPORT INFORMATION: **Eugenio María de Hostos Airport** (✉ Hwy. 2, Km 148.7, Mayagüez, ☎ 787/833–0148 or 787/265–7065). **Rafael Hernández Airport** (☎ 787/891–2286).

BOAT AND FERRY TRAVEL

Ferry service from Mayagüez to Santo Domingo leaves Mayagüez Monday, Wednesday, and Friday and returns Tuesday and Thursday. Trips are overnight leaving at 8 PM and arriving at 8 AM. Small cabins with sleeping accommodations for two, three, and four persons are provided. Tickets are usually available, but reserve well in advance if you're bringing your car. Most of the year, fares are around $149 per person and an additional $146 for cars; fares are higher December–January. Ships leave from the Zona Portuaria (Ports Zone), past the Holiday Inn on Highway 2.

▶ BOAT AND FERRY INFORMATION: **Ferry Reservations** (☎ 787/832–4800).

BUS AND VAN TRAVEL

There's no easy network of buses linking the towns in northwestern Puerto Rico. Some municipalities and private companies operate buses and large vans *(públicos)* from one city to another, but schedules are loose. It's not wise to count on them as your primary means of transportation. That said, if you're adventurous and not easily frustrated, it's possible to arrange cheap transportation from San Juan to Aguadilla, Rincón, Mayagüez, Utuado, among others towns. Prices from terminal to terminal are set, but drivers may go to another destination if arranged beforehand.

Driver Andrio Placeres has a five-passenger van (the van must be full to leave); a trip to Rincón costs $10 per person one-way. Choferes Unidos travels from San Juan to Aguadilla ($10 one-way) and will negotiate a price to go to nearby towns. Linea Sultana has vans to Mayagüez that leave San Juan every two hours, 7:30 AM–5:30 PM, and they will also drop off passengers along Highway 2 in Aguada, Quebradillas, and Isabella. Prices are $12 per person one-way. Linea Utuado leaves San Juan for Utuado daily at 1 PM; return trips are daily at 6 AM. Prices are $12 per person one-way; you must make reservations. Trips to Jayuya and Lares are also possible.

Arecibo has a bus system going in and around the city. The main Terminal del Norte is at Plaza del Mercado. Public vans go to San Juan from Terminal del Sur on Avenida Santiago Iglesias.

▶ BUS AND VAN INFORMATION: **Andrio Placeres** (☎ 787/730–5725). **Choferes Unidos** (☎ 787/751–7622). **Linea Sultana** (☎ 787/765–9377). **Linea Utuado** (☎ 787/765–1908). **Terminal del Norte** (☎ 787/880–0129). **Terminal del Sur** (☎ 787/879–3425).

CAR RENTAL

Cars can be rented at the Luis Muñoz Marín International Airport and at other locations in San Juan. You'll also find agencies in Aguadilla, Arecibo, Mayagüez, and elsewhere in the northwest. Prices vary from $25 to $65 per day.

▶ AGENCIES: **Avis** (☎ 787/890–3311 or 787/833–7070 in Aguadilla; 787/796–7243 in Dorado). **Budget** (☎ 787/890–1110 in Aguadilla). **Hertz** (☎ 787/832–3314 or 787/833–4904 in Mayagüez; 787/890–5650 in Aguadilla). **L & M Rent a Car** (☎ 787/831–4740 in Mayagüez). **Leaseway of Puerto Rico** (☎ 787/878–1606 in Arecibo).

CAR TRAVEL

Driving a car is the best way to see northwestern Puerto Rico, especially the mountain area. The toll road, Highway 22, makes it easy to reach Arecibo from San Juan. Highway 22 turns into Highway 2 just after Arecibo, swings by the northwestern tip of the island, then leads south to Mayagüez. The well-maintained and scenic Route 10, which can be accessed in Arecibo, is a main link to the central mountain region. The Ruta Panorámica runs east–west across the island and near some of the central mountain towns. It's made up of a number of small roads, many of which can be hilly and curving.

EMERGENCY SERVICES

If you rent a car, call your car rental company for assistance.

➤ CONTACTS: **Arecibo Towing Service** (⊠ 313 Av. Juan Rosado, Arecibo, ☎ 787/879–2902). **Gruas Fernandini** (⊠ 25 Rte. 135, Km 75.02, Bo Yahuecas, Adjuntas, ☎ 787/829–6102). **Gruas Sanchez** (⊠ Hwy. 2, Km 149.7, Bo Algarrobo, Mayagüez, ☎ 787/832–6704). **Gruas Warren** (⊠ 7-O Calle 11, Urb Villas Los Santos, Arecibo, ☎ 787/879–4444). **Junker Nazario** (⊠ Rte. 105, Km 1.1, Bo Limón, Mayagüez, ☎ 787/833–2755).

GASOLINE

Gas stations can be found throughout the region, but are spread out in the mountain towns. When exploring in the mountains, make sure to fill up before you head out. Prices are measured in liters instead of gallons and generally range from 30 to 40 cents per liter. The chain gas stations, Esso and Shell, are open 24 hours. Locally owned stations in small towns generally close before 6 PM.

PARKING

Parking is usually available on the street, though downtown Arecibo and Mayagüez can become congested especially in the historic districts where streets are narrower. At tourist or commercial sites, parking is normally provided.

ROAD CONDITIONS

The major highways throughout the northwest region, Highways 22 and 2, are well maintained. The Ruta Panorámica throughout the central mountains is also in good condition and has amazing vistas, but its twists and turns should be driven with caution. Road signs in the mountains may be missing—some have been blown down by storms or hurricanes and have yet to be replaced.

EMERGENCIES

➤ CONTACTS: **General emergencies** (☎ 911).

➤ HOSPITALS: **Centro de Salud** (⊠ Calle Isaac González Martínez, Utuado, ☎ 787/894–2875). **General Hospital Dr. Ramón Emeterio Betances** (⊠ Hwy. 2, Km 157, Mayagüez, ☎ 787/834–8686). **Hospital Bella Vista** (⊠ Rte. 349, Km 2.7, Mayagüez, ☎ 787/834–2350). **Hospital Regional Dr. C. Coll y Toste** (⊠ Rte. 129, Km 0.7, Arecibo, ☎ 787/878–7272). **Hospital Subregional Dr. Pedro J. Zamora** (⊠ Hwy. 2, Km 141.1, Aguadilla, ☎ 787/791–3000).

➤ PHARMACIES: **Walgreens** (⊠ Hwy. 2, Km 129.7, Aguadilla, ☎ 787/882–8035; ⊠ 342 Calle Méndez Vigo, Dorado, ☎ 787/796–1046; ⊠ Calle del Mar 547, Hatillo, ☎ 787/880–8290; ⊠ Mayagüez Mall, Hwy. 2, Km 159.4, Mayagüez, ☎ 787/831–9249; ⊠ Plaza Universitaria, Mayagüez, ☎ 787/805–4005; ⊠ Rte. 123. Bldg. 940, Utuado, ☎ 787/894–0100).

ENGLISH-LANGUAGE MEDIA

The *San Juan Star,* the only English daily newspaper published on the island, is sporadically offered in towns outside San Juan. If newspapers aren't available at your hotel, ask the concierge where you might find one. Bookstores in larger towns like Arecibo and Mayagüez have a good selection of English reading materials.

➤ BOOKSTORES: **The Bookshop** (✉ Plaza del Norte Mall, Hatillo, ☎ 787/817–4459; ✉ Mayagüez Mall, Hwy. 2, Km 159.4, Mayagüez, ☎ 787/805–3415).

HEALTH

The water on the island is generally good to drink. Always wash fruit. It's possible to catch dengue fever if bitten by an infected mosquito. Mosquitos exist everywhere (though occasionally cooler mountain temperatures make them less of a problem), so wear repellant.

MAIL AND SHIPPING

Larger towns like Arecibo and Mayagüez have a main post office with smaller branches throughout the city. You can often buy stamps in grocery and drug stores. Generally, post offices are open Monday–Friday from 7 or 8 AM until 5 or 6 PM and for a few hours in the morning on Saturday.

➤ POST OFFICES: **Arecibo Main Office** (✉ 10 Av. San Patricio, Arecibo 00612, ☎ 787/878–2775). **Dorado Main Office** (✉ 100 Rte. 698, Dorado 00646, ☎ 787/796–1052). **Mayagüez Main Office** (✉ 60 Calle McKinley W, Mayagüez 00680, ☎ 787/265–3138). **Rincón Main Office** (✉ 100 Rte. 115, Rincón 00677, ☎ 787/823–2625). **Utuado Main Office** (✉ 41 Av. Fernando L. Ribas, Utuado 00641, ☎ 787/894–2940).

OVERNIGHT SERVICES

Express Mail, overnight, and two-day service is available at all main post offices. FedEx has offices in Aguadilla at the Borinquen Airport (Hangar 404) and in Arecibo (Rte. 10, Km 83.2). There are drop boxes at the Holiday Inn Mayagüez, the Mayagüez Resort & Casino, and at CopyMax in the Mayagüez Mall. UPS has branches in Arecibo at the Domingo Ruiz Airport and in Mayagüez at Airport El Maní. Both locations close at 5 PM.

➤ MAJOR SERVICES: **FedEx** (☎ 877/838–7834). **UPS** (☎ 800/742–5877 or 787/253–2877).

MONEY MATTERS

Banks are plentiful in larger cities and smaller towns usually have at least one; banks are sometimes attached to grocery stores. All banks have ATMs (called ATHs), and many businesses accept ATM cards. Airports and most banks offer exchange services.

➤ BANKS AND EXCHANGE SERVICES: **Banco Popular** (✉ 227 Calle Paz, Aguada, ☎ 787/868–2380; ✉ Calle Mercedes Moreno, corner of Munoz Rivera, Aguadilla, ☎ 787/891–2085 or 787/891–5987; ✉ Mayagüez Mall, Hwy. 2, Km 159.4, Mayagüez, ☎ 787/834–4750; ✉ Calle Zuzuaregui Maricao, ☎ 787/838–3660; ✉ 13 Av. Agustín Ramos Calero, Isabela, ☎ 787/872–3100).

SAFETY

Unless you're camping in a recreational area, it's best to go to forest reserves during daylight hours only. Outside metro areas there's little crime, but you should take normal precautions: remember to lock your car and don't leave valuables unattended.

TAXIS

Taxis can be hailed near the main plaza in Mayagüez, but in the smaller towns they may be hard to come by. Check with your hotel or restaurant. In Mayagüez, White Taxi is reliable and charges flat rates—no meters—by location. In Arecibo, try Arecibo Taxi Cab, but note that they close at midnight. Fares to or from San Juan are steep: for example, service is $50 from Arecibo and $120 from Mayagüez.

➤ CAB COMPANIES: **Arecibo Taxi Cab** (☎ 787/878–2929). **White Taxi** (☎ 787/832–1115).

TELEPHONES

There are pay phones throughout the region, but often they're out of order. Puerto Rico's main area code is 787; a new, 939 area code is being introduced gradually. All local calls are prefaced with the area code. Many calls may be long distance, even to a nearby town. Public phones take coins or prepaid phone cards.

TOURS

AdvenTours, Desecheo Divers, Moondog Charters, and Tour Marine offer overnight camping and diving trips to Mona Island. Permits are required and reservations must be made in advance (AdvenTours requires reservations three months in advance). Trips are subject to weather and water conditions.

AdvenTours offers bird-watching, biking, and kayaking trips. Desecheo Divers has daily trips to Desecheo Island (minimum of four people) for snorkeling or scuba diving, also whale-watching trips and fishing charters. Prices range from $45 to $95. Tour Marine also goes to Desecheo Island (minimum of 10 people); you can request a cook or guide for extra. They offer diving, fishing, and whale-watching.

Expediciones Tanamá has guided hiking trips through the Tanamá River cave system. Northwestern Land Tours has trips to the Camuy Caves and the Arecibo Observatory, and will arrange other excursions.

➤ TOUR OPERATOR: **AdvenTours** (✉ 17 Calle Uroyán, Mayagüez, ☎ 787/831–6447, WEB www.angelfire.com/fl2/adventours). **Desecheo Divers** (✉ Rte. 413, Km 2.5, Rincón, ☎ 787/823–0390). **Expediciones Tanamá** (✉ Rte. 111, Km 14.5, Barrio Angeles, ☎ 787/894–7685, WEB http://home.coqui.net/albite/albite/index.html). **Moondog Charters** (✉ Black Eagle Marina, off Rte. 413 before Steps Beach, Rincón ☎ 787/823–7168). **Northwestern Land Tours** (✉ Box 215, Utuado, 00611, ☎ 787/894–7804 or 787/644–984, WEB www.puertoricoexcursions. com). **Tour Marine** (✉ Rte. 102, Km 15.4, Cabo Rojo, ☎ 787/851–9259).

TRAVEL AGENCIES

➤ CONTACTS: **Bithorn Network** (✉ 8 Calle Méndez Vigo, Mayagüez, ☎ 787/834–3300). **Liz Travel Agency** (✉ 101 Av. Interamericana, Aguadilla, ☎ 787/891–5318). **Manolin Travel Agency** (✉ 360 Av. Rotarios, Arecibo, ☎ 787/879–2245). **Sultana Travel Agency** (✉ 24 Calle Pablo Casals, Mayagüez, ☎ 787/833–5553).

VISITOR INFORMATION

The Puerto Rico Tourism Company has an office at the Rafael Hernández Airport in Aguadilla. The town of Rincón has a tourism office on Route 115; it's open weekdays 9–4. Mayagüez, Arecibo, Jayuya and Maricao have tourism offices in their towns or city halls.

➤ TOURIST INFORMATION: **Arecibo City Hall** (☎ 787/879–2232). **Jayuya Town Hall** (☎ 787/282–5010 Ext. 9704). **Maricao Town Hall** (☎ 787/838–2290)). **Mayagüez City Hall** (☎ 787/834–8585). **Puerto Rico Tourism Company** (☎ 787/890–3315, WEB www.prtourism.com or www.gotopuertorico.com). **Rincón Tourism Office** (☎ 787/823–5024).

6 BACKGROUND AND ESSENTIALS

Portraits of Puerto Rico

Puerto Rico at a Glance: A Chronology

Spanish Vocabulary

CITY OF LIGHT

THE LIGHT IS ALWAYS YELLOW in the morning streets. Even in the soft, drizzling rains of summer or the fierce, wind-driven storms of early fall, I feel bathed in that luminous yellow light. It seeps from the walls of the old houses—a light formed by the centuries, an antique light, a light that once held conquistadores and slaves, sugar kings and freebooters, the light of old gold and vanished supremacies—the light of San Juan.

When I say San Juan, I don't mean that great urban sprawl, with its population of more than a million, that makes up the modern capital of the island of Puerto Rico. That San Juan, with its office towers and traffic jams, raw concrete-block factories and heartless condominia, is just another city of the 20th century. When I think of San Juan, I mean the old town, called San Juan Antiguo by the formal, but more affectionately referred to as Viejo San Juan by those who know it and love it and have been warmed by its yellow light.

My San Juan, the old town I first saw in the late 1950s and have been visiting ever since, fills a mere seven square blocks on a promontory hooked around to face the great harbor that made the Spanish christen this island Rich Port. Across the centuries, it has been battered by unnamed tropical storms, and, in 1989, felt the power of Hurricane Hugo. But Viejo San Juan endures.

Whenever I visit Puerto Rico, arriving on a screaming jet at the airport in Isla Verde, I always go first to the old town. It centers me, in an island society that is too often culturally and politically schizophrenic. It grants me a sense of proportion. The modern city vanishes and much of the 20th century goes with it. Few places on this earth make me as happy.

The past is part of the reason. In many American cities now, we seem to be living in an eternal present tense, as insubstantial as the images on television screens. Too many events flash across our minds in unconnected fragments; today's crises are forgotten tomorrow; we hear too much and see too much and never listen for the whispering of ghosts. But there has been a San Juan since 1521, one hundred years before the first Dutchman mortared two bricks together to begin making New York. When the American Revolution began, San Juan had been there for 255 years.

SO IT IS NO ACCIDENT that when I walk from Plaza de Colón (with its statue of Columbus disguised as Dean Rusk) into Calle San Francisco, my sense of time shifts. The past asserts itself and I am reminded that for a long time before the rise of the United States this was a Spanish-speaking hemisphere. I hear the conversations of Puerto Ricans, delivered in the staccato-rhythms of port people, full of jokes and innuendo and untranslatable local words. The air is thick with vowels. From the old mortar of the walls, the past murmurs: Wait, slow down, listen, have a glass of rum, and remember old sins, the folly of man, the futility of despair.

Columbus discovered America in 1492, and on his second voyage the following year, the Admiral of the Ocean Sea landed at the site of the present town of Aguadilla on the northwest coast of the island. There were then about 30,000 Taíno Indians living on the island, which they called Borinquén. There was little gold to plunder, and those first Spaniards quickly moved on. Their first settlement was established at Caparra in 1509, but was soon abandoned to the mosquitoes. The Spaniards moved out of the marshes to the promontory beside the great bay and began to build a town they called San Juan Bautista, for St. John the Baptist, who remains the island's patron saint. They built from memory, combining the Islamic clarity and the proportions of Andalusia with houses glimpsed in the Canary Islands before the passage across the fierce Atlantic. They used brick and the axbreaking hardwood called *ausubo* as well as iron forged in their own shops. They built the place to last.

The city they made evolved over centuries, of course, and even today the urban archaeologists of the Institute of Puerto Rican Culture are trying to chart its transformations. This is no simple task. Although minibuses now move through the old town, and taxis can take you to some key points (other streets are blocked to cars), the best way to see San Juan is on foot.

As you walk the streets, you tread upon blue-slag bricks called *adoquines*. Some guides insist they were originally ballast in the sailing ships of the 17th and 18th centuries, dumped here as the ships took on cargoes of sugar and tobacco for the markets of Europe; others tell you they arrived in San Juan from England as late as 1890. But they feel as if they had been here from the beginning, glistening with spring rain, perfect complements to the suffused yellow light.

Ni modo; it doesn't matter. They are part of San Juan forever. So is the feeling that here you might be safe. Three fortresses guard the city: La Fortaleza—the oldest executive mansion in the hemisphere, now occupied by the island's governor—overlooking the bay on the southwest of the promontory; San Cristóbal, to the right as you enter the old town from the hotels of the Condado; the magnificent El Morro on the tip, its cannon pointing northwest into the Atlantic. Walls surround the city, linking the three great fortresses, walls of stone.

T HESE WALLS AND FORTS were not empty adornment; they were, like most things of beauty, a necessity. San Juan was established in an age of international gangsterism, and, since it was usually the last stop for Spanish galleons groaning with the loot of Mexico and Peru, hijackers saw it as an obvious target. Today, you can walk along the edge of El Morro, on walls that are 20 feet thick and rise 140 feet above the sea, and imagine what it was like when unfriendly sails on the horizon could mean death and destruction.

The fort was completed in 1589 by a team of military engineers headed by Juan Bautista Antonelli. The noted English gangster, Francis Drake, appeared in 1595 and was battered by the fort's six levels of cannons, along with fire from the smaller guns of La Fortaleza. Ten of Drake's ships were sunk, and more than 400 sailors were sent to the bottom of the harbor. But, three years later, another English hood, the Earl of Cumberland, arrived and came upon the city from the land side with a force of a thousand soldiers. He occupied San Juan, looted it, and then was forced to abandon it as more than 400 of his men perished from disease. El Morro never was captured again, although the Dutch tried in 1625, managing to burn a number of buildings in San Juan, including the finest private library then in existence in the New World. American naval gunners blasted away at the walls in 1898, during the war against Spain that made Puerto Rico an American colony. They never did take the fortress.

Today, you can visit El Morro on foot, with better luck than Cumberland's doomed soldiers. You go through the 27-acre park grounds, where soldiers once drilled and lovers now meet and fathers play ball with their sons. Hugo did its best against the park, damaging some 50 Australian pines that once lined its entrance. The National Park Service subsequently cut them down. The hurricane also caused minor damage to the fort, but across the centuries it has survived well. Its walls are the color of lions, its arches painted white, and you cross a dry moat to enter the interior. From the ramparts, you can look down upon crashing surf, or you can visit the museum and souvenir shop, or examine the restored lighthouse, or photograph the domed sentry boxes called *garitas*. You can watch the pretty girls. Or you can simply surrender to the sense of time.

I N THE AREA OF EL MORRO, I always save an hour to wander through the 19th-century cemetery below the fortress walls; here lie many of the most famous Puerto Rican political leaders, the martyred revolutionaries, some of the old Spanish *peninsulares* (who lived lives of leisure while slaves did the work), and ordinary folk, too; shopkeepers and blacksmiths, shoemakers and chefs, and the artisans and craftsmen who built the town and died at home. Or I visit a while in La Casa Blanca, the oldest house on the island, built for

Ponce de León in 1521. Ponce was a mixture of romantic and conqueror. He dreamed, as they all did in that generation of Spanish adventurers, of gold. In Puerto Rico, he found little of it—certainly nothing on the scale of the great treasures of Mexico. He stayed on for a while as governor, watching the Taínos die of European diseases or flee to the jungled hills or depart down through the islands in great hand-hewn boats.

They were strange, those dark-skinned pagans; they simply would not agree to be slaves. So Ponce de León departed for Florida in search of the Fountain of Youth, almost certainly a fabrication invented by an Indian. Ponce was still searching in Florida when he was killed in a skirmish with Indians much fiercer than the pacific Taínos. His body was first taken to Cuba, then to San Juan, and his bones are now in the Metropolitan Cathedral. But the elegant Casa Blanca remained in the Ponce family until the late 18th century. The town rose around them. Streets were laid out, fountains constructed, churches built. The energy of the first generation of conquistadores waned throughout the vast Spanish empire; adventurers were replaced with clerks and grandees. The family grew rich, was battered by history, and departed after 250 years. A series of Spanish and then American military commanders lived here, strutting around the lovely courtyard and the splashing fountains. The house is now occupied by the Institute for Advanced Studies.

As an object made by men, a collective work of sculpture, El Castillo de San Cristóbal is, to me, preferable to El Morro. You can walk to it along the city walls, looking down at La Perla, the most picturesque slum under the American flag (it was described in detail in anthropologist Oscar Lewis's book *La Vida*). In ordinary times, the green-tar-paper roofs of La Perla, and the flags of the island's political parties, stand precariously between the city walls and the sea. But Hugo blew the flags into eternity, ripped the tar paper from many rooftops, and battered some of the frailer structures. This was nothing new. Houses have been washed away by storms in the past, but the people of La Perla always come back and build again. Now, children run in the streets and winos flake out against the sides of houses. Years ago, I used to visit friends down here, but they don't live in

La Perla anymore. And in the age of crack cocaine I no longer have the courage to wander its impoverished streets.

INSTEAD, **I GO TO** San Cristóbal, designed by two of those Irishmen known as the "wild geese"—the men and women who scattered around the world after the English conquest of their home island. Two who came to Puerto Rico were Alejandro O'Reilly and Thomas O'Daly, and, in the employ of the Spanish Army, they designed a fort laced with tunnels, secret traps, blind walls, gates, and pickets. The intention was to protect San Juan from land invasions similar to Cumberland's. There are forts within forts here, like watertight compartments in ships. An invader might take part of the fortress, but would pay a bloody and ferocious price to take it all.

I love the view from the ramparts of this fort, looking east toward the beaches and gigantic clouds that gather above the rain forest of the mountain called El Yunque. I like to think of O'Reilly and O'Daly, with their noses peeling, standing in the great blinding light of the summer sun, far from home, on a promontory cooled by the trade winds, speaking in Irish about one final go with the hated English.

Within the city's walls, there are streets that resemble those of New Orleans, with elaborately scrolled iron balconies attached to three-story houses that loom imperiously above their smaller neighbors. Most were built in the 17th and 18th centuries by the hidalgos who grew rich from tobacco, sugar, and horses. The ceiling beams and front doors are cut from the ausubo tree, so hard that is has been known to make restoration workers cry. The austere walls are humanized by the bright colors of the Caribbean: lime green, aqua, cerulean blue, rose, and, of course, those warm ochres and yellows. In other places, such colors might seem garish; here, they are as natural and permanent as the sky and the sea.

But some things do change. When I first came to San Juan, there was always music coming from those scrolled balconies, through the open doors of apartments: The Trio Los Panchos and Tito Rodriguez, Augustin Lara and Lucho Gatica, music romantic and bittersweet, occasionally punctuated by the tougher rhythms of mambo. There is less music in the streets now because prosperity has brought air conditioning to Viejo San Juan, and, as everywhere in the world, air conditioning closes windows and doors.

But if there is less to hear, there is still much to see. You gaze into patios that are like snatches of Seville: small fountains, bird cages, polished-iron implements, flowers. All manner of flowers grow in elaborate terra-cotta pots: philodendron, orchids, the yellowing vines called canarios, bougainvillea spilling from balconies, and hibiscus— mounds, garlands, bowers of hibiscus. There is an occasional flamboyant tree, with its scarlet flowers, imprisoned in its city garden; or a flowering oleander or frangipani preening for the hibiscus. You see palm trees, too, those immigrants from Africa, with terns rattling in the fronds.

Most windows are shuttered, the mute houses implying that in the great Spanish centuries, the densest human life was lived behind them. The town was too small then, too bourgeois, too formal for public melodramas.

Today, life is more public. San Juan is not a museum, and as you wander the streets you can see old men playing dominoes in small, shaded squares, middle-aged women shopping in the boutiques or stopping in La Bombonera on Calle San Francisco for splendid coffee and oversweet pastries, and young people everywhere. I'm not much of a shopper; I'd rather look and imagine than own. So I ignore the shops and follow no set route on my wanderings through Viejo San Juan. I want to be reassured and surprised.

ALWAYS GO TO the Cristo Chapel on the city walls overlooking the harbor. Almost always it is as I saw it last, closed off by an iron gate, four potted palms within its small interior, the masonry peeled off parts of the walls to reveal the thin brick of the past. The palms were demolished by Hugo; they will be replaced. One need not share the belief that inspired the chapel to be charmed by its proportions and modesty. As always, the little park beside it is filled with children and pigeons. A plaque tells me that the chapel was built between 1753 and 1780 and that "legend traces its origin to a miraculous happening at the site." It doesn't describe the miracle, but it is said that in 1753 a rider in a holy festival made a mistake, plunged over the wall into the sea, and lived. Not exactly a major miracle, I suppose, but good enough to get the chapel built. The plaque bears the seal of Lions International.

As in most Latin countries, the sacred and the profane are at war here. All over Old San Juan, there are dozens of little bars. On the corner of San Sebastián and San Justo there is a bar called Aquí Se Puede, which means "here you can," and in its cool, dark interior the name seems more an act of reporting than of enticement.

A **FEW BLOCKS AWAY** is the Church of San José—spare, controlled, set facing a square out of de Chirico. It is the oldest church still in active use in the Americas, built by Dominican friars in the 1530s. But the mood within is of an austere European Catholicism exiled to the tropics. Plainsong comes from a hidden sound system. Natural light falls from openings in the cupolas of side chapels. The wooden pews are severe. The stations of the cross, with their ancient tale of sacrifice and pain, are bichromes of blue and white. Most afternoons, there is an eerie silence in the place, perhaps for good reason; archives suggest that as many as four thousand people—including most of the descendants of Ponce de León—might be buried beneath the tile floors.

On hot days, I used to stop for a while in the Plaza de Armas, to sit under the shade trees and talk to the taxi drivers and lounging cops and gold-toothed old men. They all told fabulous lies, and, across the street, vendors sold flowers under the arches of City Hall. There were department stores on the harbor side and pretty girls everywhere. The stores and pretty girls remain; all the rest is changed.

In 1988, a mayor named Balthasar Corrado del Río insisted on remodeling the plaza his way. Citizens protested, but he went ahead anyway—the shade trees were chain sawed at four in the morning. A cheap phone kiosk was erected. And now the Plaza de Armas is a bald, bright plain.

Now, if it's a hot day, I walk across the plaza to the corner of the New York Department Store, toward the harbor along Calle San José. I go into The Bookstore, which is air conditioned and has a fine selection of books in English, along with the latest volumes from Mexico, Buenos Aires, and Barcelona, and the works of such fine Puerto Rican writers as Pedro Juan Soto, Luis Rafael Sanchez, and Rene Marquez. Here I can also pick up a copy of the *New York Times*. Then I go next door into the Café de Los Amigos for the best coffee in the old town. A sign sets out one of the rules: *No Discuta Politica Aquí.*

There are other plazas, churches, and museums, of course; your legs will carry you to all of them, or, in revolt, will persuade you to see them at some later date. But the people are as important as the buildings. On Saturday nights, the young people of the other San Juan show up to party in Viejo San Juan; handsome young men in the pretty-boy *guapo* style—hair slicked, wearing New York fashions, playing out roles that they haven't earned; the young women, voluptuous, made up to look like Madonna or one of the stars of Spanish television, their bodies bursting from tight skirts, T-shirts, and blouses.

There is something sad about them, as they preen for each other in the ancient rituals. They seem like so many tropical flowers blooming briefly before the swift move into adulthood. On these weekend evenings, they stand outside the Daiquiri Factory on Calle San Francisco, or Joseph's Café next door, some of them drinking and dancing inside while MTV plays on giant screens. They come to Viejo San Juan from the modern city of plastic and cement, as if subconsciously seeking to discover who they are by temporarily inhabiting the places from which their families came.

The perfumed rituals are enacted amidst the colliding symbols of the island's general cultural schizophrenia: Kentucky Fried Chicken, Burger King, and McDonald's, along with El Convento and the Plaza Salvador Brau, where there is a statue of a man named Patricio Rijos, who was known in life as "Toribio, King of the Guiro." The guiro is a grooved gourd played as a rhythm instrument with a wire fork. It is never seen on MTV.

And as the children of those San Juan nights careen away to various appointments, the music gradually stops, doors are shuttered, the traffic departs. At 104 Calle Fortaleza, on one such evening, I stopped to look at a marble plaque that identified the building as: THE HOUSE WHERE IN 1963 THE PIÑA COLADA WAS CREATED BY DON RAMON PORTA MINGOT. It was now a perfume shop called Barrachina. I smiled, thinking that in Viejo San Juan, all of the important things are remembered, when a small, wiry man came up to me.

"*Es una mentira,*" he said. "It's a lie. It was the bar of the Caribe Hilton, 1958." Without another word, he walked off on unsteady legs, humming an old song. I went back to the hotel, to dream of yellow light.

— Pete Hamill

A GAMBLING PRIMER

CASINOS ARE NO LONGER as large a part of the tourism experience in Puerto Rico as they once were—but that's due more to growth in other areas than to a decline in the casinos themselves. If gambling is your thing, or if you're feeling yourself drawn to the "action" for the first time, Puerto Rico's resort-based casinos provide an attractive setting for trying your luck.

The most popular games have their rules, etiquette, odds, and strategies. If you're new to gambling, take a reconnaissance stroll through the casino, read up on the games here, and choose the one that best suits your style. If you take the time to learn the basics and fine points thoroughly, you'll be adequately prepared to play with as much of an edge as the game allows.

Baccarat

The most "glamorous" game in the casino, baccarat (pronounced *bah*-kuh-rah) is a version of *chemin de fer,* popular in European gambling halls. The Italian word *baccara* means "zero"; this refers to the point value of 10s and picture cards. The game is run by four pit personnel. Two dealers sit side by side at the middle of the table; they handle the winning and losing bets and keep track of each player's "commission" (explained below). The "caller" stands at the middle of the other side of the table and dictates the action. A pit boss supervises the game and acts as final judge if any disputes arise.

How to Play

Baccarat is played with eight decks of cards dealt from a large "shoe" (or card holder). Each player is offered a turn at handling the shoe and dealing the cards. Two two-card hands are dealt: the "player" and the "bank" hands. The player who deals the cards is called the banker, though the house, of course, banks both hands. The players bet, before the deal, on which hand, player or banker, will come closer to adding up to 9 (a "natural"). The cards are totaled as follows: Ace through 9 retain face value, while 10s and picture cards are worth zero. If a hand adds up to more than 10, the number 10 is subtracted from the total. For example, if one hand contains a 10 and a 4, the hand adds up to 4. If a hand holds an ace and 6, it adds up to 7. If a hand has a 7 and 9, it adds up to 6.

Depending on the two hands, the caller either declares a winner and loser (if either hand actually adds up to 8 or 9), or calls for another card for the player hand (if it totals 1, 2, 3, 4, 5, or 10). The bank hand then either stands pat or draws a card, determined by a complex series of rules depending on what the player's total is and dictated by the caller. When one or the other hand is declared a winner, the dealers go into action to pay off the winning wagers, collect the losing wagers, and add up the commission (usually 5%) that the house collects on the bank hand. Both bets have a house advantage of slightly more than 1%.

The player-dealer (or banker) continues to hold the shoe as long as the bank hand wins. As soon as the player hand wins, the shoe moves counterclockwise around the table. Players are not required to deal; they can refuse the shoe and pass it to the next player. Most players bet on the bank hand when they deal, since they "represent" the bank, and to do otherwise would seem as if they were betting "against" themselves. This isn't really the case.

Baccarat Strategy

Making a bet at baccarat is very simple. All you have to do is place your money in either the bank, player, or tie box on the layout, which appears directly in front of where you sit at the table. If you're betting that the bank hand will win, you put your chips in the bank box; bets for the player hand go in the player box. (Betting on a tie is a sucker bet.)

Because the caller dictates the action, the player responsibilities are minimal. It's not necessary to know any of the card-drawing rules, even if you're the banker. Playing baccarat is a simple matter of guessing whether the player or banker hand will come closer to 9, and deciding how much to bet on the outcome.

Blackjack

Blackjack is the most popular table game in the casino. It's easy to learn, it's fun to play, and it involves skill, and therefore rewards those who learn its nuances. Blackjack also has one of the lowest house advantages. Because blackjack is the only table game in the casino in which players can gain a long-term advantage over the house, it is the only table game in the casino (other than poker) that can be played professionally. And because blackjack can be played professionally, it is the most written-about and discussed casino game. Dozens of how-to books, trade journals, magazines, newsletters, computer programs, videos, theses, and novels are available on every aspect of blackjack, from how to add to 21 to how to play against a variety of shuffles, from when to stand or hit to the Level-Two Zen Count. Of course, training someone to play blackjack professionally is beyond the scope of this guide. Contact the **Gambler's Book Club** (☎ 800/552–1777) for a catalog of gambling books, software, and videotapes, including the largest selection on blackjack around.

The Rules

Basically, here's how it works: You play blackjack against a dealer, and whichever one of you comes closest to a card total of 21 without going over is the winner. Number cards are worth their face value, picture cards count as 10, and aces are worth either 1 or 11. (Hands with aces in them are known as "soft" hands. Always count the ace first as an 11; if you also have a 10, your total will be 21, not 11.) If the dealer has a 17 and you have a 16, you lose. If you have an 18 against a dealer's 17, you win (even money). If both you and the dealer have a 17, it's a tie (or "push") and no money changes hands. If you go over a total of 21 (or "bust"), you lose immediately, even if the dealer also busts later in the hand. If your first two cards add up to 21 (a "natural"), you're paid 3 to 2. However, if the dealer also has a natural, it's a push. A natural beats a total of 21 achieved with more than two cards.

You're dealt two cards, either face down or face up, depending on the custom of the particular casino. Two cards go to the dealer—one face down and one face up. Depending on your first two cards and the dealer's up card, you can:

stand, or refuse to take another card.

hit, or take as many cards as you need until you stand or bust.

double down, or double your bet and take one card.

split a like pair; if you're dealt two 8s, for example, you can double your bet and play the 8s as if they're two hands.

buy insurance if the dealer is showing an ace. Here you're wagering half your initial bet that the dealer does have a natural; if so, you lose your initial bet but are paid 2 to 1 on the insurance (which means the whole thing is a push).

surrender half your initial bet if you're holding a bad hand (known as a "stiff") such as a 15 or 16 against a high up-card like a 9 or 10.

Basic Blackjack Strategy

Playing blackjack is not only about knowing the rules—it's also about knowing *how* to play. Many people devote a great deal of time to learning strategies based on complicated statistical schemes. However, if you don't have the time, energy, or inclination to get that seriously involved, the following basic strategies, which cover more than half the situations you'll face, should allow you to play the game with a modicum of skill and a paucity of humiliation:

- When your hand is a stiff (a total of 12, 13, 14, 15, or 16) and the dealer shows 2, 3, 4, 5, or 6, always stand.
- When your hand is a stiff and the dealer shows a 7, 8, 9, 10, or ace, always hit.
- When you hold 17, 18, 19, or 20, always stand.
- When you hold a 10 or 11 and the dealer shows a 2, 3, 4, 5, 6, 7, 8, or 9, always double down.
- When you hold a pair of aces or a pair of 8s, always split.
- Never buy insurance.

Craps

Craps is a dice game played at a large rectangular table with rounded corners. Up to 12 players can crowd around the table, all standing. The layout is mounted at the bottom of a surrounding "rail," which prevents the dice from being thrown off the table and provides an opposite wall against which to bounce the dice. It's important, when you're the "shooter," to roll the dice hard enough so that they bounce off the end wall of the table; this ensures a random bounce and shows that you're not trying to control the dice with a "soft roll." The layout grid is duplicated on the right and left side of the table, so players on either end will see exactly the same design. The top of the railing is grooved to hold the bettors' chips; as always, keep a close eye on your stash to prevent victimization by rail thieves.

It can require up to four pit personnel to run an action-packed, fast-paced game of craps. Two dealers handle the bets made on either side of the layout. A "stickman" wields the long wooden stick, curved at one end, which is used to move the dice around the table; the stickman also calls the number that's rolled and books the proposition bets (☞ *below*) made in the middle of the layout. The "boxman" sits between the two dealers and oversees the game; he settles any disputes about rules, payoffs, mistakes, etc. A slow crap game is often handled by a single employee, who performs stick, box, and dealer functions. A portable end wall can be placed near the middle of the table so that only one side is functional.

How to Play

To play, just join in, standing at the table wherever you can find an open space. You can start betting casino chips immediately, but you have to wait your turn to be the shooter. The dice move around the table in a clockwise fashion: The person to your right shoots before you, the one to the left after. (The stickman will give you the dice at the appropriate time.) If you don't want to roll the bones, motion your refusal to the stickman and he'll skip you.

Playing craps is fairly straightforward; it's betting on it that's complicated. The basic concepts are as follows: If the first roll turns up a 7 or 11, that's called a "natural"—an automatic win. If a 2, 3, or 12 comes up on the first throw (called the "come-out roll"), that's termed "crapping out"—an automatic loss. Any other total on a first roll is known as a "point": The shooter keeps rolling the dice until the point comes up again. If a 7 turns up before the point does, the shooter loses. When either the point (the original number thrown) or a 7 is rolled, this is known as a "decision"; one is made on average every 3.3 rolls.

But "winning" and "losing" rolls of the dice are entirely relative in this game, depending on how you bet. There are two ways you can bet at craps: "for" the shooter or "against" the shooter. Betting for means that the shooter will "make his point" (win). Betting against means that the shooter will "seven out" (lose). (Either way, you're actually betting against the house, which books all wagers.) If you're betting "for" on the come-out, you place your chips on the layout's "pass line." If a 7 or 11 is rolled, you win even money. If a 2, 3, or 12 (craps) is rolled, you lose your bet. If you're betting "against" on the come-out, you place your chips in the "don't pass bar." A 7 or 11 loses; a 2 or 3 wins (a 12 is a push). A shooter can bet for or against himself or herself.

At the same time, you can make roughly two dozen wagers on any single roll of the dice. Besides the "for" and "against" (pass and don't pass) bets, you can also make the following wagers at craps:

Come/Don't Come: After a pass-line point is established, the come bet renders every subsequent roll of the dice a come-out roll. When you place your chips in the come box, it's the same as a pass-line bet. If a 7 or 11 is rolled, you win even money. If a 2, 3, or 12 is rolled, you've crapped out. If a 4, 5, 6, 8, 9, or 10 is rolled, it becomes another point, and the dealer moves your chips into the corresponding box on the layout. Now if that number comes up before the 7, you win the come bet. The opposite (almost) is true for the don't come box: 7 and 11 lose, 2 and 3 win (12 is a push), and if 7 is rolled before the point, you win.

Odds: The house allows you to take odds on whether or not the shooter will make his or her point, once it's established. Since the house pays off these bets at "true odds," rather than withholding a unit or two to its advantage, these are the best bets in a crap game. Odds on the 6 and 8 pay off at 6 to 5, on the 5 and 9 at 3 to 2, and on the 4 and 10 at 2 to 1. "Back up" your pass-line bets with single, double, triple, or up to 109 times odds (depending on the house rules) by placing your chips behind your line bet. For example, if the point is a 10 and your bet is $5, backing up your bet with single odds ($5) returns $25 ($5 + $5 on the line and $5 + $10 single odds);

taking triple odds returns $55 ($5 + $5 on the line and $15 + $30). To take the odds on a come bet, toss your chips onto the layout and tell the dealer, "Odds on the come."

Place: Instead of waiting for a point to be rolled on the come, you can simply lay your bet on the point of your choice. Drop your chips on the layout in front of you and tell the dealer to "place" your number. The dealer puts your chips on the point; when it's rolled you win. The 6 and 8 pay 7 to 6, the 5 and 9 pay 7 to 5, and the 4 and 10 pay 9 to 5. In other words, if you place $6 on the 8 and it hits, you win $7. Place bets don't pay off at true odds, which is how the house maintains its edge (1.51% on the 6 and 8, 4% on the 5 and 9, and 6.66% on the 4 and 10). You can "call your place bet down" (take it back) at any time; otherwise the place bet will "stay up" until a 7 is rolled.

Buy: Buy bets are the same as place bets, except that the house pays off at true odds and takes a 5% commission if it wins. Since buy bets have an edge of 4.7%, you should only buy the 4 and 10 (rather than place them at a 6.6% disadvantage).

Big 6 and 8: Place your own chips in these boxes; you win if the 6 or 8 comes up, and lose on the 7. Since they pay off at even money, rather than true odds, the house edge is large—9.09%.

Field: This is a "one-roll" bet (a bet that's decided with each roll). Numbers 3, 4, 9, 10, and 11 pay even money, while 2 and 12 pay 2 to 1. The house edge on the field is 5.5%.

Proposition Bets: All proposition bets are booked in the grid in the middle of the layout by the stickman. "Hardways" means a matching pair of numbers on the dice (two 3s for a hardways 6, two 4s for a hardways 8, etc.). A hardways 4 or 10 pays 7 to 1 (11.1% edge), and 6 or 8 pays 9 to 1 (9.09%). If a 7 or a 4, 6, 8, or 10 is rolled the "easy way," hardways bets lose. "Any seven" is a one-roll wager on the 7, paying 4 to 1 with a whopping 16.6% edge. "Yo'leven" is also a one-roll wonder paying 14 to 1 with a 16.6% edge. "Any craps" is a one-roll bet on the 2, 3, or 12, paying 7 to 1 (11.1%). Other bad proposition bets include the "horn" (one-roll bet on 2, 3, 11, or 12 separately; 16.6%), and "c and e" (craps or 11; 11.1%).

Note: The players place their own pass line, field, Big 6 and 8, and come line bets. Players must drop their chips on the table in front of the dealers and instruct them to make their place and buy bets, and to take or lay the odds on their come bets. Chips are tossed to the stickman, who makes the hardways, any craps, any seven, and c and e bets in the middle of the layout.

Roulette

Roulette is a casino game that utilizes a perfectly balanced wheel with 38 numbers (0, 00, and 1 through 36), a small white ball, a large layout with 11 different betting options, and special "wheel chips." The layout organizes the 11 different bets into six "inside bets" (the single numbers, or those closest to the dealer) and five "outside bets" (the grouped bets, or those closest to the players).

The dealer stands between the layout and the roulette wheel, and chairs for five or six players are set around the roulette table. At crowded times, players also stand among and behind those seated, reaching over and around to place their bets. *Always* keep a close eye on your chips at these times to guard against "rack thieves," clever sleight-of-hand artists who can steal from your pile of chips right from under your nose.

To buy in, place your cash on the layout near the wheel. Inform the dealer of the denomination of the individual unit you intend to play (usually 25¢ or $1, but it can go up as high as $500). Know the table limits (displayed on a sign in the dealer area); don't ask for a 25¢ denomination if the minimum is $1. The dealer gives you a stack of wheel chips of a different color from those of all the other players and places a chip marker atop one of your wheel chips on the rim of the wheel to identify its denomination. Note that you must cash in your wheel chips at the roulette table before you leave the game. Only the dealer can verify how much they're worth.

The dealer spins the wheel clockwise and the ball counterclockwise. When the ball slows, the dealer announces, "No more bets." The ball drops from the "back track" to the "bottom track," caroming off built-in brass barriers and bouncing in and out of the different cups in the wheel before settling into the cup of the winning number. Then the dealer, who knows the winning bettors by the color of their wheel chips, places a marker on the number and scoops all the losing chips into his or her corner. Depending on how crowded the game is, the casino can count on roughly 50 spins of the wheel per hour.

How to Place Inside Bets

You can lay any number of chips (depending on the table limits) on a single number, 1 through 36 or 0 or 00. If the number hits, your payoff is 35 to 1, for a return of $36 on a $1 bet. You could, conceivably, place a $1 chip on all 38 numbers, but the return of $36 would leave you $2 short, which divides out to 5.26%, the house advantage.

If you place a $1 chip on the line between two numbers and one of those numbers hits, you're paid 17 to 1 for a return of $18 (again, $2 short of the true odds).

Betting on three numbers returns 11 to 1, four numbers returns 8 to 1, five numbers pays 6 to 1 (this is the worst bet at roulette, with a 7.89% disadvantage), and six numbers pays 5 to 1.

How to Place Outside Bets

Lay a chip on one of three "columns" at the lower end of the layout next to numbers 34, 35, and 36; if the winning number falls in the column you've chosen, the payoff is 2 to 1. A bet placed in the first 12, second 12, or third 12 boxes also pays 2 to 1. A bet on red or black, odd or even, and 1 through 18 or 19 through 36 pays off at even money, 1 to 1. If you think you can bet on red *and* black, or odd *and* even, in order to play roulette and drink for free all night, think again: The green 0 or 00, which fall outside these two basic categories, will come up on average once every 19 spins of the wheel.

Slot Machines

At the beginning of the 20th century, Charlie Fey built the first mechanical slot in his San Francisco basement. Slot-machine technology has exploded in the past 20 years, and now there are hundreds of different models, which accept everything from pennies to specially minted $500 tokens. Electronically operated machines known as "multipliers" accept more than one coin (usually three to five, maximum) and have flashing lights, bells, and whistles, and spin, credit, and cash-out buttons.

Multipliers frequently have a variety of pay lines: three horizontal for example, or five horizontal and diagonal.

The major advance in the game, however, is the progressive jackpot. Banks of slots within a particular casino are connected by computer, and the jackpot total is displayed on a digital meter above the machines. Generally, the total increases by 5% of the wager. If you're playing a dollar machine, each time you pull the handle (or press the spin button), a nickel is added to the jackpot.

How to Play

To play, insert your penny, nickel, quarter, silver dollar, or dollar token into the slot at the far right edge of the machine. Pull the handle or press the spin button; then wait for the reels to spin and stop one by one, and for the machine to determine whether you're a winner (occasionally) or a loser (the rest of the time). It's pretty simple—but because there are so many different types of machines nowadays, be sure you know exactly how the one you're playing operates.

The house advantage on slots varies widely from machine to machine, between 3% and 25%. Casinos that advertise a 97% payback are telling you that at least one of their slot machines has a house advantage of 3%. Which one? There's really no way of knowing. Generally, $1 machines pay back at a higher percentage than quarter or nickel machines. On the other hand, machines with smaller jackpots pay back more money more frequently, meaning that you'll be playing with more of your winnings.

One of the all-time great myths about slot machines is that they're "due" for a jackpot. Slots, like roulette, craps, keno, and the big six, are subject to the Law of Independent Trials, which means the odds are permanently and unalterably fixed. If the odds of lining up three sevens on a 25¢ slot machine have been set by the casino at 1 in 10,000, then those odds remain 1 in 10,000 whether the three 7s have been hit three times in a row or not hit for 90,000 plays. Don't waste a lot of time playing a machine that you suspect is "ready," and don't think that if someone hits a jackpot on a particular machine only minutes after you've finished playing on it that it was "yours."

Video Poker

Like blackjack, video poker is a game of strategy and skill, and at select times on select machines, the player actually holds the advantage, however slight, over the house. Unlike with slot machines, you can determine the exact edge of video poker machines (or in gambler's lingo, "handicap" the machine). Like slots, however, video poker machines are often tied into a progressive meter; when the jackpot total reaches high enough, you can beat the casino at its own game.

The variety of video poker machines is already large, and it's growing steadily larger. All of the different machines are played in a similar fashion, but the strategies are different. This section deals only with straight-draw video poker.

How to Play

The schedule for the payback on winning hands is posted on the machine, usually above the screen. It lists the returns for a high pair (generally jacks or better), two pair, three of a kind, a straight, flush, full house, straight flush, four of a kind, and royal flush, depending on the number of coins played—usually 1, 2, 3, 4, or 5. (The machine assumes you're familiar with poker and its terminology.) Look for machines that pay, with a single coin played, 1 coin for "jacks or better" (meaning a pair of jacks, queens, kings, or aces; any other pair is a stiff), 2 coins for two pairs, 3 for three of a kind, 4 for a straight, 6 for a flush, 9 for a full house, 25 for four of a kind, 50 for a straight flush, and 250 for a royal flush. This is known as a 9/6 machine: one that gives a nine-coin payback for the full house and a six-coin payback for the flush with one coin played. Other machines are known as 8/5 (8 for the full house, 5 for the flush), 7/5, and 6/5.

You want a 9/6 machine because it gives you the best odds: The return from a standard 9/6 straight-draw machine is 99.5%; you give up a half percent to the house. An 8/5 machine returns 97.3%. On 6/5 machines, the figure drops to 95.1%, slightly better than roulette. Machines with varying paybacks are scattered throughout the casinos. In some you'll see an 8/5 machine right next to a 9/6, and someone will be blithely playing the 8/5 machine!

As with slot machines, it's always optimal to play the maximum number of coins in order to qualify for the jackpot. You insert five coins into the slot and press the "deal" button. Five cards appear on the screen—say, 5, J, Q, 5, 9. To hold the pair of 5s, you press the "hold" buttons under the first and fourth cards. The word "hold" appears underneath the two 5s. You then press the "draw" button (often the same button as "deal") and three new cards appear on the screen—say, 10, J, 5. You have three 5s; with five coins bet, the machine will give you 15 credits. If you want to continue playing, press the "max bet" button: Five units will be removed from your number of credits, and five new cards will appear on the screen. You repeat the hold and draw process; if you hit a winning hand, the proper payback will be added to your credits. Those who want coins rather than credit can hit the "cash out" button at any time. Some older machines don't have credit counters and automatically dispense coins for a winning hand.

Video Poker Strategy

Like blackjack, video poker has a basic strategy that's been formulated by the computer simulation of hundreds of millions of hands. The most effective way to learn it is with a video poker computer program that deals the cards on your screen, then tutors you in how to play each hand properly. If you don't want to devote that much time to the study of video poker, memorizing these six rules will help you make the right decision for more than half the hands you'll be dealt:

- If you're dealt a completely "stiff" hand (no like cards and no picture cards), draw five new cards.
- If you're dealt a hand with no like cards but with one jack, queen, king, or ace, always hold on to the picture card; if you're dealt two different picture cards, hold both. But if you're dealt three different picture cards, only hold two (the two of the same suit, if that's an option).
- If you're dealt a pair, always hold it, no matter what the face value.
- Never hold a picture card ("kicker") with a pair of 2s through 10s.
- Never draw two cards to try for a straight or flush.
- Never draw one card to try for an inside straight.

PUERTO RICO AT A GLANCE: A CHRONOLOGY

ca. AD 500 The first human inhabitants arrive in Puerto Rico, apparently on primitive rafts from Florida. Known today as Arcaicos (Archaics), these hunter-gatherers live near the shore, where they subsist on fish and fruit.

ca. 1000 The Arcaico are replaced by more advanced Arawak Indians who arrive by canoe from South America. The agrarian Taíno (a subgroup of the Arawak) name the island Boriquén, and thrive there in thatched villages.

1493 Christopher Columbus, on his second voyage to the New World, meets a group of Taíno on the island of Guadeloupe. The Taínos guide him to Boriquén. On November 19, Columbus claims the island for Ferdinand and Isabella of Spain, and christens it "San Juan Bautista."

1508 Caparra, the first Spanish settlement, is founded on the south shore of the island's largest bay. Juan Ponce de León, a soldier who had accompanied Columbus on his second voyage, is appointed governor by the Spanish crown.

1510 The Spanish begin mining and smelting gold on the island. In an effort to Christianize the Taíno, they also institute a program of virtual slavery: the Indians are required to work for the settlers in return for religious instruction. In November, a group of Taíno loyal to a *cacique* (chieftain) named Urayoan set out to determine whether the Spanish are gods. By drowning a young settler in a river, the Taíno prove the Spanish to be mortal.

1511 The Spanish crown grants the island a coat of arms. The town of Caparra is renamed Puerto Rico (Rich Port). The Taíno rebel against the conquistadors, but are no match for European armament. In a brutal act of reprisal, the Spanish hunt down and kill as many as 6,000 Indians.

1512 Ferdinand II of Spain issues the Edict of Burgos, intended to protect the island's surviving Indians from abuse by the settlers.

1513 The first African slaves are introduced. Setting sail from the settlement of San Germán on the island's west coast, Ponce de León heads north across the Caribbean and discovers Florida.

1521 The island's primary town moves across the bay from its original, mosquito-plagued site. It's renamed Puerto Rico, and its capital becomes known as San Juan instead of the other way around.

1523 The first sugarcane processing plant is built.

1532 Puerto Rican gold mines cease to be profitable, and Spanish settlers leave in droves for Peru. Governor Francisco Manuel de Lando declares emigration a crime punishable by the amputation of a leg.

1539 To help protect their Caribbean trade routes from pirates and competing colonial powers, the Spanish begin building the massive fortress of San Felipe del Morro (El Morro).

1542 The coconut palm is introduced.

1595 English privateer Sir Francis Drake, assigned to disrupt Spanish colonial trade, attempts unsuccessfully to capture the town of San Juan.

1598 Another Englishman, George Clifford, 3rd Earl of Cumberland, attacks the island and occupies San Juan with 4,000 men. He's forced to withdraw a few months later when his troops are decimated by disease.

1625 San Juan is again invaded, this time by Dutch forces under Bowdoin Hendrick. The attack fails when Hendrick is unable to conquer El Morro.

1680 The town of Ponce is founded on the south coast.

1736 Coffee is first cultivated in the central highlands.

1760 The west coast town of Mayagüez is founded.

1765 The Spanish crown sends Field Marshal Alejandro O'Reilly to inspect military and social conditions. He conducts a census and reports that Puerto Rico's races mix "without any repugnance whatsoever."

1776 Coffee becomes a major export item.

1797 When France and Spain declare war on England, 7,000 British troops under Sir Ralph Abercromby invade Puerto Rico. The British are driven back after a two-week campaign.

1806 The first printing press arrives.

1809 After Napoléon Bonaparte deposes the King of Spain, the Spanish Cortes (parliament) permits representatives from Spain's New World colonies to participate in the drafting of a new constitution.

1810 Ramón Power y Giralt is selected as Puerto Rico's first delegate to Spain.

1812 The Cádiz Constitution is adopted, granting Puerto Rico and other Spanish colonies the rank of provinces and extending Spanish citizenship to colonials. A brief period of social and economic optimism reigns on the island, and Puerto Rico's first newspaper is founded.

1815 With the fall of Napoléon, the monarchy is restored in Spain, and the Cádiz Constitution is revoked. Puerto Rico reverts to being merely a Spanish colony.

1825 Notorious Puerto Rican pirate Roberto Cofresi is captured by the U.S. Navy in the Caribbean and handed over to Spanish authorities, who execute him by firing squad at El Morro.

1843 Puerto Rico's first lighthouse is constructed at El Morro. The first town is founded on the outer island of Vieques.

1868 Inspired by Puerto Rican separatist Ramón Emetrio Betances, several hundred revolutionaries attempt a coup against Spanish rule. The rebels successfully occupy the town of Lares before authorities crush the revolt. The uprising comes to be known as the Grito de Lares (Cry of Lares).

1873 Slavery is abolished on Puerto Rico by decree of the Spanish king, Amedeo I de Saboya.

1876 The mountain rain forest of El Yunque is designated as a nature reserve.

1887 Journalist and patriot Luis Muñoz Rivera helps form the Puerto Rican Autonomous Party.

1897 Just prior to the Spanish-American War, Spain approves the Carta Autonómica, granting the island administrative autonomy.

1898 In February Puerto Rico's first autonomous local government is inaugurated. In April the Spanish-American War breaks out. In July American troops invade, conquering the island in 17 days with minimal casualties. In December, after 405 years of continuous rule, Spain officially cedes Puerto Rico (along with the Philippines and Guam) to the United States. No member of Puerto Rico's autonomous government is consulted.

1899 Hurricane San Ciriaco kills 3,000 people and leaves 25% of the population homeless.

1900 The U.S. Congress passes the Foraker Act, which declares Puerto Rico to be a U.S. territory. The island's elected civil government remains under the control of a U.S.-appointed governor.

1903 President Theodore Roosevelt gives the navy control over the out island of Culebra. The navy later uses it as a gunnery range.

1904 Luis Muñoz Rivera establishes the Unionist Party of Puerto Rico to combat the widely unpopular regulations imposed by the Foraker Act.

1912 As dissatisfaction with American rule increases, the Independence Party is formed. This is the first political party to claim Puerto Rican independence as its primary goal.

1917 President Woodrow Wilson signs the Jones Act, which grants U.S. citizenship to Puerto Ricans.

1930 With economic conditions bleak on the island, militant separatist Pedro Albizu Campos forms the Nationalist Party. The party demands immediate independence for Puerto Rico.

1933 Cockfighting is legalized.

1935 After a visit to the island, President Franklin Roosevelt establishes the Puerto Rican Reconstruction Administration in an effort to rehabilitate Puerto Rico's economy.

1937 A decade of occasional political violence culminates with La Masacre de Ponce (The Ponce Massacre). During a Palm Sunday parade of Nationalist Party blackshirts, police open fire on the crowd, killing 19 and injuring some 100 others.

1938 Luis Muñoz Marín, son of Luis Muñoz Rivera, creates the Democratic Popular Party.

1941 The U.S. military establishes bases on Vieques and Culebra, relocating a portion of the islands' population to St. Croix, Virgin Islands.

1945 Large numbers of Puerto Ricans begin to emigrate to the mainland United States, particularly to Florida and the New York City area.

1948 The U.S. Congress grants Puerto Ricans the right to elect their own governor. In November, Luis Muñoz Marín is voted in as the island's first elected native governor. Gambling is legalized.

1950 In July President Harry Truman signs a law permitting Puerto Rico to draft its own constitution as a commonwealth, but radical nationalists are far from satisfied. In October, violence breaks out throughout the island, leaving 31 people dead. A few days later, two Puerto Rican nationalists from New York attempt to assassinate Truman in Washington.

1952 Puerto Rican voters approve the new constitution, and the Commonwealth of Puerto Rico is born. The island's flag, based on a patriotic design dating from the time of Spanish colonialism, is officially adopted.

1953 In this peak year of emigration to the U.S. mainland, nearly 70,000 people leave the island.

1961 Puerto Rican actress Rita Moreno wins an Academy Award for her performance in the hit film *West Side Story.*

1964 Luis Muñoz Marín steps down as governor after 16 years. His career is remembered as brilliantly successful: under his governorship, the percentage of Puerto Rican children attending school rose from 50% to 90%, and per capita income increased sixfold.

1967 The question of Puerto Rico's political status is put before its voters for the first time. A 60% majority votes to maintain the commonwealth, rather than push for complete independence or U.S. statehood.

1972 Beloved Puerto Rican baseball star Roberto Clemente, an outfielder for the Pittsburgh Pirates, dies in a plane crash. He's inducted into the Baseball Hall of Fame the following year.

1974 A radical nationalist organization called the Fuerzas Armadas Liberación Nacional Puertorriqueña (Armed Forces of Puerto Rican National Liberation, or FALN) claims responsibility for five bombings in New York. Over the next decade, the group commits dozens of acts of terrorism in the United States, causing five deaths and extensive property damage.

1981 Members of the Macheteros, another radical nationalist group similar to the FALN, infiltrate a Puerto Rican Air National Guard base and blow up 11 planes, causing some $45 million in damage.

1993 In a second referendum on Puerto Rico's political status, voters again choose to maintain the commonwealth.

1998 Hurricane Georges leaves 24,000 people homeless and causes an estimated $2 billion in damage. In a third referendum on the political status issue, voters once more opt to maintain the commonwealth, although the pro-statehood vote tops 46%.

1999 Puerto Ricans of all political stripes are unified in protest against the U.S. Navy bombing range on Vieques after a civilian security guard is killed by a stray bomb. Dozens of protesters occupy the range and disrupt naval exercises. President Bill Clinton offers clemency to 16 FALN members serving time in federal prisons for a string of bombings in the U.S. during the 1970s and '80s.

2000 In May, 200 protesters encamped on the Vieques naval bombing range are forcibly removed by federal agents.

2001 In January, Sila Maria Calderón becomes the island's first woman governor. In March, Puerto Rican actor Benicio del Toro wins Academy Award for Best Supporting Actor for his role in "Traffic." In May, beauty Denise Quiñones, from the mountain town of Lares, becomes Miss Universe. Also that month, President George W. Bush announces that the navy will end training on Vieques by May 2003. After the September 11 terrorist attacks, however, congress passes legislation allowing the military to stay until another suitable site is found.

— Stephen Fowler. Updated by John Marino.

SPANISH VOCABULARY

Words and Phrases

English	Spanish	Pronunciation

Basics

English	Spanish	Pronunciation
Yes/no	Sí/no	see/no
Please	Por favor	pohr fah-**vohr**
May I?	¿Me permite?	meh pehr-**mee**-tay
Thank you (very much)	(Muchas) gracias	(**moo**-chas) **grah**-see-as
You're welcome	De nada	day **nah**-dah
Excuse me	Con permiso	con pehr-**mee**-so
Pardon me	¿Perdón?	pair-**dohn**
Could you tell me?	¿Podría decirme?	po-**dree**-ah deh-**seer**-meh
I'm sorry	Lo siento	lo see-**en**-to
Good morning!	¡Buenos días!	**bway**-nohs **dee**-ahs
Good afternoon!	¡Buenas tardes!	**bway**-nahs **tar**-dess
Good evening!	¡Buenas noches!	**bway**-nahs **no**-chess
Goodbye!	¡Adiós!/ ¡Hasta luego!	ah-dee-**ohss/ah** -stah-**lwe**-go
Mr./Mrs.	Señor/Señora	sen-**yor**/sen-**yohr**-ah
Miss	Señorita	sen-yo-**ree**-tah
Pleased to meet you	Mucho gusto	**moo**-cho **goose**-to
How are you?	¿Cómo está usted?	**ko**-mo es-**tah** oo-**sted**
Very well, thank you.	Muy bien, gracias.	**moo**-ee bee-**en, grah**-see-as
And you?	¿Y usted?	ee oos-**ted**
Hello (on the telephone)	Diga	**dee**-gah

Numbers

1	un, uno	oon, **oo**-no
2	dos	dohs
3	tres	tress
4	cuatro	**kwah**-tro
5	cinco	**sink**-oh
6	seis	saice
7	siete	see-**et**-eh
8	ocho	**o**-cho
9	nueve	new-**eh**-vey
10	diez	dee-**es**
11	once	**ohn**-seh
12	doce	**doh**-seh
13	trece	**treh**-seh
14	catorce	ka-**tohr**-seh

15	quince	**keen**-seh
16	dieciséis	dee-**es**-ee-**saice**
17	diecisiete	dee-**es**-ee-see-**et**-eh
18	dieciocho	dee-**es**-ee-**o**-cho
19	diecinueve	dee-**es**-ee-new-**ev**-eh
20	veinte	**vain**-teh
21	veinte y uno/ veintiuno	**vain**-te-oo-noh
30	treinta	**train**-tah
32	treinta y dos	train-tay-**dohs**
40	cuarenta	kwah-**ren**-tah
43	cuarenta y tres	kwah-**ren**-tay-**tress**
50	cincuenta	seen-**kwen**-tah
54	cincuenta y cuatro	seen-**kwen**-tay **kwah**-tro
60	sesenta	sess-**en**-tah
65	sesenta y cinco	sess-**en**-tay **seen**-koh
70	setenta	set-**en**-tah
76	setenta y seis	set-**en**-tay **saice**
80	ochenta	oh-**chen**-tah
87	ochenta y siete	oh-**chen**-tay see-**yet**-eh
90	noventa	no-**ven**-tah
98	noventa y ocho	no-**ven**-tay-**o**-choh
100	cien	see-**en**
101	ciento uno	see-en-toh **oo**-noh
200	doscientos	doh-see-**en**-tohss
500	quinientos	keen-**yen**-tohss
700	setecientos	set-eh-see-**en**-tohss
900	novecientos	no-veh-see-**en**-tohss
1,000	mil	meel
2,000	dos mil	dohs meel
1,000,000	un millón	oon meel-**yohn**

Colors

black	negro	**neh**-groh
blue	azul	ah-**sool**
brown	café	kah-**feh**
green	verde	**ver**-deh
pink	rosa	**ro**-sah
purple	morado	mo-**rah**-doh
orange	naranja	na-**rahn**-hah
red	rojo	**roh**-hoh
white	blanco	**blahn**-koh
yellow	amarillo	ah-mah-**ree**-yoh

Days of the Week

Sunday	domingo	doh-**meen**-goh
Monday	lunes	**loo**-ness
Tuesday	martes	**mahr**-tess
Wednesday	miércoles	me-**air**-koh-less
Thursday	jueves	hoo-**ev**-ess

Friday	viernes	vee-**air**-ness
Saturday	sábado	**sah**-bah-doh

Months

January	enero	eh-**neh**-roh
February	febrero	feh-**breh**-roh
March	marzo	**mahr**-soh
April	abril	ah-**breel**
May	mayo	**my**-oh
June	junio	**hoo**-nee-oh
July	julio	**hoo**-lee-yoh
August	agosto	ah-**ghost**-toh
September	septiembre	sep-tee-**em**-breh
October	octubre	oak-**too**-breh
November	noviembre	no-vee-**em**-breh
December	diciembre	dee-see-**em**-breh

Useful Phrases

Do you speak English?	¿Habla usted inglés?	**ah**-blah oos-**ted** in-**glehs**
I don't speak Spanish	No hablo español	no **ah**-bloh es-pahn-**yol**
I don't understand (you)	No entiendo	no en-tee-**en**-doh
I understand (you)	Entiendo	en-tee-**en**-doh
I don't know	No sé	no seh
I am American/ British	Soy americano (americana)/ inglés(a)	soy ah-meh-ree-**kah**-no (ah-meh-ree-**kah**-nah)/in-**glehs** (**ah**)
What's your name?	¿Cómo se llama usted?	**koh**-mo seh **yah**-mah oos-**ted**
My name is . . .	Me llamo . . .	meh **yah**-moh
What time is it?	¿Qué hora es?	keh **o**-rah es
It is one, two, three . . . o'clock.	Es la una. . . . Son las dos, tres	es la **oo**-nah/sohn lahs dohs, tress
Yes, please/No, thank you	Sí, por favor/No, gracias	**see** pohr fah-**vor**/no **grah**-see-ahs
How?	¿Cómo?	**koh**-mo
When?	¿Cuándo?	**kwahn**-doh
This/Next week	Esta semana/ la semana que entra	**es**-tah seh-**mah**-nah/lah seh-**mah**-nah keh **en**-trah
This/Next month	Este mes/el próximo mes	**es**-teh mehs/el **prok**-see-moh mehs
This/Next year	Este año/el año que viene	**es**-teh **ahn**-yo/el **ahn**-yo keh vee-**yen**-ay
Yesterday/today/ tomorrow	Ayer/hoy/mañana	ah-**yehr**/oy/mahn-**yah**-nah
This morning/ afternoon	Esta mañana/tarde	**es**-tah mahn-**yah**-nah/**tar**-deh

Tonight	Esta noche	es-tah no-cheh
What?	¿Qué?	keh
What is it?	¿Qué es esto?	keh es es-toh
Why?	¿Por qué?	por keh
Who?	¿Quién?	kee-yen
Where is . . . ?	¿Dónde está . . . ?	dohn-deh es-tah
the train station?	la estación del tren?	la es-tah-see-on del train
the subway station?	la estación del Tren subterráneo	la es-ta-see-on del trehn soob-tair-ron-a-o
the bus stop?	la parada del autobus?	la pah-rah-dah del oh-toh-boos
the post office?	la oficina de correos?	la oh-fee-see-nah deh-koh-reh-os
the bank?	el banco?	el bahn-koh
the hotel?	el hotel?	el oh-tel
the store?	la tienda?	la tee-en-dah
the cashier?	la caja?	la kah-hah
the museum?	el museo?	el moo-seh-oh
the hospital?	el hospital?	el ohss-pee-tal
the elevator?	el ascensor?	el ah-sen-sohr
the bathroom?	el baño?	el bahn-yoh
Here/there	Aquí/allá	ah-key/ah-yah
Open/closed	Abierto/cerrado	ah-bee-er-toh/ser-ah-doh
Left/right	Izquierda/derecha	iss-key-er-dah/dare-eh-chah
Straight ahead	Derecho	dare-eh-choh
Is it near/far?	¿Está cerca/lejos?	es-tah sehr-kah/leh-hoss
I'd like . . .	Quisiera . . .	kee-see-ehr-ah
a room	un cuarto/una habitación	oon kwahr-toh/oo-nah ah-bee-tah-see-on
the key	la llave	lah yah-veh
a newspaper	un periódico	oon pehr-ee-oh-dee-koh
a stamp	un sello de correo	oon seh-yo deh koh-reh-oh
I'd like to buy . . .	Quisiera comprar . . .	kee-see-ehr-ah kohm-prahr
cigarettes	cigarrillos	ce-ga-ree-yohs
matches	cerillos	ser-ee-ohs
a dictionary	un diccionario	oon deek-see-oh-nah-ree-oh
soap	jabón	hah-bohn
sunglasses	gafas de sol	ga-fahs deh sohl
suntan lotion	loción	loh-see-ohn-brohn-seh-ah-do-rah
a map	un mapa	oon mah-pah
a magazine	una revista	oon-ah reh-veess-tah

paper	papel	pah-**pel**
envelopes	sobres	**so**-brehs
a postcard	una tarjeta postal	**oon**-ah tar-**het**-ah post-**ahl**
How much is it?	¿Cuánto cuesta?	**kwahn**-toh **kwes**-tah
It's expensive/ cheap	Está caro/barato	es-**tah kah**-roh/ bah-**rah**-toh
A little/a lot	Un poquito/ mucho	oon poh-**kee**-toh/ **moo**-choh
More/less	Más/menos	mahss/**men**-ohss
Enough/too much/too little	Sufficiente/ demasiado/ muy poco	soo-fee-see-**en**-teh/ deh-mah-see-**ah**-doh/**moo**-ee **poh**-koh
Telephone	Teléfono	tel-**ef**-oh-no
Telegram	Telegrama	teh-leh-**grah**-mah
I am ill	Estoy enfermo(a)	es-**toy** en-**fehr**-moh(mah)
Please call a doctor	Por favor llame un medico	pohr fah-**vor ya**-meh oon **med**-ee-koh
Help!	¡Auxilio! ¡Ayuda! ¡Socorro!	owk-**see**-lee-oh/ ah-**yoo**-dah/ soh-**kohr**-roh
Fire!	¡Encendio!	en-**sen**-dee-oo
Caution!/Look out!	¡Cuidado!	kwee-**dah**-doh

On the Road

Avenue	Avenida	ah-ven-**ee**-dah
Broad, tree-lined boulevard	Bulevar	boo-leh-**var**
Fertile plain	Vega	**veh**-gah
Highway	Carretera	car-reh-**ter**-ah
Mountain pass, Street	Puerto Calle	poo-**ehr**-toh **cah**-yeh
Waterfront promenade	Rambla	**rahm**-blah
Wharf	Embarcadero	em-bar-cah-**deh**-ro

In Town

Cathedral	Catedral	cah-teh-**dral**
Church	Templo/Iglesia	**tem**-plo/ee-**glehs**-see-ah
City hall	Casa de gobierno	kah-sah deh go-bee-**ehr**-no
Door, gate	Puerta portón	poo-**ehr**-tah por-**ton**
Entrance/exit	Entrada/salida	en-**trah**-dah/sah-**lee**-dah
Inn, rustic bar, or restaurant	Taverna	tah-**ver**-nah
Main square	Plaza principal	plah-thah prin-see-**pahl**

Market	Mercado	mer-**kah**-doh
Neighborhood	Barrio	**bahr**-ree-o
Traffic circle	Glorieta	glor-ee-**eh**-tah
Wine cellar, wine bar, or wine shop	Bodega	boh-**deh**-gah

Dining Out

A bottle of . . .	Una bottella de . . .	**oo**-nah bo-**teh**-yah-deh
A cup of . . .	Una taza de . . .	**oo**-nah **tah**-thah deh
A glass of . . .	Un vaso de . . .	oon **vah**-so deh
Ashtray	Un cenicero	oon sen-ee-**seh**-roh
Bill/check	La cuenta	lah **kwen**-tah
Bread	El pan	el pahn
Breakfast	El desayuno	el deh-sah-**yoon**-oh
Butter	La mantequilla	lah man-teh-**key**-yah
Cheers!	¡Salud!	sah-**lood**
Cocktail	Un aperitivo	oon ah-pehr-ee-**tee**-voh
Dinner	La cena	lah **seh**-nah
Dish	Un plato	oon **plah**-toh
Menu of the day	Menú del día	meh-**noo** del **dee**-ah
Enjoy!	¡Buen provecho!	bwehn pro-**veh**-cho
Fixed-price menu	Menú fijo o turistico	meh-**noo** **fee**-hoh oh too-**ree**-stee-coh
Fork	El tenedor	ehl ten-eh-**dor**
Is the tip included?	¿Está incluida la propina?	es-**tah** in-cloo-**ee**-dah lah pro-**pee**-nah
Knife	El cuchillo	el koo-**chee**-yo
Large portion of savory snacks	Raciónes	rah-see-**oh**-nehs
Lunch	La comida	lah koh-**mee**-dah
Menu	La carta, el menú	lah **cart**-ah, el meh-**noo**
Napkin	La servilleta	lah sehr-vee-**yet**-ah
Pepper	La pimienta	lah pee-me-**en**-tah
Please give me	Por favor déme	pohr fah-**vor** **deh**-meh
Salt	La sal	lah sahl
Savory snacks	Tapas	**tah**-pahs
Spoon	Una cuchara	**oo**-nah koo-**chah**-rah
Sugar	El azúcar	el ah-**thu**-kar
Waiter!/Waitress!	¡Por favor Señor/Señorita!	pohr fah-**vor** sen-**yor**/sen-yor-**ee**-tah

INDEX

NOTES

Fodor's Key to the Guides

America's guidebook leader publishes guides for every kind of traveler. Check out our many series and find your perfect match.

Fodor's Gold Guides
America's favorite travel-guide series offers the most detailed insider reviews of hotels, restaurants, and attractions in all price ranges, plus great background information, smart tips, and useful maps.

Fodor's Road Guide USA
Big guides for a big country—the most comprehensive guides to America's roads, packed with places to stay, eat, and play across the U.S.A. Just right for road warriors, family vacationers, and cross-country trekkers.

COMPASS AMERICAN GUIDES
Stunning guides from top local writers and photographers, with gorgeous photos, literary excerpts, and colorful anecdotes. A must-have for culture mavens, history buffs, and new residents.

Fodor's CITYPACKS
Concise city coverage with a foldout map. The right choice for urban travelers who want everything under one cover.

Fodor's EXPLORING GUIDES
Hundreds of color photos bring your destination to life. Lively stories lend insight into the culture, history, and people.

Fodor's POCKET GUIDES
For travelers who need only the essentials. The best of Fodor's in pocket-size packages for just $9.95.

Fodor's To Go
Credit-card–size, magnetized color microguides that fit in the palm of your hand—perfect for "stealth" travelers or as gifts.

Fodor's FLASHMAPS
Every resident's map guide. 60 easy-to-follow maps of public transit, parks, museums, zip codes, and more.

Fodor's CITYGUIDES
Sourcebooks for living in the city: Thousands of in-the-know listings for restaurants, shops, sports, nightlife, and other city resources.

Fodor's AROUND THE CITY WITH KIDS
68 great ideas for family days, recommended by resident parents. Perfect for exploring in your own backyard or on the road.

Fodor's ESCAPES
Fill your trip with once-in-a-lifetime experiences, from ballooning in Chianti to overnighting in the Moroccan desert. These full-color dream books point the way.

Fodor's FYI
Get tips from the pros on planning the perfect trip. Learn how to pack, fly hassle-free, plan a honeymoon or cruise, stay healthy on the road, and travel with your baby.

Fodor's Languages for Travelers
Practice the local language before hitting the road. Available in phrase books, cassette sets, and CD sets.

Karen Brown's Guides
Engaging guides to the most charming inns and B&Bs in the U.S.A. and Europe, with easy-to-follow inn-to-inn itineraries.

Baedeker's Guides
Comprehensive guides, trusted since 1829, packed with A–Z reviews and star ratings.

At bookstores everywhere.   www.fodors.com/books